D1539743

THE COMPLETE INFORMATION BANK FOR ENTREPRENEURS AND SMALL-BUSINESS MANAGERS

THE COMPLETE INFORMATION BANK FOR ENTREPRENEURS AND SMALL-BUSINESS MANAGERS

2nd Edition

RON CHRISTY
and
BILLY M. JONES
in cooperation with the
Center for Entrepreneurship and
Small Business Management
Wichita State University

amacom
AMERICAN MANAGEMENT ASSOCIATION

Library of Congress Cataloging-in-Publication Data

Christy, Ron.
  The complete information bank for entrepreneurs
and small business managers.

  Includes index.
  1. Small business—United States—Handbooks, manuals,
etc. 2. Entrepreneurship—United States—Handbooks,
manuals, etc. 3. Small business—United States—
Bibliography. 4. Entrepreneurship—United States—
Bibliography. 5. Small business investment companies—
United States—Directories. I. Jones, Billy Mac.
II. Wichita State University. Center for Entrepre-
neurship and Small Business Management. III. Title.
HD2346.U5C45 1988   016.658'022'0973   87-47841
ISBN 0-8144-5912-9

Printing number

10 9 8 7 6 5 4 3 2 1

CONTENTS

Foreword   vii

Introduction   xi

Section 1   ***Books for Entrepreneurs***   **1**

     The Entrepreneur   3
     Women Entrepreneurs   20
     Minority Entrepreneurs   24
     Foreign Entrepreneurs   28
     Small Business Opportunities   33
     The American Enterprise System   44

Section 2   ***Books for Managers of Small Businesses***   **51**

     General Business Management   53
     Finance and Accounting   66
     Computers   74
     Financing and Venture Capital   81
     Case Studies   88
     Franchising   93
     Innovation and New-Product Development   97
     Legal   102
     Marketing, Advertising, and Sales   106
     Human Resources Management   116
     Problems and Failures   121
     Acquisitions   125
     Intrapreneurship   129

Section 3   ***Periodicals***   **133**

     Magazines and Journals   135
     Newsletters   142

Section 4   *Audiovisual Materials*   **145**

    Films   147
    Audio Tapes   152
    Videotapes   154
    Teaching Materials   163
    Records for the Blind   167

Section 5   *Computer Systems for Small Businesses*   **169**

    On-Line Information Sources   171
    Software Packages   176

Section 6   *Organizations and Associations*   **191**

Section 7   *Academic Programs*   **209**

Section 8   *Government Information and Venture Capital Firms*   **227**

    Small Business Administration   229
    National Association of Small Business
       Investment Companies   237
    Private Venture Capital Companies   281

List of Publishers   301
Author Index   322
Title Index   329
Subject Index   339

FOREWORD

Pizza Hut began in Wichita in 1958 as an entrepreneurial effort of brothers Dan and Frank Carney, and its success today continues to rely heavily on the entrepreneurial spirit of our franchise partners. Current, timely, and accurate information is critical to any business venture. For the new or small-business entrepreneur, it can mean the difference between success and failure. With this revised and expanded edition, *The Complete Information Bank for Entrepreneurs and Small Business Managers* has shown its enduring value and importance to aspiring and practicing entrepreneurs. I recommend it to anyone who owns or is contemplating starting up a business.

STEVEN S. REINEMUND
President and CEO
Pizza Hut, Inc.

This book is about entrepreneurship. It is designed as a ready sourcebook for aspiring creators of new ventures. It also is about intrapreneurship, and contains valuable materials for owner-managers of existing small businesses who wish to add new zest to their planning and operations. But most important, this book is about private enterprise, the cornerstone of an economic system that finds both continuity and self-renewal in the more than 600,000 new business corporations (as well as countless noncorporate entities) that are started every year.

Six hundred thousand new business corporations every year! There is a profound message in this statement. Something must be right about a democratic system of government that not only guarantees the widest latitude of political freedom but also ensures the broadest possible participation in a marketplace that welcomes such vast numbers of new entrants each year. Many of these new firms survive and grow. Even larger numbers falter and regrettably are discontinued. Yet one fact remains paramount: Each new venturer had the unrestrained freedom to test an idea, service, or product in the marketplace and to succeed or fail essentially from the application of his or her own entrepreneurial skills. It is our purpose in compiling the information in this book to offer encouragement and assistance to the principal actors in this unending economic drama in an effort to help increase the success ratios, thereby permitting more and more individuals to realize their own version of the American dream.

No system, however, is stronger than the collective will of its precursors to defend it, and it is our belief that America's enterprise-for-profit system is in need of better understanding and greater advocacy by those who share its rewards, consumers as well as entrepreneurs. This feeling has been the catalyst behind our drive in the W. Frank Barton School of Business Administration at Wichita State University to bring the whole world of entrepreneurship into sharper focus, to stress its importance in the perpetuation of private enterprise as an essential ingredient in our American way of life, and to identify those who wish to become business creators and help prepare them for greater success in the marketplace.

This effort began at Wichita State in 1977 when I founded, with the encouragement and support of administrators and faculty members, the Center for Entrepreneurship and Small Business Management. The Center had been a personal dream for more than a decade, and I am indebted to a number of dedicated individuals who have worked hard to help me realize it.

Our first target was the teenage group (high school seniors and university freshmen) who was invited to participate in a three-week-long, college credit class entitled "Entrepreneurship: Your Future in Business," which we offered for the first time in the summer of 1978. It was an instant success, and since that time, a total of almost 5,000 individuals have enrolled in this annual summer program. Over the past decade, the scope of the course has been broadened to include adult and continuing education students, public and private schoolteachers, and professional businesspersons at all management levels. Interestingly, these participants have ranged in age from 16 to 82, and many of them have been holders of advanced college and professional degrees.

This success led us in 1980 to develop what now has become a minor in entrepreneurial studies; it consists of course work at both the undergraduate and graduate levels. We also teach a special course in the university's general education program entitled "Introduction to Entrepreneurship," which is offered annually to more than 600 students drawn from all college divisions or major areas of study. We have begun to track the students in all these programs to determine the effectiveness of our efforts, and early tabulations unquestionably confirm our belief that entrepreneurial education can make a significant impact on the careers of our students as well as on the business life of our community.

These experiences then led us in 1984 to undertake yet another ambitious project— developing a network of students at other universities who share a strong interest in entrepreneurship. The result has been the establishment of an organization known as the Association of Collegiate Entrepreneurs (ACE), with chapters at colleges and universities throughout the world. The fourth annual ACE Convention in Chicago in February 1987 hosted more than 1,000 of these entrepreneurially minded students, almost 200 educators, and a large number of entrepreneurs and small-business owners. Even though this program is only in its infancy, its influence already spans the continents, and may yet prove to be one of the stronger catalysts in causing the world's leaders to acknowledge that nations are economically interdependent and that the entrepreneurs of all countries must be permitted unrestricted access to the global marketplace if the comprehensive needs and interests of all people are to be served adequately.

The same pride we feel in this endeavor blends well with the progress we have made in other areas. For example, each year men and women of national and international stature are invited to share their experiences with our student body through two special lectureships: an entrepreneur-in-residence program (those who have started major businesses) and an executive-in-residence program (those who are successful corporate executives of large companies). These visiting lecturers have included such outstanding entrepreneurs as T. Boone Pickens, chairman and president of Mesa Petroleum Company; Fred Smith, chairman and CEO of Federal Express; R. David Thomas, founder and senior chairman of Wendy's International; and R. E. "Ted" Turner, chairman and president of Turner Broadcasting System, Inc. Representative of the corporate executives who have delivered major addresses to campuswide audiences are Robert R. Campion, chairman of Lear Siegler, Inc.; William K. Coors, chairman of Adolph Coors Company; George Farrell, president of the Mellon National Corporation, Mellon Bank; and Don Nickelson, president of Paine, Webber, Jackson and Curtis.

The Center also sponsors a research program in both empirical and pragmatic studies as well as a Business Heritage Series, which seeks to preserve, through historical monographs, the contributions of both institutions and individuals who have made significant contributions to regional and national business development. Presently, there are ten titles in print, and others are in preparation. In addition, the forerunner of this volume, *The Complete Information Bank for Entrepreneurs and Small Business Managers*, was compiled and published in 1981 through a generous grant from Pizza Hut, Inc., and has enjoyed wide circulation in all 50 states and in 20 foreign countries.

Much progress has been made. Much remains to be accomplished. The increasing interest of students and the growing number of graduates who are moving relentlessly into private enterprise continually rekindles our enthusiasm and determination to develop new programs and goals that more clearly address their needs in a changing business arena. It is to these and future generations of students, and to the entrepreneurial spirit that motivates them, that this book is dedicated.

Appreciation is expressed to Ron Christy and Dr. Billy M. Jones, members of the Center's staff, for their work in compiling and preparing this book for publication; to the several outstanding business personalities who provided brief messages to introduce the various sections of this book; and to the editorial staff of the American Management Association for their insight, advice, and editorial support in finalizing this expanded source of information for entrepreneurs and small-business managers.

Fran D. Jabara
Founder and Director
Center for Entrepreneurship
Wichita State University

INTRODUCTION

The information in this sourcebook was compiled principally for use as general reference material by entrepreneurs and owner-managers of small businesses. It is hoped that academic researchers also will find it useful, although they undoubtedly will view it from a different perspective.

Our goal has been to provide entrepreneurs and small-business practitioners with as much relevant information on as wide a range of subjects as possible, and in a format that can help them get information as easily and quickly as possible. The purpose is obvious: We seek to enhance their chances of success, for we are aware that a major cause of small-business failures results from poor management decisions exacerbated by lack of reliable and timely information.

Although this sourcebook hardly could be termed exhaustive, it is reasonably comprehensive and can be quite valuable to those who seek solutions to practical problems. Users are required only to employ their "entrepreneurial spirit" in following the guidelines for identifying, locating, and accessing the materials contained here.

The book is divided into eight sections arranged according to medium, and each section is further subdivided to permit sufficient depth on specific aspects of the broader subjects. These eight sections, and their general points of view, are:

1. *Books for Entrepreneurs:* Books about starting a business, including the how-to's of specific ventures, the special considerations faced by women and minority entrepreneurs, and philosophical treatises on the free-enterprise system.
2. *Books for Managers of Small Businesses:* By and large, listings here pick up at the point where the new venture has been established, and provide specific information on various aspects of managing it.
3. *Periodicals:* Details many of the special-focus magazines, journals, and newsletters that provide information useful to small businesses.
4. *Audiovisual Materials:* Information for small businesses is available in the form of films, videotapes, audiotapes, and multimedia kits for teachers.
5. *Computer Systems for Small Businesses:* Describes the amazing depth of information available in the form of on-line data bases, and lists a broad range of software application packages that can revolutionize the operation of a small business.
6. *Organizations and Associations:* Individuals in a particular industry or those who share a certain business focus can gain information from one another through meetings and publications of their organizations.
7. *Academic Programs:* Formal academic training in entrepreneurship skills and practice is available across the country.
8. *Government Information and Venture Capital Firms:* Describes the programs and publications of the Small Business Administration, lists the members of the National Association of Small Business Investment Companies (financial institu-

tions that make loans to small businesses following SBA guidelines), and lists private venture capital companies.

To locate information on a specific subject, users should:

1. Start with the Table of Contents, which will point the way to general categories.
2. Consult the Subject Index, which will pinpoint listings on specific topics, and will be particularly helpful in locating items with more than one focus.
3. Check the Author Index or Title Index, if either of those is known for a specific book title; either index will inevitably lead to the location of other books on the same subject.

We used 1970 as the cutoff publication date for this volume, so most of the books listed here are still in print and readily available in bookstores and libraries. A Publisher Index is provided, with mailing addresses, for those who wish to order their own copy of a preferred volume.

The format for the book listings in Sections 1 and 2 was in essence followed for all other media categories. In designing this format, we attempted to find that delicate balance between too much information and too little. We have tried to include all that most users would find appropriate, but to avoid extraneous data of marginal value. There are listings for which full information was not available; we chose to include those entries if we believed their usefulness outweighed the inconvenience of this partial void.

Certain acknowledgments are appropriate. We received permission to use and subsequently drew liberally upon several national data bases for the information contained in this volume. Special appreciation is expressed to Gavin Claybaugh for his assistance in accessing these data bases, to Nancy Brandwein for her editorial oversight, and to Karl Vesper for giving us permission to include the results of his impressive study on current academic programs in entrepreneurship. None of them, however, bears any responsibility for whatever shortcomings this sourcebook may have.

Ron Christy
Billy M. Jones

January 1988

SECTION 1.

Books for Entrepreneurs

The Entrepreneur 3
Women Entrepreneurs 20
Minority Entrepreneurs 24
Foreign Entrepreneurs 28
Small-Business Opportunities 33
The American Enterprise System 44

THE ENTREPRENEUR

Although narrowly defined by Webster as those who assume risks for the sake of profit, entrepreneurs are characterized by modern researchers in other important ways: as innovative overachievers; as mavericks with confidence in their ability to reach a desired objective; or more appropriately, as reasoned risk-takers with a burning desire to excel in a business of their own creation. To examine the life story of any successful entrepreneur is to discover a person who found himself on the leading edge of business development with a fresh and workable idea for a new product or service—and with a determination to bring it into the market. Historically, entrepreneurs have been the cornerstones of America's "enterprise-for-profit system," and today they are being recognized as the essential self-renewing agents for both private enterprise and the American economy.

R. E. "TED" TURNER
Chairman of the Board
Turner Broadcasting System, Inc.

Although entrepreneurs have played a vital role in every historical stage of our nation's business development, there is little doubt that they have become the most dynamic, powerful, and innovative force in creating fresh growth in the United States today. In fact, many observers have labeled the late twentieth century the Age of the Entrepreneur because of a resurgence of enthusiasm and activity in developing new businesses, in marketing new products and services, and in fashioning new types of organizational structures.

In many ways, this has resulted from post-World War II influences. The baby boom brought an enormous increase in young Americans who are now in their prime years as creators of new business ventures. These baby-boomers lived through the turbulent 1960s and early 1970s, when almost every facet of American society was questioned and their values reassessed. Many changes in cultural norms emerged, the most graphic among this younger generation being a partial rejection of corporate dependency and a resurgent belief in self-reliance, independence, and confidence in one's economic energy, leading to the creation of new businesses. These expressions are the grass-roots manifestations of democratic capitalism.

Significantly, the entrepreneur is capitalism's built-in self-renewing agent, the cornerstone of America's private enterprise system. Each time a new business starts, or an innovation takes place in an existing firm, faith is expressed again in an economic system driven by competition, the profit motive, and a desire for personal excellence. The perpetuation of this entrepreneurial spirit is essential to the survival of our democratic way of life, as well as to the health and vitality of American business.

The early years of this nation's industrial growth were highlighted by corporate moguls (themselves entrepreneurs in their own pursuits) who developed giant companies with the apparent capacity for almost limitless expansion. Moreover, bigness became the accepted strategem for solving all of America's problems and needs, and corporate bigness was accompanied by bigness in all institutions—government, labor, education. The vast majority of all employment opportunities, from the Civil War days to the Vietnam era, was provided by corporate America.

Since the late 1960s, however, job creation and growth have shifted to a new sector of the economy. It is obvious that small and medium-size businesses now are providing this important function, for labor statistics clearly indicate that during the past two decades, more than 40 million new jobs have been created at a time when net corporate employment has been declining. This is not surprising. New businesses are being formed in unprecedented numbers—almost 600,000 per year, not including perhaps tens of thousands of unrecorded, untraceable proprietorships and partnerships that also start each year. Thus, entrepreneurship is serving a vital role in providing the inspiration and energy for a new economic era.

Entrepreneurship does not take place in a vacuum. Most scholars agree that it flourishes best in those countries where economic, social, and political conditions are most favorable—where new-business creators are motivated to assume a risk in quest of profit opportunities in a fair and competitive market environment. American entrepreneurs are singularly blessed, for no other country offers these conditions in greater abundance, a fact that has caused Peter Drucker to contend that "the entrepreneurial economy is purely an American phenomenon."

Never has the business climate been richer with opportunity than in the United States today, for the economic environment is alive with change—at a rate much faster than in any previous era because of what some observers have labeled the Information Age. Information once painfully compiled and disseminated through limited media outlets now floods the marketplace in a variety of usable forms. Thirty years ago, for example, parents of today's baby-boomers relied heavily on local newspapers for information and had access to only three television channels and a limited number of AM radio stations. Now they and their children have hundreds of satellite and cable television channels and a plethora of highly segmented AM and FM radio stations to supplement and reinforce the information in thousands of newspapers, magazines, journals, and business newsletters targeted to specialized audiences. As one analyst has noted, "Today, if Soviet Chairman Gorbachev gets a cold, we know of it immediately."

In addition, a vast network of statistical data bases, electronically stored and retrieved upon instant command, has exploded on the business scene with far-reaching, even frightening, impact. Statistical comparisons keep track of trends and changes in consumer lifestyles and socioeconomic behavior, revealing shifts in buying habits and suggesting new market niches. Access to this information by all marketplace participants is so widespread that business owners are forced to make decisions much more rapidly than they did a decade ago just to maintain their competitiveness.

Well-prepared entrepreneurs thrive in such a changing environment, for they are, by definition, opportunistic risk-takers in search of an unmet need for a service or product. However, just as the explosion of information has changed economic behavior in the marketplace, it also has helped forge a revised definition of the entrepreneur. Once reserved for those who created or operated small businesses, the term *entrepreneurship* has been broadened to include a range of creative individuals, now called *intrapreneurs*, who use their innovative skills while remaining employees of large corporations.

Although this concept is hardly new, its metamorphosis has been slow in developing. Joseph Schumpeter, for example, stresses that both entrepreneurs and managers experience risk, but he believes that the innovative spirit clearly distinguishes entrepreneurs from their counterparts. It has been the entrepreneurs' challenge to find and use new ideas, to develop new products or markets, to discover new sources of supply, and to create new forms of organization. Today, corporate managers increasingly are being made responsible for creating a work environment in which intrapreneurs can function with a minimum of organizational interference while performing all of Schumpeter's entrepreneurial challenges within the corporate structure. As Drucker recently summarized: "Entrepreneurship is neither a science nor an art. It is a practice. It has a knowledge base, of course. But as in all practices, medicine for instance, or engineering, knowledge in entrepreneurship is a means to an end." This applies to both individual and corporate business development.

Numerous studies have attempted to identify the attitudinal, psychological, and background characteristics of entrepreneurs. It is evident that these individuals are at least as different as they are alike, but successful entrepreneurs tend to have some traits in common: persistence; aggressiveness; ambition; low aversion to risk-taking; a confidence in personal decisions; a problem-solving attitude; a willingness to work long hours; and a high need for achievement. In addition, one of the great motivators urging entrepreneurs to start new businesses is a high level of dissatisfaction with their present employment or an inability to find happiness in working for someone else, creating the desire to develop private enterprises where personal independence and creativity can be more fully expressed.

Thus, the essence of entrepreneurship is the initiation of change, as contrasted to the essence of management, which involves controlling and planning within a given structure. Some entrepreneurs are tinkerers and inventors; others are good at putting things together and making the results work; still others are sensitized to opportunity and can readily spot viable business opportunities. Regardless of category or terminology used in identifying them, entrepreneurs are a necessary and vital ingredient in our economy, essential for improving the quality of life within our democratic system. Entrepreneurship is not unique to the American enterprise system, but the degree to which it is being exercised today certainly is unique in the history of this nation. Perhaps we are in the beginning stages of an American entrepreneurial renaissance.

1.

Adler, Bill

Bill Adler's Chance of a Lifetime

Warner Books, 1985, 212 pp., $15.50
ISBN 0-446-51327-S. Dewey Decimal No.
658.022. LC Card No. 85-40008.

2.

Archer, Maurice, and Jerry White

Starting and Managing Your Own Small Business

MacMillan of Canada, 1978, 291 pp.
ISBN 0-7705-1629-7.
Guides readers through all the basic steps
of starting and managing a business, and
lists sources needed in starting and
running an enterprise.

3.

Aronson, Charles N.

Free Enterprise

Charles Aronson, 1979, 1683 pp., $25
(cloth), $18 (paper)
ISBN 0-915736-15-2 (cloth), 0-915736-16-
0 (paper).
Compelling true story of an American
proprietorship. Tells how a small business is born and why, and shows what
changes have to be made in a company's
direction and management as it grows.

4.

Avis, Warren E.

Take a Chance to Be First

Macmillan, 1986
ISBN 0-02-504410-9. Dewey Decimal No.
650.1. LC Card No. 86-2948.

5.

Bailey, Geoffrey

Maverick

Franklin Watts, 1982, 176 pp.
ISBN 0-531-09869-9. Dewey Decimal No.
658.041. LC Card No. 82-10914.

6.

Ballas, George C., and David Hollas

The Making of an Entrepreneur: Keys to Your Success

Prentice-Hall, 1980, 245 pp.
ISBN 0-13-546788-8 (cloth), 0-13-546770-
5 (paper). Dewey Decimal No. 650.1. LC
Card No. 80-12223.

7.

Baty, Gordon B.

Entrepreneurship for the Eighties

Reston, 1981, 238 pp.
ISBN 0-8359-1745-2. Dewey Decimal No.
658.42. LC Card No. 81-2864.

8.

Baumback, Clifford Mason

How to Organize and Operate a Small Business, 7th edition

Prentice-Hall, 1985, 578 pp., $27.95
ISBN 0-13-425646-8. LC Card No. 84-
16037.
Discusses the organization and operation
of small enterprises in retailing, wholesaling, manufacturing, and the service
trades. The text looks at the importance
of small business, its status, problems,
and requirements for success.

9.

Baumback, Clifford M., and Joseph R. Mancuso

Entrepreneurship and Venture Management

Prentice-Hall, 1975, $12.95 (paper)
ISBN 0-13-283119-8.
Thirty-five articles by various well-
known authors slanted toward the tech-
nologically based manufacturing ventures
and technical entrepreneurship.

10.

Bos, Dieter, Abram Bergson, and John Robert Meyer, eds.

Entrepreneurship

Springer-Verlag, 1984, 218 pp.
ISBN 0-387-81830-8. Dewey Decimal No.
338.04. LC Card No. 84-26677.
Proceedings from the Bonn-Harvard
Schumpeter centennial, Bonn, September
1983.

11.
Brandt, Steven C.
Entrepreneuring
Addison-Wesley, 1982, 225 pp., $12.95
ISBN 0-201-10382-6. Dewey Decimal No.
   658.42. LC Card No. 82-1660.
Focus is building a company for rapid
growth. Ten main operating principles,
called the 10 Commandments for Build-
ing a Growth Company, are presented.

12.
Brooks, Julie K., and Barry A. Stevens
How to Write a Successful Business Plan
AMACOM, 1987, 231 pp., $17.95
ISBN 0-8144-5873-4.
Offers entrepreneurs step-by-step instructions for researching, organizing, and
writing a business plan, and guidance on
tailoring the plan to meet the needs of
different audiences. Includes sample
excerpts from successful real-life business plans and case studies that reveal
pitfalls and opportunities. Tips on
frequently tapped sources of capital and
some lesser-known sources.

13.
Brown, Deaver
The Entrepreneur's Guide
Macmillan, 1980, 173 pp.
ISBN 0-02-517360-X. Dewey Decimal No.
   658.1141. LC Card No. 80-459.

14.
Bunzel, John H.
The American Small Businessman
Arno Press, 1979, $22
ISBN 0-405-11460-5.
Provides a general review of the status
and role of the small businessman in
post-World War II American society.
Author's chief concern is "to analyze the
roots and qualities" of small entrepre-
neurs, to probe "the man as well as the
legend."

15.
Burch, John G.
Entrepreneurship
Wiley (Series in Management), 1986,
   493 pp., $28.95
ISBN 0-471-82522-0. LC Card No. 85-
   12455.
Comprehensive introduction to entrepreneurship. Begins with the basic characteristics of entrepreneurship, proceeds to
product ideas and evaluation, covers
startup, structuring, and financing, and
culminates with example of a complete
business plan.

16.
Burstiner, Irving
The Small Business Handbook
Prentice-Hall, 1979, $19.95 (text), $10.95
   (paper)
ISBN 0-13-814202-5 (text), 0-13-814914-0
   (paper).
Nontechnical, practical guide shows how
to start and run a profitable small busi-
ness.

17.
Casson, Mark
The Entrepreneur: An Economic Theory
Barnes & Noble, 1982, 418 pp.
ISBN 0-389-20328-9. Dewey Decimal No.
   338.04. LC Card No. 82-13802.
A study of how economic theory has
developed with the participation of the
entrepreneur.

18.
Chamberlain, John
*The Enterprising Americans: A Business
History of the United States*
Harper & Row, 1974, $14.95
ISBN 06-010702-02.
Gives a history of business from the
Revolution to the present. The heroes are
entrepreneurs who undertook risk
ventures and combined the units of
production into creative enterprises.
Covers both historical periods and
various industries, from textiles and
railroads to automotive and computer
corporations.

19.

Channing, Peter C.

Scratching Your Entrepreneurial Itch: A Guide to Business Venturing

Hawthorn Books, 1977, $4.98

ISBN 0-8015-6607-4.

Attempts to encourage and help prepare those who have sound, basic entrepreneurial attributes and motivations. Discusses the main reasons entrepreneurs fail and covers the major areas of operating a small business (finance, marketing, sales, production, and management considerations).

20.

Clifton, David S., Jr., and David E. Fyffe

Project Feasibility Analysis (A Guide to Profitable New Ventures)

Wiley, 1977, $19.95

ISBN 0-471-01611-X.

A manual for the preparation of a new-venture feasibility study and investment proposal. Includes details on how to perform the market analysis, conduct the technical analysis, and direct a financial analysis.

21.

Comiskey, James C.

How to Start, Expand and Sell a Business

Venture Perspectives Press, 1985, $17.95 (paper)

ISBN 0-932309-38-0. Dewey Decimal No. 658.42. LC Card No. 85-15814.

22.

Cook, James R.

The Start-Up Entrepreneur: How You Can Succeed in Building Your Own Company into a Major Enterprise Starting from Scratch

Dutton, 1986, 305 pp., $18.95

ISBN 0-525-24372-0. Dewey Decimal No. 658.42. LC Card No. 85-16160.

Both a handbook and a memoir of the author's own trials and triumphs in starting a business. Gives readers a shrewd pep talk and a wise set of guidelines for starting from scratch.

23.

Cook, Peter D.

Start and Run Your Own Successful Business: An Entrepreneur's Guide

Beaufort Books, 1982, 272 pp., $9.95

ISBN 0-8253-0107-6. Dewey Decimal No. 658.11. LC Card No. 82-4336.

24.

Crego, Edwin T., Jr., Brian Deaton, and Peter D. Schiffrin

How to Write a Business Plan

AMACOM, $110 AMA members, $120 nonmembers

Outlines the business planning process from start to finish.

25.

Crimmins, C. E.

Entrechic: The Mega-Guide to Entrepreneurial Excellence

AMACOM, 1985, 143 pp., $6.95 (paper)

ISBN 0-8144-7635-X. Dewey Decimal No. 818.5402. LC Card No. 85-47669.

26.

Deeks, John

The Small Firm Owner-Manager: Entrepreneurial Behavior and Management Practice

Praeger, 1976, $24.95

ISBN 0-275-5550-X.

Examines empirical data on the characteristics and behavior of small-business owner-managers and in the process highlights the gap that exists between theories about entrepreneurial behavior and the management practices of owner-managers.

27.

Dible, Donald

Business Start-Up Basics

Entrepreneur Press, 1978, $10.95

Answers to basic questions a person may have when contemplating a business startup.

28.
Dorland, Gilbert N., and John Van Der Wal
The Business Idea—From Birth to Profitable Company
Van Nostrand Reinhold, 1978, $14.95
ISBN 0-442-22163-0.
Describes the business plan and the purpose, format, and research factors that go into its formation, including market surveys, product feasibility studies, and distribution, pricing, and timing considerations.

29.
Doughtery, David E.
From Technical Professional to Entrepreneur
Wiley, 1986, $19.95
ISBN 0-471-83042-9. Dewey Decimal No. 346.73048. LC Card No. 86-1501.
A guide to industrial property rights.

30.
Drake Publishers, Inc.
How to Start Your Own Small Business, vol. 1
Drake Publishers, 1973, $5.95
ISBN 0-87749-498-3.
Details practical aspects of beginning a successful business: securing capital, finding your market, solving the problems of distribution and labor supply, and dealing with competition. Accent on results rather than theory.

31.
Dressler, Fritz R. S., and John W. Seybold
The Entrepreneurial Age: The Twenty-first Century Renaissance of the Individual
Seybold Publications, 1985, 224 pp.
ISBN 0-918514-10-X. Dewey Decimal No. 338.040973. LC Card No. 85-232719.
Entrepreneurism as it relates to technological innovation, the competitive nature of industry, and overall U.S. economic policy.

32.
Drucker, Peter F.
Innovation and Entrepreneurship

Harper & Row, 320 pp., $8.95
ISBN 0-06-091360-6. LC Card No. 84-048593.
The great challenges and opportunities of entrepreneurship presented as a systematic discipline.

33.
Easton, Thomas A., and Ralph Wendall Conant
Cutting Loose
Probus, 1985, 202 pp., $17.95
ISBN 0-917253-14-0. Dewey Decimal No. 658.42. LC Card No. 85-17040.
Making the transition from employee to entrepreneur.

34
Entrepreneurship Development Programme
Kerala
Dewey Decimanl No. 338.642. LC Card No. 80-904325.
Development Commissioner, Small Scale Industries, Minister of Industry, 1980, 53 pp.

35.
Fierro, Robert Daniel
The New American Entrepreneur
Morrow, 1982, 286 pp.
ISBN 0-688-00806-2. Dewey Decimal No. 658.022. LC Card No. 81-14218.
How to get off the fast track into a business of your own.

36.
Fiffer, Steve
So You've Got a Great Idea
Addison-Wesley, 1986, 192 pp., $8.95 (paper)
ISBN 0-201-11536-0.
How-to book with practical advice on going from idea to reality. Entertaining profiles of people who followed through successfully on a new idea. Very informative; full of examples.

37.
Flexman, Nancy A., and Thomas J. Scanlan
Running Your Own Business
Argus, 1982, 204 pp., $5.95 (paper)
ISBN 0-89505-091-9. Dewey Decimal No.
658.041. LC Card No. 82-72622.

38.
Fritz, Roger
No One Gets Rich Working for Somebody Else
Dodd, Mead, $17.95 (cloth), $8.90 (paper)
Complete with case histories, this guide offers information on testing one's own potential, selecting the right business, formulating a business plan, financing a startup, managing the business, and preparing for growth.

39.
Fucini, Joseph J., and Suzy Fucini
Entrepreneurs
G. K. Hall, 1985, 297 pp.
ISBN 0-8161-8708-8. Dewey Decimal No.
338.0409. LC Card No. 84-15846.
The men and women behind famous brand names and how they made it.

40.
Gallup, George, Jr., Alec M. Gallup, and William Proctor
The Great American Success Story
Dow Jones–Irwin, 256 pp., $14.95
Ingredients such as education, family life, influential advisers, luck, talent, and time management have played important parts in the success of these achievers.

41.
Gardner, Ralph
Young, Gifted, and Rich
Simon & Schuster, 1984, 207 pp., $7.95
(paper)
ISBN 0-671-47046-9. Dewey Decimal No.
338.040. LC Card No. 83-26018.
The secrets of America's most successful entrepreneurs.

42.
Goldstein, Arnold S.
Starting on a Shoestring: Building a Business Without a Bank Roll
Wiley, 1984
ISBN 0-471-88439-1. LC Card No. 83-23-
23379.
Guide for starting any type of business with little or no investment capital. What it takes to be a successful small-business entrepreneur, the economic fundamentals of building a business venture, proven ways to reduce risk, how to find money, how to buy starting inventory on terms, the techniques for taking over a going business without up-front money, and the best ways to expand.

43.
Goldstein, Jerome
How to Start a Family Business and Make It Work
Evans, 1984, 156 pp.
ISBN 0-87131-435-5. Dewey Decimal No.
658.022. LC Card No. 84-3995.

44.
Goldstein, Jerome
In Business for Yourself
Scribner's, 1982, 176 pp., $12.95
ISBN 0-684-17436-7. Dewey Decimal No.
658.022. LC Card No. 81-21256.
A guide to starting a small business and running it your way.

45.
Gough, J. W.
The Rise of the Entrepreneur
Schocken Books, 1970, 325 pp.
Dewey Decimal No. 338.70942. LC Card
No. 73-85677.

46.
Gray, Bob
How Entrepreneurs Make Business Profits
Cordovan Press, 1982, 173 pp. (paper)

ISBN 0-89123-018-1. Dewey Decimal No.
658.42. LC Card No. 82-71922.
A study of personal success stories from
Cordovan Business Journals.

47.
Greene, Gardner G.
*How to Start and Manage Your Own Small
Business*
McGraw-Hill, 1975
ISBN 07-024350-6.

48.
Greenfield, Sidney M., Arnold Strickon, and
Robert Aubey
Entrepreneurs in Cultural Context
University of New Mexico Press, 1979,
373 pp., $22.50
ISBN 0-8263-0504-0. Dewey Decimal No.
301.1832. LC Card No. 78-21433.

49.
Griffin, Barbara C.
*A Successful Business of Your Own and The
Speculators Handbook*
U.S. News and World Report Books, 1976,
$6.95
ISBN 0-8202-0167.
Two books in one. *A Successful Business
of Your Own* contains guidance on every
aspect of setting yourself up in business.
The Speculators Handbook introduces
exotic areas for investments.

50.
Guthrie, Michael, and Clifford D. Stromberg
*Entrepreneurial Health Care: How to Struc-
ture Successful New Ventures*
Harcourt Brace Jovanovich, 1985, 316 pp.
Dewey Decimal No. 344.73. LC Card No.
85-205403.

51.
Hammer, Marian Behan
*The Complete Handbook of How to Start and
Run a Money-Making Business in Your Home*
Parker Publishing Co., 1975, $9.95

ISBN 0-13-161265-4.
Chapters on finance, promotion, advertising, franchising, mail order, and other
specialized business activities. Many
examples, checklists, trade publications,
government helps, and reference materials are also listed.

52.
Harmon, Paul
*Small Business Management: A Practical
Approach*
Van Nostrand Reinhold, 1979
Provides the practical information a
person needs to start his or her own busi-
ness. It offers guidelines, warning signals,
and sources of help to keep the inexperi-
enced from stumbling.

53.
Henderson, Carter F.
Winners
Holt, Rinehart & Winston, 1985, 245 pp.,
$15.95
ISBN 0-03-001887-0. Dewey Decimal No.
658.1141. LC Card No. 85-5511.
The successful strategies entrepreneurs
use to build new businesses.

54.
Hennessy, Elizabeth
The Entrepreneurs
Scope Books, 1980
ISBN 0-906619-02-5 (cloth), 0-906619-03-
3 (paper). Dewey Decimal No.
338.0924. LC Card No. 80-476239.

55.
Hisrich, Robert D.
*Entrepreneurship, Intrapreneurship, and
Venture Capital*
Lexington Books, 1986, 160 pp., $21
ISBN 0-669-11867-2. Dewey Decimal No.
338.04. LC Card No. 85-45519.
How to attract seed money and venture
capital to support the development of
new ideas and introduce them to the
marketplace.

56.

Holland, Philip
The Entrepreneur's Guide
Putnam's, 1984, 252 pp., $17.95
ISBN 0-399-13005-5. Dewey Decimal No.
  658.1141. LC Card No. 84-9837.
How to start and succeed in your own
business.

57.

Holtz, Herman
Profit From Your Money-Making Ideas
AMACOM, 1982, 370 pp., $14.95 (cloth),
  $8.95 (paper)
ISBN 0-8144-5590-5 (cloth), 0-8144-7553-
  1 (paper). Dewey Decimal No. 658.041.
  LC Card No. 80-65880.
How to build a new business or expand
an existing one.

58.

Hosmer, LaRue T., and Roger Guiles
*Creating the Successful Business Plan for New
Ventures*
McGraw-Hill, 1985, 213 pp., $19.95
ISBN 0-07-030452-1. Dewey Decimal No.
  658.022. LC Card No. 84-19472.
Contains sections on the business plan,
industry analysis, market planning,
production planning, financial planning,
organizational planning, and presentation of written reports.

59.

*How to Start Your Own Business . . . and
Succeed*
McGraw-Hill, 1978, 320 pp., $39.95.
  Paperback edition 1981, 367 pp.,
  $16.95
ISBN 0-07-035648-3 (cloth); 0-07-035650-
  5 (paper). Dewey Decimal No.
  658.1141. LC Card No. 80-13058.
A three-ring looseleaf workbook/resource
manual for the person considering
starting a service, retail, or manufacturing
business. Filled with practical information and suggestions.

60.

Kent, Calvin A.
The Environment for Entrepreneurship
Lexington Books, 1984, 191 pp.
ISBN 0-669-07507-8. Dewey Decimal No.
  338.04. LC Card No. 83-48736.
Includes expanded versions of a series of
lectures given during 1982–83 at the
Center for Private Enterprise and Entre-
preneurship, Baylor University.

61.

Kent, Calvin A., Donald L. Sexton, and Karl
H. Vesper
Encyclopedia of Entrepreneurship
Prentice-Hall, 1982, 425 pp., $24.95
ISBN 0-13-275826-1. Dewey Decimal No.
  338.04. LC Card No. 81-10602.

62.

Kiam, Victor
*Going for It! How to Succeed as an
Entrepreneur*
Morrow, 1986, 260 pp., $16.95
ISBN 0-688-06060-9. Dewey Decimal No.
  338.040924. LC Card No. 85-61762.

63.

Kirzner, Israel M.
Competition and Entrepreneur
University of Chicago Press, 1973,
  242 pp., $5.95
ISBN 0-226-437760.
Attempts to show how the theory of
entrepreneurship and the theory of
competition coincide. It also offers a new
perspective on quality competition, on
selling effort, and on the fundamental
weakness of contemporary welfare
economics.

64.

Kirzner, Israel M.
Perception, Opportunity, and Profit
University of Chicago Press, 1979,
  274 pp.

ISBN 0-226-43773-6. Dewey Decimal No.
338.5201. LC Card No. 79-11765.
Studies in the theory of entrepreneurship.

65.
Kishel, Gregory F., and Patricia Gunter
Kishel
How to Start, Run and Stay in Business
Wiley, 1981, 200 pp., $9.95
ISBN 0-471-08274-0. LC Card No. 81-
3389.
A complete, step-by-step guide to forming and operating a small business.
Includes information on selecting a
business, selecting a site, financing,
insuring, and promoting the business.
Covers the advantages and disadvantages
of owning a small business, information
on structuring the business, physical
plant, ordering and inventory control,
pricing, record keeping, management, advertising, and promotion.

66.
Kling, John R.
The Basic Book of Business
CBI Publishing, 1977, $24.50
ISBN 0-84360751-3.
This book covers the broad general areas
of how to organize a new business, how
to operate it, how to sell out, and how to
prepare for retirement and plan your
estate. Includes case studies.

67.
Kreider, Carl Jonas
The Christian Entrepreneur
Herald Press, 1980, 220 pp., $7.95 (paper)
ISBN 0-8361-1936-3. Dewey Decimal No.
248.4897. LC Card No. 80-16836.

68.
Kuriloff, Arthur H., and John M. Hemphill
Starting and Managing the Small Business
McGraw-Hill, 1983, 592 pp., $22.95
ISBN 0-07-035662-9. Dewey Decimal No.
658.022. LC Card No. 82-18012.

Explores the fundamentals of going into
business and the psychic rejuvenation
it provides for those involved.

69.
Lane, Byron
Free Yourself in a Business of Your Own
Guild of Tutors Press, 1979

70.
Leavitt, Harold J.
*Corporate Pathfinders: Building Vision and
Values into Organizations*
Dow Jones-Irwin, $19.95
Pathfinders include the visionary, the
dreamer, the creator, and the entrepre-
neur. Managing with values, esthetics,
and beliefs.

71.
Levinson, Jay Conrad
Earning Money Without a Job
Holt, Rinehart & Winston, 1979, 204 pp.
ISBN 0-03-047606-2 (cloth), 0-03-
0476110-9 (paper).

72.
Mancuso, Joseph
The Entrepreneurship Handbook, 2 vols.
Artech House, 1974, $22.95 (per volume),
$35.50 (both)
ISBN 0-89006-040-1 (vol. 1), 0-89006-041-
X (vol. 2). Dewey Decimal No.
658.1141. LC Card No. 74-82601.
A collection of articles written by experts
in the various segments of the business
arena. Compiled specifically for manag-
ers in technology-based enterprises.
Focuses on the problems of managing a
significant manufacturing enterprise.

73.
Mancuso, Joseph
Fun and Guts
Center for Entrepreneurial Management,
1977
ISBN 0-201-04414-5.

A quick and painless way to gather the core ideas of entrepreneurship. Through a mixture of humorous and serious messages, provides background about the process of managing a small venture. Contains information on the characteristics of an entrepreneur, the life cycle of a small business, marketing the product, and much more.

74.

Mancuso, Joseph
Have You Got What It Takes?
Prentice-Hall, 1982, 230 pp., $16.95
  (cloth), $7.95 (paper)
ISBN 0-13-383893-5 (cloth), 0-13-383885-
  4 (paper). Dewey Decimal No. 658.022.
  LC Card No. 81-15686.
How to tell if you should start your own business.

75.

Mancuso, Joseph
How to Start, Finance and Manage Your Own Small Business
Prentice-Hall, 1978, 420 pp., $18.95
  (cloth), $9.95 (paper)
ISBN 0-13-434928-8 (cloth), 0-13-434910-
  5 (paper).
Focuses on the entrepreneur and the business plan. A guide for existing enterprises and a textbook on starting, financing, and managing aspects of business management. "Entrepreneur's Quiz" helps readers identify their entrepreneurial ability. Covers raising capital and preparing an effective business plan; five business plans and commentaries included.

76.

Mancuso, Joseph
The Small Business Survival Guide
Prentice-Hall, 1980, 422 pp.
ISBN 0-13-814228-9 (cloth), 0-13-814210-
  6 (paper). Dewey Decimal No. 658.022.
  LC Card No. 80-19061.
Sources of help for entrepreneur.

77.

McKiernan, John
Planning and Financing Your New Business: A Guide to Venture Capital
Technology Management, 1978, 166 pp.,
  $15.95
ISBN 0-686-14350-7.
Designed as an entrepreneur's handbook for starting a business enterprise. Describes entrepreneurs, what they are like, how they think, what motivates them, and the skills or characteristics they need to be successful. Also deals with marketing and conducting marketing research, planning, and venture capital—what it is, how it works, and why it exists.

78.

McLaughlin, Harold
Building Your Business Plan: A Step-by-Step Approach
Wiley, 1985, 297 pp., $24.95
A comprehensive, step-by-step guide for developing a business plan from A to Z. Includes checklists and model plans.

79.

Meredith, G. G., Robert E. Nelson, and Philip A. Neck
The Practice of Entrepreneurship
International Labour Office, 1982, 196
  pp.
ISBN 92-210-2839-9 (cloth), 92-210-2846-
  1 (paper). Dewey Decimal No. 658.42.
  LC Card No. 82-186539.

80.

Metcalf, Wendell
Starting and Managing a Small Business of Your Own
US Gov't Printing Office, 1973, 97 pp.,
  $3.50
ISBN 045-000-00124-7.
Takes readers through the steps of starting and managing a small business, from selecting the right business to how to launch the new enterprise.

81.
Minkow, Barry
Making It in America
B. Minkow, 1985, 136 pp.
ISBN 0-9615900-0-9. LC Card No. 85-
  51822.

82.
Morrison, Robert H.
Greedy Bastard's Business Manual
Morrison, Butterfield & Boyle, 1981, 666
  pp., $19.95
ISBN 0-936062-02-9. Dewey Decimal No.
  658.022. LC Card No. 81-14217.
Small-business wealth-building for the
1980s.

83.
Morrison, Robert S.
Handbook for Manufacturing Entrepreneurs
Western Reserve, 1973, 571 pp., $17.50
ISBN 0-686-05578-0.
A discussion of owner-managed manufacturing from the decision to go into the
business to maintaining the operation
after the owner-manager retires. Covers
all the various phases of starting up,
operations, and maintaining an owner-
managed manufacturing company.

84.
Mucciolo, Louis
Small Business: Look Before You Leap
Arco, 1981, 290 pp., $8.95
ISBN 0-668-05173-6. Dewey Decimal No.
  658.022. LC Card No. 80-26082.
A catalog of sources of information to
help start a small business.

85.
Mucciolo, Louis
Starting and Winning in Small Business
Arco, 1982, 208 pp., $8.95
ISBN 0-668-05239-2. Dewey Decimal No.
  658.022. LC Card No. 81-12913.

86.
Osgood, William R., and Victoria Thompson
Business Resource Directory

Federal Reserve Bank of Boston, 1974,
  169 pp.
Dewey Decimal No. 658.403. LC Card No.
  75-601428.
A source of assistance groups for the New
England entrepreneur.

87.
Ronen, Joshua
Entrepreneurship
Lexington Books, 1983, 323 pp.
ISBN 0-669-05715-0. Dewey Decimal No.
  338.04. LC Card No. 82-47950.

88.
Rosefsky, Robert S.
*Getting Free: How to Profit Most Out of
Working for Yourself*
Quadrangle, 1977, 256 pp., $9.95
ISBN 0-8129-0663-2.
Helps readers to evaluate present career
to determine whether they are happy.
If not, the book suggests specific steps
that can be taken, and some that should
be avoided, in establishing a new career.
It discusses financing, professional
assistance, taxes, and much more.

89.
Scarborogh, Norman M., and Thomas W.
Zimmerer
Effective Small Business Management
Merrill, 544 pp.
ISBN 0-675-20101-2. Dewey Decimal No.
  658.022. LC Card No. 84-60046.
Introductory text, combining theory with
the actual concerns of businesspeople,
for starting and operating a successful
small business. Includes 40 case studies
and 4 appendices on SBA publication
and office locations.

90.
Scase, Richard, and Robert Goffee
The Entrepreneurial Middle Class
Croom Helm, 1982, 212 pp.

ISBN 0-7099-0450-9. Dewey Decimal No.
305.554. LC Card No. 81-208110.

91.

Schollhammer, Hans, and Arthur H. Kuriloff
Entrepreneurship and Small Business Management, 2nd edition
Wiley, 1987, $39.95
ISBN 0-471-89860-0.
Integrates the concepts of starting a small
business and managing small firms. A
step-by-step look at small business from
the new-venture idea through its implementation and management. Stresses
legal considerations and financing, and
explains how to avoid common pitfalls.
Includes real-life cases from actual small-
business management.

92.

Sexton, Donald L., and Raymond W. Smilor
The Art and Science of Entrepreneurship
Ballinger, 1986, 422 pp.
ISBN 0-88730-070-7. Dewey Decimal No.
338.04. LC Card No. 85-22843.
Papers from a conference held in Febru-
ary 1985 sponsored by the RGK Founda-
tion, the IC2 Institute at the University of
Texas at Austin, and the Center for
Entrepreneurship at Baylor University.

93.

Shilling, Dana
Be Your Own Boss
Penguin, 1984, 385 pp., $8.95
ISBN 0-14-046631-2. Dewey Decimal No.
658.041. LC Card No. 83-19515.
The complete, indispensable, hands-on
guide to starting and running your
own business.

94.

Silver, A. David
*Entrepreneurial Life: How to Go for It and
Get It*
Ronald Press/Wiley, 244 pp., $19.15

ISBN 0-471-87382-9. LC Card No. 82-
24838.
Profiles of successful entrepreneurs, from
key personality traits and characteristics
to the critical, step-by-step process they
follow in launching a new company.

95.

Siropolis, Nicholas C.
*Small Business Management: A Guide to
Entrepreneurship,* 2nd edition
Houghton Mifflin, 1982, 570 pp.
ISBN 0-395-31732-0. Dewey Decimal No.
658.022. LC Card No. 81-82561.
For those who are contemplating the
startup of a business or for those already
in business. Contains overview of entrepreneurship, problems of launching a
new venture, and problems connected
with managing a new venture.

96.

Small, Samuel
Starting a Business After 50
Pilot Books, 1977, $2.50
ISBN 0-87576-008-2.
Shows how to establish a small business,
a franchised business, and a business at
home. A comprehensive listing of 175
franchise opportunities.

97.

Smith, Randy Baca
Setting Up Shop
Warner Books, 1983, 274 pp.
ISBN 0-446-37533-0. Dewey Decimal No.
658.114. LC Card No. 82-20084.
The do's and don'ts of starting a small
business.

98.

Sobel, Robert
*The Entrepreneurs: Explorations Within the
American Business Tradition*
Longman Financial Services, 1974, 383
pp., $6.95

ISBN 0-679-40066-4. Dewey Decimal No.
338.009. LC Card No. 74-76157.
Takes a look at major figures who were
entrepreneurs in the business world—
their leadership, influence, and many
other important characteristics.

99.
Sonfield, Matthew C.
Small Business in the 1980's
Hofstra University, 1984, 569 pp.
Dewey Decimal No. 658.022. LC Card No.
84-80399.
An analysis of entrepreneurial traits and
the decision to start a business. Consists
of MBA theses written by Hofstra Univer-
sity students during 1982–83.

100.
Sterling Publishing Co.
How to Start Your Own Small Business
Sterling, 1982, 320 pp., $6.95
ISBN 0-8069-7600-4. Dewey Decimal No.
658.022. LC Card No. 81-85067.
Practical information about the facts and
figures of starting and managing a small
business.

101.
Stevens, Mark
*How to Pyramid Small Business Ventures into
a Personal Fortune*
Prentice-Hall, 1977, $9.95
ISBN 0-13-430686-4.
Covers a wide variety of areas, including
how to pick the most lucrative fields, how
to obtain and use free government research, how to apply leveraging. Detailed
case histories.

102.
Stevens, Mark
The 10-Minute Entrepreneur
Warner Books, 1985, 250 pp.
ISBN 0-446-38069-5. Dewey Decimal No.
658.159. LC Card No. 84-21890.

103.
Stevenson, Howard H., Michael J. Roberts,
and H. Irving Grousbeck
New Business Ventures and the Entrepreneur
Irwin, 1985, 738 pp.
ISBN 0-256-02166-X. Dewey Decimal No.
658.11. LC Card No. 84-81414.

104.
Stickney, John
*Self-Made: Braving an Independent Career in
a Corporate Age*
Putnam's, 1980, 222 pp., $10.95
ISBN 0-399-11931-0. Dewey Decimal No.
650.102. LC Card No. 80-12525.

105.
Storey, D. J.
Entrepreneurship and the New Firm
Croom Helm, 1982, 233 pp., $13.95
ISBN 0-7099-2347-3. Dewey Decimal No.
338.642. LC Card No. 82-165361.

106.
Taffi, Donald J.
*The Entrepreneur, a Corporate Strategy for
the '80s*
AMACOM, 1981, 44 pp., $7.50 ($5 to
members)
ISBN 0-8144-2264-0. Dewey Decimal No.
658.42. LC Card No. 81-4443.

107.
Tarrant, John J.
Making It Big on Your Own
Playboy Press, 1981, 248 pp.
ISBN 0-87223-676-5. Dewey Decimal No.
658.114. LC Card No. 81-566.
How to start, finance, and manage a new
business in the 1980s.

108.
Tate, Curtis E., Jr.
The Complete Guide to Your Own Business
Dow Jones–Irwin, 1977, 384 pp., $30
ISBN 0-87094-144-5.

Step-by-step guide to establishing a new business and running it for profit and growth. Also includes information on how to enter an existing business and how to go about getting a franchise.

109.
Taylor, Charlotte
The Entrepreneurial Workbook
New American Library, 1985
ISBN 0-452-25660-7. Dewey Decimal No.
   658.022. LC Card No. 84-29439.

110.
Taylor, Frederick John
How to Be Your Own Boss: A Complete Guide to Starting and Running Your Own Business
Business Books, 1975, 171 pp.
Covers all topics needed to successfully start your own business—everything from where to look for financing to how to organize time properly.

111.
Tetreault, Wilfred, and Robert W. Clements
Starting Right in Your New Business
Addison-Wesley, 1982, 242 pp., $7.95
   (paper)
ISBN 0-201-07709-4. Dewey Decimal No.
   658.114. LC Card No. 81-512.
Learn to finance a business with little or no money down, avoid costly mistakes, ensure the future earning power of a business, and more. A straight, honest book that answers questions of those starting a new business.

112.
Timmons, Jeffry A., and Leonard E. Smollen
New Venture Creation: A Guide to Entrepreneurship
Irwin, 1985, 700 pp.
ISBN 0-256-03476-1. Dewey Decimal No.
   658.11. LC Card No. 85-60245.

113.
Torrence, Ronald W.
In the Owner's Chair

Prentice-Hall, 1986, 286 pp., $28.95
ISBN 0-8359-3203-6. Dewey Decimal No.
   658.022. LC Card No. 85-14545.
Proven techniques for taking a business from $0.00 to $10 million.

114.
Van Voorhis, Kenneth R.
Entrepreneurship and Small Business Management
Allyn & Bacon, 1980, 565 pp.
ISBN 0-205-06682-8. Dewey Decimal No.
   658.022. LC Card No. 79-12636.
Covers all the practical tools and techniques for launching and operating a successful small business. Includes initial person assessment, understanding entrepreneurship, a feasibility study, the startup of venture, major decision areas of running a firm, and problem solving. Two case examples.

115.
Vesper, Karl H.
New Venture Strategies
Prentice-Hall, 1980, 303 pp., $16.95
   (cloth), $10.95 (paper)
ISBN 0-13-615948-6 (cloth), 0-13-615930-
   3 (paper). Dewey Decimal No. 658.11.
   LC Card No. 79-1336.
Describes strategies—both personal and commercial—that can be used to embark on new business ventures effectively.

116.
Weaver, Peter
Your Inc.: A Detailed Escape Route to Being Your Own Boss
Doubleday, 1975, 284 pp., $3.95
ISBN 0-385-09895-2.
For those considering leaving a present secure job and starting a new business.

117.
Welsh, John A., and Jerry F. White
The Entrepreneur's Master Planning Guide

Prentice-Hall, 1983, 408 pp., $11.95
 (paper), $21.95 (cloth)
ISBN 0-13-282806-5 (paper), 0-13-
 282814-6 (cloth). Dewey Decimal No.
 658.42. LC Card No. 82-18112.
How to launch a successful business.

118.
White, Richard M.
The Entrepreneur's Manual
Chilton, 1977, 419 pp., $21.50
ISBN 0-8019-6454-7. LC Card No. 76-
 55520.
How to operate a business; company
management.

119.
Wilken, Paul H.
*Entrepreneurship: A Comparative and
Historical Study*
Ablex, 1979, 306 pp.
ISBN 0-89391-020-1. Dewey Decimal No.
 338.04. LC Card No. 79-4236.

120.
Williams, Edward E., and Salvatore E.
Manzo
Business Planning for the Entrepreneur
Van Nostrand Reinhold, 1983, 200 pp.
ISBN 0-442-28970-7. Dewey Decimal No.
 658.401. LC Card No. 82-8658.
How to write and execute a business
plan.

WOMEN ENTREPRENEURS

Businesses created or owned by women are the fastest-growing segment of America's private enterprises. Sociological changes, economic necessity, and personal ambition are bringing women into the business arena in increasing numbers, and they are succeeding in a marketplace long thought to be dominated by men. As with their male counterparts, however, success has come only to those whose vision and courage have been conditioned by training and experience. The business arena is a difficult and exacting environment, but personal preparation and careful planning will engender confidence, make complications more manageable, and increase the personal satisfaction of operating a privately owned business.

MURIEL SIEBERT
Muriel Siebert & Co.
New York City

"What do you call most new entrepreneurs?"

"Madam president!"

The question is rhetorical, and the answer is deliberately humorous, but the implication is a very real fact of life in today's small-business world. The word *entrepreneurship*, once used almost exclusively to identify certain masculine business activities, is but another in a long list of terms that have been stripped of gender in recent years. This is not surprising, for women in increasing numbers are becoming small-business owners—at an annual growth rate three times that of men—and many are surviving in a highly competitive marketplace that consistently devours 70 percent of its first-time entrants.

This surge in female entrepreneurship is a recent phenomenon. Indeed, four decades ago women composed less than 26 percent of the total American work force and owned only a small portion of the nation's businesses. In earlier times, women were expected to be wives and mothers first, and those who found it necessary or desirable to seek employment outside this framework could do so only in a limited number of "female" career fields, such as teaching, nursing, and secretarial activities. Then World War II gave women the opportunity to demonstrate proficiency at "men's work." Thereafter, the concept of what constituted a "proper role" for women never reverted to its former rigidity.

The evidence is indisputable. Today, more than 50 percent of American women of working age are engaged in business activities, and the number of women small-business owners has risen sharply in recent years. Why this persistent surge? A realistic explanation involves much more than a recap of the changes wrought by the women's liberation movement, significant though they have been. Rather, the true reasons are to be found in the will and determination of women themselves, who now view the entrepreneurial world as men always have—a window of opportunity for self-expression and individual achievement.

This window, however, has yet to become an open door. Women still suffer from being "the new kid on the block," for the business support systems developed and used mostly by men through the years have been slow in addressing the needs of women entrepreneurs. For example, women often experience greater problems in finding options for financing their businesses because many of them have not established credit histories or accumulated the assets or savings needed for leveraging or collateralizing loans. In addition, the business referral network remains essentially a male-oriented environment, and so does the array of checklists (such as the *Fortune 500*) used as measures of success.

The major stumbling blocks continue to be a lack of experience and undeveloped business-related skills, deficiencies that can be bridged only by time and persistence. There are other problems as well. Marriage and parenthood continue to influence the timing and selection of careers, and many discover that combining jobs with parenthood limits career growth, especially when divorce results in single-parent households. Nonetheless, women have shown a remarkable resiliency in coping with these conditions.

The road of upward mobility for women entrepreneurs is more difficult than the one men travel, but it is becoming more manageable because women are committing the time and energy needed to prepare themselves for careers in business. Far more of them than ever before are now earning college degrees in business, economics, law, medicine, and engineering, and they are using these educational skills to enter the professions and to start service-related enterprises in record numbers.

Because of this growth, considerable attention is being devoted to the study of female business ownership and to analyzing the characteristics of "typical" women entrepreneurs. Studies show that most firms owned by women have been in existence for fewer than five years, that they have fewer than five employees, that gross annual sales average less than $500,000, and that women entrepreneurs start their businesses a decade later than men, usually between the ages of 35 and 45. This research also reveals that there is a high concentration of women in service-related businesses, especially those associated with certain types of sales activities such as real estate, insurance, retailing, and manufacturers' representatives.

The future for women entrepreneurs appears exceptionally bright, and as more and more of them start and manage successful small businesses, a greater number will emerge as role models and mentors. This unquestionably will affect the overall character of the marketplace. Change will not come overnight, but when the critical mass of women participants becomes great enough, some of the male-dominated overtones of the marketplace will begin to soften, and its rewards will be shared more equitably among those men and women whose performances justify greater consideration.

121.
Boehm, Helen F., and Nancy Dunnan
With a Little Luck—An American Odyssey
Rawson, 1985, 219 pp., $17.95
ISBN 0-89256-277-3. Dewey Decimal No. 338.766. LC Card No. 84-42928.

122.
Goffee, Robert, and Richard Scase
Women in Charge: The Experiences of Female Entrepreneurs
Allen & Unwin, 1985
ISBN 0-04-301189-6 (paper). Dewey Decimal No. 338.040. LC Card No. 84-24449.

123.
Hilton, Terri
Small Business Ideas for Women and How to Get Started
Pilot Books, 1975, $2 (paper)
ISBN 0-87576-050-3.
A guide to the field of self-employment. Provides information on businesses that can be started with a modest investment, including many that can be operated from the home on a part-time basis. Shows how to make extra income by judicious use of spare time.

124.
Hisrich, Robert D., and Candida G. Brush
The Woman Entrepreneur: Starting, Financing, and Managing a Successful Business
Lexington Books, 1986, 216 pp., $14.95
ISBN 0-669-09189-8. LC Card No. 84-48256.
Guidebook for starting a business, with a close look at the special problems women face. Covers sources of capital, developing marketing plans, hiring, test marketing, promotion, taxes, and more.

125.
Jessup, Claudia, and Genie Chipps
Supergirls

Harper & Row, 1972
A lighthearted narrative of the trial and error of two college-trained young women who started and operated their own small businesses in New York City. Covers four years of their particular experiences. Some good checklists are incorporated in the text.

126.
Jessup, Claudia, and Genie Chipps
The Woman's Guide to Starting a Business
Holt, Rinehart & Winston, 1976, $8.95 (cloth), $4.95 (paper)
ISBN 0-03-014606-2 (cloth), 0-03-017611-5 (paper).
Information and sources needed for striking out on your own. Case studies of successful women entrepreneurs. Appendix of additional sources of information.

127.
Leslie, Mary, and David Seltz
New Businesses Women Can Start and Successfully Operate
Barnes & Noble, 1979, $2.95 (paper)
ISBN 0-06-463487-6.
Food, writing, research, selling, animals, and promotion are some of the topics evaluated in the book's 16 chapters. Good appendix of information sources.

128.
Lester, Mary
A Woman's Guide to Starting a Small Business
Pilot Books, $2.50
The 7 basic steps in starting a business, along with a 20-point beginner's checklist. Main thrust: low-overhead businesses, evaluating your potential, and finding business management assistance.

129.
McVicar, Marjorie, and Julia F. Craig
Minding My Own Business

Marek, 1981, 348 pp., $13.95
ISBN 0-399-90116-7. Dewey Decimal No.
   650.108. LC Card No. 80-29423.
Entrepreneurial women share their
secrets for success.

130.
Riccardi, Betty Rinehart, and Elizabeth Crow
Dayani
The Nurse Entrepreneur
Reston, 1982, 204 pp., $18.95
ISBN 0-8359-5018-2. Dewey Decimal No.
   362.173. LC Card No. 82-5415.

131.
Small, Anne
A Woman's Guide to Her Own Franchised
Business
Pilot Books, $3.50
Peculiarly adaptable to women of all
ages, franchising is taking off across the
country.

132.
U.S. Congress, Senate Committee on Small
Business
Women Entrepreneurs, Their Success and
Problems

US Gov't Printing Office, 1984, 98 pp.
Dewey Decimal No. 338.040. LC Card No.
   84-603429.
Hearing before the Committee on Small
Business, United States Senate, Ninety-
eighth Congress, second session.

133.
Wilkens, Joanne
Her Own Business: Success Secrets of Entre-
preneurial Women
McGraw-Hill, 1987, 240 pp., $16.95
ISBN 0-07-050854-2.
Manual for any woman considering a
self-employment venture. Contains
interviews with successful businesswomen, self-help assessments, and
appropriate guidelines and advice.

134.
Winston, Sandra
Entrepreneurial Woman
Newsweek Books, 1979, 238 pp., $8.95
ISBN 0-88225-259-3.
Shows women how to become an entre-
preneur with proper preparation, and
how to overcome obstacles.

MINORITY ENTREPRENEURS

The need for more minority-owned businesses should be of pressing concern to all Americans if we are to successfully combat the problems of minority unemployment and economic disadvantage. Some encouraging signs are emerging. There is a measurable increase in interest among minorities for careers in business, and the number of new enterprises is growing at a steady rate, thanks in large measure to special programs that have been developed to help with planning and raising startup capital. Although minority entrepreneurs may face some discouraging problems, the doors of economic opportunity nonetheless remain uniquely open to them because of their understanding and sensitivity to the basic needs of their potential customers.

A. G. GASTON
Chairman and CEO
Citizens Federal Savings Bank
Birmingham, Alabama

Two decades ago, *minority enterprise* was a term that aroused little interest. Today, it is considered one of the most vital subjects in the overall development of the American economy because minority entrepreneurship represents a ladder of upward mobility for those ethnic groups that traditionally have not enjoyed wide participation in business activities. Increased attention now is being devoted to studying the reasons why some minority groups have been poorly represented in the nation's total entrepreneurial endeavors, and recent findings offer both hope and encouragement.

Some U.S. minorities have succeeded well in the marketplace while others have not, and this poses some interesting psychological and sociological questions. In seeking explanations for this phenomenon, researchers have learned that a controlling consideration usually is found in social pressures, particularly those felt within home environments. Entrepreneurs come most often from families who insist on high performance standards for their children and who stress self-reliance. Education is paramount to these families, and they are willing to endure many hardships to help their children achieve the highest professional preparation possible.

In the past, the absence of such social pressures, as well as the lack of career education and prior business exposure, unquestionably caused many members of minority groups to develop a sense of hopelessness and frustration when considering business opportunities. Fortunately, however, these educational and economic disadvantages are dissipating. Statistics show a steady increase in the number of minority students in undergraduate business subjects and courses leading to graduate professional certification. Moreover, the number of new businesses started by these "disadvantaged" groups is rising sharply, owing in some measure to a raft of assistance and incentive programs created by government and the business community.

The most visible example of federal assistance is the Small Business Administration, an agency created in 1957 for the express purpose of encouraging and aiding the development of small businesses. Through its "participating loan" program, the SBA has been responsible for helping countless new businesses find appropriate startup capital by guaranteeing up to 90 percent of individual loan packages obtained through private financial institutions. The agency also oversees other key programs, such as the provisions in Section 8 of the Small Business Act that reserve to small firms a percentage of all government purchases, and the Minority Set-Aside Program, which requires the allotment of a portion of these government purchases specifically to minority-owned companies. The SBA also provides loans at low interest rates to two types of private investment firms. One of these, Minority Enterprise Small Business Investment Companies (MESBICs), extend loan opportunities only to minority-owned enterprises. See Section 8 for more details.

Corporate America also has shown increasing sensitivity to the disproportionate representation of certain minorities at the upper professional levels. Companies large and small have developed programs that provide for a systematic increase in the number of minorities in both executive and management positions, and many national food and service chains have recognized the wisdom of awarding new franchises to entrepreneurs who will operate businesses in their own neighborhoods. Such efforts benefit both the businesses and the minority groups; the bottom line in economic endeavors is profits, and the ability to penetrate the more ethnically oriented markets not only helps increase corporate earnings but also allows minority owners the opportunity to share in these profits.

Government and corporate assistance programs notwithstanding, pride accounts for much of the recent surge in minority enterprises and professional advancements. Those men and women who historically have been underrepresented in the business world are now succeeding in record numbers because they are helping themselves, and they are doing so in the finest traditions of our immigrant forebears—through hard work, perseverance, and sacrifice—and by developing an increased sophistication and knowledge about the workings of the competitive marketplace.

135.
Bailey, Ronald W., ed.
Black Business Enterprise
Basic Books, 1971
Collection of articles on black business, its successes and failures, with emphasis on the future.

136.
Cross, Theodore L.
Black Capitalism: Strategy for Business in the Ghetto
Atheneum, 1971, 174 pp., $3.95 (paper)
ISBN 0-689-70266-3.
Written by a trained lawyer, a relatively

young man, who describes the community as he found it in the late 1960s. Contains suggestions for action.

137.

Gupta, Brijen, and Arthur D. Lopatin
Starting and Succeeding in Small Business: A Guide for the Inner City Businessman
Council on International and Public
  Affairs, 1978
Answers basic questions of existing and prospective minority entrepreneurs in the inner-city areas of Rochester; sources for further help and information.

138.

Halliday, Thelma Y.
Minorities in the Field of Business (An Annotated Bibliography)
Howard University Press, 1975

139.

Huff, Ann S., and Samuel I. Doctors
Minority Enterprise and the President's Council
Ballinger Publishing, 1973, 201 pp.
ISBN 0-88410-002-2.
Documents experiences of the President's Council on Minority Business Enterprise, an advisory group; presents the minority economic development program it recommended to President Nixon and assesses the impact from the program.

140.

Hund, James M.
Black Entrepreneurship
Wadsworth, 1970, 157 pp.
Dewey Decimal No. 338.7. LC Card No.
  76-135348.

141.

Jones, Thomas B.
A Franchising Guide for Blacks
Pilot Books, 1973, $2 (paper)
ISBN 0-87576-004-X.

Written with special interest for black entrepreneurs. Details the pitfalls of franchising and how to avoid them. Helps readers identify their own potential and evaluate whether this potential can be brought out in franchising.

142.

Lee, Roy F.
The Setting for Black Business Development
New York State School of Industrial and
  Labor Relations, 1973, $7 (paper),
  $10 (cloth)
ISBN 0-87546-039-9 (paper), 0-87546-
  275-8 (cloth).
Discusses the sociological and economic development of blacks from a macro perspective.

143.

Levitan, Sar. A., Garth L. Mangum, and Robert Taggert III
Economic Opportunity in the Ghetto: The Partnership of Government and Business
Johns Hopkins Press, 1970, $7 (cloth),
  $1.95 (paper)
ISBN 0-80108-1163-5 (cloth), 0-80108-
  1144-9 (paper).
A dispassionate and factual study of the economic situation in the ghetto and some of the possible solutions. Included are sections explaining the need to create new private-sector jobs near the ghetto business, and the need for government-business partnership.

144.

Light, Ivan H.
Ethnic Enterprise in America
University of California Press, 1972,
  $12.75 (cloth), $3.95 (paper)
ISBN 0-520-01738-2 (cloth), 0-520-02485-
  0 (paper).
A sociological study of the underrepresentation in small business by black Americans, including their special difficulty in securing business loans.

145.
MacDonald, Stephen, ed.
Business and Blacks
Dow Jones-Irwin, 1970, 150 pp.
ISBN 0-87128-456-1. Dewey Decimal No.
   331.639. LC Card No. 74-121050.
Selected articles from the *Wall Street
Journal* on minorities as employees and
entrepreneurs.

146.
Office of Minority Business Enterprise
Minority Business Enterprise—A Bibliography
U.S. Department of Commerce, 1973
Intended as a comprehensive and useful
resource tool dealing with minority
business enterprise. Each of the 1,413
items is numbered consecutively for easy
reference, and a subject index is provided.

147.
Purcell, Theodore V., and Gerald F.
Cavanaugh
Blacks in the Industrial World
Free Press, 1972, $15.95 (cloth), $5.95
   (paper)
ISBN 0-02-925520-1 (cloth), 0-02-925470-
   9 (paper).

Presents black business in its macro
setting.

148.
Seder, John, and Berkeley G. Burrell
*Getting It Together (Black Businessmen in
America)*
Harcourt Brace Jovanovich, 1971
Case histories of black people who have
been successful in many different areas
of business as owners.

149.
Venable, Abraham S.
Building Black Business
Crowell, 1972
Written by a U.S. Government official
directly responsible for the improvement
of minority business in the United States.

150.
Wichita State University
*A Small and Minority Business Management
and Procurement Study for the Kansas
Department of Economic Development*
Wichita State University, 1979
Report of research conducted to determine the desire of small and minority
businesses to get involved in a state set-
aside program and to generally encourage
economic development.

FOREIGN ENTREPRENEURS

Foreign markets are a fertile source of business opportunities, even though some of the entrepreneurial qualities that lead to success in home markets often are constrained by business practices and regulations in the foreign environment. The large number of small U.S. firms that do business abroad and compete favorably with home-grown or produced goods offer unquestioned encouragement to any entrepreneur who is willing to plan carefully and do the homework, including consulting with legal advisers and the appropriate government agencies offering assistance to foreign venturers.

SHELDON COLEMAN
Chairman and CEO
The Coleman Company, Inc.

Peter Drucker refers to entrepreneurial practice as "fundamentally an American phenomenon." History substantiates this notion. The spirit of free enterprise in the United States predates even Adam Smith's seminal work, *The Wealth of Nations*, for the American colonists regarded the right to flex one's economic muscles as inseparable from all other freedoms guaranteed by English law. Indeed, the American Revolution was grounded partly in a prolonged dispute over limiting colonial entrepreneurial activities.

After the United States gained its independence, the right to pursue happiness in whatever legal endeavor an individual might choose became a dominant characteristic in this wilderness nation, constitutionally indistinguishable from political liberty. Thus, American businessmen and women have grown up with the freedom to pursue economic dreams in an environment purposely adjusted periodically through the years to ensure equal opportunity in the marketplace for all participants. As a result, the ingenuity of Yankee entrepreneurs oftentimes set an enviable pace throughout the world.

This is decreasingly true. The growing awareness of the interdependency of nations has motivated many countries to acknowledge the essential role entrepreneurs play in promoting the general welfare of their people. Even the People's Republic of China, long the proponent of collectivist ideology, has relaxed its grip on enterprise-for-profit in its move toward *scientific socialism*, a term that belies the anomaly it reflects.

Certainly mainland China has numerous examples of what private enterprise can do for a nation's economy. Some of her neighbors, such as Japan, Taiwan, and Korea, as well as cities like Hong Kong and Shanghai, have developed economies that compete favorably with the larger industrial nations of the world—and often tip the balance of trade in their favor. Businesspeople in these countries enjoy the advantage of cooperative governments that provide financial support as well as leadership in economic planning. Understandably, foreign entrepreneurs frequently suffer in this type of support system because such national planning often erects a protective shield around home markets and makes it more difficult for goods of other nations to penetrate them.

American firms historically have found easier access to the markets of those European countries in which compatible political and economic philosophies exist. Although some of these nations experimented with state ownership of basic industries after World War II, they fortunately did not discard the fundamental concepts of democratic capitalism. Thus, the spirit of entrepreneurship and private enterprise remains integral to their economic development; indeed, nations such as France, Italy, West Germany, and even Yugoslavia have demonstrated remarkable (sometimes surprising) expertise in producing goods and services that challenge those of any country.

Most of these countries discovered long ago that the U.S. consumer market, the strongest and most developed in the world, is an international magnet. The products of almost every nation are to be found throughout the United States. Presently, foreign entrepreneurs enjoy far greater access to the U.S. marketplace than their American counterparts do in other nations. Perhaps the day may not be too distant when all nations will acknowledge their interdependency and when innovative and creative individuals, regardless of ethnicity, sex, or national origin, will be free to assume risks in any of the world's markets and be afforded the opportunity to receive an equitable return from their efforts.

151.
Aslund, Anders
Private Enterprise in Eastern Europe
Macmillan, 1985, 294 pp.
ISBN 0-333-37412-6. Dewey Decimal No. 338.610.

152.
Barth, Frederick
The Role of the Entrepreneur in Social Change in Northern Norway
Scandinavian University Books, 1963
Four essays by anthropologists about the northern Norway entrepreneur.

153.
Campbell, John Creighton, ed.
Entrepreneurship in a Mature Industry
Center for Japanese Studies, University of Michigan, 1985, $9
ISBN 0-939512-22-X. Dewey Decimal No. 338.476. LC Card No. 85-29128.
Proceedings of the Fifth U.S.-Japan Automotive Industry Conference, held at the University of Michigan in March 1985.

154.
Clarke, Philip
Small Businesses in Britain: How They Survive and Succeed
Barnes & Noble, 1973, 380 pp.
Looks at all general aspects of small business. Reviews reasons for failure, money problems, government.

155.
Copeland, Lennie, and Lewis Griggs
Going International
Random House, 279 pp., $21
Provides universal truths and rules that
apply anywhere and in almost any
situation. Includes country summary,
do's and don'ts, special sensitivities at a
glance. Provides fundamental information for international transactions.

156.
Coutarelli, Spiro A.
Venture Capital in Europe
Praeger, 1977, 164 pp., $19.95
ISBN 0-275-56680-3.
How venture capital is raised in Europe,
what lending organizations are looking
for in a borrower, and the process
through which a company goes when
lending money. Includes appendix on
how to raise venture capital and a list of
European capitalists.

157.
Europa Publications Ltd.
International Who's Who 1985–86
Unipub, 1985, 1530 pp., $130
ISBN 0-905118-86-3.
An international biographic reference
source for essential facts on the most
outstanding men and women in every
country of the world today.

158.
Gauld, Charles A.
*The Last Titan: Percival Farquhar, American
Entrepreneur in Latin America*
Hispanic American Luso-Brazilian
   Studies Institute of California, 1972,
   $5.50
ISBN 0-912098-04-X.
Biography of well-known American
responsible for developing many rail-
roads, utilities, and other industries in
Latin America.

159.
Gautam, Vinayshil
Enterprise and Society
Concept Publishing Co., 1979, 118 pp.,
   $7
Dewey Decimal No. 658.400. LC Card No.
   79-901126.
A study of some aspects of entrepreneur-
ship and management in India.

160.
Granick, David
The European Executive
Doubleday, 1979, $25
ISBN 0-405-12093-1.
Analysis of postwar European executive.
Sections on entrepreneurship and owner-
managers show the difference between
American and European executives.

161.
Harper, Malcolm
Consultancy for Small Business
Intermediate Technology Pubs., 1977,
   254 pp., $19.95 (paper)
ISBN 0-903031-42-6.
Summarizes results of five years of
experiments to provide economic on-the-
spot consultancy to small businesses in
developing countries.

162.
Harper, Malcolm
*Small Business in the Third World: Guidelines
for Practical Assistance*
Wiley, 1984
ISBN 0-471-90210-1. LC Card No. 83-
   25960.
Guidelines for promoting new and small
enterprises in developing countries.
Treats issues such as the roles of small
business in social and economic development and appropriate administrative and
funding institutions.

163.
Haskins, Gay, Allan Gibb, and Tony Hubert,
eds.
A Guide to Small Firms Assistance in Europe

Gower, 1986, 263 pp., $71.95
ISBN 0-566-05082-X. Dewey Decimal No.
   338.642. LC Card No. 85-27307.
Contributors from 17 countries.

164.

Ichimura, Shin'ichi
Japanese Entrepreneurship in the Early Stage
of Economic Development
Center for Southeast Asian Studies, Kyoto
   University, 1973
Dewey Decimal No. 338.040. LC Card No.
   80-473440.

165.

Japan Economic Journal
High-Tech Start-Up Ventures in Japan
Unipub, 1984, 256 pp., $149.50
Five hundred of the most promising high-
tech venture companies in Japan are
listed in alphabetical format. Includes
strengths and weaknesses, overseas
strategies, capitalization, R&D capabilities, and prospective financial sources.

166.

Johns, B. L., W. D. Shealan, and W. J.
Dunlop
Small Business in Australia: Problems and
Prospects
Allen & Unwin, 1978, 204 pp., $14.95
Economic and social aspects of small
business in Australia.

167.

Jones, Leroy P., and Il SaKong
Government, Business, and Entrepreneurship
in Economic Development
Council on East Asian Studies, Harvard
   University, 1980, 434 pp.
ISBN 0-674-35791-4. Dewey Decimal No.
   338.951. LC Card No. 79-28671.
Studies in the modernization of the
Republic of Korea, 1945–75.

168.

Kurzweil, Edith
Italian Entrepreneurs: Rearguard of Progress
Praeger, 1983, 221 pp., $23.95

169.

Melo, Jose Luiz, Anamaria Ladeira Aragao,
and Yoichi Koiko
Business Leaders in Brazil
Institute of Developing Economies, 1982,
   163 pp.
Dewey Decimal No. 338.040. LC Card No.
   85-157036.

170.

Oakey, R. P.
High Technology Small Firms Regional
Development in Britain and the U.S.
St. Martin's Press, 1984, 179 pp., $25

171.

O'Connor, Joyce, and Mary Lyons
Venture Initiation in Irish Society
Industrial Development Authority Ire-
   land, 1982, 235 pp., $9.95
ISBN 0-902647-23-7. Dewey Decimal No.
   338.040. LC Card No. 83-177713.
A pilot study of the entrepreneurial
process.

172.

Porter, Michael E.
Competition in Global Industry
Harper & Row, 640 pp., $29.95
ISBN 0-87584-140-6.
Strategic implications of global competition for firms and the historical transformation of international competition. An
aid for managers coping with global
competition.

173.

Storey, David
The Small Firm: An International Survey
St. Martin's, 1983, 274 pp.
ISBN 0-7099-2351-1. LC Card No.
   83-40075.

174.
Wik, Philip
How to Do Business with the People's Republic of China
Reston, 1984, 322 pp., $17 (cloth), $12.95
   (paper)
ISBN 0-8359-2919-1 (cloth), 0-8359-2918-
   3 (paper). Dewey Decimal No. 346.510.
   LC Card No. 83-24796.

SMALL-BUSINESS OPPORTUNITIES

There is no hard and fast rule for determining the appropriate business a person should enter. Normally, in making such a choice, one should start with an analysis of his or her basic skills and specialized knowledge, and then choose the business endeavor that most closely complements those attributes. Nonetheless, some of the most successful entrepreneurs have started in a field totally unrelated to their basic skills. A careful study of books on starting a wide variety of businesses will be very valuable to the new-venture creator. But remember, very few of us know what our capacity for ultimate achievement is until we're challenged. The task is to *prepare* ourselves.

MOYA OLSEN LEAR
Chairman of the Board
Lear Avia Corporation

Books in this category normally are known as how-to or nuts-and-bolts publications. Many describe how to start a specific business, ranging from mail-order firms to computer companies, food-service shops, art galleries, and even goatkeeping farms. There is no standard format. A typical entry might contain data on starting and managing a specific kind of business; on general business information about an industry or one of its special market segments; or on niches in the market not being served adequately by existing firms—which may provide the entrepreneur with an alternative business idea.

Most important, these works often provide a set of instructions or a step-by-step guide to a proven method of starting and managing a particular type of business. The practical "rules" outlined in these books are based on someone else's experiences and may have to be tailored to the individual needs of a specific enterprise, but they represent an invaluable source of information on how the authors adjusted to the idiosyncrasies of an industry and its marketplace. Such descriptions may assist entrepreneurs in recognizing potential dangers and avoiding mistakes.

175.
Albert, Kenneth J.
How to Pick the Right Small Business Opportunity: The Key to Success in Your Own Business
McGraw-Hill, 1977, $13.95
ISBN 0-07-000947-3.
Tells how to evaluate personal capabilities and limitations, develop business-selection criteria, make a list of business types, and select the right business opportunity by getting the facts.

176.
American Entrepreneurs Association
Start-Up Manuals Series
American Entrepreneurs Association
This is not a single book, but actually a collection of over 200 different manuals and reports with detailed instructions and market studies for each business researched. Much valuable information.

177.
Baker, Nancy C.
Cashing in on Cooking
Contemporary Books, 1982, 163 pp.
ISBN 0-8092-5873-0. Dewey Decimal No. 642.068. LC Card No. 81-69604.

178.
Bell, Chip R., and Leonard Nadler
Clients and Consultants: Meeting and Exceeding Expectations
Gulf Publishing, 1985, 346 pp., $21.95
ISBN 0-87201-119-4.
How to manage client-consultant relationships.

179.
Bermont, Hubert
How to Become a Successful Consultant in Your Own Field

Consultant's Library, 148 pp., $29
ISBN 0-930686-22-5.
The story of the author's consulting career, starting on the day he was fired from a high executive position. Describes elements of success, how to get started, business operations, tricks of the trade, what to charge the client, why you should never work on a contingency basis, contracts, ways to promote yourself innovatively, and how to get your first client.

180.
Blanchard, Marjorie P.
Cater From Your Kitchen: Income From Your Own Home Business
Bobbs-Merrill, 1981, 244 pp.
ISBN 0-672-52688-3. Dewey Decimal No. 642.406. LC Card No. 80-675.

181.
Breen, James J., and William D. Sanderson
How to Start a Successful Restaurant: An Entrepreneur's Guide
Lebhar-Friedman Books, 1981, 117 pp., $11.50
ISBN 0-86730-242-9. Dewey Decimal No. 647.950. LC Card No. 81-18089.
Step-by-step guide to achieving and maintaining profitability.

182.
Brownstone, David M.
How to Run a Successful Specialty Food Store
Wiley, 1978, 124 pp.
ISBN 0-471-04031-2.
Discusses all aspects of selling specialty foods and the operations of a specialty food store. Covers getting business ideas together, finding the right suppliers, ordering and receiving, trade credit and pricing, design and layout, sidelines, location and equipment, and the grand opening. For the entrepreneur just starting in business or looking to expand.

183.
Brunner, Marguerite
Goldmine of Money-Making Ideas
Lorenz Press, 1977, $7.95 (cloth), $4.95
   (paper)
ISBN 0-89328-015-1 (cloth), 0-89328-017-
   8 (paper).
This book offers many moneymaking
possibilities that can be started in your
own home with very little investment.

184.
Canape, Charlene
How to Capitalize on the Video Revolution
Holt, Rinehart & Winston, 1984, 196 pp.
ISBN 0-03-070343-3. Dewey Decimal No.
   621.388. LC Card No. 83-26534.

185.
Cantor, Mike
Open and Operate Your Own Small Store
Prentice-Hall, 1982, 226 pp.
ISBN 0-13-637496-4 (cloth), 0-13-637488-
   3 (paper). Dewey Decimal No. 658.870.
   LC Card No. 82-5265.

186.
Cassell, Dana K.
Making Money with Your Home Computer
Dodd, Mead, 1984, 143 pp., $5.95 (paper)
ISBN 0-396-08448-6. Dewey Decimal No.
   001.64. LC Card No. 84-13529.

187.
Cate, Joan M.
How to Start Your Own Home Typing Business
Calabasas, 1984, 102 pp., $21.95 (paper)
ISBN 0-930025-00-8. LC Card No. 84-
   71562.

188.
Chidakel, Susan
Starting and Operating a Playgroup for Profit
Pilot Books, $3.95
Turn play into pay while working with
small children out of your own home.
Learn to make an enjoyable pastime into
a profitable business.

189.
Clark, Leta
How to Open Your Own Shop or Gallery
St. Martin's Gallery, $8.95
ISBN 0-312-39607-4.
Questions to consider before and during
opening an art gallery. Includes a list of
lawyers, nationwide, who have volun-
teered their services for arts organiza-
tions.

190.
Cummings, Richard
Make Your Own Comics for Fun and Profit
McKay, 1975, $8.95
ISBN 0-8098-3929-6.

191.
Faivre, Milton I.
How to Raise Rabbits for Fun and Profit
Nelson Hall, 1973, $14.95 (cloth), $8.95
   (paper)
ISBN 0-911012-47-8 (cloth), 0-88229-493-
   8 (paper).
Gives explicit instruction on selecting
stock, housing, breeding, processing,
tanning, marketing, joining clubs. For
beginners.

192.
Faux, Marian
Successful Free-Lancing
St. Martin's Press, 1982, 241 pp., $11.95
ISBN 0-312-77478-8. Dewey Decimal No.
   658.041. LC Card No. 82-5595.
The complete guide to establishing and
running any kind of free-lance business.

193.
Feinman, Jeffrey
*100 Sure-Fire Businesses You Can Start with
Little or No Investment: The Opportunity
Guide to Starting Part-Time Businesses and
Building Financial Independence*
Playboy Press, 1976, $1.95
ISBN 0-87216-368-7.

Short discussions on 100 different
business alternatives.

194.
Feldstein, Stuart
Home, Inc.
Grosset & Dunlap, 1981, 249 pp., $12.95
ISBN 0-448-12021-6. Dewey Decimal No.
  658.041. LC Card No. 81-47700.
How to start and operate a successful
business from your home.

195.
Fox, Jack
*Starting and Building Your Own Accounting
Business*
Ronald Press/Wiley, 1984, 257 pp.
ISBN 0-471-80053-8. LC Card No. 84-
  7336.
A practically oriented textbook explaining how to start and run an accounting
business. Contains a full menu of information from marketing to maintaining
client relations. Detailed information on
charging and collecting, the need for
certification and maintaining professional standards, and direct solicitation,
including how to run a direct mail
campaign. Contains weekly action plans
and numerous charts and graphs.

196.
Frantz, Forrest H., Sr.
*Big-Time Opportunities and Strategies That
Turn Pennies into Millions*
Prentice-Hall, 1973
Contains hundreds of different business
ideas that can be started with little or no
capital. Includes author's proven meth-
ods for discovering, assembling, and
promoting big deals.

197.
Friedberg, Ardy
The Computer Freelancer's Handbook
New American Library, 1984, 138 pp..

ISBN 0-452-25562-7. Dewey Decimal No.
  658.041. LC Card No. 84-9855.
Moonlighting with your home computer.

198.
Gazvoda, Edward A., William M. Haney,
and John Greenya
*The Harvard Entrepreneurs Society's Guide to
Making Money*
Little, Brown, 1983, 186 pp., $6.95
  (paper)
ISBN 0-316-30590-1 (paper). Dewey
  Decimal No. 658.42. LC Card No. 83-
  12075.

199.
Gearing, Phillip J., and Evelyn V. Brunson
*Breaking into Print (How to Get Your Work
Published)*
Prentice-Hall, 1977, $11.95 (cloth), $3.45
  (paper)
ISBN 0-13-081687-6 (cloth), 0-13-081679-
  5 (paper).
Everything you need to know to get
published, from developing a worthwhile
project to finding the right publishers to
managing royalties wisely. Includes a list
of specific criteria against which you can
evaluate your work in terms of vocabulary, reading level, and tone.

200.
Genfan, Herb, and Taetzch Genfan
How to Start Your Own Craft Business
Watson-Guptill, 1974, 208 pp., $7.95
Explains everything about a craft busi-
ness; includes pricing, inventory, produc-
tion, shipping, billing, collection, and
taxes.

201.
Goldstein, Arnold S.
*Own Your Own: The No-Cash-Down Business
Guide*
Prentice-Hall, 1983, 208 pp.
ISBN 0-13-647487-X (cloth), 0-13-647479-
  9 (paper). Dewey Decimal No. 658.11.
  LC Card No. 82-22973.

202.
Grenier, Mildred
The Quick and Easy Guide to Making Money at Home
Frederick Fell, 1974, 269 pp., $7.95
ISBN 0-8119-0230-7.
Suggests hundreds of ways to earn easy and quick money.

203.
Gross, Len, and John T. Stirling
How to Build a Small Advertising Agency and Run It at a Profit
Kentwood Publications, 1984, 103 pp.,
    $48 (paper)
ISBN 0-917855-00-0. Dewey Decimal No.
    659.112. LC Card No. 84-10088.

204.
Gumpert, David E., and Jeffry A. Timmons
The Encyclopedia of Small Business Resources
Harper & Row, 1984, 407 pp., $9.95
    (paper)
ISBN 0-06-091111-5. Dewey Decimal No.
    658.022. LC Card No. 83-48350.
A directory of small-business resources in the United States.

205.
Handy, Jim
How to Uncover Hidden Business Opportunities That Make Money
Parker Publishing Co., 1983, 216 pp.
ISBN 0-13-436071-0 (cloth), 0-13-436063-
    X (paper). Dewey Decimal No. 658.022.
    LC Card No. 82-12574.

206.
Harmon, Charlotte
How to Make Money Selling at Flea Markets and Antique Fairs
Pilot Books, 1974, $2 (paper)
ISBN 0-87576-048-1.
Shows, step by step, how to get started and cash in. Covers what to sell, where to find merchandise, setting up your display, and selling techniques.

207.
Harris, Herby, and Lucien Farrar
How to Make Money in Music: A Guidebook for Success in Today's Music Business
Arco, 1978, $5.95
ISBN 0-668-04089.
For the musically inclined—whether performer, composer, technician, or entrepreneur—who wants to make it in show business and recording, with information on the market, the procedures, the techniques, and the legal and financial sides of the industry.

208.
Henke, Thomas R.
Managing Your Private Trucking Operation
Traffic Service Corp., 1976, $8 (paper)
ISBN 0-87408-005-3.
Starting a private trucking operation calls for new management skills and a certain knowledge of transportation costs, techniques, and laws and regulations not usually found in the smaller firm.

209.
Hilburn, R. E.
Successful Electronics Servicing Business
Prentice-Hall, 1977, 224 pp., $10.15
ISBN 0-13-860809-1.

210.
Holt, Robert Lawrence
How to Publish, Promote, and Sell Your Own Book
St. Martin's Press, 1985, 366 pp., $16.95
ISBN 0-312-39618-X. Dewey Decimal No.
    070.5. LC Card No. 85-11748.

211.
Holtz, Herman
Advice, a High Profit Business
Prentice-Hall, 1986
ISBN 0-13-011958-X. Dewey Decimal No.
    658.460. LC Card No. 85-24405.
A guide for consultants and other entrepreneurs.

212.

Holtz, Herman

How to Make Money with Your Microcomputer

Wiley, 1984, 324 pp., $14.95

ISBN 0-471-88455-3. LC Card No. 84-3589.

Suggests ideas for business ventures using a microcomputer. How to instantly access the needs of a local market, how to use the micro to manage company finances, and how to exploit the growing market for word processing services.

213.

Katchen, Carole

Promoting and Selling Your Art

Watson-Guptill, 1978, $10.95

ISBN 0-8230-4422-X.

Down-to-earth advice on getting started, building a reputation, finding buyers, and promoting and selling your work.

214.

Kirkpatrick, Frank

How to Find and Buy Your Business in the Country

Storey Communications, 1985, 199 pp., $19.95 (cloth), $14.95 (paper)

ISBN 0-88266-372-0 (cloth), 0-88266-373-9 (paper). Dewey Decimal No. 658.11. LC Card No. 84-51489.

215.

Kishel, Patricia Gunter, and Gregory F. Kishel

Dollars on Your Doorstep: The Complete Guide to Homebased Businesses

Wiley, 1984, 183 pp., $8.95

ISBN 0-471-88452-9. LC Card No. 83-21890.

How to choose, set up, and run a successful small business out of the home. Detailed guidance on getting organized and handling all critical details of a profitable enterprise. Examines specific issues facing entrepreneurs as well as general issues. Anecdotes about successful and unsuccessful entrepreneurs serve to illustrate points.

216.

Klein, Howard J.

How to Test Your Million Dollar Idea

Bobbs-Merrill, 1982, 210 pp.

ISBN 0-672-52700-6. Dewey Decimal No. 650.12. LC Card No. 81-17998.

217.

Kracke, Don, and Rogers Honkanen

How to Turn Your Idea into a Million Dollars

Doubleday, 1977, $7.95

ISBN 0-385-11608-X.

218.

Krause, William H.

How to Get Started as a Manufacturer's Representative

AMACOM

ISBN 0-8144-5584-0.

This book is intended primarily for the person who wants to start his or her own sales agency but doesn't know how to begin. Explains the essential ingredients for entering this field.

219.

Kryszak, Wayne D.

The Small Business Index, vol. 2

Scarecrow Press, 1985, 320 pp., $22.50

ISBN 0-8108-1150-2. LC Card No. 78-17540.

Information on small-business enterprises and opportunities. Five hundred specific types of business are listed, with bibliographic information for each entry, an extensive bibliography, and a list of publishers.

220.

Kuecken, John A.

Starting and Managing Your Own Engineering Practice

Van Nostrand Reinhold, 1978, $13.95

ISBN 0-442-24513-0.

Financing, income, financial survival, and credit. Computer tables and graphs showing how to make financial projections and gauge progress against the chances of success or failure.

221.
Lane, Thorne
How to Own Your Own Newspaper
Exposition Press, 1976, $4.50
ISBN 0-682-48513-6.
Pointers that can make a success out of a newspaper.

222.
Lee, Albert
How to Profit from Your Arts and Crafts
McKay, 1978, $9.95
ISBN 0-679-50831-7.
Information on defining what you want your art to do for you, calculating overhead prices, marketing one-of-a-kind artifacts, selling your craft concept to businesspeople.

223.
Liebers, Arthur
How to Start a Profitable Retirement Business
Pilot Books, 1975, 56 pp., $2.50
ISBN 0-87576-009-0.
Businesses that can be started with a minimum investment, many for $500 or less; many can be operated from the home, and most on less than a full-time basis.

224.
Luisi, Billie
A Practical Guide to Small Scale Goatkeeping
Rodale Press, 240 pp., $8.95
ISBN 0-87857-239-2.
Selecting stock; breeding, birthing, and milking; housing, feeding, and health; the business of goat dairying.

225.
Lulow, Kalia
The Freelancer's Business Book
Ballantine Books, 1984, 152 pp., $2.95 (paper)
ISBN 0-345-30355-5. Dewey Decimal No. 658.041. LC Card No. 84-90861.

226.
Masser, Barry Z.
Thirty-Six Thousand Dollars a Year in Your Own Home Merchandising Business
Prentice-Hall, 1978, 217 pp., $9.95
ISBN 0-13-918987-4.
Suggests ways and plans to make quick profit from various types of creative businesses with little investment. Includes many case histories.

227.
Miller, Murray, and Franz Serdahely
How to Win the Battle Against Inflation with a Small Business.
Enterprise Publishing, 1980, 163 pp., $14.95
ISBN 0-913864-33-1. Dewey Decimal No. 658.159. LC Card No. 79-53799.

228.
Muffet, Deborah
Be Your Own Boss
Ashton Scholastic, 1984, 187 pp., $6.95
ISBN 0-86896-237-6.
Creative ideas for self-employment.

229.
Murray, Jean Wilson
Starting and Operating a Word Processing Service
Pilot Books, $3.50
How to select the right equipment, define the right market, and develop promotional plans, including the right price structure. All this can be done out of the home.

230.
Newcomb, Dwayne G.
Spare-Time Fortune Guide
Prentice-Hall, 1973, $8.95
ISBN 0-13-824185-6.
Shows how to find moneymaking possibilities, how to fit your schedule to particular moneymaking areas, how to find moneymaking opportunities in your local newspaper or Yellow Pages, how to consumer-test your business before it gets started, and how to get a list of money sources.

231.

Ossin, Archie, and Myrna Ossin

How to Start and Run a Profitable Craft Business

Ossin Publishing, 1977, 77 pp., $7.95

ISBN 0-930912-00-4.

Covers every aspect of doing business, from legal information to improving marketing, production, and selling techniques. A general reference for anyone concerned with a manufacturing business. Applications for home-based business as well as expanding to a national sales level.

232.

Poynter, Dan

The Self-Publishing Manual—How to Write, Print and Sell Your Own Book

Parachuting Publications, 1979, $14.95 (cloth), $9.95 (paper)

ISBN 0-915516-22-5 (cloth), 0-915516-21-7 (paper).

Describes how to successfully write, publish, promote, market, and distribute your own books. Emphasis on promotion and marketing.

233.

Price, Laurence W.

How to Start Your Own Horticulture Business

Botany Books, 1983, $4.95 (paper)

ISBN 0-9611966-0-2. Dewey Decimal No. 635.906. LC Card No. 83-17918.

Landscape maintenance, lawn renovation, landscaping services, home nursery.

234.

Revel, Chase

168 More Businesses Anyone Can Start and Make a Lot of Money

Bantam, 1984, 296 pp., $8.95 (paper)

ISBN 0-553-34104-9. Dewey Decimal No. 658.114. LC Card No. 83-46008.

235.

Revel, Chase, and John Hiatt

The Newest, Most Unique Ways People Are Making Money

Baronbrook, 1979, 223 pp., $9.95

ISBN 0-932362-03-6. Dewey Decimal No. 658.11. LC Card No. 79-52286.

236.

Rice, Donald L.

How to Publish Your Own Magazine

McKay, 1978, 116 pp.

A step-by-step process to publishing your own magazine. Success depends on your ability to write, edit, organize, prepare, and distribute the finished product.

237.

Richard, Clement C.

How to Make Money with Your Home Computer

Warner Books, 1984, 236 pp., $3.95 (paper)

ISBN 0-446-32567-8.

238.

Ruhe-Schoen, Janet

Organizing and Operating Profitable Workshop Classes

Pilot Books, $2.50

The various steps in getting started: development of the curriculum, what to charge, where to set up classes, how to sign up students, and how to promote your workshop in your community. Suggests nearly 50 teachable subjects.

239.

Schabacker, Joseph Charles

Small Business Information Sources: An Annotated Bibliography

National Council for Small Business, 1976, $10

Over 1,100 publications that tell the story of starting, managing, advising, or conducting research on small business.

240.

Seltz, David D.

The Entrepreneur's Guide to Restaurant Expansion

Lebhar-Friedman Books, 1982, 238 pp., $11.50
ISBN 0-86730-241-0. Dewey Decimal No. 647.950. LC Card No. 82-1174.
All expansion options and alternate growth financing are available in this concise guide for the restaurateur.

241.
Shebar, Sharon Sigmond, and Judith Schoder
How to Make Money at Home
Simon & Schuster, 1982, 196 pp., $7.95 (paper)
ISBN 0-671-44814-5.

242.
Shenson, Howard L.
How to Create and Market a Successful Seminar or Workshop
Consultant's Library, 180 pp., $27.00
ISBN 0-930686-25-4.
Describes the factors required to prepare a successful seminar or workshop. Analyzes the failures, then explains the rules that guarantee participant and sponsor acceptance.

243.
Shenson, Howard L.
The Successful Consultant's Guide to Fee Setting
Consultant's Library, 72 pp., $29
ISBN 0-930686-27-6.
Why a successful consultant's fee is no arbitrary matter and must be calculated carefully for client acceptance. Hourly, daily, fixed-price, contingency, and cost-plus fees are discussed.

244.
Simon, Julian L.
How to Start and Operate a Mail-Order Business
McGraw-Hill, 1976

Tells how and when to use mailing lists; how to get quick favorable responses to your campaign, how to handle orders, how to deal with supplies, how and where to get free advertising, how to run one-inch ads that sell, ways not to compete with large mail-order houses, how to handle guarantees, credit card orders, trial offers, and current laws.

245.
Smith, Dennis C.
Starting and Operating a Clipping Service
Pilot Books, $2.95
Detailed instructions on what to look for in the newspapers, and how and where to submit clippings. Age and education are not factors.

246.
Starchild, Adam
Start Your Own Construction and Land Development Business
Nelson Hall Publishers, 1983, 216 pp.
ISBN 0-8304-1013-9. Dewey Decimal No. 690.068. LC Card No. 83-2366.

247.
Starr, Douglas P.
How to Handle Speechwriting Assignments
Pilot Books, $3.95
Business, political, government, military, public relations are used in this guide as examples for writing speeches.

248.
Steckel, Robert C.
Profitable Telephone Sales Operations
Arco Publishing Company, 1975, 192 pp., $15 (paper)
ISBN 0-668-03649-4.
How to develop and manage a dynamic telephone sales operation; the ten keys to outstanding results.

249.
Stern, Alfred
How Mail Order Fortunes Are Made

Arco Publishing Company, 1977, 259 pp., $12.50

Chapters on locating salable products, how they should be priced, where to contact sources for mail order, direct mail vs. the publication approach, preparing hard-hitting sales literature, how to write ads that sell, building a mailing list, shipping and recordkeeping systems, expansion and capitalization.

250.

Stevens, Lawrence
Guide to Buying, Selling and Starting a Travel Agency
Chicago Review Press, 1979, $9.95 (paper)
ISBN 0-916032-00-0.
How to establish a new agency: advertising and publicity, budgeting, and acquiring accreditation. How to buy an existing agency: criteria, establishing the market value of the agency, and negotiating the sale.

251.

Taetzsch, Lyn
Opening Your Own Retail Store
Contemporary Books, Inc., 1977, 194 pp., $14.95 (cloth), $6.95 (paper)
ISBN 0-8092-8285-2 (cloth), 0-8092-7981-9 (paper).
Choosing a location, buying fixtures, purchasing stock, planning your advertising campaign, setting up a bookkeeping system, hiring employees, and applying for a loan.

252.

Telchin, Charles S., and Seymour Helfant
Planning Your Store for Maximum Sales and Profits
National Retail Merchants Assn., 1975, 153 pp.
Practical advice on style, beauty, customer attraction, space utilization, lease negotiations, construction techniques, and maintenance expense.

253.

Temple, Mary
How to Start a Secretarial and Business Service
Pilot Books, 1978, $2.50 (paper)
ISBN 0-87576-069-4.
How to start and operate a public secretarial service. Choosing the right location, advertising, obtaining clients, purchasing equipment, and how to expand in other fields.

254.

Tepper, Ron
Become a Top Consultant: How the Experts Do It
Wiley, 243 pp., $21
Ten of the most successful consultants explain how to determine your market, set up your practice, and obtain clients and keep them satisfied.

255.

Thomsett, Michael C.
Fundamentals of Bookkeeping and Accounting for the Successful Consultant
Consultant's Library, 136 pp.
ISBN 0-930686-07-1.
Two points of view are expressed in this book: (1) proper compliance with Internal Revenue Service regulations to avoid penalties and (2) setting up and keeping simplified records that assist in the financial planning and control of the consultancy.

256.

Townsend, Carl, and Merl K. Miller
How to Make Money With Your Microcomputer
TAB Books, 1982, 154 pp., $14.95
ISBN 0-8306-4335-4. Dewey Decimal No. 001.64. LC Card No. 81-21398.

257.

Traister, Robert J., and Rich Ingram
Making Money with Your Microcomputer

TAB Books, 1982, 152 pp.
ISBN 0-8306-2506-2. Dewey Decimal No.
001.64. LC Card No. 82-5828.

258.
Whitis, Rose Freeman
Starting and Operating a Vintage Clothing Shop
Pilot Books, $3.50
Step-by-step guide that gives information on store layout, gathering merchandise, financing, customer relations, and more.

259.
Wilbanks, Patricia M.
How to Start a Typing Service in Your Own Home
Arco, 1972, 97 pp., $5 (paper)

A practical guide to setting up a profitable home typing service and letter shop.

260.
Williams, W. P., and Joseph H. Van Zandt
How to Start Your Own Magazine
Contemporary Books, 1978, 108 pp.,
    $8.95 (cloth), $4.95 (paper)
ISBN 0-8092-7444-2 (cloth), 0-8092-7443-4 (paper).
How to turn your magazine ideas into a viable business. Covers everything from creating a format to building circulation, including how to fill your pages with articles from top authors and journalists at little or no cost to you, how to arrange for retail distribution and maneuver your magazine to the front of the racks, and how to get free publicity for your magazine.

THE AMERICAN ENTERPRISE SYSTEM

The American private enterprise system is unique among the world's economic systems. Founded on the concepts of individual freedom, the inviolability of private property, a free market driven by the profit motive, and a business environment unrestrained by political interference, this system has spawned the strongest industrial economy in history. Despite the restrictive encroachment of governmental regulations, the lamp of economic opportunity still burns brightly because it is fueled by the initiative and determination of risk-taking entrepreneurs who consistently find better ways to supply basic human needs for goods and services.

WILLIAM K. COORS
Chairman of the Board
Adolph Coors Company

The American enterprise-for-profit system, more often labeled as capitalism, is sometimes referred to as the free enterprise, private enterprise, or competitive market system. Other terms used to describe its contemporary status include "modified capitalism," "democratic capitalism," and "a mixed economy." Regardless of designation, it is by all measures the best economic system yet devised by theorists and pragmatists in the history of the world. It has produced more goods and services, greater social and financial security, and a higher standard of living and the enjoyable qualities of life) for more people than any other economic system. It is emulated by many nations, envied by others, and disdained by those which cannot keep pace with its achievements.

The ideals of the American Enterprise System are to be found in Adam Smith's classic, *The Wealth of Nations*, in which the concept of free trade (laissez-faire) was advanced as the theoretical cornerstone of personal and national wealth. A basic Smith premise is that if we are given the protected freedom to pursue our own selfish goals, we will in turn maximize the welfare of society as a whole. To him, political liberty and economic freedom are essential elements, and the role of responsible government is to guarantee protection of both in a marketplace unencumbered by political interference or regulation.

Such thought patterns certainly were integral to business philosophies in wilderness America, for colonial merchants regarded trade regulations and other abridgements of freedom as worthy of the most demanding of sacrifices. Over time, however, the growth of the U.S. economy has been accompanied by government regulations that seek to protect the openness of the marketplace by restricting the behavior of those who would divert its "freedoms" to gain personal advantages. It no longer is, and probably never was, what Smith envisioned it should be in his laissez-faire concepts. Thus, the realization of the purest interpretation of Smith's theory perhaps is impractical of achievement, but it nonetheless remains the spiritual and intellectual yardstick by which the so-called free-enterprise–mixed-economy system is measured.

What matters most is that America's current economic structure has retained, and continues to encourage, the enterprise-for-profit notions that historically have stoked the fires of capitalism. Despite increasing regulation, the marketplace remains surprisingly open to everyone (to the consternation of many domestic producers who must compete against foreign imports), and the myriad new business opportunities that consistently surface become magnets for countless men and women who are motivated to create new businesses in order to compete against the older firms for a share of the profits.

This entrepreneurial spirit is the lifeblood of the enterprise-for-profit system and is playing a vital role in America's twentieth-century transformation from the industrial age to what is being called the information age. Reliance upon entrepreneurial attitudes and philosophies has become the identifying hallmark of those on the cutting edge of this dramatic change. Only time will tell just how great an impact this ultimately will have on the U.S. economy, but the effects already have been substantial. Indeed, analysts are beginning to refer to the last decades of the twentieth century as the age of the entrepreneur because of the expanding, positive influence by men and women whose creativity tends to maximize opportunities wherever they exist.

The American enterprise system works in spite of its wrenching problems. Recessions sometimes plague its stability as do runaway inflationary spirals. Seldom does the economy experience a "normal" cycle. Periodically, it pauses to disgorge some of its weaker participants—only to greet a host of new profit-seeking, risk-taking aspirants who believe in their business ideas, trust their own instincts, and measure their rewards more in terms of accomplishment than in dollars. This cyclical entrepreneurial process is economic poetry in motion—and proof that the enterprise-for-profit system not only works but is also alive and well.

261.
Bartlett, Roland W.
Success of Modern Private Enterprise
Interstate, 1970, $7.95 (text edition $5.95)
ISBN 0-8134-1148-3, 0-685-12687-0 (text edition).

262.
Benson, John
The Penny Capitalists
Gill and Macmillan, 1983, 172 pp.
ISBN 0-7171-1084-2. Dewey Decimal No. 305.554. LC Card No. 84-125840.
A study of nineteenth-century working-class entrepreneurs.

263.
Berger, Peter L.
The Capitalist Revolution
Harper & Row, 304 pp., $17.95

ISBN 0-465-00867-4. LC Card No. 85-73882.

Fifty propositions about prosperity, equality, and liberty. Focuses on how capitalism has revolutionized modern life.

264.

Bernstein, Ilene Nagel, and Howard E. Freeman

Academic and Entrepreneurial Research

Russell Sage Foundation, 1975, 187 pp.

ISBN 0-87154-109-2. Dewey Decimal No. 300.72. LC Card No. 74-83208.

The consequences of diversity in federal evaluation studies. The evaluation and research of entrepreneurial research and social action programs.

265.

Brophy, David J.

Finance, Entrepreneurship, and Economic Development

University of Michigan, 1974, 200 pp.

Dewey Decimal No. 338.642. LC Card No. 75-622248.

A discussion of entrepreneurship as it relates to economic and industrial development in the state of Michigan.

266.

Cain, Louis P., and Paul J. Uselding

Business Enterprise and Economic Change

Kent State University Press, 1973, $14

ISBN 0-87338-134-3.

A series of essays compiled as a tribute to Professor Harold Williamson. Includes a section on the role of entrepreneurship in economic development.

267.

Cantrell, J. A.

James Nasmyth and the Bridgewater Foundry

Manchester University Press, 1985, $33

ISBN 0-7190-1339-9. Dewey Decimal No. 942.714. LC Card No. 84-25415.

A study of entrepreneurship in the early engineering industry.

268.

Casey, William L., John E. Marthinsen, and Laurence S. Moss

Entrepreneurship, Productivity, and the Freedom of Information Act

Lexington Books, 1983, 224 pp.

ISBN 0-669-06349-5. Dewey Decimal No. 342.730. LC Card No. 82-48609.

How the Freedom of Information Act and the protection of relevant business information affected the entrepreneur in the United States.

269.

Chamberlain, Neil W.

The Place of Business in America's Future

Basic Books, 1973, 355 pp.

A study of the social values of Americans and businesses alike, past and present.

270.

Cramer, Clarence H.

American Enterprise—Free and Not So Free

Little, Brown, 1972

A history of the American enterprise system from the colonization of the New World to the managed money supply of the twentieth century. Points out the benefits and hazards of our American enterprise system.

271.

Dahlberg, Arthur

How to Save Free Enterprise

Devin-Adair, 1975, $9.95

ISBN 0-8159-5708-4.

This book maintains that the form of contract agreements now used is slightly defective, and that it is in itself occasionally disruptive of the aggregate private monetary demand for goods. To eliminate the defect, the author outlines two easy remedies.

272.
Deal, Terrence E., and Allan A. Kennedy
Corporate Cultures: The Rites and Rituals of Corporate Life
Addison-Wesley, 1985, $9.95 (paper)
A behind-the-scenes approach on the nation's best-known companies and how they have created business cultures that work.

273.
Ferguson, James Milton
Advertising and Competition: Theory, Management, Fact
Ballinger Publishing, 1974, 190 pp., $17.50
Investigates the relationship between advertising and competition.

274.
Folsom, Burton W., Jr.
Urban Capitalists
Johns Hopkins Press, 1981, 191 pp.
ISBN 0-8018-2520-2. Dewey Decimal No. 338.9748. LC Card No. 80-8864.
Entrepreneurs and city growth in Pennsylvania's Lackawanna and Lehigh regions, 1800–1920.

275.
Friedman, Robert E.
Expanding the Opportunity to Produce
Corporation for Enterprise Development, 1981, 549 pp., $19.95
ISBN 0-9605804-0-9. Dewey Decimal No. 338.642. LC Card No. 81-66853.
Discusses how to revitalize the American economy through new-enterprise development.

276.
Gevirtz, Don
Business Plan for America
Putnam's, 1984, 223 pp., $15.95
ISBN 0-399-12844-1. Dewey Decimal No. 658.42. LC Card No. 83-21114.

277.
Gilder, George F.
The Spirit of Enterprise
Simon & Schuster, 1984, 274 pp.
ISBN 0-671-45482-X. Dewey Decimal No. 338.04. LC Card No. 84-10612.

278.
Goelz, Paul C., ed.
An Economic Philosophy for a Free People
St. Mary's University Press, 1980, 180 pp., $15
Report of the 1979 National Symposium on the Philosophy of Free Enterprise.

279.
Gross, Eugene L., Adrian R. Cancel, and Oscar Figueroa
Small Business Works! How to Compete and Win in the Free Enterprise System
AMACOM, 1977
What business is really all about, and what the businessperson must know to run a business successfully and competitively. Based on thousands of actual case studies.

280.
Hebert, Robert F., and Albert N. Link
The Entrepreneur: Mainstream Views and Radical Critiques
Praeger, 1982, 128 pp., $21.95
ISBN 0-03-059589-4. Dewey Decimal No. 338.040. LC Card No. 81-21134.

281.
Hughes, Jonathan R. T.
The Vital Few: The Entrepreneur and American Economic Progress
Oxford University Press, 1986
ISBN 0-19-504038-4. Dewey Decimal No. 330.973. LC Card No. 85-28504.

282.
Jewkes, John
A Return to Free Market Economies?
Holmes and Meier, 1978, 241 pp., $27.50

ISBN 0-8419-5028-8.
Critical essays on government intervention.

283.
Kelley, Robert E.
The Gold Collar Worker
Addison-Wesley, $16.95
ISBN 11739-8.
Harnessing the brainpower of the new work force. Hard look at the new breed of workers that will make up 60 percent of the work force by 1990.

284.
Kirzner, Israel M.
Discovery and the Capitalist Process
University of Chicago Press, 1985, 183
   pp., $22.50
ISBN 0-226-43777-9. Dewey Decimal No.
   338.04. LC Card No. 85-5799.
Entrepreneurship in a capitalistic society.

285.
Magaziner, Ira C.
Minding America's Business
Harcourt Brace Jovanovich, 387 pp.
ISBN 0-15-558835-4.
This text documents America's declining competitiveness in the world economy. Discussion focuses around the need to increase competitive productivity in American industry by developing an industrial policy.

286.
Meyer, John Robert, Clinton V. Oster, and Marni Clippinger
Deregulation and the New Airline Entrepreneurs
MIT Press, 1984, 240 pp.
ISBN 0-262-13198-6. Dewey Decimal No.
   387.712. LC Card No. 84-7935.
A look at deregulation of the airline industry and its effects.

287.
Miller, William, ed.
Men in Business

Greenwood Press, 1979
ISBN 0-313-20867-0. Dewey Decimal No.
   338.092. LC Card No. 78-21159.
A collection of biographies that includes essays on the historical role of the entrepreneur.

288.
Moore, Barbara H.
The Entrepreneur in Local Government
International City Management Association, 1983, 214 pp., $19.50
ISBN 0-87326-039-2. Dewey Decimal No.
   352.073. LC Card No. 83-10806.
The spirit of entrepreneurship: how the entrepreneur participates in local, state, and federal government.

289.
Neels, Kevin, and Michael N. Caggiano
The Entrepreneurial City: Innovations in Finance and Management for St. Paul
Ford Foundation, 1984, 135 pp.
ISBN 0-8330-0603-7. Dewey Decimal No.
   352.109. LC Card No. 84-18217.
Entrepreneurship as it is seen in government practice in St. Paul, Minnesota.

290.
Ouchi, William
The M-Form Society
Addison-Wesley, $19.95
ISBN 05533-3.
How American teamwork can recapture the competitive edge with the successful use of M-form management teamwork.

291.
Puth, Robert C.
American Economic History
CBS Publishing, 1982, 650 pp.
ISBN 0-03-050556-9.
A comprehensive account of U.S. economic history.

292.
Sevareid, Eric, and John Case
Enterprise: The Making of Business in America

McGraw-Hill, 1983, 225 pp.
ISBN 0-07-056336-5. LC Card No. 82-
   17930.
Based on a PBS television series.

293.
Smith, Jerald R., and Peggy A. Golden
Enterprise: A Simulation
Houghton Mifflin, 1985, 179 pp.
ISBN 0-395-35596-6. Dewey Decimal No.
   658.11. LC Card No. 85-147054.

294.
Stankiewicz, Rikard
Academic Entrepreneurs
St. Martin's Press, 1985, $25
ISBN 0-312-00200-9. Dewey Decimal No.
   378.103. LC Card No. 85-22227.
A look at the entrepreneurial process as it
operates in academe.

295.
Starling, Grover
The Changing Environment of Business
Kent Publishing, 1984, 641 pp.
The day-to-day decision-making concerns
of managers. Suggests that management's
understanding of the changing business
environment is crucial to the survival of
corporations.

296.
Starling, Grover
*Issues in Business and Society: Capitalism
and Public Purpose*
Kent Publishing, 1985, 499 pp.
College text on managing external rela-
tions and government-public policy
issues.

297.
U.S. Congress, House Committee on Bank-
ing, Finance, and Urban Affairs
National Entrepreneurship Act: Hearings
U.S. Gov't Printing Office, 1984, 106 pp.
Dewey Decimal No. 346.73. LC Card
   No. 84-603571.

The National Entrepreneurship Act
hearing before the Subcommittee on
Economic Stabilization of the Committee
on Banking, Finance, and Urban Affairs,
House of Representatives, Ninety-Eighth
Congress.

298.
U.S. Congress, Joint Economic Committee
*Climate for Entrepreneurship and Innovation
in the United States*
U.S. Gov't. Printing Office, 1985
Dewey Decimal No. 338.973. LC Card No.
   85-601475.
Hearings before the Joint Economic
Committee, Congress of the United
States, Ninety-eighth Congress, second
session.

299.
Vaughan, Roger J., Robert Pollard, and
Barbara Dyer
*The Wealth of States: Policies for a Dynamic
Economy*
Council of State Planning Agencies, 1985
ISBN 0-934842-23-X. Dewey Decimal No.
   338.9. LC Card No. 85-29082.

300.
Vesper, Karl H.
Entrepreneurship and National Policy
Heller, 1983, 95 pp.
Dewey Decimal No. 338.04. LC Card No.
   83-60963.

301.
Walthall, Wylie A.
Getting into Business
Harper & Row, 1979, 330 pp., $11.50
ISBN 0-06-389125-5.
Introductory college text on the American business system. Includes importance of business to society, organization
and management of the firm, accounting
as the tool of management, and marketing.

302.

Webb, Terry, Thelma Quince, and David Watkins
Small Business Research: The Development of Entrepreneurs
Gower, 1982, 218 pp.
ISBN 0-566-00381-3. Dewey Decimal No. 658.022. LC Card No. 82-227833.
A look at small-business research as it relates to the development of entrepreneurial enterprises in Great Britain.

303.

Young, Dennis R.
If Not for Profit, for What?
Lexington Books, 1983, 170 pp.
ISBN 0-669-06154-9. Dewey Decimal No. 302.35. LC Card No. 82-48482.
A behavioral theory of the nonprofit sector based on entrepreneurship.

304.

Zeigler, Harmon
The Politics of Small Business
Arno Press, 1979, $12
ISBN 0-405-11511-3.
An analysis of the political activities of organized groups representing the interests of small businesspeople. The tactics of leading organizations, including the Small Business Administration, are described and appraised, and their values and interests are noted.

SECTION 2.

Books for Managers of Small Businesses

General Business Management　　53

Finance and Accounting　　66

Computers　　74

Financing and Venture Capital　　81

Case Studies　　88

Franchising　　93

Innovation and New-Product Development　　97

Legal　　102

Marketing, Advertising, and Sales　　106

Human Resources Management　　116

Problems and Failures　　121

Acquisitions　　125

Intrapreneurship　　129

GENERAL BUSINESS MANAGEMENT

For success in any business, big or small, the entrepreneurial spirit is essential. However, drive must be tempered by a working knowledge of sound managerial practices. National studies clearly indicate that poor management accounts for the vast majority of failures among new businesses. Management, then, is the fiber that holds all businesses together and the substance from which all success is generated. Prospective entrepreneurs should avail themselves of every opportunity, formal and informal, to improve their understanding of successful managerial theories and practices.

FRANK L. CARNEY
President, Carney Enterprises
Cofounder, Pizza Hut, Inc.

A common misconception about business is that all firms, regardless of size, rely essentially upon the same management techniques. However, those who have owned or managed a small enterprise understand clearly that smallness presents an entirely different set of management conditions from those encountered by the directors of larger firms. At no time in the history of an enterprise is this more true than in the startup phase of a new business, or during periods of financial crisis or unexpected growth immediately following startup, when pressures demand that priorities and strategies be reshaped (*bent* may be a more appropriate term) to the needs of the moment. Some analysts refer to this phenomenon as entrepreneurial carpentry; others describe it as resource poverty management.

Resource poverty can arise from any number of deficiencies, such as limited assets, a shortage of working capital, unpredictable cash flow, employees with few problem-solving skills, and inadequate data bases or information sources on which to base decisions. These deficiencies can lead to other monumental headaches, ranging from the difficulty of recruiting key employees and compensating them competitively to an inability to respond forthrightly to sudden changes in the economic environment. The ability to cope with these conditions often determines the staying power of small firms, for managerial mistakes or errors in judgment affect the survival rate of smaller enterprises much more directly than they do larger companies.

Once the early hurdles to survival have been cleared, a new and even more challenging experience awaits the small-business owner: managing the dynamics of growth. Increasing complexity accompanies each new phase of an enterprise's life cycle, requiring greater and greater managerial versatility in directing these changes. For example, a small company may begin with a simple "pegboard" (or single-entry) form of bookkeeping and control. As the business expands, however, it must move at appropriate stages to a greater sophistication in its accounting procedures, ranging from a manual, double-entry type of accrual accounting to a complex integrated system of computerized recordkeeping and control. Choosing the right moment for making such changes is a function of both need and available resources, conditions that oftentimes prove to be incompatible and thus force small-business managers to continue exercising their "jack-of-all-trades, master-of-none" versatility indefinitely.

Some business owners avoid many of these complications because they elect to keep their enterprises small, simple, and stable, but all of them face fiscal and legal hassles that would test the virtues of a saint. Indeed, everyday management does not come naturally for many entrepreneurs, especially those who derive their greatest challenges from conceptualizing and bringing a business into existence. Yet business growth inevitably instills in the small-business owner a sobering realization of the urgency for leadership, organizational structure, and professional management procedures, lest the young enterprise falter in its transition to early stability.

In this section are found books that detail general business management skills particularly relevant to small businesses. Readers are encouraged also to peruse the listings under The Entrepreneur in Section 1, which include books that describe the process of starting a new enterprise. However, many excellent books have a dual focus: how to start a new business *and* how to manage it once it is a reality. These dual-focus books are located in Section 1, and readers will find in them many useful management ideas.

305.

Aaker, David A.

Developing Business Strategies

Wiley, 1984, 391 pp., $24.95

A comprehensive review of the strategic planning process: sales and marketing, finance, accounting, and managerial processes.

306.

Alcorn, Pat

Success and Survival in the Family-Owned Business

McGraw-Hill, 1981, 256 pp.

ISBN 07-000961-9.

The pros and cons of family concerns. Discusses the problems of a family business that has grown out of family control. Special issues covered: generational transfer of power, inheritance taxes, keeping control and ownership despite the death of the founder, and coping with nepotism.

307.

Alves, Jeffrey R., and Dennis Curtin

Planning and Budgeting for Higher Profits

Van Nostrand Reinhold, 1984, 218 pp.,
   $17.50
ISBN 0-930764-74-9. Dewey Decimal No.
   658.401. LC Card No. 83-21046.

308.
American Management Associations
AMA Management Handbook, 2nd edition
American Management Associations,
   1,600 pp., $79.95, AMA members
   $71.95
Every business area, from accounting and
computer systems to marketing and
personnel, is covered in this one-volume
business library. Fourteen sections, 163
chapters.

309.
Ames, Michael D., and Norval L. Wellsfry
Small Business Management
West Publishing, 1983, 492 pp., $19.95
ISBN 0-314-69631-8. Dewey Decimal No.
   658.022. LC Card No. 82-20139.

310.
Archer, Maurice, and Jerry White
*Starting and Managing Your Own Small
Business*
MacMillan of Canada, 1978, 291 pp.
ISBN 0-7705-1629-7.
Guides readers through all the basic steps
of starting and managing a business, and
lists sources needed in starting and
running an enterprise.

311.
Armstrong, Donald R.
Strategies for Success in Small Business
Bookman House, 1977
ISBN 0-918464-15-3.
Includes all aspects of managing a small
business: management, finance, manufac-
turing controls, and how you should
prepare yourself for a small-business
career.

312.
Balderston, Jack
*Improving Office Operations: A Primer for
Professionals*

Van Nostrand Reinhold, 1985, 304 pp.,
   $34.95
ISBN 0-442-21310-7.
A practical, how-to-do-it guide for
expediting the paperwork part of any
position.

313.
Becker, Benjamin Max
The Family Owned Business
Commerce Clearing House, 1978, 381 pp.
The problems that lead to business
failure and the opportunities that, if
acted upon, are more likely to lead to
success. From planning and startup of
business enterprises through the sale or
merger of a company. Advice on operating problems (including financing),
expansion and growth, and decisions
regarding selling, merging, or retaining
the family business.

314.
Bennis, Warren, and Burt Nanus
Leaders: The Strategies for Taking Charge
Harper & Row, $18.00 ASTD National
   Members, $20.00 Nonmembers
An in-depth analysis of 90 top leaders.
Main focus is on the qualities that enable
managers to take charge and lead.

315.
Blake, Robert R., and Jane S. Mouton
The Managerial Grid III
Gulf Publishing, 1985, 244 pp., $17

316.
Bracey, Hyler J., Aubrey Sanford, and
James C. Quick
*Basic Management: An Experience-Based
Approach,* 3rd edition
Dow Jones–Irwin, $20.95
Outlines a group approach designed to
bolster skills in planning, organizing,
directing, and controlling.

317.
Brandt, Steven C.
Strategic Planning in Emerging Companies

Addison-Wesley, 1981, 160 pp., $18.95
The management of growth dynamics;
offers concise and professional advice on
how to get and keep a 1980s enterprise
focused.

318.
Brodie, Earl D.
When Your Name Is on the Door
Books in Focus, 1981, 264 pp., $24.95
ISBN 0-916728-45-5. LC Card No. 80-
  66756.

319.
Broom, H. N.
Small-Business Management, 6th edition
South-Western Publishing, 1983, 632 pp.
ISBN 0-538-07250-4. Dewey Decimal
  No. 658.022. LC Card No. 81-51803.
Covers strategy determination, planning,
organizing, actuating, and controlling
small-business operations, with emphasis
on management aspects uniquely important to small firms. Also includes a
comprehensive case study and 27 shorter
case problems.

320.
Brownstone, David
*The Small Business Owner's Practical Hand-
book*
Wiley, 1986
ISBN 0-471-89864-3.

321.
Brunsson, Nils
*The Irrational Organization: Irrationality as a
Basis for Organizational Action and Change*
Wiley, 1985, 193 pp., $18.95
Illustrates why and in what ways organi-
zations should be irrational. Examples
cast new light on such factors as organi-
zational ideology, expectations, motiva-
tion, and commitment.

322.
Buskirk, Richard Hobart, and Percy J.
Vaughn, Jr.
Managing New Enterprises

West Publishing, 1976, $11.95 (text)
ISBN 0-8299-0071-3.

323.
Champion, John M., and John H. James
*Critical Incidents in Management: Decisions
and Policy Issues*
Dow Jones–Irwin, $17.95
Cites real-world incidents that help
illustrate management philosophy and
decision-making strategy.

324.
Church, Olive D.
*Small Business Management and
Entrepreneurship*
Science Research Associates, 1984, 514
  pp., $21.95
ISBN 0-574-20715-5. Dewey Decimal No.
  658.022. LC Card No. 83-16444.

325.
Chute, Phillip B.
American Independent Business
Chute, 1985, 407 pp., $14.95
ISBN 0-930981-00-6. LC Card No. 84-
  072826.
Independent business: formation, opera-
tions, and philosophy for the 1980s.

326.
Cohen, William A.
*The Entrepreneur and Small Business Problem
Solver: An Encyclopedic Reference and Guide*
Wiley, 1984, 655 pp., $22.95
ISBN 0-471-80795-8.
A complete guide to owning and operating one's own business. Saves business
owners time and money finding the
answers to common business problems.
Offers comprehensive step-by-step
guidance to legal aspects of business
ownership, sources of capital, business
insurance, planning, recruiting employees, buying a business, protecting one's
ideas, leasing equipment, record keeping,
personnel and financial management,

credit and collections, advertising and
publicity, marketing, selling, pricing.
Extensive forms, worksheets, and checklists for each topic.

327.

Cohn, Theodore, and Roy A. Lindberg
Survival and Growth: Management Strategies
for Small Firms
AMACOM, 1974, 220 pp., $17.50
ISBN 0-451-61624-3.
For managers of small companies who
wish to improve the performance of their
firms or to keep them healthy as they
grow. Provides guidelines for the user of
managerial time in small firms.

328.

Coleman, Bob
The Small Business Survival Guide:
A Handbook
Norton, 1984, 350 pp., $18.95
ISBN 0-393-01768-0. Dewey Decimal No.
658.022. LC Card No. 83-17228.

329.

Conder, Joseph M., and Gilbert N. Hopkins
The Self-Insurance Decision
National Association of Accountants,
119 pp.
ISBN 0-86641-002-3.
A study based on a survey of 400 companies. Helps business managers perform
the function of risk management with
respect to self-insurance. The study
includes self-insurance approaches,
techniques, and procedures.

330.

Curran, James, John Stanworth, and David
Watkins, eds.
Survival of the Small Firm, 2 vols.
Gower, 1986, $35 each
ISBN 0-566-00725-8 (vol. 1), 0-566-00726-
6 (vol. 2). Dewey Decimal No. 338.642.
LC Card No. 85-27035.

331.

Curtin, Richard T.
Running Your Own Show: Mastering the Basics
of Small Business
Ronald Press, 1982, 226 pp.
ISBN 0-471-86074-3. LC Card No. 81-
14746.
A step-by-step handbook on finding,
buying, and operating a small business,
with emphasis on the major decisions
that must be made at each phase. Analyzes both financial and emotional
commitments, and includes case problems that assist in coping with a wide
range of frequently encountered business
problems.

332.

Dailey, Charles A.
Entrepreneurial Management: Going All Out
for Results
McGraw-Hill, 1971, $23
ISBN 0-07-015-85-0.
The risk-taking "entrepreneurial manager" has emerged as the most essential
manager of today's multi-echelon management team. Book also explores how
entrepreneurial techniques can be used
for role management problems, and
outlines the techniques of the entrepreneur.

333.

Danco, Leon A.
Beyond Survival: A Business Owner's Guide
for Success
Prentice-Hall, 1982, 196 pp., $19.95
ISBN 0-13-072074-7.
How to plan for your company's continuity, develop and install responsible
successors, attract and hold key managerial talent, gain commitment from compe-
tent advisers, create a working board of
outside directors, and balance personal
and company goals.

334.

Danco, Leon A.
Inside the Family Business

Prentice-Hall, 1982, 250 pp., $19.95
ISBN 0-13-467407-3. LC Card No. 80-
  23512.

335.
Day, William
Maximizing Small Business Profits With
Precision Management
Spectrum, 1978, $13.95
ISBN 0-13-566257-5.
Covers tax laws, financing techniques,
physical layout plans, legal requirements,
and more.

336.
Dible, Donald M.
Up Your Own Organization!
Reston, 1986, 423 pp., $18.95
ISBN 0-8359-8086-3. Dewey Decimal No.
  658.022. LC Card No. 85-8293.
A handbook for today's entrepreneur.

337.
Dollar, William E.
Effective Purchasing and Inventory Control for
Small Business
CBI Publishing, 1983, 143 pp., $22.95
ISBN 0-8436-0893-5. Dewey Decimal No.
  658.7. LC Card No. 82-24293.

338.
Earl, Michael J., ed.
Perspectives on Management: a Multidisciplin-
ary Analysis
Oxford University Press, 1983, 248 pp.
ISBN 0-19-827257-X. Dewey Decimal No.
  658. LC Card No. 84-167713.
British management and industrial
relations; entrepreneurship and economic history; management and economic performance; accounting and
management.

339.
Eckert, Lee A., J. D. Ryan, and Robert J.
Ray
Small Business: An Entrepreneur's Plan

Harcourt Brace Jovanovich, 1985, 115 pp.
ISBN 0-15-581220-3. Dewey Decimal No.
  658.022. LC Card No. 85-115519.

340.
Elster, Robert J., ed.
Small Business Sourcebook
Gale Research, 1985
ISBN 0-8103-1472-X.
A guide to the information services and
sources provided to small businesses by
associations, consultants, educational
programs, franchisers, government
agencies (federal, state, and local),
reference works, statisticians, suppliers,
trade shows, and venture capital firms.

341.
Engel, Herbert M.
How to Delegate: A Guide to Getting Things
Done
Gulf Publishing, 1983, 254 pp., $17.95
ISBN 0-87201-170-4.
Many examples and illustrative cases
drawn from experience are cited. Pros
and cons of each technique are ex-
plained.

342.
Flamholtz, Eric
How to Make the Transition from an Entrepre-
neurship to a Professionally Managed Firm
Jossey-Bass, 1986
ISBN 0-87589-679-0. Dewey Decimal No.
  658.406. LC Card No. 85-45902.

343.
Frantz, Forrest H.
Successful Small Business Management
Prentice-Hall, 1978, $15.95
ISBN 0-13-872119.
Principles and theories of business and
management as well as the how-to's
needed to start a business.

344.
Fregly, Bert
How to Be Self-Employed: Introduction to
Small Business Management

ETC Publications, 1977, 654 pp., $17.95
ISBN 0-88280-031-0.
Includes narrow as well as broad-range techniques of business management. The reader is literally led by the hand through all the phases of self-appraisal, innovation, business procedures, and financing.

345.
Freiermuth, Edmond P.
Revitalizing Your Business
Probus, 1985, 171 pp., $19.95
ISBN 0-917253-05-1. Dewey Decimal No.
    658.159. LC Card No. 85-3375.

346.
Friday, William
Successful Management for One to Ten Employee Businesses
Prudential Pub. Company, 1979, $14.50
ISBN 0-934434-04-X.

347.
Gitman, Lawrence J., and Carl McDaniel
Business World, 2nd edition
Wiley, 1987, 608 pp.
ISBN 0-471-80596-3.
Introduces the basic business functions of management, marketing, and finance; also treats such topics as information management, the legal environment, and international concerns. Includes practical career planning information, emphasizing small business.

348.
Greisman, Bernard
How to Run a Small Business
McGraw-Hill, 1982, 298 pp., $17.95
ISBN 0-07-036566-0. Dewey Decimal No.
    658.022. LC Card No. 81-15584.

349.
Grieco, Victor A.
Management of Small Business: Text, Incidents and Cases
Merrill Publishing, 1975, $15.95

ISBN 0-675-08731-7.
This book is designed to assist persons who are contemplating going into business or are in the process of setting up their own small business. About half text and half cases.

350.
Gumpert, David E., and Jeffry A. Timmons
The Encyclopedia of Small Business Resources
Harper & Row, 1984, 407 pp., $9.95
ISBN 0-06-091111-5. Dewey Decimal No.
    658.022. LC Card No. 83-48350.
A directory of small-business resources in the United States.

351.
Hall, William E.
The New Capitalism: How Cutting Edge Companies Are Managing the Future
Wiley, 1986
ISBN 0-471-87472-8. Dewey Decimal No.
    658.401. LC Card No. 86-1643.

352.
Harrigan, Kathryn Rudie
Managing for Joint Venture Success
Lexington Books, 1986, 240 pp., $19.95
ISBN 0-669-11617-3. LC Card No. 85-
    45417.
Describes the dynamic interactions between organizations. Pooling the capabilities of two or more companies is sometimes necessary, especially when penetration of the international market is the focus.

353.
Harrigan, Kathryn Rudie
Strategies for Joint Ventures
Lexington Books, 1985, 448 pp., $52.00
ISBN 0-669-10448-5. LC Card No. 85-
    40110.
A how-to approach to keep the joint venture economically and competitively viable.

354.
Harvard Business Review Executive Books
Series
*Growing Concerns: Building and Managing
the Smaller Business*
Wiley, 1984, 418 pp., $24.95
Advice and analyses that cover every
small-business concern from acquiring a
new business to selling an old one.

355.
Harvard Business Review Executive Books
Series
Strategic Management
Wiley, 1983, 560 pp., $24.95
Peter Drucker and other top experts offer
suggestions for planning and implement-
ing organizational, market, and business
strategies, including specific strategies for
small businesses.

356.
Hazel, A. C., and A. S. Reid
Managing the Survival of Smaller Companies
Business Books, 1973, $13.95
ISBN 0-220-66215-0.
A guide to the causes of company decline
and their prevention and cure. It exam-
ines the impact of inflation and the
difficulties of establishing an even cash
flow, and suggests remedies.

357.
Heyel, Carl
The Encyclopedia of Management, 3rd
edition
Van Nostrand Reinhold, 1982, 1,500 pp.,
    $59.95
ISBN 0-442-25165-3.
This revised volume contains information ranging from alternate work schedules to women in management, business
ethics, dynamic programming, engineering management, the legal aspects of
franchising, etc. Every specialized aspect
of management is provided.

358.
Ianni, Francis A. J.
Family Business
Russell Sage, 1972, $8.50
ISBN 0-87154-396-6.
An in-depth assessment of one family's
activities in running a small business.

359.
Kao, Raymond W. Y.
*Small Business Management: A Strategic
Emphasis*
Holt, Rinehart & Winston, 1984, 383 pp.,
    $19.95 (Canada)
ISBN 0-03-921677-2.

360.
Kishel, Gregory F., and Patricia Gunter
Your Business Is Success, Now What?
Wiley, 1983, 154 pp., $8.95
ISBN 0-471-87699-2. Dewey Decimal No.
    658.022. LC Card No. 82-24745.

361.
Klatt, Lawrence A.
*Small Business Management: Essentials of
Entrepreneurship*
Wadsworth, 1973, $9.95
ISBN 0-534-00324-9.
The essential concepts and techniques
related to managerial problems of a
smaller firm. Provides a framework for
management aspects basic to small-
business operations, and recognizes the
need for individual application to problems unique to certain types of businesses.

362.
Krentzman, Harvey C., L. T. White, and
Joseph C. Schaberker
*Technique and Strategies for Effective
Business Management*
Entrepreneur Press, 1979, 314 pp., $12.95
The fundamental aspects of small busi-
ness: finance and marketing, as well as
how to find new customers, manage
yourself, etc.

363.

Kuhn, Robert Lawrence

To Flourish Among Giants: Creative Management for Mid-Size Firms

Wiley, 1985, 494 pp., $19.95

ISBN 0-471-80911-X.

Hands-on guide offers step-by-step advice on how mid-size companies can make it in a tough economic world. Author compares successful mid-size enterprises with failing businesses, drawing from that analysis ten creative strategies that serve as the foundation for an optimal mid-size performance model. Shows how mid-size entrepreneurs can effectively position products, evaluate options, and structure organizations to build winning mid-size firms.

364.

Lasser, J. K.

How to Run a Small Business, 5th edition

McGraw-Hill, 1982, 250 pp.

ISBN 0-07-36565-2.

A detailed analysis of various aspects of establishing and operating a business, such as financing, choosing a location, accounting and record systems, tax management, hiring and managing personnel, office management and efficiency, selling the product, extending credit to your customers, and comprehensive insurance planning.

365.

Lauenstein, Milton C.

What's Your Game Plan? Creating Business Strategies That Work

Dow Jones–Irwin, $19.95

A look at strategic and long-range planning. Helps executives articulate bold steps to define their business, design an appropriate system, and formulate a strategy.

366.

Levinson, Robert E.

The Decentralized Company: Making the Most of Entrepreneurial Management

AMACOM, 1983, 196 pp.

ISBN 0-8144-5674-X. Dewey Decimal No. 658.402. LC Card No. 82-16470.

367.

Linneman, Robert F.

Shirt-Sleeve Approach to Long-Range Planning for the Smaller, Growing Corporation

Prentice-Hall, 1980, $15.95

ISBN 0-13-808972-8.

A how-to manual for the owner of a company with annual sales ranging from $2 to $75 million. Presents general procedures for adapting strategic planning into corporate structure.

368.

MacFarlane, William N.

Principles of Small Business Management

McGraw-Hill, 1977, $15.95

ISBN 0-07-044380-7.

An overview of the major problems and pitfalls of managing a small business.

369.

McCaskey, Michael B.

The Executive Challenge: Managing Change and Ambiguity

Pitman, 231 pp., $24

Shows how to make creative, clearheaded decisions when issues are blurred.

370.

McLaughlin, Curtis P.

The Management of Nonprofit Organizations

Wiley, 1986, 516 pp., $34.95

ISBN 0-471-87765-4. LC Card No. 85-9601.

Nonprofit management from both a macro and micro perspective. Explores the full range of management functions: strategic management, marketing, accounting, finance, operations, and personnel. Offers a selection of cases dealing with private, nonprofit, and autonomous agencies handling health, social work, aging, education, and entrepreneurial ventures.

371.
Merril, Ronald E., and Henry D. Sedgwick
The New Venture Handbook
AMACOM, 1987, 400 pp., $25.00 (cloth) $19.95 (paper)
ISBN 0-8144-5895-5. LC Card No. 86-47818.
Entrepreneurial practices, procedures, and pitfalls. Penetrates to the reality behind glib success stories.

372.
Meyers, Herbert S.
Minding Your Own Business: A Contemporary Guide to Small Business Success
Dow Jones–Irwin, 1984, 128 pp., $9.95
ISBN 0-87094-563-7. LC Card No. 84-70599.

373.
Mills, D. Quinn
The New Competitors
Wiley, 1985, 391 pp., $19.95
Drawing on interviews with 300 managers, author explains the modern-day manager. Discusses competitiveness thinking and explains what it means to be *people oriented* and *market driven*.

374.
Mintzberg, Henry
Impediments to the Use of Management Information
National Association of Accountants, 27 pp., $6.95
ISBN 0-86641-041-4.
Analysis of why managers use informal rather than formal management information systems, as well as why the information is not used as it should be.

375.
Morrisey, George L.
Management by Objectives and Results for Business and Industry, 2nd edition

Addison-Wesley, 1976, 260 pp., $10.95
Using case histories, examples, concepts, and other applications, author backs up his claim that the human element is necessary to make MOR work in organizations.

376.
Olson, Dean F., and Omer L. Carey
Opportunity Management: Strategic Planning for Smaller Businesses
Reston, 1985, 232 pp., $18.95 (cloth), $14.95 (paper)
ISBN 0-8359-5260-6 (cloth), 0-8359-5259-2 (paper). Dewey Decimal No. 658.4012. LC Card No. 84-8297.

377.
Park, William R., and Sue Chapin-Park
How to Succeed in Your Own Business
Wiley, 1978, 346 pp.
ISBN 0-471-03189-5.
Removes much of the uncertainty from the small-business venture by giving the first-time, untested entrepreneur a look at what to expect. For those already established in a small business, it provides ways to analyze its operation and compare it to other successful ventures in the field. Brings together all the basic financial and management principles for succeeding in a small business, along with a wealth of specific operating data for over 80 different kinds of businesses.

378.
Petrol, John V., Peter S. Carusone, and John E. McDavid
Small Business Management: Concepts and Techniques for Improving Decisions
McGraw-Hill, 1972, $16.95
ISBN 0-07-049672-2.
For those who own their own business but lack the necessary management skills.

379.
Pickle, Hal B.
Small Business Management, 3rd edition

Wiley, 1984, 645 pp., $30.45
ISBN 0-471-89129-0. LC Card No. 83-
  16821.
Overview of entrepreneurship and small-
business management. Covers the practical, day-to-day operation of a small
business.

380.
Proxmire, William
Can Small Business Survive?
Arno Press, 1979, 219 pp., $16
ISBN 0-405-11477-X.
Intended to prevent the small businessperson from becoming "as extinct as the
village blacksmith" by providing him
or her with suggestions on how to improve economic, managerial, and competitive position.

381.
Rose, Tom
How to Succeed in Business: A Resource Unit
on Understanding Business and Getting
Ahead in the Business World
American Enterprise Institute, 1975,
  $4.95 (cloth), $1.95 (paper)
ISBN 0-686-10503-6 (cloth), 0-686-10504-
  4 (paper).
Deals with the economics of the employee-employer relationship. Emphasizes the principles necessary to improve
productivity and thereby raise both
profits and wages.

382.
Sandberg, William R.
New Venture Performance: The Role of
Strategy and Industry Structure
Lexington Books, 1986, 184 pp.
ISBN 0-669-10919-3. Dewey Decimal No.
  658.42. LC Card No. 85-40193.

383.
Schabacker, Joseph, ed.
Strengthening Small Business Management
U.S. Gov't Printing Office, 1971, 158 pp.

ISBN 045-000-00114-8.
Twenty-one chapters on small-business
management. This collection reflects the
experience the author gained in a lifetime
of work with the small-business community.

384.
Seigel, David, and Harold L. Goldman
Successful Small Business Management
Fairchild, 350 pp., $17.50
Provides information on raising capital
and choosing the right location. The
complete why, where, and how-to of
making a small business work. A comprehensive examination of all aspects of
retailing, wholesale, manufacturing,
mail-order, and franchising businesses.

385.
Sexton, Donald L., and Philip M. Van Auken
Experiences in Entrepreneurship and Small
Business Management
Prentice-Hall, 1982, 248 pp., $14.95
ISBN 0-13-294884-2. Dewey Decimal No.
  658.022. LC Card No. 81-13803.

386.
Shames, William H.
Venture Management: The Business of the
Inventor, Entrepreneur, Venture Capitalist and
Established Company
Free Press, 1974
ISBN 0-02-928400-7.
Concerned with starting a new venture,
with emphasis on its early administra-
tion.

387.
Smith, Brian R.
How to Prosper in Your Own Business
Lewis Publishing, 1983, 323 pp., $11.95
ISBN 0-86616-025-6 (paper). LC Card No.
  80-19917.
Getting started and staying on course.

388.
Sondeno, Stanley R.
Small Business Management Principles

Business Publications, 1985, 505 pp.
ISBN 0-256-03168-1. Dewey Decimal No.
658.022. LC Card No. 84-71561.

389.
Stanford, Melvin J.
New Enterprise Management
Reston, 1982, 361 pp.
ISBN 0-8359-4886-2. Dewey Decimal No.
658.022. LC Card No. 81-13953.
This book is a spectrum of new-enterprise development, from planning a prospective business through startup, operations, growth and development, new directions, innovation, merger, and sellout.

390.
Stegall, Donald P., Lawrence L. Steinmetz, and John B. Kline
Managing the Small Business
Irwin, 1976, 500 pp., $18.50
ISBN 0-256-01784-0.
Assembles and analyzes material important in starting and managing a small business.

391.
Steinhoff, Dan
Small Business Management Fundamentals, 3rd edition
McGraw-Hill, 1982, 426 pp., $19.95
ISBN 0-07-061146-7. Dewey Decimal No.
658.022. LC Card No. 81-8412.
Text covers all aspects of small-business management. Describes the small-business scene and then examines planning and operational areas for a contemplated firm. Special management areas and problems are discussed; management consultants' checklist included.

392.
Steinhoff, Dan, B. A. Deitzer, and K. A. Schiliff
Small Business Management

Grid Publishing, 1976, 351 pp., $9.95
ISBN 0-88244-087-X.
This textbook covers the major areas of business from accounting and finance to production, marketing, and personnel.

393.
Tashakori, Maryam
Management Succession
Praeger, 1980, 126 pp., $16.50
ISBN 0-03-047076-5. Dewey Decimal No.
658.407. LC Card No. 80-13722.
From the owner-founder to the professional president.

394.
Tate, Curtis E.
Successful Small Business Management, 4th edition
Business Publications, 1985, 654 pp.
ISBN 0-256-03278-5. Dewey Decimal No.
658.022. LC Card No. 84-71758.

395.
Taylor, John R.
How to Start and Succeed in a Business of Your Own
Reston, 1978, $13.95
ISBN 0-8359-2927-2.
Contains more illustrations of failure and more "do not" advice than most standard works. The illustration stories are true.

396.
U.S. Government Printing Office
Handbook for Small Business
US Gov't Printing Office, 1980, $5.50
ISBN 052-071-00600-1.
Designed to arm small-business entrepreneurs with up-to-date information. Contains information and helpful hints about tax benefits, financing, management assistance, buying from and selling to the government, research, and technical matters. The dozens of federal programs available to small business are described in detail.

397.
Walker, Ernest W.
The Dynamic Small Firm: Selected Readings
Austin Press, 1975, 484 pp., $6.95
ISBN 0-914872-03-6.
Contains several of the more important articles on planning, evaluation, investment decision making, financial aspects of distribution, and procurement of funds.

398.
Watkins, David, John Stanworth, and Ava Westrip, eds.
Stimulating Small Firms
Gower, 1982, 273 pp., $41.50
ISBN 0-566-00513-1.

399.
Welsh, John, and Jerry F. White
Administering the Closely-Held Company
Prentice-Hall, $39.50
A straightforward reference guide that delivers new strategic information to help you improve your management skills and increase your profitability.

400.
Wilson, Brian, ed.
Small Business Handbook
Blackwell, 1986, 241 pp., $34.95 (cloth), $14.95 (paper)
ISBN 0-631-14403-X (cloth), 0-631-14612-1 (paper). Dewey Decimal No. 658.022. LC Card No. 85-15681.

401.
Wortman, Leon A.
Successful Small Business Management
AMACOM, 272 pp., $12.95
ISBN 0-8144-5394-5.
Provides techniques and practices, not theories, that have helped many managers make decisions and take actions to steer their business in profitable directions. Covers most areas of business: marketing, finance, and planning.

402.
Young, Jerrald F.
Decision Making for Small Business Management
Krieger, 1982, 248 pp., $15.50
ISBN 0-89874-346-X. LC Card No. 81-1214.
Ways to make successful analyses and decisions in all areas of business: organizing, financing, marketing, and community relations.

FINANCE AND ACCOUNTING

It is often said that accounting is the universal language of business. If that is so, financial information is the vocabulary of this language, and financial statements are the history of business.

Most companies' decisions are based, in large part, on the information that is conveyed in financial statements. Therefore, to be successful, managers must have a thorough understanding of the elements in the financial statements and the relationships among those elements that express the performance, status, and trends of a company.

To understand and to make the best use of financial statements as tools for business planning and decision making requires a sound working knowledge of accounting principles and practices, which the entrepreneur should strive to obtain.

LARRY HORNER
Chairman of Board and CEO
Peat, Marwick & Main Co.

An organized system of fiscal responsibility and control is important at all stages in the life of a business, yet most entrepreneurs tend to ignore this fact until the pressures of growth force them to adopt formal recordkeeping procedures. Far too many are prone to rely on intuition and memory during startup periods and simply "wing it," only to discover that many headaches might have been avoided had they taken time for some up-front financial planning.

According to a Dun & Bradstreet study, proper fiscal control begins with determining what types of information are necessary in managing an enterprise and how this data can be obtained in a timely, usable format. An estimated 80 percent of all retail and service company failures result from an inability to avoid conditions that adequate records would have disclosed in time for corrective action. By contrast, most successful businesses, it was found, take the time to install—and believe in—high-quality accounting and infor-mation-retrieval systems.

Yet, as in all responses to the dynamics of growth, the method of meeting the needs for accounting controls changes in direct relationship to the increasing complexity of managerial responsibilities. To be useful, accounting and reporting must be done with speed and reasonable accuracy; it must also be understandable, in format as well as information.

Beginning accounting students often complain that they are required to learn a foreign language before proceeding to master the discipline. This "language of business" is equally essential to owner-managers if they expect to survive in a marketplace governed by numbers—and the relationship between numbers—as defined and controlled by specific terminology. As one observer has stated humorously, "Entrepreneurs ultimately must give up the urge to keep important records on the backs of envelopes (which they usually file in shirt pockets) and adopt a systematized record-reporting system that provides data with which to evaluate the performance of their businesses." The most critical of these accounting reports monitors cash flow, the lifeblood of fledgling enter-prises. There seldom is enough cash generated from early sales to satisfy day-to-day needs, and the wise manager constantly reviews, and learns to rely on, cash-flow statements.

Other extremely valuable accounting reports bear such names as income statements, balance sheets, and breakeven charts, and these are supplemented by a raft of journals and ledgers that keep track of such functions as purchases, inventories, production, and payrolls, as well as the all-important accounts known as receivables and payables. To the novice, these records represent a confusing and meaningless maze, but to the serious-minded entrepreneur, they are the stepping-stones to successful decision making.

Indeed, these interrelated accounting records represent the most effective way of understanding what is happening within a business, and of measuring the progress toward "where you planned to be" from "where you were." With these accumulated records, managers can make statistical comparisons between the achievements of a current month or quarter and those of related periods in previous years; such comparisons are an effective tool for developing goals as well as maintaining control over a small business.

There is another important reason for thorough and systematic record-keeping. All business owners soon discover that they have a partner in their operations—the Internal Revenue Service—to whom periodic and detailed accountings must be made. Some may view this obligation with disdain, but it is a small price to pay to sustain a form of government that encourages the broadest possible participation in a marketplace based on the enterprise-for-profit system.

Books in this section present a wide range of information on finance and financial management, accounting, and bookkeeping, from the big picture to day-to-day specifics. Individual managers will have to decide, however, whether to invest their own time in performing these activities in their businesses, or whether to engage the services of accounting professionals.

403.

AMACOM

Fundamentals of Finance and Accounting for Nonfinancial Managers

AMACOM, $84.95 AMA members, $94.95 nonmembers

Provides basic financial skills that every manager, regardless of functional area, needs for success. Emphasizes how financial tools can be used in day-to-day decisions.

404.

American Institute of Certified Public Accountants

Audits of Small Business

American Institute of Certified Public Accountants, 1985, 94 pp.

Dewey Decimal No. 657.45. LC Card No. 85-171942.

405.

American Institute of Certified Public Accountants

Report of the Committee on Generally Accepted Accounting Principles for Smaller and/or Closely Held Businesses

American Institute of Certified Public Accountants, 1976

Report intended to influence standards for accounting and for reporting by CPAs in directions the committee believes are in the public interest.

406.

Anthony, Robert N.

A Reference Guide to Essentials of Accounting

Addison-Wesley, 1985, 128 pp., $12.95

Formatted as reference for businesspeople. Contains overview of basic concepts and elements of accounting.

407.

Behan, Raymond J.

How to Develop, Install and Maintain Cost-Reduction/Productivity-Improvement Programs

Van Nostrand Reinhold, 224 pp.

ISBN 0-442-21280-1. LC Card No. 83-1299.

Proven techniques for analyzing all aspects of a company's operations to uncover costs that are controllable and set up programs that ensure profits.

408.

Butler, David H.

An Income Tax Planning Model for Small Business

UMI Research Press, 1981, 324 pp.

ISBN 0-8357-1131-5. Dewey Decimal No. 343.730. LC Card No. 81-582.

Describes a convenient planning method to guide the small-business owner in organizing the firm for the greatest tax advantage. Five computerized models forecast the tax consequences of the common forms of small-business organization.

409.

Carey, Omer L., and Dean Francis Olson

Financial Tools for Small Business

Reston, 1983, 269 pp., $15 (cloth), $10 (paper)

ISBN 0-8359-2043-7 (cloth), 0-8359-2042-9 (paper). Dewey Decimal No. 658.159. LC Card No. 82-16146.

410.

Carsberg, Bryan

Small Company Financial Reporting

Prentice-Hall, 1985, 101 pp., $15.95

ISBN 0-13-814252-1. Dewey Decimal No. 658.151.

411.

Day, Theodore D., Hans R. Stoll, and Robert E. Whaley

Taxes, Financial Policy, and Small Business

Lexington Books, 1985, 192 pp., $24

ISBN 0-669-10393-4. Dewey Decimal No. 338.642. LC Card No. 85-40016.

Effects of tax policies on small businesses and how small firms set their financial policies. Explores why small firms prefer bank loans to public financing. Dividend payout policy and the relationship between taxes and the firm's financial policies.

412.
Donoghue, William E.
Financial Forecasting
Donoghue, 1974
Designed to assist small-business owners in improving their financial forecasting skills.

413.
Donoghue, William E., ed.
Cash Management
Donoghue, 1974
A manual on cash management, printed privately by a management consulting firm, to assist the small-business owner in doing a better job of managing cash resources.

414.
Droms, William G.
Finance and Accounting for Nonfinancial Managers
Addison-Wesley, $17.95
If you need to acquire a basic and working understanding of finance and accounting, this book is invaluable. Important key points, questions, answers are highlighted at the end of each chapter.

415.
Dyer, Mary L.
Practical Bookkeeping for the Small Business
Contemporary Books, 1976, $7.95
ISBN 0-8092-8206-2.
A combined textbook and workbook, designed to meet the needs of the small-business owner or manager for keeping accurate financial records, through a system that can be learned quickly and adapted easily to almost any kind of business.

416.
Ellerbach, Richard J.
Tax Reduction Strategies for Small Business
Prentice-Hall, 1982, 145 pp.
ISBN 0-13-885228-6 (cloth), 0-13-885219-3 (paper). Dewey Decimal No. 343.7300. LC Card No. 82-7544.

417.
Figgie, Harry E., Jr.
The Cost Reduction and Profit Improvement Handbook
Van Nostrand Reinhold, 1985, 228 pp., $23.95
ISBN 0-442-22584-9.
A how-to approach.

418.
Gargan, John Joseph
Milking Your Business for All It's Worth
Prentice-Hall, 1982, 137 pp.
ISBN 0-13-583005-2 (cloth), 0-13-582999-2 (paper). Dewey Decimal No. 343.730. LC Card No. 82-3687.
Tax-saving opportunities for small business.

419.
Haller, Leon
Making Sense of Accounting Information: A Practical Guide for Understanding Financial Reports and Their Use
Van Nostrand Reinhold, 1985, 208 pp., $27.95
ISBN 0-442-23249-7.
A guide for the nonaccountant. Helps in understanding all the flows of resources and financing through business, including the risks of creditors and investors.

420.
Harris, Clifford C.
The Break-Even Handbook
Prentice-Hall, $24.95
ISBN 0-13-081489-X.

Practical, field-tested breakeven techniques that have proved profitable when used in tough, real-life situations. For those who tackle complex operating problems needing complex volume-cost-profit analysis.

421.
Hogsett, Robert N.
Profit Planning for Small Business
Van Nostrand Reinhold, 1981, 231 pp.
ISBN 0-442-24907-1. Dewey Decimal No. 658.155. LC Card No. 80-24346.

422.
Hribar, Zvonimir
Accounting Practice Management for Small Businesses
Commerce Clearing House, 1985, 154 pp.
ISBN 0-86903-596-7.

423.
Internal Revenue Service
Tax Guide for Small Business
US Gov't Printing Office
Tax consequences and operating regulations for sole proprietorships, partnerships, and corporations.

424.
Jones, Seymour, and M. Bruce Cohen
Emerging Business: Managing for Growth
Wiley, 1983, 425 pp., $41.95

425.
Kamoroff, Berhard
Small Time Operator: How to Start Your Own Small Business, Keep Your Books, Pay Your Taxes, and Stay Out of Trouble
Bell Springs Publishing, 1980, $7.95
ISBN 0-91715-00-3.
This book is a technical manual, a step-by-step guide to help you set up the "machinery" of your own business—the "business" end of your business—and keep it well maintained.

426.
Kaufman, Bob
Cost-Effective Telecommunications Management
Van Nostrand Reinhold, 1983, 288 pp., $26.95
ISBN 0-843-61609-1.
A step-by-step how-to approach for saving on telephone expenses and increasing profitability.

427.
Lane, Marc J.
Taxation for Small Business, 2nd edition
Wiley, 1982, 284 pp.
ISBN 0-471-86774-8. LC Card No. 82-70353.
Traces tax decision making from organizational issues through all kinds of operational questions, and concludes with the tax side of merger and acquisition, all from the vantage point of the small entrepreneur. A guide to virtually every tax aspect of setting up and running a business, with checklists for performing all the vital steps that can lead to tax success.

428.
Lipay, Raymond J.
Accounting Services for Your Small Business
Wiley, 1983, 258 pp.
ISBN 0-471-09160-X. LC Card No. 82-13647.
Shows small-business owners and managers how to use compilation and review financial services as an alternative to costly audits. Explains the financial statements most frequently issued by profit-oriented companies: the income statement, balance sheet, and statement of changes in financial position. Offers guidance on how to select a CPA and how to organize the company for a CPA's service.

429.
McGee, Robert W.
Accounting for Software Costs

National Association of Accountants, 200 pp., $11.95
ISBN 0-86641-104-6.
For financial executives of software manufacturing companies and software users. Focuses on financial reporting issues, internal accounting, and tax policies.

430.
Moscove, Stephen, and Mark G. Simkin
Accounting Information Systems
Wiley, 1981, 616 pp.
ISBN 0-471-03369-3. LC Card No. 80-15445.
Analyzes the important role of accounting information systems within an organization's operating environment. Provides accounting students necessary tools to examine a given company's current system, identify problems within it, design changes to solve any existing problems, implement required changes, and perform follow-up analyses.

431.
National Association of Accountants Library
Industry Accounting Manuals,
1983–1984 edition
National Association of Accountants, 46 pp., $5.95
ISBN 0-86641-058-9.
A listing of literature from many different industries.

432.
Ragan, Robert
Step-by-Step Bookkeeping
Sterling Publishing, 128 pp., $5.95
ISBN 0-8069-8690-5.
Written for the small-store owner whose business does not require a trained, full-time bookkeeper.

433.
Ragan, Robert C., and Jack Zwick
Fundamentals of Recordkeeping and Finance for Small Business

Entrepreneur Press, 1978, 63 pp., $4.95
Explains basic record keeping: how the money comes in and goes out, how to maintain records and prepare monthly financial statements, other accounting and taxing information you need to know as a small-business owner-manager.

434.
Rausch, Edward N.
Financial Keys to Small Business Profitability
AMACOM, 1982, 166 pp., $15.95
ISBN 0-8144-5615-4. Dewey Decimal No. 658.159. LC Card No. 81-69354.

435.
Rausch, Edward N.
Financial Management for Small Business
AMACOM, 1979, 184 pp., $12.95
ISBN 0-8144-5499-2.
Financial management for owners or operators of small businesses.

436.
Ruland, William
Managers Guide to Corporate Tax
Ronald Press, 1984, 370 pp.
ISBN 0-471-88179-1. LC Card No. 84-7344.
For executives and entrepreneurs with no formal legal or tax training. Examines the tax ramifications of inventory methods, timing of sales to minimize tax risk, and choice of compensation plan alternatives. Shows how to minimize double taxation and maximize earnings, and alternative forms of corporate acquisitions and dispositions. Demonstrates how investors and lenders can determine tax liabilities and estimate cash flow.

437.
Seder, John W.
Credit and Collections
Wiley, 1977, 121 pp.

A basic overview: advantages and disadvantages of extending credit, how to get insurance against credit losses, and numerous other aspects of credit management.

438.
Spsiro, Herbert T.
Finance for the Non-Financial Manager
Wiley, 1977, $16.50
ISBN 0-471-01188-4.
Helps readers decipher a financial statement, answer tough questions about costs, see the true profit picture in a new project, put together a budget that withstands scrutiny by financial management, do a better job of keeping track of income and expenses, and learn the basic language of finance.

439.
Starchild, Adam
Tax Havens for Corporations
Gulf Publishing, 1979, 176 pp., $25
ISBN 0-87201-818-0.
Two fundamental questions are addressed: Is the organization of a business in a foreign country for the purpose of tax avoidance legal? If it is legal but takes funds from the country of residence, is it also moral?

440.
Steiner, Barry R., and David W. Kenney
Perfectly Legal: 450 Foolproof Methods for Paying Less Taxes
Wiley, 1986, 293 pp.
ISBN 0-471-83448-3. LC Card No. 85-22457.
Legal tax dodges presented in a question-and-answer format, covering audits to business deductions and pensions.

441.
Still, Jack W.
A Guide to Managerial Accounting in Small Companies

Arno Press, 1979, 271 pp., $18
ISBN 0-405-11480-X.
Intended for accountants in small companies and for public accountants who advise small companies, this book shows how the managerial accounting techniques employed by larger business can be profitably used by smaller companies. Explains how accounting can be made a relevant part of the decision-making process.

442.
Tompkins, Bill G.
Project Cost Control for Managers
Gulf Publishing, 1985, 162 pp., $26.95
ISBN 0-87201-684-6.
This book presents guidelines for involving all levels of management in order to induce a successful cost-control program. Geared toward engineering, construction, operating, and manufacturing companies. Offers an inside track to management on understanding and applying the concepts of effective project cost control.

443.
Vaughan, Roger J.
State Tax Policy and the Development of Small and New Business
Coalition of Northeastern Governors, 1983, 144 pp.
ISBN 0-914193-01. LC Card No. 83-179310.

444.
Walker, Ernest W., and J. William Petty II
Financial Management of the Small Firm
Prentice-Hall, 382 pp., $16.95
ISBN 0-13-316091-2.
Provides managers of small firms the same financial theories used by large firms. Offers suitable techniques and models to improve the efficiency of the small firm.

445.

Zabalaoui, Judith Cowan

How to Use Your Business or Profession as a Tax Shelter

Reston, 1983, 401 pp., $18 (cloth), $14.95 (paper)

ISBN 0-8359-2985-X (cloth), 0-8359-2988-4 (paper). Dewey Decimal No. 343.730. LC Card No. 83-2963.

COMPUTERS

Because of recent developments in electronic technology, the business world is poised on the edge of a quantum leap forward in computer hardware capability. Computers, properly programmed, now operate much of the industrial machinery once regarded as labor intensive. Their capacity for storing, processing, and retrieving mountains of information with lightning speed also threatens to revolutionize traditional patterns of analyzing and using all such data. Moreover, the impact of future developments unquestionably will be even more awesome, given the fact that computer manufacturers and software specialists tend to leapfrog each new achievement with frightening ease. The entrepreneur faces a severe challenge in merely keeping abreast of them.

K. PHILIP HWANG
Chairman
Televideo Systems, Inc.

The technological milestone of the twentieth century has been the development of low-cost, high-capacity, operationally uncomplicated computer systems. Indeed, computer hardware/software technology has expanded so dramatically in the last five years that it has become feasible, both economically and logistically, for even the smallest of businesses to acquire or use. Management benefits are almost unlimited, for the smallest of personal computers now offers a variety of standardized programs ranging from word processing, accounting, payroll, and inventory control to even more complicated applications such as spreadsheet analysis, data base management, point-of-sale entry and control, and even telecommunications.

The development of the personal computer (PC) has been more than the emergence of another office tool; potentially, it has placed electronic record analysis and management control on the desk of every business executive. The turnaround time in retrieving stored information is measured in seconds, and spreadsheet data immediately become available in preprogrammed and formatted displays or printouts that facilitate timely and appropriate decision making. The multipurpose usage of the PC is mind-boggling, for it is entirely possible that, in the near future, small businesses will be able to communicate via computer terminals with customers, suppliers, and even financial institutions.

A word of caution, however. Computers often are purchased with the thought of saving money, and this may well be an important long-term result of their acquisition. More often, however, this is *not* the case, for the process of implementing an information storage and retrieval system comes with a price tag of significant dimensions. In addition to mainframe hardware costs, other related expenses include software programs, training of user or support personnel, and sometimes even the retention of a systems analyst. Additionally, computer hardwares require special space accommodations, furniture, and security.

It becomes, therefore, a cost-benefit decision, especially for the small-businessperson whose capitalization posture may be thin, but it is important that this decision not be overly influenced by a lack of computer literacy. Computers increasingly are becoming "user-friendly," for the gap of understanding between man and machine has significantly narrowed in recent years. Program formats and operating terminology have been simplified, and computer language compatibility allows the machines of many competing manufacturers to interface or use the same software programs. Moreover, channels of distribution have been improved, both for acquiring and servicing computer units and for obtaining software and other operating supplies.

There is an inexplicable mystique that surrounds the computer: some fear its unknown characteristics and are slow to investigate its potential; others are lured by the challenge to master its mysteries and purchase units without trying to match operational needs with the most appropriate system available. Wise entrepreneurs make certain they obtain the right computer system to meet the requirements of their business, within economic parameters that complement their financial status. Many systems are designed to accommodate "add-on" components, which permit an expansion of storage capacity and retrieval speed as well as adaptation to periodic improvements in software.

Design advancements in software packages undoubtedly will accelerate dramatically in the next decade and move businesses ever closer to total automation of most sales, management, marketing, and accounting functions. As attractive as this phenomenon may seem to small-business owners, it eventually may be greeted by a type of employee resistance called cyberphobia (fear of computers), derived in part from a temporary dread of computer illiteracy but also from a mounting, more realistic fear—that of ultimately being replaced by computers. Given the industry's trend of leapfrogging old technologies with new ones within increasingly compressed time frames, holding back the advancements in computer systems is as unlikely as holding back the dawn.

In this section readers will find books discussing the impact of computers in business, and offering ideas on how to choose and set up the most appropriate system. Ideas for moneymaking ventures using a computer you already own are included in Small Business Opportunities in Section 1. Also refer to Section 5, which describes both on-line information systems and a wide range of software packages.

446.
Bates, Timothy, and Judith Wright
Choosing the Right Small Business Computer
Hayden, 1984, 129 pp.
ISBN 0-8104-6200-1. Dewey Decimal No.
001.64. LC Card No. 84-586.

447.
Bennett, Wilma E.
Checklist/Guide to Selecting a Small Computer
Pilot Books, $5
Contains a 332-point checklist for selecting the proper equipment to ensure increased productivity and improved management decisions. A glossary of 163 computer terms and abbreviations is included.

448.
Berkery, Michael J., and Raymond W. Bolek
Touche Ross Guide to Selecting a Small Business Computer
Prentice-Hall, 1985, 338 pp., $19.95
ISBN 0-13-925744-6. Dewey Decimal No.
658.054. LC Card No. 84-26528.

449.
Birnbaum, Mark, and John Sickman
How to Choose Your Small Business Computer
Addison-Wesley, 1983, 150 pp., $9.95
ISBN 0-201-10187-4. Dewey Decimal No.
001.640. LC Card No. 82-11665.

450.
Blumenthal, Susan
Understanding and Buying a Small-Business Computer
Sams, 1982, 157 pp., $8.95
ISBN 0-672-21890-9. Dewey Decimal No.
001.640. LC Card No. 81-86553.

451.
Bradley, Charles W.
Manager's Guide to Small Computers
Holt, Rinehart & Winston, 1984, 352 pp.

ISBN 0-03-059538-X. Dewey Decimal No.
001.64. LC Card No. 84-19222.
Guide for evaluating, selecting, financing, and installing a business computer that works.

452.
Christie, Linda Gail
Managing Today and Tomorrow with On-Line Information
Dow Jones–Irwin, $25
How to take advantage of strategic business information available from on-line data base services. Helps you design and implement a system that will meet your company's specific information needs.

453.
Connell, Stephen, and Ian A. Galbraith
Electronic Mail: A Revolution in Business Communications
Van Nostrand Reinhold, 1983, 152 pp., $17.95
ISBN 0-442-21691-2.
A guide for choosing the products and systems for electronic mail.

454.
Curry, Jess W., and David M. Bonner
Up and Running: The Small Business Computer Implementation Cookbook
Prentice-Hall, 1984, 145 pp., $17.95
(cloth), $9.95 (paper)

455.
Dataquest
Small Computer Industry Service
Dataquest, 1982
Dewey Decimal No. 381.450. LC Card No.
82-229937.
Four-volume set covering general-purpose minicomputers, small commercial systems.

456.

Enockson, Paul G.
A Guide for Selecting Computers and Software for Small Businesses
Reston, 1983, 109 pp., $19.95
ISBN 0-8359-2642-7. Dewey Decimal No. 001.64. LC Card No. 82-21478.

457.

Falk, Howard
Handbook of Computer Applications for the Small or Medium-Size Business
Chilton, 1983, 331 pp., $19.95
ISBN 0-8019-7393-7. Dewey Decimal No. 658.054. LC Card No. 83-70782.

458.

Gibson, Glenn A., and Mary L. Gibson
Understanding and Selecting Small Business Computers
Prentice-Hall, 1986, 418 pp., $28.95
ISBN 0-13-937046-3. Dewey Decimal No. 658.022. LC Card No. 85-12324.

459.

Hockney, Donald
Personal Computers for the Successful Small Business
Macmillan, 1984, 202 pp., $19.95
ISBN 0-02-5518704. Dewey Decimal No. 658.022. LC Card No. 84-7174.

460.

Installing a Small Business Computer
Wiley, 1982, 111 pp.
ISBN 0-471-89459-1.
Covers the responsibilities of staff, manufacturer's and supplier's costs, insurance, documentation, site preparation and layout, and other practical aspects of establishing a small computer system.

461.

Isshiki, Koichiro R.
Small Business Computers
Prentice-Hall, 1982, 478 pp., $26.95
ISBN 0-13-8141525. Dewey Decimal No. 658.054. LC Card No. 81-11836.
A guide to evaluation and selection of a small-business computer.

462.

Jong, Steven F.
Word Processing for Small Businesses
Sams, 1983, 190 pp., $11.95
ISBN 0-672-21929-8. Dewey Decimal No. 652. LC Card No. 82-61964.

463.

Keim, Robert T.
Business Computers: Planning, Selecting and Implementing Your First Computer System
Merrill Publishing, 384 pp.
Written for the nontechnical, management-oriented student. Offers a complete step-by-step program for choosing the right computer system for any business. Comprehensive checklists guide you through the planning stages, through the choice and purchase of a computer system, to its operation on the job.

464.

Kolve, Carolee Nance
How to Buy [and Survive!] Your First Computer
McGraw-Hill, 1983, 204 pp., $14.95
ISBN 0-07-035130-9. Dewey Decimal No. 001.64. LC Card No. 83-795.

465.

McGlynn, Daniel R.
Personal Computing: Home, Professional and Small Business Applications, 2nd edition
Wiley, 1982, 335 pp.
ISBN 0-471-86164-2. LC Card No. 81-16146.
Guide to the capabilities and operating features of personal computers. Provides detailed, critical coverage of the limitations of hardware and software commercially available today, and explains various programming languages, from BASIC to Pascal and APL. Contains photos, tables, and charts that list and compare equipment.

466.

McGlynn, Daniel R.

Simplified Guide to Small Computers for Business

Wiley, 1983, 241 pp.

ISBN 0-471-86853-1. LC Card No. 82-24812.

Provides an overview of small-business computer systems for the first-time user with no previous computer experience. Introduces today's new technologies and systems, and explains, in layman's terms, the computer jargon used in describing these systems. Stresses the capabilities and limitations of available hardware and software. Provides guidelines and criteria for evaluating and selecting computing equipment.

467.

McNichols, Charles W., and Thomas D. Clark

Microcomputer-Based Information and Decision Support Systems for Small Businesses

Reston, 1983, 198 pp., $24.95 (cloth), $15.95 (paper)

ISBN 0-8359-4359-3 (cloth), 0-8359-4358-5 (paper). Dewey Decimal No. 658.022. LC Card No. 82-16556.

A guide to design and implementation of micro-based information and decision support systems specifically for small business.

468.

McNitt, Jim

The Art of Computer Management

Simon & Schuster, 1984, 272 pp., $15.95

ISBN 0-671-46471-X. Dewey Decimal No. 658.022. LC Card No. 83-20432.

How small firms increase their productivity and profits with personal computers.

469.

Porochnia, Leonard

The Minicomputer: To Buy or Not to Buy?

National Association of Accountants, 122 pp., $15.95

ISBN 0-86641-085-6.

Familiarizes prospective users of minicomputers with the steps necessary for selecting a minicomputer. A glossary of computer terminology and a listing of manufacturers are included.

470.

Poynter, Dan

Computer Selection Guide

Parachute Publications, 1983, 168 pp., $11.95

ISBN 0-915516-33-0. LC Card No. 83-8084.

A sourcebook for finding the system that meets your needs. Includes checklist for every function and feature.

471.

Predicasts

Small Business Systems Software

Predicasts, 1983, 93 pp.

Dewey Decimal No. 380.145. LC Card No. 83-191648.

472.

Randall, Robert D.

Microcomputers in Small Business

Prentice-Hall, 1982, 134 pp.

ISBN 0-13-580753-0 (cloth), 0-13-580746-8 (paper). Dewey Decimal No. 658.022. LC Card No. 82-12221.

473.

Rosa, Nicholas, and Sharon Rosa

Small Computers for the Small Businessman

TAB Books, 1982, 334 pp., $19.95

ISBN 0-8306-4337-0. Dewey Decimal No. 001.64. LC Card No. 81-21392.

474.

Salm, Walter

Beginner's Guide to Small Business Computers

Van Nostrand Reinhold, 232 pp.

Guide to small-business computers featuring instructions on using CP/M and Wordstar.

475.
Schadewald, Robert J., and Bill Dickey
dBASE II Guide for Small Business
Ashton-Tate, 1984, 350 pp., $24.95
ISBN 0-912677-07-4. Dewey Decimal No.
650.028. LC Card No. 84-196281.

476.
Silberstein, Judith A., and F. Warren Benton
Bringing High Tech Home
Wiley, 1985, 202 pp.
ISBN 0-471-80018-X. Dewey Decimal No.
658.041. LC Card No. 84-19547.
How to create a computer-based home
office.

477.
Silver, Gerald A.
Small Computer Systems for Business
McGraw-Hill, 1978, 264 pp., $11.95
ISBN 0-07-057463-4.
An overview of microcomputers and
minicomputers for students, businesspeople, managers, and small-business
operators; discusses the full range of
small computer hardware, languages,
software, and applications.

478.
Sipple, Charles J., and Fred Dahl
Computer Power for the Small Business
Prentice-Hall, 1979, $15.95 (cloth), $8.95
(paper)
ISBN 0-13-165373-3 (cloth), 0-13-165373-
2 (paper).
Explains how computers work and how
they can perform many functions in a
small business: measuring inventory,
calculating profit and loss statements,
and controlling energy. Includes charts,
tables, and illustrations.

479.
Small Business Computer News
How Small Businesses Use Computers, 3rd
edition

Management Information Corp., 1982,
92 pp.
Dewey Decimal No. 658.022. LC Card No.
82-181595.

480.
*Small Business Programs for the
Commodore 64*
Elcomp Publishing

481.
Small Business Programs for the IBM PC
Elcomp Publishing
Book of program listings of small-busi-
ness software for the IBM PC. Disk of
software available.

482.
Small Business Systems for First-Time Users
Wiley, 1982, 180 pp.
ISBN 0-471-89427-3.
Discusses the elements of a small-
business computer system and its typical
applications, and provides guidelines
for acquiring a system and associated
applications packages.

483.
Smolin, Roger C.
*How to Buy the Right Small Business Com-
puter System*
Wiley, 1981, 156 pp.
ISBN 0-471-08494-8. LC Card No. 81-
4276.
An introduction to the use of microcomputers in business, for those with no
previous computer background. Shows
how computers are used by small businesses, when they are cost effective, how
to get the most out of a computer, what to
look for, and how to select hardware and
software. Includes sample business
applications programs. Emphasizes common business software systems and how
they work.

484.
So You Think You Need Your Own Business Computer
Computer BookBase
Selecting, installing, and using a small-business system.

485.
Strosberg, Linda
Big Decisions for Small Business
Harper & Row, 1984, 144 pp., $15.95
ISBN 0-06-046485-2. Dewey Decimal No. 001.64. LC Card No. 83-18478.
What you should know before you buy a computer.

486.
Wiatrowski, Claude A.
A Kiss for Your Computer
MAC Publishing, 1984, 96 pp., $4.95
ISBN 0-936206-17-9. Dewey Decimal No. 658.022. LC Card No. 83-22285.
The small-business guide to successful computing.

FINANCING
AND VENTURE CAPITAL

New ventures require "up-front" money that assures an appropriate capitalization of the business. Such resources most often come for small business from personal, family, or private associates, but large financial packages that provide venture capital may come from a variety of financial institutions or the federal Small Business Administration. Determining the best source and the amount of needed financing requires careful planning and execution.

FREDERICK W. SMITH
Founder, Chairman, and CEO
Federal Express Corporation

By far the most formidable problem entrepreneurs and small-business owners face today is the lack of access to sources of affordable capital. This is not surprising, given the fact that the risk factors inherent in operating small enterprises often make it difficult for financial institutions to approve loan applications. All too frequently, entrepreneurs are told that they have insufficient collaterable assets, too little net worth, a shortage of operating experience, or a lack of adequate formal planning—or all four.

Successful capital formation begins with an assessment of needs and the drafting of a business plan that accurately reflects these needs in relationship to the goals and operating strengths of a proposed enterprise. This business plan examines in detail all the functions of an enterprise, ranging from a statement of business objectives to a description of management, marketing, production, and financing strategies. Moreover, it contains sales forecasts and financial statements that reflect both market analysis and the probability of generating sufficient cash flow to meet financial obligations. It is more than a wish list; it is a proposed blueprint for the successful operation of a business. Few successful loans have ever been negotiated without such a business plan. (Readers should also note that many of the listings under The Entrepreneur in Section 1 also provide information on developing a business plan.)

Equally essential in capital formation is entrepreneurs' knowledge of the different methods of raising funds and an ability to judge which is best suited to their needs. Capital may be derived from at least four major sources: debt (such as arranging a loan at a bank); equity (selling shares of stock); internal financing (recycling current earnings); and personal savings. Typically, existing small businesses tend to rely more heavily upon earnings for capital needs than on any other source.

For those seeking outside funding (debt or equity), a formal business plan substantially increases the likelihood of obtaining favorable loan considerations. This is especially true of debt capital, because borrowed money must be repaid according to the terms of a loan agreement. Thus, a business plan containing well-thought-out sales projections that reflect sufficient cash flow to retire an indebtedness undoubtedly will add strength to any entrepreneur's loan application.

Equity capital may come from a variety of sources, including private investors (friends, relatives, or personal investors); partnerships; venture capital firms; and initial public stock offerings. This type of capital investment usually involves partial ownership in a firm as well as a participation in a pro rata share of its earnings. Although such paid-in capital is retained by the enterprise and need not be repaid, it represents a different type of obligation in that shareholders are entitled not only to a systematic reporting of business activities and achievements but also to a voice in management commensurate with their shares of ownership.

The most common source of new-venture financing belongs to a category known as personal or owner savings, which include paid-in equities in bonds, real estate, whole life insurance policies, and pension funds. Yet, for a majority of individuals, aggregate net worth from such personal equities is limited, and the businesses started with personal capital usually end up being limited in scope as well. Thus, an early assessment of needs may result in reshaping (indeed, reducing) one's goals unless sources of outside capital can be tapped.

As formidable as the obstacles seem in arranging adequate financing for new-venture startups, there is an overriding, compensatory condition that offers hope to any aggressive entrepreneur. Many individuals and companies have cash reserves that they wish (and need) to invest. To penetrate this investors' circle, the wise entrepreneur must begin with an assessment of "who loans money to whom and for what purposes." Banks and financial institutions have policy guidelines that give specific answers to this question, as do the investment managers of industrial portfolios, insurance companies, and venture capital firms. These guidelines need not be discouraging, because they are usually not inflexible. Nevertheless, any loan request to a lending institution must meet basic qualifying expectations, especially in the area of collaterable assets.

Additional opportunities for raising equity capital are found in a variety of partnership categories; general and limited partnerships are the most frequently used. Growing rapidly in popularity is the limited partnership arrangement, which attracts profit-seeking investors to a business venture without subjecting them to the unattractive liabilities associated with a general partnership. Moreover, a business owner may obtain needed capital without inviting interference from the investing partner in the management of the enterprise.

There is yet another area of nontraditional capital formation that is limited only by the imagination of the entrepreneur. Commonly referred to as creative financing, this type of funding involves such unique sources as customer financing, middleman financing, supplier buy-back agreements, subcontracting, and leasing. The key to creative financing is to match the proprietary needs of both lender and borrower, be they owner, user, jobber, purchaser, or supplier, in an arrangement that "goes down well on both sides of the table."

Many businesses never start because of an inability to secure initial financing; others fail for lack of working or expansion capital that might have become available had the entrepreneurs taken the right steps in obtaining it. Providing adequate funding for a business is a never-ending process and requires careful and creative thought at every stage of development.

487.
Alexander, Don H.
How to Borrow Money from a Bank
Beaufort Book Co., 1984, 92 pp.
ISBN 0-8253-0228-5. Dewey Decimal No.
  658.152. LC Card No. 84-9327.
Banking for the nonbanker.

488.
Altman, Edward I., ed.
Financial Handbook, 5th edition
Wiley, 1981, 1,344 pp., $69.95
All-inclusive text on modern finance encompasses such topics as short- and long-term money markets and instruments, financial institutions, real estate and public utility finance, performance measurement and modern portfolio theory, international topics for markets and firms, corporate finance, small-business finance, corporate bankruptcy, and reorganization, and managing in an inflationary environment.

489.
Batterson, Leonard A.
Raising Venture Capital and the Entrepreneur
Prentice-Hall, 1986, $27.50
ISBN 0-13-752684-9. Dewey Decimal No.
  658.152. LC Card No. 85-30095.

490.
Belew, Richard
How to Negotiate a Business Loan
Van Nostrand Reinhold, 1975, 176 pp.,
  $8.50

ISBN 0-442-20666-6.
For those responsible for preparing financial forecasts in order to borrow money for funding company objectives. Describes in detail how to develop financial projections, gives step-by-step explanations and examples for developing forecasts of operations and, related cash flow and for preparing the resulting pro forma balance sheets and estimated borrowing requirements.

491.
Belew, Richard C.
How to Win Profits and Influence Bankers:
The Art of Practical Projecting
Van Nostrand Reinhold, 1973
For men and women who desire to be entrepreneurs and are far enough along with their dreams to realize that bankers play vital roles in the affairs of business enterprises. Describes in detail how to develop financial projections, with step-by-step explanations and 108 exhibits of projections, cash flows, pro forma statements, and related loan data.

492.
Chase, Anthony G.
Small Business Financing: Federal Assistance and Contracts
McGraw-Hill, 1983, 398 pp., $65
ISBN 0-07-010676-2. Dewey Decimal No.
  346.73. LC Card No. 83-10127.

493.

Competere Group

Everything You Need to Know About Raising Money for a New Business

Competere Group, $100

More than 30 different methods of raising money for a new business are provided, along with more than 3,000 different sources of money, their names, addresses, telephone numbers, and names of key decision makers.

494.

Competere Group

Preparing a Business Plan for Lenders or Investors

Competere Group, $22.50

Detailed description of the full-disclosure financing memorandum and exhibits typically required by lenders and investors; numerous specific examples.

495.

Competere Group

Talking to Lenders or Investors

Competere Group, $20

How to speak with a lender or investor. Special section on body language, and the do's and don'ts of conversation.

496.

Dible, Donald M.

How to Plan and Finance a Growing Business

Entrepreneur Press, 1980, 311 pp., $12.95

ISBN 0-88205-020-6. Dewey Decimal No. 658.022. LC Card No. 79-57045.

497.

Gladstone, David John

Venture Capital Handbook

Reston, 1983, 402 pp., $35

ISBN 0-8359-8303-X. Dewey Decimal No. 658.152. LC Card No. 82-25488.

498.

Haft, Robert J.

Venture Capital and Small Financings

Boardman, 1984

ISBN 0-87632-447-2. Dewey Decimal No. 346.73. LC Card No. 84-14514.

499.

Hayes, Rick Stephan

Business Loans: A Guide to Money Sources and How to Approach Them Successfully

CBI Publishing, 1977, 180 pp.

Dedicated to understanding the lending game, from "Where do I go to get money?" to "How do I prepare my request to get the maximum response?"

500.

Hayes, Stephen Rick, and John Cotton Howell

How to Finance Your Small Business with Government Money: SBA and Other Loans

Wiley, 1983, 258 pp., $19.95

ISBN 0-471-86563-X. LC Card No. 82-1606.

A comprehensive guide to dealing with the bureaucracy, rules, regulations, and special documentation requirements involved in acquiring government-sponsored loans for small businesses. Describes how to do a complete loan proposal, from projected cash flow to presentation format to selecting the best bank.

501.

Henderson, James William

Principles of Venture Financing: Theory and Practice

Lexington Books, 1986, $29

ISBN 0-669-10931-2. LC Card No. 85-40234.

Leads readers through the preparation of the business plan, including prospective financial statements, and helps them determine reliable financial forecasts and projections. Information on the decision to go public and valuing the business for merger or acquisition.

502.

Holtz, Herman

2001 Sources of Financing for Small Business

Arco, 1983, 173 pp., $14.95 (cloth), $9.95 (paper)

ISBN 0-668-05468-9 (cloth), 0-668-05470-0 (paper). Dewey Decimal No. 658.152. LC Card No. 82-11366.

503.

Horvitz, Paul M., and R. Richardson Pettit, eds.

Small Business Finance, 2 vols.

JAI Press, 1984, $40 each

ISBN 0-89232-390-6 (Part A), 0-89232-391-4 (Part B). Dewey Decimal No. 332.742. LC Card No. 83-48089.

Problems in financing and sources of financing for small businesses.

504.

Kozmetsky, G., M. D. Gill, Jr., and R. W. Smilor

Financing and Managing Fast-Growth Companies

Lexington Books, 1985, 176 pp., $16.95

ISBN 0-669-09481-1. LC Card No. 84-48473.

Explains the venture capital process and how it works. A clear definition of the venture capitalist and the investment analysis process.

505.

Kravitt, Gregory I., and others

How to Raise Capital: Preparing and Presenting the Business Plan

Business Publications, 250 pp., $40

Guide to writing a quality proposal that will attract potential investors and lenders. Workbook format.

506.

Lindsey, Jennifer

The Entrepreneur's Guide to Capital

Probus, 1986, $18.95

ISBN 0-917253-34-5. Dewey Decimal No. 658.15. LC Card No. 86-4930.

More than 40 techniques for capitalizing and refinancing new and growing businesses.

507.

Loffel, E. W.

Financing Your Business

Wiley, 1978, 110 pp.

ISBN 0-471-05045-8. LC Card No. 78-12243.

A complete treatment of money in your business: how to tell how much you really need, how to get it when you want it, and what it will cost you. Explains how to estimate your money needs, kinds of money, and financial records you will need. Many money sources.

508.

Mancuso, Joseph R.

Small Business Survival Guide: Sources of Help for Entrepreneurs

Prentice-Hall, 1980

ISBN 0-13-814228-9.

An extensive list of over 700 sources of available capital and an industry-by-industry directory of marketing aids. Contains a complete index of sources on the Small Business Administration.

509.

McKeever, Mike P.

Start-Up Money

Nolo Press, 1984, 201 pp., $17.95

ISBN 0-917316-86-X. Dewey Decimal No. 658.152. LC Card No. 84-61578.

How to finance your new small business.

510.

O'Flaherty, Joseph S.

Going Public: The Entrepreneur's Guide

Wiley, 1984, 304 pp., $34.95

ISBN 0-471-086981-3. LC Card No. 83-23255.

A reference guide for entrepreneurs who are considering going public and who head businesses with annual sales between $5 million and $50 million. Presents realistic evaluations of the various financial and equity alternatives facing management, the stock market mechanism for initial public offerings, and the many aftermarket considerations.

511.
Pilot Books
Directory for State and Federal Funds for Business Development
Pilot Books, $5
ISBN 87576-011-2.
Provides basic data on the financial assistance programs of the 50 states and 12 federal agencies.

512.
Pratt, Stanley E., and Jane K. Morris
Pratt's Guide to Venture Capital Sources,
9th edition
Unipub, 1985, 588 pp., $95
Offers information on how to raise from $25,000 to $10 million in venture capital. Key data on over 700 active U.S. and Canadian venture capital firms. Learn how to approach and deal with a venture capitalist.

513.
Richards, Judith W.
Fundamentals of Development Finance: A Practitioner's Guide
Praeger, 1983, 210 pp., $28.95
ISBN 0-03-062191-7. Dewey Decimal No. 658.159. LC Card No. 82-18958.

514.
Roberts, E. Wilson
How, When and Where to Go Public with a Small Company
Exposition Press, 1972, $10
ISBN 0-682-47648-X.

Spells out the advantages—and pitfalls—inherent in taking a small company public. Detailed appendix of firms handling small companies.

515.
Rubel, Stanley
Guide to Venture Capital Sources
Capital Publishing
ISBN 0-914470-08-6.
Summarizes key developments in the industry, lists all major venture capitalists, and provides a bibliography. Published every two years.

516.
Rubel, Stanley M., and Edward G. Novotny
How to Raise and Invest Venture Capital
Presidents Publishing House, 1971
A variety of business situations requiring financing are reviewed. The importance of owner-financier relationships is discussed in a number of independent articles.

517.
Shames, William H.
Venture Management: The Business of the Inventor, Entrepreneur, Venture Capitalist and Established Company
Free Press, 1974
ISBN 0-02-928400-7.
Concerned with starting a new venture, with emphasis upon its early administration.

518.
Silver, A. David
Up Front Financing: The Entrepreneur's Guide
Ronald Press, 1982, 245 pp., $17.95
ISBN 0-471-86386-6. LC Card No. 81-21985.
Describes approximately 20 different financing options and how they can enable entrepreneurs to launch, expand, turn around, or acquire a small business. Explains how to prepare persuasive business plans and how to give presentations to potential investors. Case histories illustrate how various methods can be used and misused.

519.

Silver, A. David

Venture Capital: The Complete Guide for Investors

Ronald Press, 1985, 259 pp., $19.95

ISBN 0-471-88029-9. LC Card No. 84-19479.

A guide through the principles and process of successful investing in entrepreneurial companies, from the viewpoint of a venture capitalist. Silver's Four Laws of Venture Capital, plus in-depth discussions on forming the management team, raising funds to invest, and generating a local deal.

520.

Silver, A. David

Who's Who in Venture Capital

Ronald Press, 1984, 378 pp., $90

ISBN 0-471-89125-8. LC Card No. 83-19802.

A directory of venture capitalists, not venture capital funds. Allows the entrepreneur to select the appropriate venture capitalist to call on. Explains how to approach venture capitalists, negotiate with them, and maintain their interest, and gives their points of view, aims, and goals. Provides the names, addresses, and telephone numbers of all the venture capital funds in the country and includes biographical data on the 650 people who work for them.

521.

Smith, Brian R.

Raising Seed Money for Your Own Business

Lewis Publishing, 1984, 133 pp.

ISBN 0-86616-041-8 (cloth), 0-86616-043-4 (paper). Dewey Decimal No. 658.152. LC Card No. 84-791.

522.

Smith, Richard D.

Getting Money: A Practical Guide to Financing Your Business

Smith Assocs., 1981, 158 pp., $14.95 (Canada)

ISBN 0-919031-01-3.

523.

U.S. Small Business Administration

Directory of Operating Small Business Investment Companies

U.S. Small Business Administration

524.

Wilton, John W.

The New Ventures: Inside the High-Stakes World of Venture Capital

Addison-Wesley, 256 pp., $10.95

ISBN 0-201-09679-X.

Behind-the-scenes tour of the venture capital world, focusing on the big deals, combining hard-core business savvy with a gambler's risk of winner take all. Intimate profiles of Apple, Intel, Minute Maid, Genentech, to name a few.

525.

Woods, Ronald L.

How to Win SBA Loans

Citizens Law Library, $14.95

This book explains in detail about the Small Business Administration, the basic keys to eligibility for SBA loans, how the SBA grants financial aid, simple credit requirements necessary for SBA assistance, and the purposes for which the SBA will help small businesses secure government R&D contracts.

CASE STUDIES

The value of the case study method has long been established and the number of such studies available to businesses as training documents has increased dramatically in recent years. By using the histories of actual situations involving real people, the prospective entrepreneur can gain important insights into how others dealt with a wide range of problems, from startup situations to business-threatening conditions. Case studies can be an effective tool for developing the habit of diagnosing problems and shaping decisions about what should be done to resolve them—without having to pay the emotional and financial costs of actually experiencing them.

BERNARD GOLDHIRSH
Chairman and Publisher
Inc. Magazine.

The listings in this section embrace two important sources of information for the aspiring small-businessperson. For entrepreneurs in the earliest stages of conceptualizing a new business, who are seeking to learn from the experiences of successful business developers, there are a number of biographies of men and women who started from scratch and built companies that have contributed significantly to the quality of life we enjoy. For advanced business owners who wish to sharpen their decision-making skills, there are books that attempt to teach by reflective reasoning in problem-solving situations commonly referred to as case studies.

A word of caution. It is impossible to provide the perfect source on bringing an idea to business reality or on managing a business through a particular type of crisis. There is, however, a growing assortment of books and materials written by or about individuals who have left a record of what they learned while developing successful new enterprises. Some of the books in this section were written by academic or professional authors, others by practitioners who learned the hard way about how to start a business or how to perform a special market function under difficult circumstances.

Because biographical data usually are presented in narrative form, they are easy to read and can be highly informative as well as inspirational. The decisions and techniques used by the entrepreneur are more understandable because they are explained in the historical context of goals and achievements as expressed during the various stages of business development.

A case study, on the other hand, is more challenging. It is an account of a situation, problem, or series of events that have occurred in an actual business situation. Recorded by a case writer, the treatise portrays real people and describes their activities in dealing with problems confronting their enterprises. The value to the reader derives from having the opportunity to become involved in the case and to learn vicariously from it without actually having to live through a crucial problem. Said differently, it is the closest approximation to the confrontation of real-life situations, and a valuable educational medium for an inexperienced entrepreneur.

To obtain maximum instructional benefit from such case studies, it is important that you be more than just a receiver of facts; strive to use them in diagnosing a problem, evaluating alternative solutions, and deciding upon the most appropriate plan for solving it. The case-study approach is a departure from the traditional method of classroom instruction where the student is a passive recipient of facts and principles; the case reader immediately becomes a participant in a real-life problem by identifying and weighing the facts, and deciding upon a solution for a problem to which an actual solution already has been applied and is available for appraisal at the end of the exercise. Used correctly, case studies can assist the entrepreneur in developing the habit of becoming a decision maker by systematically analyzing facts in terms of the possible short- and long-term effects of a preferred solution.

There are no ready-made answers for business problems, and each situation may present what seems to be a unique set of conditions that requires special understanding and imaginative problem-solving skills. Oftentimes, decisions must be made with a degree of uncertainty because of incomplete facts, yet no problem exists in a vacuum. What has happened before in all likelihood will occur again in one form or another. The case study is a useful method of accumulating a backlog of valuable experiences others have faced, and of acquiring experience in making decisions in a highly competitive and demanding marketplace.

526.
Bender, Marylin, and Selig Altschul
The Chosen Instrument
Simon & Schuster, 1982, 605 pp.
ISBN 0-671-22464-6. Dewey Decimal No. 387.706. LC Card No. 81-21427.
A biography of Juan Trippe of Pan Am. The rise and fall of an American entrepreneur.

527.
Bhandari, Narendra C.
Cases in Small Business Management

South-Western Publishing Co., 1979, 200 pp., $10.30
Contains 26 cases covering a wide variety of real decision-making problems from a cross section of small businesses; the problems cover both functional and process areas, and are organized and written with emphasis on relevant material.

528.
Breuer, Miklos M.
Milton Harris: Chemist, Innovator and Entrepreneur

American Chemical Society, 1982,
   170 pp.
ISBN 0-8412-0740-2. Dewey Decimal No.
   677.028. LC Card No. 82-13926.

529.
Carter, John Mack, and Joan Fenney
Starting at the Top
Morrow, 1985, 252 pp.
ISBN 0-688-04520-0. Dewey Decimal No.
   338.040. LC Card No. 85-4826.
America's new achievers: twenty-three
success stories told by men and women
whose dreams of being boss came true.

530.
Church, Olive D.
Stanley Junction
Science Research Associates, 1984, 55
   pp., $7.95
ISBN 0-574-20717-1. Dewey Decimal No.
   658.022. LC Card No. 83-20063.
A case study in small-business manage-
ment and entrepreneurship.

531.
Hosmer, LaRue T., Arnold C. Cooper, and
Karl H. Verper
The Entrepreneurial Function
Prentice-Hall, 1977, $16.95
ISBN 0-13-283093-0.
Selection of cases for students and small-
business managers.

532.
Jones, Billy M.
The Chandlers of Kansas, a Banking Family
Wichita State University, 1983, 265 pp.
ISBN 0-865460948-5.
The biography of an entrepreneurial
banking family.

533.
Jones, Billy M.
L. E. Phillips: Banker, Oil Man, Civic Leader
Wichita State University, 1981, 206 pp.
ISBN 0-86546-016-7.

The life story of the cofounder of the
Phillips Petroleum Company of Bartlesville, Oklahoma.

534.
Jones, Billy M.
Magic with Sand: AFG Industries, Inc.
Wichita State University, 1984, 171 pp.
ISBN 0-86546-016-8.
The story of the flat-glass industry and
the contributions of R. Dee Hubbard and
AFG Industries, Inc.

535.
Jones, Billy M.
Olive White Garvey: Uncommon Citizen
Wichita State University, 1985, 242 pp.
ISBN 0-86546-066-3.
The biography of a courageous woman
who became a highly successful business
owner after assuming the leadership of an
enormous family enterprise founded by
her late husband.

536.
Keuls, Henry P. C.
*Uncle Henry: The Autobiography of an
Irrepressible Entrepreneur*
Phoenix Publishing, 1981, $14.95
ISBN 0-914016-88-1. Dewey Decimal No.
   338.060. LC Card No. 82-7687.

537.
Levering, Robert, Michael Katz, and Milton
Moskowitz
The Computer Entrepreneurs
New American Library, 1984, 481 pp.
ISBN 0-453-00477-6. Dewey Decimal No.
   338.761. LC Card No. 84-19057.
Making it big in America's upstart
industry. The names, faces, and ideas
behind today's computer revolution.

538.
Liles, Patrick R.
New Business Ventures and the Entrepreneur
Irwin, 1974, $18.50

ISBN 0-256-01560-0.
Case studies of 14 actual venture situations.

539.
Mahin, Philip William
Entrepreneurial Skills: Cases in Small Business Management
Irwin, 1981, 234 pp.
ISBN 0-256-02562-2. Dewey Decimal No. 658.022. LC Card No. 80-84532.

540.
Miller, Harry M., and Denis O'Brien
My Story
Macmillan, 1983, 322 pp.
ISBN 0-333-35644-6. Dewey Decimal No. 338.040. LC Card No. 83-201822.

541.
Moriarity, Shane
Cases from Management Accounting Practice, vol. 1
National Association of Accountants, 35 pp., $4.95
ISBN 0-86641-133-X.
Contains eight cases involving currently practiced management accounting issues in actual situations faced by the company that prepared the case.

542.
Nestlebaum, Karen
House of Diamonds
AMACOM, 1987, 240 pp.
ISBN 0-8144-5879-3. LC Card No. 86-47821.
The story of the most successful cartel in history, the worldwide diamond and mineral empire of the DeBeers. Tells how the small firm of DeBeers Consolidate Mines, under the leadership of the notorious magnate Cecil Rhodes, gradually gained control over 80 percent of the world's diamond supply.

543.
Reagan, Alice E.
H. I. Kimball, Entrepreneur

Cherokee Publishing, 1983
ISBN 0-87797-064-5. Dewey Decimal No. 338.040. LC Card No. 82-73598.

544.
Schellenberger, Robert E., and Glenn Boseman
Policy Formulation and Strategy Management: Text and Cases
Wiley, 1982, 760 pp., $38
ISBN 0-471-08215-5. LC Card No. 81-14739.
Provides a general overview of all the functional areas of management. Features a balanced selection of cases in terms of size, complexity, and types of organizations represented.

545.
Schmitz, Hubert
Manufacturing in the Backyard
Pinter, 1982, 232 pp., $26.50
ISBN 0-86598-076-4. Dewey Decimal No. 338.642. LC Card No. 81-17604.
Case studies on accumulation and employment in small-scale Brazilian industry.

546.
Shook, Robert L.
The Entrepreneurs
Harper & Row, 1980, 181 pp.
ISBN 0-06-014025-9. Dewey Decimal No. 338.040. LC Card No. 79-2735.
Twelve who took risks and succeeded.

547.
Silver, A. David
Entrepreneurial Megabucks: 100 Greatest Entrepreneurs of the Last 25 Years
Ronald Press
ISBN 0-471-82184-5. LC Card No. 85-12089.
Collage of stories about our most successful entrepreneurs—individuals who have made $25 million or more launching new enterprises.

548.
Smith, Irene
Diary of a Small Business
Scribner's, 1982, 178 pp., $14.95
ISBN 0-684-17656-4. Dewey Decimal No.
658.022. LC Card No. 82-10378.

549.
Swann, Leonard Alexander
John Roach, Maritime Entrepreneur
Arno Press, 1980, 301 pp.
ISBN 0-405-13078-3. Dewey Decimal No.
623.809. LC Card No. 79-6124.

550.
Thomas, James, and Loren Schweninger
From Tennessee Slave to St. Louis Entrepreneur
University of Missouri Press, 1984,
225 pp.
ISBN 0-8622-0431-7. Dewey Decimal No.
976.8. LC Card No. 83-16676.
The autobiography of James Thomas
Hope Franklin.

551.
Van Buren, Ernestine Orrick
Clint: The Biography of Clinton Williams Murchison, 1895–1969
Eakin Publishing, 1986
ISBN 0-89015-549-6. Dewey Decimal No.
001.64. LC Card No. 81-21398.

552.
Wagener, Elaine Hoffman
George C. Vaughan: Early Entrepreneur
Watercress Press, 1984, 165 pp.
Dewey Decimal No. 338.767. LC Card No.
84-51740.

553.
Wang, Dr. An, and Eugene Linden
Lessons, An Autobiography
Addison-Wesley, 288 pp.
ISBN 0-201-09400-2.
The biography of a man who, in 1951
with $600 in savings and no business
plan, opened a one-man electronics
consulting firm in Boston, which he
called Wang Laboratories.

554.
Webster, Bryce
Winner Take All
AMACOM, 1987, 224 pp., $10.95
ISBN 0-8144-7689-9.
Shows how successful business owners
identify opportunities, minimize risks,
and then act decisively at the right
moment. Each chapter contains a look at
decisive moments in the life of a top
small-business owner and the "lessons
learned" that readers can apply to their
own business.

FRANCHISING

A recent study commissioned by the International Franchise Association predicts an enormous growth in franchising during the next two decades. It has been, and increasingly is, a popular way of becoming a business owner. Chief among the attractions is the higher success ratios most franchises enjoy in comparison to other types of business ventures. However, some entrepreneurs may find a franchise organization too restrictive. Products, advertising, and management philosophies are all standardized, and royalties must be paid to the parent company. Nevertheless, franchisees who work hard, plan, and give creative direction to their enterprises consistently earn handsome profits.

R. DAVID THOMAS
Founder and Chairman of the Board
Wendy's International, Inc.

Whether you drink a Pepsi Cola, eat a priazzo at Pizza Hut, or lease an automobile at Thrifty Rent-a-Car, you are buying goods and services from one of the fastest-growing distribution systems in the United States—the franchise. Almost nonexistent in the early twentieth century, franchised businesses today have become a significant contributor to the overall American economy, accounting for almost one-third of all retail sales. Projected growth over the next 25 years also appears to be bright, for analysts predict that franchising will produce approximately one-half of total retail sales by the year 2000, and that the aggregate dollar value of franchise sales will reach $1.3 trillion by 2010.

Franchising is a unique concept that, in effect, permits the cloning of a successful enterprise by allowing entrepreneurs, through licensing agreements, to own and operate units of the business similar or identical in format to the one originally established by the founding franchisor. Under the right circumstances, a franchise arrangement can be quite attractive to both franchisor and franchisee. For the franchisor, it provides a means of expanding the business without having to supply the capital to construct branches. For the franchisee, it significantly improves chances of success, since the franchisor already has endured the hassles of starting the business and has developed proven, brand-name products or services that have achieved a degree of customer recognition and predictable profitability.

A typical franchise contract embraces a variety of legal agreements. In exchange for the exclusive right to a specified territory or location, franchisees normally are obliged to pay a fixed assessment, known as a franchise fee, as well as a stipulated percentage of annual sales, commonly referred to as a royalty fee. The franchisor in turn authorizes the use of the company's logo and extends a number of benefits related to the operation of the business, including a number of well-researched and standardized brand-name products, opportunities for centralized procurement of supplies, management training and assistance, advertising expertise, and ongoing, up-to-date marketing advice.

Some parts of a franchise agreement may be considered disadvantageous to franchisees. The required up-front fees and royalties lower the entrepreneur's profits. Additionally, strict controls over products as well as the services to be performed normally are stipulated in any contractual arrangement, and serious or uncorrected deviations from these standards may result in the termination of a franchise agreement and a subsequent buyout by the parent company. Such performance requirements constitute a diminution of an entrepreneur's independence and satisfaction, but most franchisees regard these disadvantages as inconsequential when compared to the broader considerations and rewards they receive.

The world of franchising is evolving rapidly. In a recent study commissioned by the International Franchise Association, John Naisbitt predicted enormous growth for franchised companies during the next quarter century. His analysis of the American economy points clearly to several trends that should spur the growth of franchising opportunities: a rising demand for all types of services; the persistent cry for consumer convenience products of consistent quality; the obvious need for new opportunities for minority groups and women; a growing consumer preference for specialty items; and an emerging foreign market for franchised goods. He also identified five areas with the most promising growth potential: construction and home services, recreation, business services, nonfood retailing, and fast-food restaurants—the most successful of all franchising categories.

Franchising has proved to be a popular and reliable business form whose survival ratios greatly exceed those of independently started enterprises. Name affiliation alone, however, does not assure success. The achievement of desired goals and objectives in any business endeavor, including a franchised enterprise, most often occurs when the owner-manager possesses the talents and instincts of an entrepreneur who understands and appreciates the value of the work ethic.

555.

Church, Nancy Sunway
Future Opportunities in Franchising
Pilot Books, $3.50
Covers trend analysis, opportunities for the prospective franchisee, types of franchising, franchise systems, and current laws that affect franchising.

556.

Finn, Richard P.
Your Fortune in Franchises
Contemporary Books, 1979, 200 pp.,
 $9.95 (cloth), $4.95 (paper)
ISBN 0-8092-7449-3 (cloth), 0-8092-7448-5 (paper).

Covers all the important aspects of the franchising business: choosing a good location, promoting and advertising, insuring your business premises, franchises for women and minority group members. Includes a directory of established franchises.

557.
Gross, Harry
Franchise Investigation and Contract Negotiation
Pilot Books, $3.95
The facts you need, the moneymaking factors to consider, how to read available financial information, how to project sales costs, and what to look for in the franchise contract before making a final decision.

558.
Hammond, Alexander
Franchisee Rights: A Self-Defense Manual
Fairchild Books, 360 pp., $31.45
For dealers, distributors, retailers, wholesalers, and other franchisees. Case histories and detail problems involving coercion, termination, contract rights, litigation, federal antitrust laws, and price-fixing.

559.
Henward, DeBanks M., III, and William Ginalski
The Franchising Option: Expanding Your Business Through Franchising
Franchise Group Publishers, 1979, 186 pp., $34.50
ISBN 0-936898-00-4.
Written for those who are thinking of franchising a business, for those who have started franchising and want to expand their franchise systems, and for those who simply want to know more about franchising. It describes what franchising is, how it works, what it takes to be a successful franchiser, and how to undertake the development of a franchise system.

560.
Hjelmfelt, David C.
Understanding Franchise Contracts
Pilot Books, $3.95
Various aspects of a sample franchise contract are analyzed.

561.
Info Press, Inc.
1986 Franchise Annual
Info Press
ISBN 0-9692267-0-5. LC Card No. 76-17321.
Franchise directory and handbook: 3,006 total listings, 2,102 American, 579 Canadian, and 325 overseas listings. Each includes full description of franchisor's business; number of franchised units, company-owned units; how long established; initial investment required; total investment required; royalty; contact information; financing availability. Sample franchise contract clauses.

562.
Lewis, Mack O.
How to Franchise Your Business
Pilot Books, 1981, $3.50
ISBN 0-87576-007-4.
Successful franchising techniques are offered to prevent sacrificing ownership or control. Shows the procedures to follow to franchise a business.

563.
Mendelson, Martin
The Guide to Franchising, 2nd edition
Pergamon Press, 1979, 177 pp., $27.50
Reference guide to the basic principles of franchising.

564.
Norback, Peter G., and Craig T. Norback
The Dow Jones–Irwin Guide to Franchises
Dow Jones–Irwin, 1978, 271 pp.

Lists almost 500 franchises with detailed explanations on what the franchise is, how much capital is required, the type of financing available, if any, what training is provided, and what managerial assistance is offered during the life of the franchise contract.

565.

Pilot Books
Directory of Franchising Organizations
Pilot Books, 1986, $5
The nation's top moneymaking franchises, with facts, evaluation checklist, concise description, and approximate investment.

566.

Pilot Books
Pilot's Question and Answer Guide to Successful Franchising
Pilot Books, $2
Stresses proper investigation before money is expended or a decision is made to buy a franchise. Contains helpful hints to avert failure.

567.

Scherer, Daniel J.
Financial Security and Independence Through a Small Business Franchise
Pilot Books, 1977, 47 pp.
ISBN 0-87576-002-3.
Establishing and operating a profitable franchised business, with limited investment and minimum risk. Includes where to find opportunities, how to raise capital, investment protection, and pitfalls to avoid.

568.

Seltz, David D.
Complete Handbook of Franchising
Addison-Wesley, 1982, 254 pp., $49.95
Examines franchisor-franchisee relationship, how to determine franchise feasibility, blueprinting and packaging the program, capital requirements, contract preparations, and state regulations.

569.

Seltz, David
How to Get Started in Your Own Franchise Business
Farnsworth Publishing Co., 1979, $9.95
ISBN 0-87863-172-0.
Provides the information needed to help franchisees to select the franchise most compatible with their qualifications, with excellent potential for success and within their financial capacities.

570.

Sterling Publishing Co., Inc.
Franchise Opportunities: A Business of Your Own, 16th edition
Sterling Publishing, 416 pp., $9.95
ISBN 0-8069-6232-1.
Over 900 franchises are described in great detail.

571.

Vaughn, Charles L.
Franchising
Lexington Books, 1979, 304 pp., $21.95
ISBN 0-669-02852-5.
A how-to approach to franchising; details financial arrangements, the recruitment and training of franchises, the selection and acquisition of franchise sites, international franchises, and the importance of franchisee-franchisor relations.

INNOVATION AND NEW-PRODUCT DEVELOPMENT

With the steel industry unable to compete with foreign producers, 200,000 of its former employees will never get those jobs back. The textile and garment industries in this country have laid off over 350,000 workers. It is therefore most important for our future entrepreneurs to start new businesses, particularly in high technology. Never has there been so much venture capital available in the United States to finance startups and to provide investment funds for the expansion of new growth industries.

It is the future entrepreneurs of America whose courage to risk, whose ability to create, and whose determination to achieve will ensure the survival of the free enterprise system in this country.

ROYAL LITTLE
Founder
Textron, Inc.

By virtue of size and scale, small businesses are natural research and development entities. Indeed, from the moment an entrepreneur conceptualizes an enterprise, it becomes, from idea to implementation and beyond, an experiment in "how to make it work." Unlike large corporations, smaller firms have neither the time nor finances to introduce a product in selected test markets, but they do enjoy the advantage of being able to commercialize a product more rapidly with minimal development costs and usually at a lower selling price.

Inventions are not the domain of any group of people, but they most often occur in an environment where creative individuals can function with great flexibility. This may be in a tinkerer's shop, an entrepreneur's home, or a corporate laboratory where intrapreneurs are encouraged to "do their thing." Yet, as important as the creation of new products is to the business world, they often are developed by people who know little about how to commercialize them. Inventors generally concede that "inventing does not pay." Most new products, especially those devised by unaffiliated individuals, end up being purchased by other companies that have the expertise to bring them into the marketplace in an effective, competitive manner. Thus, inventors would be well advised to broaden their business skills if they desire to profit more equitably from their creations.

There is an equally important aspect of new-product development—innovation. Perhaps America's greatest innovator was Thomas Alva Edison, to whom an incredible 1,000-plus patents were issued. He understood in 1882, as do the Japanese today, that innovation is the handmaiden of the inventive process, the marriage of a new idea and its technology to market insight. In his judgment, the best way to determine whether an invention would sell was to allow the marketplace to function. Consumer acceptance represented the cardinal test for all of his new products, many of which often had to be adapted or redesigned innovatively in order to meet customer expectations or gain survival market share.

So it is with all new products, then and now. Edison's "incubator" approach to invention/innovation may have fostered many new products in his Menlo Park laboratories, but recent experiences by large companies using his "hyperorganized" research-and-development approach to new-product creation have not always resulted in an outpouring of new products or patents. Thomas J. Peters in his *In Search of Excellence* cautions that highly detailed strategic and technological planning greatly increases the odds of "no-surprise" outcomes and suggests that the "sloppy side" of innovation (the unstructured, contemplative, trial-and-error approach) still holds great promise both in terms of the number of new products developed and in the cost-effectiveness of their creation.

Indeed, statistics generated by the National Science Foundation show that small enterprises produce 24 times more new products per dollar expended than larger, more mature companies. This is attributed to the greater flexibility of action enjoyed by small firms, which affords them the freedom to conceive, develop, innovate, and move a product to market more quickly because they are not encumbered by structured processes of administrative approval. Little wonder that large organizations have sought to replicate the entrepreneurial environment within (but independent of) the corporate structure by allowing creative individuals to function as intrapreneurs in a setting funded separately from other corporate activities and only loosely connected to the formal organizational chart; see Intrapreneurship listings at the end of Section 2.

Companies such as 3M, General Electric, and Westinghouse have enjoyed significant gains from encouraging internal creativity. Art Fry's Post-It note, developed for 3M, is an excellent example of intrapreneurship at work. The prototype was developed in his home shop in a single night—a sharp contrast to the six months 3M officials estimated it most likely would have taken under corporate direction.

Newly developing technologies such as robotics, computerization, biogenetic engineering, lasers, and space exploration offer tremendous opportunities for the truly creative mind, and encouragement to those entrepreneurs/intrapreneurs who dare to venture on the frontiers of scientific and technological research. Growth in these areas is inevitable, and each new breakthrough fosters fresh opportunities for an expanded base of additional technologies and profitable innovations for the perceptive small-business person.

572.
Boston Public Library
Lectures for Inventors
Boston Public Library, 1983, 172 pp.
LC Card No. 83-467.
Lectures delivered at the Boston Public
Library, December 1981–June 1982.
Contents include: developments and
plans at the patent and trademark office;
starting your own business; experiences
with inventions; protecting your ideas;
bringing inventions to the marketplace;
invention evaluation; and the role of the
entrepreneur.

573.
Botkin, James, Dan Dimancescu, and Ray
Stata
The Innovators: Rediscovering America's
Creative Energy
University of Pennsylvania Press, 1986,
   319 pp., $11.95
ISBN 0-8122-1224-X.
Case studies illustrate the rapid changes
taking place in the economy. Offers the
premise that high tech is the new tool
maker, not the cause of a general "de-
skilling" of the U.S. work force.

574.
Braden, Patricia L.
Technological Entrepreneurship
University of Michigan, 1977, 86 pp., $5
ISBN 0-87712-187-7. Dewey Decimal No.
   658.4. LC Card No. 78-623036.
Part of an ongoing program of research on
technological entrepreneurship designed
to improve the contribution of small
business to the economic development of
Michigan.

575.
Drucker, Peter Ferdinand
Innovation and Entrepreneurship: Practice
and Principles
Harper & Row, 1985, 277 pp., $19.95
ISBN 0-06-015428-4. Dewey Decimal No.
   658.4. LC Card No. 84-48593.

Contends that the spirit of entrepreneurship is not only for business creators
but for corporate managers, institutional
administrators, and others.

576.
Gevirtz, Don
The New Entrepreneurs: Innovation in Ameri-
can Business
Penguin, 1985, 223 pp., $6.95
ISBN 0-14-007973-4. Dewey Decimal No.
   658.4. LC Card No. 84-26581.

577.
Gould Staff Editors
Patents
Gould Publications, 1979, 175 pp.,
   $77.50
This book is a practical guide to the laws
and procedures involved in understand-
ing and obtaining patents.

578.
Green, Orville M., and Frank L. Durr
The Practical Inventor's Handbook
McGraw-Hill, 1979, $19.95
ISBN 0-07-024320-4.
Discusses the opportunities and pitfalls
in developing your own invention. Gives
amateur inventors the practical how-to
guidance they need to develop, protect,
and profit from their ideas and creations.

579.
Gruenwald, George
New Product Development: What Really
Works
NTC Business Books, 432 pp.
ISBN 0-8442-3085-5.
An invaluable volume with all details
relating to the conception of new prod-
ucts and how they are introduced into
the marketplace. Discover how to boost
your own business while reading case
histories of Land O' Lakes Margarine,
Fisher-Price, etc.

580.

Holt, K., H. Geschka, and G. Peterlongo

Need Assessment: A Key to User-Oriented Product Innovation

Wiley, 1984, 187 pp., $31.95

Provides systematic methods for assessing user needs. Demonstrates the importance of user-need assessment in product development, and tells you how to select and apply the proper methods.

581.

Krauser, Peter M.

New Products and Diversification

Business Books, 1977, 212 pp., $19.75

ISBN 0-330-66308-4.

Explains the need for new products or for diversification, new-product failure and success, planning and promotion of your new products.

582.

Lowe, Julian, and Nick Crawford, eds.

Technology Licensing and the Small Firm

Gower, 1984, 115 pp., $32.50

ISBN 0-566-00665-0. Dewey Decimal No. 346.410. LC Card No. 84-5955.

583.

Mancuso, Joseph

Managing Technology Products and Marketing Technology Products

Artech House, 1975

A compilation of 50 significant readings for entrepreneurs launching new products. This set of books applies to independent entrepreneurs and the "international entrepreneur," usually a product manager charged with planning, developing, and introducing a new product.

584.

Martin, Michael J. C.

Managing Technological Innovation and Entrepreneurship

Reston, 1984, 340 pp., $22.95

ISBN 0-8359-4201-5. Dewey Decimal No. 658.406. LC Card No. 83-21220.

585.

Piage, Richard E.

Complete Guide to Making Money with Your Ideas and Inventions

Barnes & Noble, 215 pp., $2.95

ISBN 0-06-463446-9.

Step-by-step guide shows you how to develop your idea, protect it, finance it, and get it on the market.

586.

Pilot Books

Protecting and Profiting from Your Business Ideas

Pilot Books, $2.95

ISBN 87576-021-X.

This book shows the individual or company with a worthwhile idea how to protect, develop, and profit from that idea. Written by a prominent attorney, the book explains the traditional methods of protection plus additional methods made available through recent statutes and technology.

587.

Rivkin, Bernard

Patenting and Marketing Your Invention

Van Nostrand Reinhold, 1985, 264 pp., $34.95

ISBN 0-442-27824-1.

Information on how to protect, develop, finance, and market new inventions. An all-purpose inventor's manual that includes addresses and telephone numbers of useful sources and services as well as a glossary of patents and trademarks.

588.

Rosenau, Milton D., Jr.

Innovation: Managing the Developments of Profitable New Products

Van Nostrand Reinhold, 1982, 220 pp.,
    $27.95
ISBN 0-534-97934-3.
Information on how to develop innovative new products for a profit. With
illustrations, case studies, and checklists.

589.
Smilor, Raymond W., and Michael A.
Gill, Jr.
The New Business Incubator: Linking Talent,
Technology, Capital, and Know-How
Lexington Books, 1986, 192 pp., $19.95
ISBN 0-669-11096-5. LC Card No. 85-
    45009.
A new approach to economic develop-
ment, the new-business incubator, links
technological innovation and entrepre-
neurship. Describes in detail how new-
business incubators serve and support
new businesses in many ways.

590.
Smilor, Raymond W., and Robert Lawrence
Kuhn
Managing Take-Off in Fast Growth Compa-
nies

Praeger, 1985
ISBN 0-03-005709-4. Dewey Decimal No.
    658.4. LC Card No. 85-16745.
Innovation in entrepreneurial firms.

591.
Stanworth, John
Perspectives on a Decade of Small Business
Research
Gower, 1982, 199 pp.
ISBN 0-566-000587-5.

592.
Taylor, Clarence R.
How to Be a Successful Inventor: Patenting,
Protecting, Marketing, and Selling Your
Invention
Exposition Press, 1972, $6.50
ISBN 0-682-47473-8.
Explains how to take your invention from
the drawing board to market, how to
choose a patent lawyer and evaluate your
market, and information on the new
transfer industry.

LEGAL

All businesses have rights and responsibilities, some of which are inherent in the unstated ethical standards of the owners. Others are codified in local, state, and national enactments that seek to preserve a basic fairness within the marketplace and to spread the costs of maintaining our free-enterprise–democratic process as equitably as possible among all participants. To be successful, entrepreneurs must respect and observe all existing laws regulating business activities and must use intelligent judgment in matters relating to tax determination. To avoid unnecessary problems, the use of consultants is highly recommended.

DONALD NICKELSON
President and CEO
Paine, Webber, Jackson and Curtis, Inc.

There is an old saying: "Any man who attempts to be his own lawyer has a fool for a client." Experienced small-business owners know the wisdom inherent in this statement, for they discovered very early in the startup phase of their enterprises that there are countless laws and regulations—federal, state, county, and municipal—with which to comply and whose interpretations frequently require professional expertise. Indeed, it is rare when any business decision escapes legal implication, and this is especially true for two-party agreements such as leases, mortgages, licenses, contracts, bills of sale, and stock issuances.

For example, one of the earliest decisions for entrepreneurs is the legal form of ownership most appropriate for the type of business they are forming. The choices initially appear uncomplicated. They may choose a proprietorship because it is the simplest to form and permits total independence of operation; or a partnership because two or more individuals suggest broader business and management skills as well as an expanded base of capital; or perhaps even a corporate structure because of a variety of important considerations, including an even greater potential for capital formation through stock sales, the possibility of increased flexibility of operations, and the financial strength to attract and retain high-quality management personnel.

The fact that almost 80 percent of all business enterprises are sole proprietorships supports the thesis that entrepreneurs opt for ease of formation because they wish to direct their own fortunes with a minimum of external interference. There unquestionably are fewer regulations with which they must contend, but all businesses, regardless of legal form, must comply with a surprising range of laws and ordinances. Proprietorships certainly are not exempted from them, and the complexity of compliance greatly increases with partnerships and corporations. Yet the advantages gained from selecting either of these two forms may far outweigh the hassle of having to observe stricter regulations. This decision, like all others involving legal implications, becomes more comprehensible when the advantages and disadvantages are explained in detail by professionals who understand them.

Books in this section discuss—either in broad-stroke format or in specific detail—many of the legal considerations small businesses will face. They are excellent sources for enabling business owners or managers to get a general understanding of these legal issues. However, owners of business enterprises never escape the need for legal counseling. Managers of stable companies usually learn by experience that applicable laws remain fairly constant and that their observance borders on routine—until a legislative body makes one of its inevitable and periodic revisions. Those who manage small companies, especially during periods of growth, experience an expanding need for professional advice about conditions that result from the dynamics of growth, such as employee insurance and retirement programs, equal opportunity recruiting policies, and employee participation in stock ownership. Certain types of business opportunities for small firms are set forth in federal and state laws that regulate government procurement programs, many of which require legal interpretation in order to sift through the numerous definitions and exemptions that control participation.

In summary, attorneys can offer invaluable service to small-business owners. The wisdom of maintaining legal propriety in all phases of business decision making more than offsets the expenses incurred in doing so, and can lead to a peace of mind that makes operational responsibilities a pleasure.

593.

Adama, Paul

The Complete Legal Guide for Small Business
Wiley, 1982, 218 pp.
ISBN 0-471-09436-6. LC Card No. 81-11445.
Presents contract law in a pragmatic context for small businesses. Supplies all relevant forms and explains what each paragraph means. Designed as a reference work for drafting purchase orders, sales orders, employment contracts, marketing agreements, etc. Can be used to critically examine a contract that is presented by a third party.

594.

Allen, Paul A., ed.

How to Keep Your Company Out of Court
Prentice-Hall, 1984, 282 pp., $22.50 (cloth)
ISBN 0-13-411132-X (cloth), 0-13-411140-0 (paper). Dewey Decimal No. 346.730. LC Card No. 83-11176.
The practical legal guide for growing businesses.

595.

Davidson, Marion, and Martha Blue

Making It Legal: A Law Primer for the Craftmaker

McGraw-Hill, 1979, 320 pp., $8.95
ISBN 0-07-015431-7.
Written by two lawyers, this book covers a variety of topics including: the legal steps in surfacing a business, legal restrictions on content and materials, making contracts, copyright laws, and others.

596.
Diamond, Sidney A.
Trademark Problems and How to Avoid Them
NTC Business Books, 285 pp., $22.95
ISBN 0-8442-3059-6.
Register a trademark, but avoid the pitfalls in the process. This book offers certain techniques to anticipate and solve potential snags. New material is available on nicknames, package and design, comparative advertising.

597.
Faber, Peter L., and Martin E. Holbrook
Subchapter S Manual
Prentice-Hall, 1983, 221 pp., $24.95
ISBN 0-13-859124-5. Dewey Decimal No. 343.730. LC Card No. 83-128142.
A manual on special tax breaks for small-business corporations.

598.
Goldstein, Arnold S.
The Small Business Legal Problem Solver
Van Nostrand Reinhold, 1984, 270 pp.
ISBN 0-442-22808-2. Dewey Decimal No. 346.73. LC Card No. 83-27374.

599.
Hancock, William A.
The Small Business Legal Advisor
McGraw-Hill, 1986, 258 pp., $9.95
ISBN 0-07-025999-2. Dewey Decimal No. 346.73. LC Card No. 81-12400.

600.
Hess, Robert P.
Desk Book for Setting Up a Closely-Held Corporation

Institute for Business Planning, 1979, 451 pp.
ISBN 0-87624-113-5.
Analyzes the tax aspects of operating a business in the form of a closely held corporation, shows how to determine the proper capital structure for a corporation, provides a discussion of the advantages of various employee benefits, and contains step-by-step procedures for preparing corporate documentation, including sample forms.

601.
Hicks, J. William
1983 Limited Offering Exemptions:
Regulation D
Boardman, 1983, 347 pp.
ISBN 0-87632-345-X. Dewey Decimal No. 346.73. LC Card No. 83-187848.

602.
Jackson, Stanley G.
How to Proceed in Business—Legally: The Entrepreneur's Preventive Law Guide
Prentice-Hall, 1984, 232 pp.
ISBN 0-13-429332-0 (cloth), 0-13-429324-X (paper). Dewey Decimal No. 346.73. LC Card No. 83-21163.

603.
Kirk, John
Incorporating Your Business: The Complete Guide to Establishing and Operating a Small Corporation
Contemporary Books, 192 pp., $9.95
ISBN 0-8092-5902-8.
Every step of incorporation is covered. Costs, state regulations, number of officers required, sample proxy forms, tax benefits, and various types of organizations that can be constructed to bypass tax regulations.

604.
Lane, Marc J.
Legal Handbook for Small Business

AMACOM, 1978, $14.95
ISBN 0-8144-5452-6.
Traces the legal decision making through all the operational challenges a business is likely to meet; concludes with the yes-and-no factors that lead the small enterprise to go public or not.

605.
Lane, Marc J.
Purchase and Sale of Small Businesses: Tax and Legal Aspects
Wiley, 1985, 737 pp.
ISBN 0-471-89070-7. Dewey Decimal No. 346.73. LC Card No. 84-19693.

606.
Neely, Richard
Judicial Jeopardy: When Business Collides with the Courts
Addison-Wesley, 288 pp., $19.95
ISBN 0-201-05736-0.
An analysis of how business can improve its performance in court. Includes cases from author's experience as a judge, illustrating ways for business to reduce its legal liabilities.

607.
Nicholas, Ted
How to Form Your Own Corporation Without a Lawyer for Under $50
Enterprise Publishing, 1979, $14.95 (cloth), $2.95 (paper)
ISBN 0-913864-31-5 (cloth), 0-913864-3 (paper).
Discusses Subchapter S corporations, what they are and how to set one up. Includes tear-out forms for minutes, bylaws, and the certificate of incorporation.

608.
Prentice-Hall, Inc.
S Corporations
Prentice-Hall, 1983
Dewey Decimal No. 343.73. LC Card No. 83-216121.
Tax choices for business planning: explanation, laws and regulations, legislative history, cases and rulings, indexes.

609.
Rohrlich, Chester
Organizing Corporate and Other Business Enterprises
Bender, 1975, $50
ISBN 0-685-02524-1.
A guide, from a lawyer's point of view, to dealing with problems such as how initial assets should be acquired; how to capitalize venture; and a discussion of the various tax and other consequences. Yearly cumulative supplements.

610.
Steingold, Fred
Legal Master Guide for Small Business
Prentice-Hall, 1983, 242 pp.
ISBN 0-13-528422-8 (cloth), 0-13-528414-7 (paper). Dewey Decimal No. 346.73. LC Card No. 82-13185.

611.
Vella, Carolyn M., and John J. McGonagle, Jr.
Incorporating: A Guide for Small-Business Owners
AMACOM, 1984, 185 pp.
ISBN 0-8144-7608-2. Dewey Decimal No. 346.73. LC Card No. 83-45206.

MARKETING, ADVERTISING, AND SALES

The marketplace is like an altar around which many participants gather—some to present their wares, others their private resources—in a ritual that features a free-will exchange of property rights. Developing a sales advantage in such an environment requires a marketing strategy that tends to focus greater attention on your product than on those of your competitors, but determining the right mix of promotional techniques is a wrenching, sometimes costly, but absolutely essential process in creating a competitive edge. Marketing strategies are the cornerstone of prudent sales management.

DONALD M. KOLL
President
The Koll Company

It has been said that "a business doesn't exist until the first sale has been made." The importance of sales cannot be overstated, for sales and marketing are the lifeblood of any business. Indeed, most small-business owners spend the largest share of their time trying to discover ways to increase total market share by developing strategies or revising sales objectives that focus on targeted customers. This entails a constant study of product variations, pricing structures, promotional efforts, and channels of distribution as they relate to shifting consumer behavior and demand.

Because purchasers' interests often change quickly and sometimes dramatically, one analyst has remarked that entrepreneurs should "not set out to grab just a share of the market but rather to capture all of it before any part of it gets away." This is a recognition of the fact that consumer sophistication has risen so sharply in recent years that things once regarded as intangible are now paramount in determining customer behavior—manufacturer's reputation, seller's image, attention before and during sales transactions, and post-purchase service, to mention only a few.

In today's consumer-conscious environment, competitive selling has been further complicated by a raft of new media options that make it possible to fine-tune an advertising campaign and aim it like a rifle at the narrowest of target audiences. This poses a significant problem for small businesses that may be forced, because of limited advertising budgets, to rely heavily on word of mouth in promoting their products. Research indicates that supporting testimonials from ten satisfied customers are required to offset the negative impact of one that has expressed dissatisfaction.

Thus, marketing strategies provide an important link between internal operations and external markets, and all firms, large and small, should give careful attention to their development. Such strategies essentially are a function of what must be accomplished in order to survive competitively and of what resources can be committed to various promotional alternatives at different intervals in the life of an enterprise. Strategizing involves the development of plans that intelligently integrate the four classical marketing components: product or service, price, promotion, and distribution. The result is what is termed a marketing mix that provides comprehensible plans and alternatives for an overall company marketing model.

Decisions on the proper mix of product or service in the marketing model include product development, merchandise-service mix, warranties and guarantees, branding, and packaging. Pricing decisions include pricing strategies, price adjustments, credit availability and cost, and costs for such services as delivery, handling, or storage. Decisions on promotional efforts entail advertising, special sales, training and staffing for direct sales presentations, and various public relations activities that bring special attention to both company and product. Finally, decisions on matters relating to distribution involve developing market channels (methods of delivering products to customers), inventory controls, selecting efficient and cost-effective methods of receiving and delivering products, and choosing appropriate storage facilities for warehousing products.

Businesses fail in many cases because management either incorrectly measures market demand or inappropriately directs advertising and sales management efforts—or both. Market strategies begin with market assessments and focus all promotional efforts on the best methods of gaining market acceptance of certain products or services among customers in targeted segments. To make such strategies consistently successful requires a sound understanding of customer behavior, and a reflective knowledge about both present and potential markets so that a periodic freshness can be injected into yesterday's marketing model.

612.

Ballas, George C., and David Hollas

The Making of an Entrepreneur: Keys to Your Success

Prentice-Hall, 1980, 244 pp., $6.95
ISBN 0-13-546670-5.

Generating an idea and then getting the idea into the marketplace as a successful product. Emphasizes the marketing of a new product idea, but many strategies apply to marketing a new service idea.

613.

Berman, Steve

How to Create Your Own Publicity and Get It Free

Fredrick Fell, 1977, $7.95

A comprehensive guide for those who want to create their own publicity, whether in a letter to the editor of the local newspaper or as a guest on a radio or TV show.

614.
Blake, Gary, and Robert W. Bly
How to Promote Your Own Business
New American Library, 1983, 241 pp.,
$10.95
ISBN 0-452-25456-6. Dewey Decimal No.
659.2. LC Card No. 83-12093.

615.
Bradway, Bruce M., Robert E. Pritchard,
and Mary Anne Frenzel
Strategic Marketing
Addison-Wesley, 1982, 272 pp., $27.95
ISBN 0-201-00079-2. Dewey Decimal No.
658.8. LC Card No. 81-3638.
Practical and proven planning strategies
are presented, along with all the necessary elements to ensure a successful
business.

616.
Brannen, William H.
Advertising and Sales Promotion
Prentice-Hall, 1983, 247 pp., $9.95
ISBN 0-13-015016-9. Dewey Decimal No.
659.1. LC Card No. 83-4415.
Cost-effective techniques for small
business.

617.
Brannen, William H.
*Practical Marketing for Your Small Retail
Business*
Prentice-Hall, 1981, 232 pp.
ISBN 0-13-69276. 0-13-692756. Dewey
Decimal No. 658.8. LC Card No. 81-92.

618.
Brannen, William H.
*Small Business Marketing: A Selected and
Annotated Bibliography*
American Marketing Association, 1978,
79 pp., $8
ISBN 0-87757-112-0.
Sourcebook for the small businessperson.
Lists and annotates over 200 references
on the subject of small-business market-
ing. Broken down into ten subject area
categories.

619.
Breen, George Edward
Do-It-Yourself Marketing Research
McGraw-Hill, 1977, 258 pp., $22.50
ISBN 0-07-007445-3.
How to develop effective market research
techniques without the mystique, mathe-
matics, and complex "intelligence-
gathering" that have made a mystery out
of a basic business tool.

620.
Brownstone, David M.
Successful Selling Skills for Small Business
Wiley, 1978, 112 pp.
ISBN 0-471-04029-0.
Presents, in case history format, the
essential combination of high motivation
and basic skills for consistently successful selling. Guides the reader through the
steps of the sales process, from selling
benefits to product knowledge, appear-
ance, communication, and listening.
Covers aspects of the first sales contact,
including presentation, techniques,
strategies for overcoming hurdles that
might arise, and after-sale considerations.

621.
Calvin, Robert J.
*Profitable Sales Management and Marketing
for Growing Businesses*
Van Nostrand Reinhold, 1984, 326 pp.
ISBN 0-442-21502-9. Dewey Decimal No.
658.8. LC Card No. 83-25888.

622.
Carlson, Linda C.
The Publicity and Promotion Handbook
CBI Publishing, 1982, 261 pp., $19.95
ISBN 0-8436-0865-X. Dewey Decimal No.
659.2. LC Card No. 81-10060.
A complete guide for small business.

623.
Cassell, Dana K.
*How to Advertise and Promote Your Retail
Store*

AMACOM, 1985, 202 pp., $14.95 (paper)
ISBN 0-8144-7637-6.
Shows store owners and managers how to keep their store in the public eye, build traffic, and boost sales. Describes how and when to use local newspapers, radio, TV, and direct mail—and how to double ad space without paying a penny extra.

624.

Chappe, Eli
Winning Government Contracts
Prentice-Hall, 1984, 274 pp., $69.95
ISBN 0-13-960998-9. Dewey Decimal No.
   353.007. LC Card No. 83-22954.
A complete 27-step guide for small businesses.

625.

Cohen, William A.
Direct Response Marketing: An Entrepreneurial Approach
Wiley, 1984, 496 pp., $36.45
ISBN 0-471-88684-X. Dewey Decimal No.
   658.8. LC Card No. 83-19825.
Textbook on direct response/direct mail marketing written from the entrepreneur's viewpoint. Instructs the student in techniques and concepts needed for a successful mail-order business.

626.

Cohen, William A.
How to Sell to the Government: A Step-by-Step Guide to Success
Wiley, 1981, 434 pp.
ISBN 0-471-08103-5. LC Card No. 80-
   22997.
Provides step-by-step guidance through the process of locating business opportunities, marketing, organizing for the proposal effort, writing the proposal, and negotiating the government contract. Describes specific techniques and gives leads for thousands of potential government contracts, as well as necessary bidding forms, names, addresses, and phone numbers of potential government customers.

627.

Connor, Richard A., Jr., and Jeffrey P. Davidson
Marketing Your Consulting and Professional Services
Wiley, 220 pp., $20
Meant for the professional business-person or technical specialist who wants to enter the consulting field. Shows how to generate more profits.

628.

Coxe, Weld
Marketing Architectural and Engineering Services, 2nd edition
Van Nostrand Reinhold, 1982, 272 pp.,
   $27.95
ISBN 0-442-22011-1.
A thorough discussion of the elements required to make a business succeed: comprehensive marketing plan, organization strategies, management roles, research of new business markets, identification of prospective clients, oral presentations, as well as negotiating and closing commissions.

629.

Dickinson, John R.
The Bibliography of Marketing Research Methods, 2nd edition
Lexington Books, 1986, 832 pp., $49.95
ISBN 0-669-12373-0. LC Card No. 85-
   45895.
A compilation of material from popular marketing and marketing research periodicals; more than 9,000 entries.

630.

Dorff, Ralph L.
Marketing for the Small Manufacturer
Prentice-Hall, 1983, 193 pp.
ISBN 0-13-557298-3 (cloth), 0-13-557280-
   0 (paper). Dewey Decimal No. 658.8. LC
   Card No. 82-24046.

How to turn the disadvantages of being small into big business advantage.

631.
Fisk, Raymond P., and Patriya S. Tansuhaj, eds.
Services Marketing: An Annotated Bibliography
American Marketing Association, 1985, 256 pp., $10 member, $14 nonmember
A bibliography with over 1,900 references in two major categories: conceptual insights and services fields.

632.
Fenno, Brooks
Helping Your Business Grow
AMACOM, 1984
ISBN 0-8144-7622-8.
Explains how to outmaneuver competition in the business world. Covers all aspects of small-business marketing. Includes sample forms, letters, and illustrations.

633.
Fuld, Leonard M.
Competitor Intelligence: How to Get It, How to Use It
Wiley, 1985, 496 pp., $24.95
ISBN 0-471-80967-5. LC Card No. 84-19539.
Brings together intelligence-gathering techniques and sources for keeping informed on the marketing activities and products of business competition. Reveals both traditional and creative methods for obtaining detailed insider information, such as marketing plans, plant capacity, and distribution networks, in an honest, ethical way.

634.
Graham, John W., and Susan K. Jones
Selling by Mail
Scribner's, 1985, 309 pp., $24.95

ISBN 0-684-18215-7. Dewey Decimal No. 658.8. LC Card No. 85-14267.
An entrepreneurial guide to direct marketing.

635.
Gray, Ernest A.
Profitable Methods for Small Business Advertising
Wiley, 1984, 285 pp.
ISBN 0-471-86962-7. LC Card No. 83-19884.
Advertising for the small-business owner-operator, with techniques for getting maximum returns at minimum cost. Step-by-step approach through market planning, sales strategy, creative ad-making, tactical media scheduling, goal-based budgeting, and performance proof. Shows how to cut costs while increasing exposure, and shows how to pre-test and post-test advertising. Contains flow-charts, illustrations, and "success stories." Uses case histories to show how advertisers achieve optimum returns.

636.
Hayes, Rick Stephen, and Gregory Brooks Elmore
Marketing for Your Growing Business
Ronald Press, 1985, 283 pp.
ISBN 0-471-09199-5. LC Card No. 84-25645.
A hands-on guide to developing a marketing plan, geared to small-business owners and managers. Step-by-step workbook approach, with fill-in blanks, checklists, and questions that lead readers through all the stages involved in developing and implementing the marketing plan, including market research, strategic planning, advertising, sales, pricing, and budgeting. Includes illustrations, glossary, directory of resources, and full-length examples.

637.
Haynes, W. Warren
Pricing Decisions in Small Business

Greenwood Publishing, 1973, $8.95
ISBN 0-8371-7089-3.
The problems of pricing in small business demand a variety of practices seldom used in larger operations. The book reports the results of intensive interviews with the managers of 88 small businesses.

638.
Hisrich, R. D., and M. P. Peters
Marketing a New Product: Its Planning, Development and Control
Addison-Wesley, 1978, 358 pp.
ISBN 0-8053-4102-1.
Fundamentals of new-product marketing; focuses on the management of all the activities involved in this process.

639.
Hodgson, Richard S.
Direct Mail and Mail Order Handbook
American Marketing Association, 1,555
    pp., $45.35 member, $63.50 nonmember
Shows how to create, plan, and produce a results-getting direct mail/mail order program. Useful tips on how to use the computer to save time and money, make reliable market projections.

640.
Holtz, Herman
Consultant's Edge: Using the Computer as a Marketing Tool
Wiley, 1985, 364 pp.
ISBN 0-471-81190-4. LC Card No. 85-5117.
A guide for consultants who want to use computers to boost the efficiency, productivity, and profitability of their consulting practice, with emphasis on the computer's power as a marketing tool. Shows how to use integrated word processing, data base, graphics, and spreadsheet software to write proposals, launch direct mail campaigns, develop new profit centers, and make everyday paperwork a nonactivity. Provides a comprehensive worksheet to help consultants select the personal computer best suited to their special needs, and features dozens of examples to illustrate each application.

641.
Holtz, Herman
The Secrets of Practical Marketing for Small Business
Prentice-Hall, 1982, 192 pp., $15.95
    (cloth), $7.95 (paper)
ISBN 0-13-798223-2 (cloth), 0-13-798215-1 (paper). Dewey Decimal No. 658.8. LC Card No. 82-9016.

642.
Imhoff, Eugene A., Jr.
Sales Forecasting Systems
National Association of Accountants,
    104 pp.
ISBN 0-86641-127-5.

643.
Kelleher, Robert F.
Industrial Marketing and Sales Management in the Computer Age
Van Nostrand Reinhold, 1983, 180 pp.,
    $23.95
ISBN 0-843-6087-6.
Developing a marketing information system that increases efficiency and total sales.

644.
Konikow, Robert B.
How to Participate Profitably in Trade Shows
American Marketing Association, 254
    pp., $57.95 member, $78.50 nonmember
Shows how to design, build, and staff business-producing exhibits at low cost with the use of a 16-point planning guide. Lists 4,500 trade shows.

645.
Kuswa, Webster
Big Paybacks from Small Budget Advertising

American Marketing Association, 350
   pp., $64 member, $91.50 nonmember
Tips for creating an advertising budget
that eliminates costly mistakes. How
much market research should be done?
What makes good advertising copy?
Trade or consumer publications: what to
look for and look out for when considering ad space.

646.
Lee, Donald D.
*Industrial Marketing Research: Techniques and
Practices,* 2nd edition
Van Nostrand Reinhold, 1984, 208 pp.,
   $32.95
ISBN 0-442-25922-0.
Marketing research specifically for
industrial goods and services.

647.
Levine, Mindy N., and Susan Frank
In Print
Prentice-Hall, 1984, 145 pp.
ISBN 0-13-453960-5 (cloth), 0-13-453952-
   4 (paper). Dewey Decimal No. 686.2. LC
   Card No. 84-7231.
Guide to graphic arts and printing for
small businesses and nonprofit organiza-
tions.

648.
Levinson, Jay Conrad
Guerrilla Marketing
Houghton Mifflin, 1985, 226 pp., $7.95
ISBN 0-395-38314-5. Dewey Decimal No.
   658.8. LC Card No. 83-18507.
Secrets for making big profits from small
business.

649.
Lewis, H. Gordon
How to Handle Your Own Public Relations
Nelson Hall, 1976, $12.95 (cloth), $8.95
   (paper)
ISBN 0-88229-319-2 (cloth), 0-88229-408-
   3 (paper).

Describes specific public relations
campaigns tailored to suit the needs of
over 70 different business, professional,
and institutional outlets. Shows how to
capitalize on promotional opportunities
using the tools of the trade—news releases and photos, awards, celebrities,
speaking engagements, news conferences.
Samples of news releases, press kit,
model release form.

650.
Lewis, H. G.
*How to Make Your Advertising Twice as
Effective at Half the Cost*
Nelson Hall, 1979, $16.95 (cloth), $8.95
   (paper)
ISBN 0-88229-536-5 (cloth), 0-88229-694-
   9 (paper).
Guidebook and how-to manual on
creating an ad for the Yellow Pages,
producing a television commercial, or
developing an attention-getting campaign
for a product. Presents a framework that
can be used successfully by anyone to
write competitively acceptable copy,
place an ad in the right medium, and buy
space for the right price.

651.
Lindberg, Roy A., and Theodore Cohn
*The Marketing Book for Growing Companies
That Want to Excel*
Van Nostrand Reinhold, 232 pp., $32.50
ISBN 0-442-21838-9.

652.
Lumley, James E.
*Sell It by Mail: Making Your Product the One
They Buy*
Ronald Press, 1986, 382 pp.
ISBN 0-471-87908-8. LC Card No. 85-
   16362.
A blueprint that shows businesses selling
a product or service by mail how to
multiply their earnings.

653.
Luther, William M.
How to Write a Marketing Plan
AMACOM, $110 AMA member, $120
   nonmember
Teaches readers how to fuse all the vital
elements to create a marketing plan that
is right for their product line or company;
explores basic planning concepts and
provides the practical tools needed to put
these concepts to work.

654.
Luther, William M.
*The Marketing Plan: How to Prepare and
Implement It*
AMACOM, $20.65 AMA members,
   $22.95 nonmembers
Positioning products and services for
success, developing a broader profit base
in established markets, and entering new
markets.

655.
McCready, Gerald B.
*Marketing Tactics Master Guide for Small
Business*
Prentice-Hall, 1982, 139 pp., $17.95
   (cloth), $9.95 (paper)
ISBN 0-13-558148-6 (cloth), 0-13-558130-
   3 (paper). Dewey Decimal No. 658.8. LC
   Card No. 81-13952.

656.
McKenna, Regis
*The Regis Touch: New Marketing Strategies
for Uncertain Times*
Addison-Wesley, 192 pp., $9.95
ISBN 0-201-13964-2.
Marketing techniques for today's fast-
changing environment. Written by a top
marketing consultant.

657.
Midgley, David
Innovation and New Product Marketing
Wiley, 1977, 296 pp.

This book is concerned with the diffu-
sion of innovations, and more specifically
with the management of new-product
introductions.

658.
O'Brien, Richard E.
Publicity: How to Get It
Harper & Row, 1977, 176 pp., $9.95
ISBN 0-06-013199-3.
A how-to book spelling out all the
possible ways to obtain publicity, and
how to do it without hiring a professional
publicist.

659.
Poppe, Fred C.
*The 100 Greatest Corporate and Industrial
Ads*
Van Nostrand Reinhold, 1983, 208 pp.,
   $27.95
How each of the 100 ads was written and
laid out; includes some famous award-
winning examples.

660.
Porter, Michael E.
Competitive Strategy
Free Press, 1980, $15.95
ISBN 0-02-925360-8.
Tools and techniques needed to conduct
an industry and competitors analysis.
Charts, bulletins, and checklists.

661.
Roman, Murray
*Telephone Marketing: How to Build Your
Business by Phone*
McGraw-Hill, 1976, $24.95
ISBN 0-07-053595-7.
Concepts, strategies, and techniques of
telephone marketing. For marketing
professionals.

662.
Scheuing, E. E.
New Product Management

Holt, Rinehart & Winston, 1974, 307 pp.
ISBN 0-03-085004-5.
Marketing mix, marketing concept, innovation, and product life cycles. Case examples.

663.
Serif, Med
Business Building Ideas for Franchising and Small Business
Pilot Books, 1977, $2.50
ISBN 0-87576-006-6.
This book shows how to issue successful news releases to the community press, how to cope with the constant problems of community. A well-planned and well-executed promotion program is one of the most important operations in any business. This book provides some ideas in this area.

664.
Siegel, G. M.
How to Advertise and Promote Your Small Business
Wiley, 1978, 124 pp.
ISBN 0-471-04032-0.
How to plan successful advertising and direct mail campaigns, establish good community relations, write ad copy, measure the effectiveness of promotions.

665.
Smith, Brian R.
Successful Marketing for Small Business
Greene Press/Lewis, 1984, 237 pp.
ISBN 0-86616-032-9 (cloth), 0-86616-033-7 (paper). Dewey Decimal No. 658.8. LC Card No. 83-22219.

666.
Smith, Cynthia S.
How to Get Big Results from a Small Advertising Budget
Hawthorn Books, 1973, $4.50
ISBN 0-8015-3648-0.

Do-it-yourself guide to handling smaller advertising budgets; shows simple and often ingenious ways of getting more out of every dollar spent.

667.
Smith, Roger F.
Entrepreneur's Marketing Guide
Reston, 1984, 239 pp., $19.95 (cloth), $13.95 (paper)
ISBN 0-8359-1743-6 (cloth), 0-8359-1742-8 (paper). Dewey Decimal No. 658.8. LC Card No. 84-3295.

668.
Soderberg, Norman R.
Public Relations for the Entrepreneur and the Growing Business
Probus, 1986, $17.95
ISBN 0-917253-35-3. Dewey Decimal No. 659.2. LC Card No. 86-4931.
How to use public relations to increase visibility and create opportunities for you and your company.

669.
Stansfield, Richard H.
The Advertising Manager's Handbook
American Marketing Association, 1,088 pp., $45.35 member, $63.50 nonmember
Covers 2,600 subjects, with over 500 illustrations and hundreds of case histories of ads and campaigns. Details on copy; layout approaches; money-saving tips on choosing the right media.

670.
Stone, Bob
Successful Direct Marketing Methods
Crain Books, 1979, $24.95
ISBN 0-87251-040-9.
Information on creating and producing direct marketing materials and managing your direct marketing business.

671.

Webb, Terry, Thelma Quince, and David
Watkins, eds.
Small Business Research: The Development of
Entrepreneurs
Gower, 1982, 218 pp., $34
ISBN 0-566-00381-3.

672.

West, C.
Marketing on a Small Budget
Wiley, 1975, 210 pp.

Shows how firms with limited funds can
take advantage of modern marketing
theory and practice; how to optimize the
yield from any given budget allocation.

673.

Wheelwright, Steven C., and Spyros Makridakis
Forecasting Methods for Management, 4th
edition
Wiley, 1985, 404 pp., $36.95
Covers the most important forecasting
techniques now in use, with suggestions
on how to apply them in marketing,
sales, and strategic planning.

HUMAN RESOURCES MANAGEMENT

To be successful, the small-business owner must be able to maintain high morale among employees while making maximum use of their talents. This requires intelligent managerial leadership and an effective system of communicating company goals, employment expectations, employee benefits, and individual performance ratings. Sensitivity to all such conditions strengthens any business operation.

THOMAS DEVLIN
Chairman
Rent-A-Center

Easily the single most important asset of a small business is its personnel. This fact is underscored when owners realize that most of the functions of their firm are performed by employees. Nothing is more important in posturing a small enterprise for success than to develop winning guidelines for recruiting, hiring, and retaining key staff members. Size of operations and limited financial resources often strain an owner's best intentions, but there are many ways in which imaginative employers can encourage talented individuals to remain in their employ.

Overcoming the disadvantages of smallness requires creativity. Hiring quality personnel at salaries less than the going rate sometimes is a wrenching process, but the perceptive entrepreneur often meets this challenge by offering, in association with a minimum starting salary, an incentive package that includes an attractive bonus plan based on preestablished performance criteria. This bonus plan may involve a percentage of profits or the opportunity to acquire an equity (stock) in the firm and thereby to become a part owner.

Frequent personnel changes also may characterize small businesses. The key to successful management in such an environment is to remain flexible, to develop job descriptions based on the skills of staff members presently on hand rather than attempting to recruit personnel to some idealistic job model. Also, it often is necessary to employ individuals with little or no direct experience, so an ongoing employee training program is essential.

Such a training program should not be regarded as a onetime event; a successful training program is continuous, blending new recruits with seasoned employees in an ongoing learning experience that builds on the past and seeks a broadened understanding and knowledge of a firm's position in the competitive marketplace. Periodic sessions during which performances are evaluated are extremely helpful, for they tend to focus again on company goals and on how well each individual is contributing to them. This is especially true for firms that find it necessary to employ part-time personnel. Even with a persistent in-service training program, the owner-manager must be prepared for another frustrating reality: Once trained, the better or more experienced employees often move on to other positions that appear to offer greater rewards.

The secret of retaining key employees is to develop a strong rapport with them and to discover (and discuss) ways to help them realize their professional ambitions within your organization. Many times, their short-term goals may essentially involve financial security, and a compensation package that includes a reasonable salary or bonus plan plus standard employee benefits may be sufficient. A more attractive plan, however, embraces a range of economic, philosophical, and psychological considerations that equate compensation with performance, job worth, and external market forces.

Integral to this mix is what industrial psychologists refer to as psychic income, a nonmonetary benefit of critical importance to the employee's feeling of personal worth. It derives from interpersonal relationships, interpretation of company policies and style of enforcing them, attitudes in the workplace toward dress and personal demeanor, and attention to on-the-job working conditions. Smallness facilitates this type of communication and closeness, and this advantage should not be lost by an insensitive regard for the psychological needs of those who can make or break an enterprise.

A note of caution: There is a growing list of laws and regulations that deal with labor relations and human resources management. Past failures of business firms, large and small, to protect employee rights have led to an increasing scrutiny of all working conditions and employee-employer relations by federal and state legislatures, with the result that some businesses occasionally find themselves in a position of noncompliance with existing regulations. This may prove costly and damaging to a firm's reputation, and the small-businessperson should become as familiar with potential noncompliance areas as possible and use common sense, judgment, and a sense of fairness in dealing with them.

674.

Anthony, William P.

Participative Management

Addison-Wesley, 1978, 240 pp., $9.95

Shows managers how to become more responsive and effective in working with people to achieve organizational goals.

675.

Bergash, Robert

Investment in People: A Small Business Perspective

AMACOM, 1974

Discusses the cost and the economics of better human relations in business.

676.

Cohn, Theodore, and Roy A. Lindberg

Compensating Key Executives in the Smaller Company

AMACOM, 1980, $16.95

Suggests that only through "creative compensation" can the smaller company compete with larger concerns in motivating its top officers. By thinking of pay as a resource, like working capital to be managed toward selected objectives, a smaller firm can build opportunities to realize its aims more efficiently.

677.

Cohn, Theodore, and Roy A. Lindberg

Practical Personnel Policies for Small Business

Van Nostrand Reinhold, 1984, 216 pp., $21.95

ISBN 0-442-21699-8. Dewey Decimal No. 658.303. LC Card No. 82-20696.

A practical guide for helping managers make the most of their most important assets: people. How to tailor personnel management programs that match employee capability, ambition, personality, and style with the demands of a particular job.

678.

Copperman, Lois, and Fred D. Keast

Adjusting to an Older Work Force

Van Nostrand Reinhold, 1983, 140 pp., $24.95

ISBN 0-442-21493-6.

A description of innovative programs, with changes in fringe benefits, pensions, work/leisure combinations, and part-time work options designed to extend careers of the older work force. Primary focus on practices and policies of retirement.

679.

Dougherty, James L.

Union-Free Labor Relations: A Step-by-Step Guide to Staying Union Free

Gulf Publishing, 1980, 227 pp., $69

ISBN 0-87201-302-2.

How-to approach to avoiding union infiltration successfully. The do's and don'ts of employee relations are reviewed.

680.

Dougherty, James L.

Union-Free Supervisor

Gulf Publishing, 1974, 230 pp., $19

ISBN 0-87201-882-2.

Focus on first-line supervisors and their responsibilities in keeping employees union-free.

681.

Dyer, William G.

Team Building: Issues and Alternatives

Addison-Wesley, 1977, 160 pp., $10.50

Emphasizes team-building programs and the importance of differing personalities and backgrounds of individuals.

682.

Ellman, Edgar S.

Put It in Writing

Van Nostrand Reinhold, 1984, 160 pp., $59.95

ISBN 0-442-22171-1.

Geared to the small-business owner, this is a guide to writing a personnel policy manual tailored to fit the company's needs. Fill-in-the-blank forms are provided.

683.
Fournies, Ferdinand F.
Coaching for Improved Work Performance
Van Nostrand Reinhold, 1978, 224 pp., $19.95
ISBN 0-442-22460-5.
For the manager. Face-to-face coaching techniques are described to help obtain immediate, positive results and eliminate self-destructive behavior within subordinates.

684.
Kellogg, Marion S.
Talking with Employees: A Guide for Managers
Gulf Publishing, 1979, 162 pp., $19
ISBN 0-87201-825-1.
Ten critical discussions between managers and employees. Suggestions and sample dialogue on work standards, goal setting, performance appraisal, salary, and career discussions.

685.
Lund, Robert T., and John A. Hansen
Keeping America at Work: Strategies for Employing the New Technologies
Wiley, 1985, 272 pp., $19.95
How organizations can benefit from the new technologies by making work more meaningful and satisfying for all employees. Also provides strategies for job placement and relocation programs.

686.
Meyers, M. Scott
Managing with Unions
Addison-Wesley, 1978, 180 pp., $11.95
Discusses various labor-management relationships and offers new worker-boss models for companies facing union problems.

687.
Nadler, Leonard
Corporate Human Resource Development
Van Nostrand Reinhold, 1980, 224 pp., $18.95
ISBN 0-442-25624-8.

688.
Rice, Craig S.
People par Excellence: How Smaller Firms Can Get Them and Keep Them
AMACOM, 1984, 50 pp., $10
ISBN 0-8144-2307-8. LC Card No. 84-16945.

689.
Siegel, William Lairy
People Management for Small Business
Wiley, 1978, 130 pp., $4.95
ISBN 0-471-04030-4.
Describes ways to train the large number of managers needed to lead the industrial revolution in underdeveloped countries. Three types of training are envisaged: short courses to typical managers of small factories, advanced management courses to exceptional managers of rapidly expanding semimodern factories, and preparatory courses to manager candidates.

690.
Slimmon, Robert F.
Successful Pension Design for Small- to Medium-Sized Businesses
Reston, 1985, 461 pp., $34.95
ISBN 0-8359-7146-5. Dewey Decimal No. 658.3. LC Card No. 84-15100.

691.
Tjosvold, Dean
Working Together to Get Things Done: Managing for Organizational Productivity
Lexington Books, 1986, $24
ISBN 0-669-10834-0.
This book identifies ideas, strategies, and procedures that will improve collaboration, leading to organizational productivity and a better quality of work life.

692.
Uris, Auren
The Executive Interviewer's Deskbook
Gulf Publishing, 1978, 210 pp., $69
ISBN 0-87201-395-2.
Helpful, practical insights into one-on-one communication.

PROBLEMS AND FAILURES

Entrepreneurs, by nature, are independent thinkers who believe in themselves. Yet an uncontrolled ego can cause many problems, especially if danger signs are ignored. The "can-do" spirit should be tempered with a careful attention to detail and conditioned by the development and execution of sound management techniques. No one can walk on water; don't wait until you are halfway across the lake before you discover it.

JACK DeBOER
Chairman and CEO
The Residence Inn Company

Murphy certainly must have had small businesses in mind when he fashioned his oft-used law of probability, for whatever can possibly go wrong in the life of an enterprise undoubtedly will go wrong. Indeed, managing a small business can be characterized as an attempt to run through a minefield with potential disaster awaiting the entrepreneur's every step. Such dangers, though real, are but "the nature of the beast"; without problems, business involvement would lose most of its challenges and much of the excitement that continually lures the creative mind into the marketplace.

Nor do serious problems always result in failure, despite persistent claims that eight out of ten new businesses will fail within the first five years of their existence. Such statistics, in today's vernacular, simply do not wash. Recent studies in leading business journals note that the case for business failures obviously has been overstated, for in 1985 alone, approximately 660,000 new incorporations were registered and only 56,000 bankruptcies filed.

Admittedly, businesses cease to exist for reasons other than bankruptcy. Some are discontinued because they have not achieved sufficient profitability to encourage further investment of risk capital. Others close because of the death or disability of the owners;

still others are capitalized (liquidated) and the money reinvested in savings or other enterprises. In other words, the closing or discontinuation of a business, in many cases, is something other than its failure.

The debate over failure rates undoubtedly will continue until serious research can provide a more definitive analysis of business closings, but one feature of the issue is indisputable: Businesses do fail, and at a much higher rate among new startups than at other stages of business development. A strong case can be made for proper, up-front planning if the entrepreneur desires to avoid as many booby traps in the economic minefields as possible. Such planning begins with a feasibility study, i.e., a detailed business plan. This includes the preparation of operational methods and goals, appropriate financial data, and sources of probable funding. Its ultimate objective is to help an entrepreneur determine if his or her business idea makes economic sense.

Even though many of today's successful entrepreneurs started businesses without a feasibility study, an even larger number of their contemporaries have long since been relegated to economic obscurity. These facts may speak more poignantly about the lack of effective entrepreneurial education than about the failure to conduct preopening planning, but the net effect of either condition unfortunately is the same: a greater potential for business failure because of the absence of an adequate, up-front feasibility analysis.

A feasibility study requires that a business idea be reduced to a formal, black-and-white paper analysis, and includes both quantitative and qualitative assessments of goals, operations, competition, and growth potential in a specific market. It forces even the overly optimistic entrepreneur to become more objective about potential startup problems and to develop a set of guidelines or standards by which the progress of the business may be evaluated once it becomes operational.

Inexperienced entrepreneurs who have difficulty understanding some of the problems identified in a feasibility study should not proceed on blind faith when time, the greatest of equalizers, will absorb or resolve them. Prudent planners will seek the advice of other entrepreneurs, consultants, and business associates for help in assessing the problems and suggesting solutions. Many times they can identify the entrepreneur's managerial inadequacies (lack of experiences or training) and recommend steps to overcome them.

According to studies conducted by Dun & Bradstreet, a lack of management skills accounts for most business failures. Every phase of business operations—sales, personnel management, advertising, promotion, inventory, or finance—requires leadership, direction, and control. Trouble most often arises when the entrepreneur lacks formal education in business management techniques and is thereby constrained in learning and adapting to changing business conditions; or he or she may have general management experience in a related industry but none in the specific field of the new business venture, or an overconcentration of skills in a narrowly defined area (such as an engineer-inventor who is skilled in production but inexperienced in the management of people).

Without experience or formal training in the principles of management, entrepreneurs may be unable to grasp the importance of the day-to-day problems that tend to compound as time passes. Common among them are poor records management, inadequate inventory control, lack of focus on customer satisfaction, poor quality control in both products and services, improper handling of cash and receivables, and the neglect of financial and tax obligations. Yet the most critical of the entrepreneurs' problems may be self-management—controlling their own egos, time, and goals. An uncontrolled ego may result in an unwillingness to face the reality of a threatening economic situation until a solution becomes impossible; it may cause the diversion of much-needed cash from business operations to personal and private use; or it may create an insensitivity to external environmental changes and cause the loss of a competitive edge in the marketplace. If one wishes to be successful in business, the most significant maxim would seem to be "To thine own self be true."

A final word about failure. One of today's most successful entrepreneurs has noted that of approximately 40 businesses he has started since 1950, fewer than 10 are still in existence. "From this," he states, "you could say that I have failed and failed again, but I have never regarded myself as a failure." Nor has anyone else who has analyzed his current investment portfolio. Like other successful entrepreneurs, he regards errors in judgment and mistakes in management as a part of the process of learning how to succeed in business. Mistakes understandably are enervating and consequential, but the only permanent damage is to be found in an unwillingness or inability to learn from them.

693.

Bork, David

Family Business, Risky Business: How to Make It Work

AMACOM, 1986, 186 pp., $17.95

ISBN 0-8144-5878-5.

An inside look at the trials and triumphs of America's 13 million family businesses, this book shows how the entrepreneurial founder can sow the seeds of lasting success—or sudden collapse—for the family business. Provides guidance for developing a workable succession plan, and shows how in-laws, children, spouses, and outsiders can be effectively integrated into the business.

694.

Boswell, Jonathan

The Rise and Decline of Small Firms

Allen & Unwin, 1973

Reports a two-year study of economic performance of smaller firms, mainly in relation to their types of management, their goals and problems, and their ownership and control.

695.

Delaney, William A.

Why Small Businesses Fail—Don't Make the Same Mistake Once

Prentice-Hall, 1984, 208 pp., $16.95 (cloth), $9.95 (paper)

ISBN 0-13-959016-1 (cloth), 0-13-959008-0 (paper). Dewey Decimal No. 658.022. LC Card No. 84-11704.

696.

Frost, Ted S.

Where Have All the Wooly Mammoths Gone? A Small Business Survival Manual

Parker, 1976, $12.95 (cloth), $3.45 (paper)

ISBN 0-13-057142-6 (cloth), 0-13-957159-0 (paper).

The author is a CPA, and this book has been distilled from the painful experience of thousands of small-business clients through the years. Although some suggestions are unorthodox, they are realistic and practical.

697.

Gerber, Michael E., and Patrick O'Heffernan

The E-Myth: Why Most Businesses Don't Work and What to Do About It

Ballinger Publishing, 1986, 162 pp.

ISBN 0-88730-040-5. Dewey Decimal No. 658.022. LC Card No. 85-4002.

698.

Goldstein, Arnold S.

How to Save Your Business

Enterprise Publishing, 1983, 233 pp.

ISBN 0-913864-74-9. Dewey Decimal No. 658.159. LC Card No. 82-83243.

Winning ways to put any financially troubled business together again.

699.
Goldstein, Arnold S.
Strategies and Techniques for Saving the Financially-Distressed Small Business
Pilot Books, 1976, $3.95

700.
Klein, Howard J.
Stop! You're Killing the Business
Mason & Lipscomb, 1974
ISBN 0-87576-054-6.
An overview of some of the remedies available to save the weak or failing company.

701.
Lewis, John, John Stanworth, and Allan Gibb
Success and Failure in Small Business
Gower, 1984, 275 pp., $33.90
ISBN 0-566-00645-6. Dewey Decimal No. 338.642. LC Card No. 83-16447.

702.
Mirvis, Philip H., and David N. Berg, eds.
Failures in Organization Development and Change
Wiley, 1977, 346 pp.
ISBN 0-471-02405-8.
Essays on change, organizational development, and management.

703.
Platt, Harlan D.
Why Companies Fail: Strategies for Detecting, Avoiding and Profiting from Bankruptcy
Lexington Books, 1985, 176 pp., $16.95
ISBN 0-669-09748-9. LC Card No. 84-48692.
Identifies five major financial traps that lead businesses to failure. Causes of business failure and solutions to avoid bankruptcy.

704.
Stevens, Mark
36 Small Business Mistakes and How to Avoid Them

Parker, 1978, $10.95 (cloth), $3.45 (paper)
ISBN 0-13-918946-7 (cloth), 0-13-918920-3 (paper).
A guide through the dangers that threaten novice and seasoned entrepreneurs alike. All observations and recommendations are based on actual case histories.

705.
Stewart, John, Jr.
Managing a Successful Business Turnaround
AMACOM, 1984, $26.95
ISBN 0-8144-5784-3.

706.
Vatter, Harold G.
Some Aspects of the Problem of Small Enterprise As Seen in Four Selected Industries
Arno Press, 1978, 666 pp., $10
ISBN 0-405-11508-3.
Studies the problems in the creamer butter industry, the flour milling industry, the automobile industry, and the glass container industry; doctoral dissertation.

707.
Wayne, William
How to Succeed in Business When the Chips Are Down
McGraw-Hill, 1971
The everyday problems that determine the success or failure of small businesses. Shows how to avoid the bankruptcy court.

708.
Wingate, John W., Elmer O. Schaller, and Robert W. Bell
Problems in Retail Merchandising, 6th edition
Prentice-Hall, 1973, 300 pp., $10.95
ISBN 0-13-720680-1.
A collection of problems and decision-making situations covering various phases of retail merchandising. Largely of the mathematical nature. Includes thumbnail cases involving managerial decisions.

ACQUISITIONS

Whether to buy an existing firm or start a new one is a question that only entrepreneurs can answer for themselves. The costs of entry normally are greater in a buyout situation but may be offset by the advantages of acquiring a business with a proven record of sales and service. Yet the greater entrepreneurial challenge and satisfaction may attend the creation of a new enterprise. Either way, success usually comes to those who study all factors and analyze the alternatives before finalizing their plans.

R. DEE HUBBARD
Chairman of the Board
AFG Industries, Inc.

When aspiring entrepreneurs decide to enter into the ownership of a business, they have at least three options from which to choose: purchasing an enterprise that already exists; starting one from scratch; or acquiring the rights to own and operate one or more units of a franchised company. The process of starting a company is described in the first unit of Section 1, and franchising is in a separate part of Section 2. Here are included books that describe the advantages and disadvantages of buying a firm, along with some of the specifics involved.

Although there is no precise definition for the "right time" to enter the competitive marketplace, small-business consultants stress the importance of becoming familiar with certain economic and environmental factors before embarking upon a business venture. Entry opportunities may surface almost constantly, but there are times when conditions seem more favorable than others. For example, in periods of economic turndown, many small, undercapitalized businesses struggle to survive, and inevitably some owners find it necessary to close their companies and sell all tangible assets. These "distress sales," though painfully expedient to the owners, nonetheless offer other hopeful investors the opportunity to acquire assets at reduced and sometimes bargain-basement prices.

125

However, a warning flag hovers over such buyouts. Why does the owner want to sell? What is the physical status of building, equipment, fixtures, and inventory? Are there unexplained ramifications of lease rights, franchising agreements, and other legal considerations? Does the purchase price reflect the value of the business? The prudent entrepreneur knows to examine all the reasons why owner divestiture has become necessary. Otherwise, one person's failure may contribute directly to a second failure unless the prospective buyer understands the problems and develops plans to overcome them *before* finalizing the purchase.

On the other hand, periods of economic upswing or market expansion could present conditions favorable to new startups, provided entrepreneurs study and understand the market continuum, plan their enterprises carefully, and know and respect their competitors. A rising consumer economy often allows inexperienced owners the chance to learn the art of survival without being penalized severely for early mistakes. However, because national statistics are almost alarmingly unfavorable on new-business startups, it follows that the warning flag, though driven in this case by a different mix of economic currents, still delivers its indelible message of caution to those who are considering a first-time entry into the marketplace.

Other decisions must be weighed carefully. Whether buying a business or starting one, entrepreneurs must find a way to finance their companies. Putting together a capital package for a new business venture often requires creativity, but it usually involves a combination of funds or leveraged assets obtained from bank financing, leasing, and owner's equity. Bank loans normally are obtained on collaterable assets; leasing assists in acquiring equipment. Owner's equity, used typically as operating capital or for short-term leveraging, most frequently is derived from personal savings or from friends or other outside investors through the sale of equity shares in the company. The financial options remain essentially the same for those desiring to purchase an existing firm, although the costs of entry may be somewhat higher than a new startup because the firm's intangible assets, such as goodwill, must be considered in the purchase price. However, the potential buyer may also enjoy another unique funding alternative: persuading the owner to carry a part of the purchase price in the form of a personally held, interest-bearing note that can be retired in installments over a specified number of months.

Weighing the good and bad features of an acquisition and assessing their potential impact on the operation of a business, are significant exercises in the overall decision. The ultimate test is: Would your goals be better achieved by creating a new enterprise whose staying power and nonexistent customer base are yet to be developed, or would it be better to purchase an existing firm with a track record and presumably an established customer loyalty but perhaps also significant operational problems. Neither method is devoid of risks, and the probability of success in either case most likely will be determined by the commitment, preparation, and creativity of the entrepreneur.

709.
Baumer, William H., and Leo J. Northart
Buy, Sell, Merge: How to Do It
Prentice-Hall, 1971, 168 pp., $21.50
ISBN 0-13-109553-6.

Gulf Publishing, 1980, 248 pp., $25
ISBN 0-87201-009-0.
Provides information on proven approaches to negotiating merger agreements, as well as pitfalls.

710.
Bing, Gordon
Corporate Acquisitions

711.
Clark, John J.
Business Merger and Acquisition Strategies

Prentice-Hall, 1985, 223 pp.
ISBN 0-13-106345-6. Dewey Decimal No.
    658.16. LC Card No. 84-15963.
A handbook for entrepreneurs and
managers.

712.
Davis, F. T., Jr.
*Business Acquisitions Deskbook with Check-
lists and Forms*
Institute for Business Planning, 264 pp.
ISBN 0-87624-050-3.
This book is based on the concept that
there are unique acquisition and recapi-
talization possibilities in today's market.
Provides quick access to tested tax-saving
and moneymaking techniques, and
general discussion of acquisition possibilities in today's market.

713.
Drake Publishers
How to Buy and Sell a Small Business
Drake Publishers, 1977, 122 pp., $4.95
Covers the buy-sell transaction, sources
of information for buy-sell decisions,
financial statements, analyzing the
market position of the economy.

714.
Freier, Jerold L.
Acquisition Search Programs
Pilot Books, $3.95
Explains how to pinpoint acquisition
objectives and avoid costly unformulated
search programs by using key organizing
and planning methodologies.

715.
Hanson, James M.
Guide to Buying or Selling a Business
Prentice-Hall, 1975, 269 pp.

716.
Harold, Victor
A Checklist Guide to Successful Acquisitions
Pilot Books, 1980, $3.50

ISBN 0-87576-039-2.
Checklist of the more important and most
often asked questions. Helps avoid
surprises and arrive at a correct decision.

717.
Lee, Steven J., and Robert D. Colman
*Handbook of Mergers, Acquisitions and
Buyouts*
Business Publications, 747 pp., $75
Topics include leveraged financing, nego-
tiating strategies, antitrust law, human
impact, financial analysis.

718.
Manhgold, Maxwell J.
How to Buy a Small Business
Pilot Books, 1976, $1.50
ISBN 0-87576-010-4.
A step-by-step guide for the person
seeking to own and operate a business of
his or her own.

719.
Miles, Raymond C.
Basic Business Appraisal
Ronald Press, 1984, 399 pp., $59.95
ISBN 0-471-88555-X. LC Card No. 83-
    23368.
A comprehensive treatment of business
appraisal theory, offering detailed expla-
nations, step-by-step instructions for
applying theory, and examples of actual
business appraisal reports.

720.
Miles, Raymond C.
How to Price a Business
Business Publications, 131 pp., $60
For owners thinking about selling their
companies. Explains two crucial princi-
ples of pricing, and includes a checklist
of key questions that should be asked.
Case histories.

721.
Pratt, Shannon
*Valuing a Business: The Analysis and Ap-
praisal of Closely-Held Companies*

Dow Jones–Irwin, 410 pp., $55
Valuation mechanics are described: data assembly, financial statement analysis, and presentation of the valuation report.

722.

Pratt, Shannon P.

Valuing Small Businesses and Professional Practices

Dow Jones–Irwin, 512 pp., $45
ISBN 0-87094-598-X. LC Card No. 85-72255.

Valuing small businesses or professional practices differs greatly from valuing larger operations. Explores key issues such as working with business brokers or an appraiser, drafting a purchase agreement, and estate-planning considerations.

723.

Rubel, Stanley

Guide to Selling a Business

Capital Publishing, 1977, 344 pp., $49.50
ISBN 0-914470-10-8.

Designed to assist those who are selling their companies or are beginning to think about it. Directories of corporate acquirers and merger intermediaries.

724.

Scharf, Charles A.

Acquisitions, Mergers, Sales, and Takeovers

Prentice-Hall, 1971, 317 pp., $34.95
ISBN 0-13-003053-8.

Describes how to acquire, sell, merge, and take over businesses. Sets forth the rules governing the legal, tax, securities, and accounting aspects of acquisitions.

725.

Smith, Brian R., and Thomas L. West

Buying Your Own Small Business

Greene Press/Lewis, 1985, 118 pp.
ISBN 0-86616-047-7. Dewey Decimal No. 658.114. LC Card No. 84-19390.

726.

Sterling Publishing Co.

How to Buy and Sell a Small Business

Sterling Publishing, 132 pp., $5.95
ISBN 0-8069-7592-X.

A resource tool for forming sound judgments, saving time, effort, and money in the buying and selling aspects of small business.

727.

Webb, Ian

Management Buy-Out: A Guide for the Prospective Entrepreneur

Gower, 1985, 175 pp., $27
ISBN 0-566-02519-1. Dewey Decimal No. 658.16. LC Card No. 84-27940.

728.

Woods, Gordon

The Acquisition Decision

National Association of Accountants, 102 pp., $15.95
ISBN 0-86641-110-0.

Senior executives of 29 companies in the United States and Canada give their ideas on how to become a successful acquirer. Identifies and interprets the information needs of management accountants in the acquisition decision-making process.

INTRAPRENEURSHIP

Corporate managers increasingly are recognizing the importance of encouraging an entrepreneurial spirit within their organizations; hence the new term *intrapreneurship*. Indeed, many large businesses are reinventing themselves, discarding old-line industrial structures in favor of flexible organizations that can respond more readily to product innovation and change. This trend gives new meaning to "small is beautiful"—and new significance to the role entrepreneurs historically have assumed and are now playing in shaping the contemporary business environment.

VICTOR K. KIAM II
Chairman and President
Remington Products, Inc.

Corporate efforts to capture the spirit of entrepreneurship—its spontaneity, energy, and creativity—have been going on for more than a decade. Although large corporations and institutions long have followed the historic pattern of performing what they do best within organizational structures that emphasize stability and a conservative attitude toward change and risk management, their managers have become increasingly aware that the economic sands around these traditional foundations are shifting. Many of them now recognize that one of the most important keys to their competitive future rests on an ability to develop and encourage the growth of a spirit of new enterprise. This philosophical and organizational innovation, generally referred to as intrapreneurship, is a fast-growing phenomenon that strives to place a premium on entrepreneurial creativity within what once might have been regarded as a hostile environment—the corporate structure.

As a concept, intrapreneurship is easy to embrace; in practice, however, it poses many problems. Professional corporate managers normally perform best in situations of structured control, established procedures, and planned, even predictable, outcomes. On the other hand, creative individuals perform best in unstructured settings as devoid as possible of the constraints of time, finances, and pressure to produce. For some companies, this paradox in attitudes and functional expectations has been difficult to overcome, but many others have used maturity of judgment, long-term vision, and courage to accommodate the needs of an extremely valuable colleague (intrapreneur) or group of innovative individuals whose goals are identical to those of the company but whose methods of contributing to it differ significantly from the expected norm.

Intrapreneurs are not conventional project leaders; rather, they appropriately might be described as a cross between an employee and an independent entrepreneur whose special status within a corporate structure is justified and defended because of certain unique and recognizable talents. In a sense, they select themselves by drawing attention to skills that managers find compatible with company goals and wish to exploit. To realize the full potential of such individuals requires vision and risk. The most successful experiments with the intrapreneurial concept have involved the creation of a separate division or profit center, virtually independent of the corporate structure, featuring a narrowed focus or objective, a separate budget, and a flexible, team-style management.

The success of these experiences has caused many large companies to adopt Peter Drucker's contention that entrepreneurship is not antithetical to the corporate structure if a clear understanding of functions is recognized: A manager's duty is to control and plan; the entrepreneur's role is to be creative and initiate change. Yet there exists considerable debate among the leading analysts about the best methods of achieving a compatibility of these functions.

Gustaf Delin recognizes that there are no established norms for setting up an intrapreneur's relationship with a corporation and suggests that a preferred association is best established through negotiation. Thus, each "set of rules" governing such relationships will be unique to the individuals involved, but a few general, overriding principles are applicable:

1. The intrapreneur should be permitted to undertake a well-defined risk with the full support of management.
2. A clear agreement should be made on the intrapreneur's reward structure, including an incentive compensation plan.
3. The project should be defined as an intrabusiness endeavor, complete with separate funding and independent decision making.

Once established, such relationships have delivered definite advantages to entrepreneurs who have chosen to do their creative work within the corporate structure. Among them: the virtual elimination of personal financial risks in developing an idea; the use of existing equipment, know-how, and support systems; and the opportunity to test market a product within well-developed company strategies. Because of these facts, Gifford Pinchot III contends that intrapreneuring often makes better sense than entrepreneuring, as it also permits creative individuals the opportunity to conduct their work among friends and within the confines of the secure corporate setting.

As in all experimental endeavors, corporations have had to absorb numerous failures in their efforts to establish successful intrapreneurial project divisions. Emerging from the ashes of defeat, however, are some encouraging lessons and hopeful guidelines for the future. Projects cannot be made too "cushy" (devoid of risks or responsibilities) for the intrapreneur; neither projects nor the individuals involved should be tied too closely to corporate management strings; ideas for new products should be more the creative function of intrapreneurs than the brainchild of top management; and leadership and control of a project should be entrusted to a special group of involved and dedicated individuals, not to teams selected and appointed by management.

Although the lessons learned may have been expensive in some cases, corporations nonetheless have begun to reap some sweeping rewards from their efforts. These successes undoubtedly will engender an even greater expansion of the practice of harnessing entrepreneurial firepower by encouraging the development of attractive alternative outlets for creative energy within a corporate intrapreneurial environment.

729.
Brandt, Steven C.
Entrepreneuring in Established Companies: Managing Toward the Year 2000
Dow Jones–Irwin, 1986, 252 pp., $19.95
ISBN 0-87094-664-1. Dewey Decimal No. 658.42. LC Card No. 85-71433.
Ways to deal with issues such as leading from behind, funding ideas, and surprise management.

730.
Copulsky, William, and Herbert W. McNulty
Entrepreneurship and the Corporation
AMACOM, 1974, 152 pp., $13.95
Entrepreneurship is the spark of small-company operations that can help large companies to be more effective in certain areas, especially new ventures, and to improve results in all areas.

731.
Hanan, Mack
Fast-Growth Management
AMACOM, 1979, 145 pp., $14.95
ISBN 0-8144-5559-X. Dewey Decimal No. 658.1. LC Card No. 79-18344.
How to improve profits with entrepreneurial strategies.

732.
Levinson, Robert E.
Making the Most of Entrepreneurial Management
AMACOM, 1986
ISBN 0-8144-7656-2. Dewey Decimal No. 658.402. LC Card No. 85-30615.

733.
Naisbitt, John
Reinventing the Corporation
Warner Books, 1985
ISBN 0-446-51284-2. LC Card No. 85-40007.
Transforming your job and your company for the new information society.

734.
Pinchot, Gifford
Intrapreneuring
Harper & Row, 1985, 368 pp., $19.95
ISBN 0-06-015305-9. Dewey Decimal No. 658.42. LC Card No. 83-48800.
Learn how to choose an idea, get it approved by your company, where to find funds, and make your project succeed. For the future thinkers who want their innovative ideas to stay within the organization.

SECTION 3.

Periodicals

Magazines and Journals   135
Newsletters   142

The essential requirement for successful entrepreneuring, other than high level of motivation, is the intelligent acquisition and use of information. In our increasingly information-dependent society, the entrepreneur must learn how best to access the information with the greatest relevance and profit potential. A resource like this volume has the potential for making a significant and critical difference for the aware entrepreneur.

ARTHUR LIPPER III
Chairman
Venture Magazine

MAGAZINES AND JOURNALS

Magazines and journals provide virtually unlimited resources for information. Hundreds are published each year, with many designed specifically for the entrepreneur and small-business owner. Some provide information on specific industries; others specialize in material for entrepreneurs and small-business managers. Examples are *Entrepreneur, Venture, Inc., Franchise Adviser,* and the *Journal of Small Business Management.*

Included here are more than 70 journals and magazines of importance to small-business owners, listed in alphabetical order by title. Listings include the title of the magazine, publisher's name and mailing address, frequency of publication (monthly, quarterly, etc.), circulation, year founded, price, and ISSN number.

735.

Alliance
National Alliance of Homebased Businesswomen, Box 306, Midland Park, NJ 07432 (201) 423-9131
Bimonthly. Circ. 1,200. Founded 1981.
Price included in membership.
ISSN 0734-2837.

736.

American Journal of Small Business
University of Baltimore, School of Business, 1420 N. Charles St., Baltimore, MD 21201 (301) 659-3262
Quarterly. Circ. 1,000. Founded 1976.
$10.
ISSN 0363-9428.

737.

America's Fastest Growing Companies
(formerly *Johnson Survey*)*
$124.

738.

Barter Update
Update Publicare Co., Box 570122, Houston, TX 77257

Semiannual. Circ. 1,000. Loose-leaf.
Founded 1983. $4.
ISSN 0736-1904.

739.

Behind Small Business
Dona M. Risdall, Box 37147, Minneapolis, MN 55431 (612) 881-5364
Bimonthly. $14.

740.

Big Farmer Entrepreneur (formerly *Big Farmer;* incorporating *Big Farmer Cattle Guide*)
National Farm Databank, 131 Lincoln Hwy., Frankfort, IL 60423 (815) 469-2163
10 per year. Circ. 200,000. Vol. 42, 1970.
$10.
ISSN 0274-6050.

741.

*Black Enterprise**
Monthly. $15.

---

*Can be purchased through EBSCO Subscription Services, International Headquarters, Box 1943, Birmingham, AL 35201, (205) 991-6725.

742.

Brown's Business Reporter

Comp-Graphics, Inc., 30 E. 13th St., Box 1376, Eugene, OR 97440 (503) 345-8665

Weekly. Circ. 1,200. Founded 1959. $35.

743.

Business Franchise Guide

Commerce Clearing House, Inc., 4025 W. Peterson Ave., Chicago, IL 60646 (312) 583-8500

Base volume plus monthly reports. $435.

744.

Business Digest of Delaware Valley

Business Digest of Philadelphia Inc., 2449 Golf Rd., Philadelphia, PA 19131 (215) 477-8620

Monthly. Circ. 43,508. Founded 1977. $12.

745.

Business News

Sunrise Communications, 4805 Mercury St., Suite E, San Diego, CA 92111 (619) 565-2636

Sponsor: Business News San Diego Co.

Fortnightly. Circ. 10,000. Founded 1981. $26.

ISSN 0738-6869.

746.

Business: North Carolina

Shaw Communications, Inc., 1450 Johnston Bldg., Charlotte, NC 28281 (704) 372-9794

Monthly. Circ. 22,597. Founded 1981. $15.

747.

Business Opportunities Digest: Clearing House of Business Opportunities Information

Straw Enterprises, Inc., 3110 Maple Dr., N.E., Suite 114, Atlanta, GA 30305

Monthly. Founded 1963. $36.

ISSN 0007-6953.

748.

Center City Report

International Downtown Executives Association, 915 15th St., N.W., Suite 900, Washington, DC 20005

Monthly. Circ. 1,500. $32.

749.

Choices: For Entrepreneurial Women

Entrepreneur Group Inc., 2311 Pontius Ave., Los Angeles, CA 90064 (213) 478-0437

Quarterly. Circ. 90,000. Founded 1985. $11.97.

ISSN 0884-0989.

750.

CityBusiness (formerly Citibusiness)

CityBusiness–New Orleans, Inc., Heritage Plaza, 111 Veterans Blvd., Ste. 750, Metairie, LA 70005 (504) 834-9292

Fortnightly. Circ. 22,000. Founded 1980. $20.

751.

Commerce Journal of Minority Business

U.S. Department of Commerce, 14th St. between Constitution Ave. & E St., N.W., Washington, DC 20230 (202) 377-2000

Quarterly. Founded 1981.

752.

Computer Entrepreneur

Computer Entrepreneur Publishing Company, Box 456, Grand Central Station, New York, NY 10163

Monthly. Circ. 10,000. Founded 1983. $36.

753.

Consumer and Retailer (formerly Retailer)

754.

*Continental Franchise Review**

Biweekly. $135.

---

*Can be purchased through EBSCO Subscription Services, International Headquarters, Box 1943, Birmingham, AL 35201, (205) 991-6725.

755.

*Culture Sculpture, A Magazine of Philan-
thropy, Women's Entrepreneurship and New
Lifestyles*
Performing Arts Social Society, 543
    Frederick St., San Francisco, CA 94117
    (415) 753-1314
Quarterly. Circ. 10,000. Founded 1984.
    $18.
ISSN 0748-7649.

756.

Do It Yourself Retailing*
Monthly. $26.72.

757.

*Dynamic Business (formerly Smaller Manufac-
turer)*
Smaller Manufacturers Council, 339
    Blvd. of the Allies, Pittsburgh, PA
    15222 (412) 391-1622
11 per year Circ. 4,400 controlled.
    Founded 1945. $25.
ISSN 0279-4039.

758.

Entrepreneur
Entrepreneurial Group, Inc., 2311 Pontius
    Ave., Los Angeles, CA 90064 (213) 479-
    3987
Monthly. Circ. 200,000. Founded 1973.
    $24.50.
ISSN 0163-3341.

759.

Entrepreneur
London-Manhattan Ltd., 33-41 Dallington
    St., London E.C.1, England
Quarterly. Circ. 10,600. Founded 1978.
    £10 ($36).

760.

Executive Report
Riverview Publications, Inc., Bigelow Sq.,
    Pittsburgh, PA 15219-3028 (412) 471-
    4585
Monthly. Circ. 19,760. Founded 1981.
    $24.

761.

*Explorations in Economic History (formerly
Explorations in Entrepreneurial History)*
Academic Press, Inc., Journal Division,
    1250 Sixth Ave., San Diego, CA 92101
    (619) 230-1840
Quarterly. Founded 1963. $87.
ISSN 0014-4983.

762.

Franchising in the Economy
US Department of Commerce. I T A
    Service Industries Division, Washing-
    ton, DC 20230. Orders to Supt. of
    Documents, Washington, DC 20402
    (202) 566-8611
Annual. $4.75.

763.

Free Enterprise: Australia*
Monthly. $12.45.

764.

*Guide to Obtaining Local Minority Business
Directories**
Annual. $7.

765.

*Home Business: The Management Magazine
for Home Business Owners*
Home Business, Inc., 2 Broadlawn Ave.,
    Great Neck, NY 11023-1537
Sponsor: Home Business Research Center
Bimonthly. Circ. 100,000. Founded 1984.
    $9.95.

766.

Illinois Business
Crain Communications, Inc., 740 N. Rush
    St., Chicago, IL 60611 (312) 649-5294
Quarterly. Circ. 28,233. Founded 1982.
    $10.

---

*Can be purchased through EBSCO Subscrip-
tion Services, International Headquarters, Box
1943, Birmingham, AL 35201, (205) 991-6725.

767.

In Business: For Independent, Innovative Individuals
J G Press, Inc., Box 351, Emmaus, PA 18049 (215) 967-4135
Bimonthly. Circ. 55,000. Founded 1979. $18.
ISSN 0190-2458.

768.

Inc.: The Magazine for Growing Companies
Inc. Publishing Corp., 38 Commercial Wharf, Boston, MA 02109. Subscr. to Box 2538, Boulder, CO 80321
Monthly. Circ. 401,088. Founded 1979. $18.
ISSN 0162-8968.

769.

International Business Proposals*
Quarterly.

770.

International Marketing Data and Statistics*
Annual. $160.

771.

Itek News
Itek Corporation, 10 Maguire Rd., Lexington, MA 02173 (617) 276-2000
10 per year.

772.

Journal of Retailing*
Quarterly. $25.

773.

Journal of Small Business Management
West Virginia University, Bureau of Business Research, Box 6025, Morgantown, WV 26506-6025 (304) 293-5837
Sponsor: International Council for Small Business. Cosponsor: Small Business Institute Director's Association
Quarterly. Circ. 37,000. Founded 1963. $25.
ISSN 0047-2778.

774.

Mail Order Business Directory for United States*
Irregular.

775.

Mail Order Business Directory for Western United States and All Other Countries*
Biennial.

776.

Marketing News, collegiate edition
American Marketing Association, 250 S. Wacker Dr., Chicago, IL 60606
Monthly (except summer). Professional members $10; nonmembers (individuals) $20; nonmembers (corporate) $30. One-year subscription included with two-year student membership dues.

777.

Minority Business Entrepreneur
924 N. Market, Inglewood, CA 90302 (213) 673-9398
Bimonthly. Circ. 16,000. Founded 1984. $12.

778.

Minority Business Today (formerly Commerce: The Journal of Minority Business)
US Department of Commerce, Minority Business Development Agency, Washington, DC 20230
Monthly.

779.

Mississippi Business Journal
Downhome Publications, Inc., Box 16445, Highland Village, Suite 254, Jackson, MS 39211 (601) 982-8418
Monthly. $24.

---

*Can be purchased through EBSCO Subscription Services, International Headquarters, Box 1943, Birmingham, AL 35201, (205) 991-6725.

780.
Missouri Business
Missouri Chamber of Commerce, Box
149, Jefferson City, MO 65102
10 per year. Circ. 5,000. Founded 1952.
$3.

781.
NFIB
National Federation of Independent
Business, 150 W. 20 Ave., San Mateo,
CA 94403 (415) 341-7441
Monthly.
ISSN 0195-1513.

782.
*NFIB Quarterly Economic Report for Small
Business* (Report #50)
National Federation of Independent
Business, 600 Maryland Ave., S.W.,
Suite 700, Washington, DC 20024
Quarterly.

783.
*Photolife U.S.A.: Magazine of the Entrepre-
neur Photographer*
Dyno Publishing Corp., 26903 W. Eight
Mile Rd., Detroit, MI 48240
Monthly. Founded 1979. $15.

784.
Popular Woodworker (formerly *Pacific
Woodworker*)
E G W International Corp., 1300 Galaxy
Way, Concord, CA 94520 (415) 671-
9852
6 per year. Circ. 10,000. Founded 1981.
$9.
ISSN 0277-576X.

785.
Professional Quilter
Oliver Press, Box 4096, St. Paul, MN
55104-4096
Bimonthly. Circ. 2,000. Founded 1983.
$15.

786.
Profitable Craft Merchandising (formerly
Profitable Hobby Merchandising)
P J S Publications, Inc., News Plaza, Box
1790, Peoria, IL 61656 (516) 626-0650
Quarterly. Circ. 25,000. Founded 1965.
$12.

787.
Ram Report
Rome Arnold & Company, 1127 Thorn-
dale Ave., Chicago, IL 60660 (312) 334-
2100
Monthly.

788.
*Retail Business**
Monthly.

789.
*Retailing Today**
Monthly. $36.

790.
SBANE Enterprise
Smaller Business Association of New
England, 69 Hickory Dr., Waltham, MA
02154 (617) 890-9070
Monthly. Circ. 2,700. Founded 1984. $10.

791.
*SBIC Directory and Handbook of Small
Business Finance*
International Wealth Success, Inc., Box
186, Rockville Center, NY 11570 (516)
766-5850
Annual. Founded 1970. $15.

792.
Small Business Magazine
Richboro Press, Box 1, Richboro, PA
18954
Monthly. Founded 1979. $39.

---

*Can be purchased through EBSCO Subscrip-
tion Services, International Headquarters, Box
1943, Birmingham, AL 35201 (205) 991-6725.

793.
Small Business Report (Hawthorne)
Northrop Corporation, Aircraft Division,
    One Northrop Ave., Hawthorne, CA
    90250 (213) 970-3266
Quarterly.

794.
Small Business Report (Monterey)*: For*
Decisionmakers in Small and Midsize
Companies
Business Research and Communications,
    203 Calle de Oaks, Monterey, CA 93940
    (408) 649-1691
Monthly. Circ. 100,000. Founded 1976.
    $68.
ISSN 0164-5382.

795.
Small Business Reporter
Bank of America, Small Business Re-
    porter Department, Box 37000, San
    Francisco, CA 94137 (415) 622-3456
4–6 per year. Founded 1958. $2 per issue.

796.
*Small Business Research Library Series**
Irregular.

797.
Small Time Operator: How to Start Your Own
Small Business, Keep Your Books, Pay Your
Taxes and Stay Out of Trouble
Bell Springs Publishing, Box 640, Layton-
    ville, CA 95454 (707) 984-6746
Annual. Circ. 40,000. Founded 1976.
    $10.95.

798.
Starting and Managing Series
US Small Business Administration, 1441
    L St., N.W., Washington, DC 20005.
    Orders to Supt. of Documents, Wash-
    ington, DC 20402 (202) 653-6914
Irregular. Price varies.
ISSN 0081-4415.

799.
States and Small Business: Programs and
Activities
US Small Business Administration, Office
    of the Chief Counsel for Advocacy,
    1441 L St., N.W., Washington, DC
    20005 (202) 634-6098
Annual.

800.
*Strategic Planning Management**
Monthly. $125.

801.
Success and Money!
Beninda Books, Box 9251, Canton, OH
    44711
Quarterly. Founded 1981. $12.

802.
Successful Business: The Magazine for
Independent Business
Presidential Advisory Committee on
    Small Minority Business Ownership,
    1441 L St., N.W., Room 602, Washing-
    ton, DC 20005
Sponsor: Control Data Corporation
Annual.

803.
Technovation: An International Journal of
Technical Innovation and Entrepreneurship
Elsevier Science Publishers B.V., Box 211,
    1000 AE Amsterdam, Netherlands
Quarterly. Founded 1980. 175 florins.
ISSN 0166-4972.

804.
Tennessee Business and Economic Review
Middle Tennessee State University,
    School of Business, Murfreesboro, TN
    37132
Bimonthly. Circ. 2,500. Founded 1984.

---

*Can be purchased through EBSCO Subscrip-
tion Services, International Headquarters, Box
1943, Birmingham, AL 35201, (205) 991-6725.

805.

*Trademark Register of the U.S.**
Annual. $247.

806.

Venture Capital Journal (formerly Venture
Capital, SBIC/Venture Capital, SBIC—
Venture Capital Service)
Venture Economics, Inc., 16 Laurel Ave.,
   Wellesley Hills, MA 02181. Orders to
   Box 348, Wellesley Hills, MA 02181
   (617) 431-8100
Monthly. Founded 1961. $495.

807.

Venture Magazine: The Magazine for
*Entrepreneurs**
Monthly. $18.

808.

Voice of Small Business (formerly Small
Business Bulletin)
National Small Business Association,
   1604 K St., N.W., Washington, DC
   20006 (202) 293-8830
Monthly. Circ. 50,000. Founded 1937.
   Price included in membership.
ISSN 0037-7198.

809.

Washington Business Journal
Scripps Howard Business Publications,
   8321 Old Court House Rd., Suite 200,
   Tysons Corner, Vienna, VA 22180 (703)
   442-4900
Weekly. Circ. 20,073. Founded 1982. $26.
ISSN 0737-3147.

---

*Can be purchased through EBSCO Subscrip-
tion Services, International Headquarters, Box
1943, Birmingham, AL 35201, (205) 991-6725.

NEWSLETTERS

Companies large and small provide an almost inexhaustible amount of pertinent information in the form of newsletters. Newsletters can select and tap a source of information in a highly specific area, so entrepreneurs can subscribe to the ones that coincide with their business activities.

Newsletters are listed alphabetically by title, with the following information, where available: title, publisher's name and address, frequency of publication, circulation, year founded, price, and description of content.

A number of newsletters are available only to members of the organizations that publish them. Costs of memberships vary; some are free. Contact the appropriate organization for membership information. Also note that many of the professional organizations and business-related associations described in Section 6 produce publications for their members.

810.

Business Trends Forecaster (formerly Chase Econometrics Letter)
Newsletter Management Corporation, 10076 Boca Entrada Blvd., Boca Raton, FL 33428-5897 (305) 483-2600
Semimonthly. Founded 1984. $97.

811.

Cash Newsletter: To Help You Make, Save, Invest and Keep Money
Cashco, Box 1999, Brooksville, FL 33512
Monthly. Circ. 5,000. Founded 1977. $36.

812.

Entrepreneurial Economy: Monthly Review of Enterprise Development Strategies
Corporation for Enterprise Development, 1725 K St., N.W., Suite 1401, Washington, DC 20006 (202) 293-7963
Monthly. Circ. 1,000. Founded 1982. $78.
ISSN 0741-6776.

813.

Entrepreneurial Manager's Newsletter: For the Entrepreneurial Manager and the Professionals Who Advise Him
Center for Entrepreneurial Management, Inc., 83 Spring St., New York, NY 10012 (212) 925-7304
Monthly. Circ. 3,000. Founded 1979. $96.
ISSN 0272-0396.

814.

Entrepreneurial Woman Newsletter
Sunshine Press, 3221 Bloomfield Park Dr., West Bloomfield, MI 48033 (313) 626-3248
Bimonthly. Inactive. $18.
ISSN 0732-4642.

815.

Franchise Adviser
New Ventures Publishing Co., 2430 Pennsylvania Ave., N.W., Suite 106, Washington, DC 20037 (202) 659-3800

Semimonthly. Founded 1979. $87.
ISSN 0196-0660.

816.

*Growth Capital: The Newsletter of Entrepre-
neurial Finance*
Howard & Company, 1528 Walnut St.,
   Suite 2020, Philadelphia, PA 19102
   (215) 735-2815
Monthly. Founded 1981. $145.
ISSN 0278-7601.

817.

Hospital Entrepreneur's Newsletter
Aspen Publishers, Inc., 1600 Research
   Blvd., Rockville, MD 20850 (301) 251-
   5000
Monthly. Founded 1985. $99.50.

818.

Info Franchise Newsletter
Info Press, Inc., 736 Center St., Lewiston,
   NY 14092
Monthly. Founded 1977. $60.
ISSN 0147-5924.

819.

Insight Newsletter
National Federation of Independent
   Business, Research and Education
   Foundation, 150 W. 20th Ave., San
   Mateo, CA 94403 (415) 341-7441
Quarterly. $10.
For employers interested in providing
economic awareness programs for their
employees.

820.

International New Product Newsletter*
Monthly. $115.

821.

Jack O'Dwyer's Newsletter
J. R. O'Dwyer Company Inc., 271 Madison Ave., New York, NY 10016 (212)
   679-2471
Biweekly. $120.
Covers breaking news and trends in the
field of public relations and related
topics.

822.

Marble & Ivy Review
224 Thayer St., ESC Box 110, Providence,
   RI 02906
Monthly. Circ. 119, Loose-leaf. Founded
   1984. $60.
ISSN 0749-3967.

823.

Marketing News
American Marketing Association, 250 S.
   Wacker Dr., Chicago, IL 60606
Biweekly. Price included with AMA
   membership; nonmembers (individ-
   uals) $30; nonmembers (corporate) $40.
Business newspaper dedicated to report-
ing on new ideas in marketing.

824.

Mind Your Own Business
224 S. Michigan Ave., Chicago, IL 60604
Bimonthly. Founded 1981. $24.

825.

Moneymaker Reporter
Chris Clayton, Box 3573, Modesto, CA
   95352
Monthly. Circ. 100. Founded 1974. $5.

826.

Money Making Opportunities
Success Publishing Co. Inc., 542 W. Park
   Ave., Long Beach, NY 11561 (516) 432-
   2293
8 per year. $6.
ISSN 0192-9399.

827.

NASBIC News
National Association of Small Business
   Investment Companies, 1156 15th St.,

---

*Can be purchased through EBSCO Subscrip-
tion Services, International Headquarters, Box
1943, Birmingham, AL 35201, (205) 991-6725.

N.W., No. 1101, Washington, DC 20005
(202) 833-8230
Semimonthly. Circ. 1,500. Founded 1959.
$100.
ISSN 0469-323X.

828.
*National Home Business Report (formerly
Sharing Barbara's Mail)*
Barbara Brabec Productions, Box 2137,
Naperville, IL 60566
Bimonthly. Circ. 3,000. Founded 1984.
$18.
News, information, and guidance for
home-based workers.

829.
New York Alive
Business Council of New York State, Inc.,
152 Washington Ave., Albany, NY
12210. Subscr. to: Box 6389, Syracuse,
NY 13217 (518) 465-7511
Bimonthly. Circ. 34,000. Founded 1981.
$9.
ISSN 0734-0265.

830.
Retail Management Letter*
Monthly. $67.

831.
Retail Operations News Bulletin*
Quarterly. $30.

832.
Retailer and Marketing News*
Monthly. $12.

833.
Sideline Business Newsletter
J G Press, Inc., 18 S. Seventh St., Box 351,
Emmaus, PA 18049
Monthly. Circ. 2,000. Loose-leaf. Founded
1982. $30.

834.
*Small Business Preferential Subcontracts
Opportunities Monthly*
Government Data Publications, 1120

Connecticut Ave., N.W., Washington,
DC 20036
Monthly. $72.

835.
*Small Business Report (formerly Small
Business)*
Small Business Service Bureau, Inc., Box
1441, 544 Main St., Worcester, MA
01601 (617) 262-2981
Every 6 weeks. Circ. 35,000. Founded
1978. $75.

836.
Small Business Tax Control
Capitol Publications, Inc., 1300 N. 17th
St., Arlington, VA 22209 (703) 528-
1100
Monthly. Founded 1970. $89.
ISSN 0162-8658.

837.
Small Business Tax Saver
Enterprise Publishing, Inc., 725 Market
St., Wilmington, DE 19801
Monthly. $72.

838.
Small Businessman's Clinic
113 Vista del Lago, Scotts Valley, CA
95066 (408) 438-1411
Monthly. Circ. 300. Duplicated. Founded
1972. $28.
ISSN 0094-2464.

839.
Washington Business Journal
Scripps-Howard Business Publications,
5314 Bingle Rd., Houston, TX 77092
Monthly. $26.
ISSN 0737-3147.
An information tool for decision-making
executives, investors, and managers.
Lends insight into trends, growth, and
new ideas important to commerce and
industry.

---

*Can be purchased through EBSCO Subscrip-
tion Services, International Headquarters, Box
1943, Birmingham, AL 35201, (205) 991-6725.

SECTION 4.

Audiovisual Materials

Films   147
Audio Tapes   152
Videotapes   154
Teaching Materials   163
Records for the Blind   167

The explosion of information now available to entrepreneurs and small-business owners includes a large volume of materials on audio- and videotapes. These can be of inestimable value in promoting an understanding of a wide range of subjects and problem areas. Many libraries, reference centers, and trade associations have collections of these tapes as well as the electronic equipment needed to make effective use of them. Some charge nominal rental fees; others none. Additionally, many private companies now produce instructional tapes that may be bought or leased. In the aggregate, these tapes represent a significant education tool that can strengthen any business.

JOSEPH R. MANCUSO
President
Center for Entrepre-
neurial Management
New York, New York

People acquire knowledge through a variety of experiences and media; some learn better from reading, others from listening, still others by observing. Whatever medium provides the most favorable learning experiences, whether for psychological reasons or personal convenience, should be used to develop skills or bridge obvious weaknesses.

Audiovisual materials are excellent motivational devices for larger groups. Some may be rented from local libraries at nominal cost, and others are available for purchase.

Entries in this section are grouped by medium; with the Subject Index you can locate materials on topics of your interest. The five general media categories are:

1. Films
2. Audio tapes
3. Videotapes
4. Teaching materials
5. Records for the blind

The listings include the following information, as available: title; name and address of producer; name and address of distributor (if different); relevant technical data; length; date produced; audience/grade level; Library of Congress number; and description. Individual films and tapes that are part of a series are grouped together under the series title.

Symbols used are for grade levels as follows:

E	Elementary	JC	Junior college
I	Intermediate	C	College
H	High school	A	Adult

FILMS

840.

The American Character, a series
Encyclopedia Britannica Educational
  Corporation, 425 N. Michigan Ave.,
  Chicago, IL 60611
16mm film, optical sound. Color.
    "Jerry's Restaurant." 12 min. 1977.
Level JC, A. LC Card No. 78-700240.
Introduces Jerry and his unconventional
restaurant. Follows him during a frantic
and noisy lunch hour as he shouts to
greet his customer, brusquely propels
him to the counter, hollers to ask for the
order, and shares some jokes.
    "Trader Vic's Used Cars." 10 min.
1976. Level JC. LC Card No. 76-701794.
Presents a film portrait of Victor Snyder,
a Southern California used car dealer.
Portrays Trader Vic and talks frankly
about his business and shares his secrets
of success.

841.

"Another Bad Month at Grey's Grocery"
Coronet Instructional Films, 65 E. South
  Water St., Chicago, IL 60601
16mm film, optical sound. 21 min. Color.
  1977. Level H, C, A. LC Card No. 77-
  703191.
Interviews with store owners, customers,
and a supermarket manager give insight
into changing social values and increasing economic pressure that face small
businesses.

842.

"Burglary Is Your Business"
Producer: Small Business Administration, 1441 L St. NW, Washington, DC
  20416
Distributor: U.S. National Audiovisual
  Center, General Services Administration, Washington, DC 20409
16mm film, optical sound. 15 min. Black/
  white. 1969. LC Card No. 74-704255.
Points out security measures that retailers
should take to prevent burglaries. Shows
an investigation by a police detective
following a burglary at a home furnish-
ings and appliance store.

843.

"The Business Plan for Small Businessmen"
Producer: Small Business Administration, 1441 L St. NW, Washington, DC
  20416
Distributor: U.S. National Audiovisual
  Center, General Services Administration, Washington, DC 20409
16mm film, optical sound. 15 min. Color.
  1972. LC Card No. 74-704256.
Dramatizes the need for a business plan
as a management tool for successful
business operation, through a dialogue
between two small businessmen.

844.

"The Calendar Game"
Producer: Small Business Administration, 1441 L St. NW, Washington, DC
  20416
Distributor: U.S. National Audiovisual

Center, General Services Administration, Washington, DC 20409
16mm film, optical sound. 14 min. Color. 1967. LC Card No. 74-704263.
Emphasizes the need for planning and budgeting by small retail and service businesses.

845.
"Chef's Special"
Producer: WGBH-TV, 125 Western Ave., Boston, MA 02134
Distributor: Learning Corporation of America, 1350 Ave. of the Americas, New York, NY 10019
16mm film, optical sound. 30 min. Color. 1983. Level C, A. LC Card No. 83-700087.
The establishment of a small restaurant shows what is involved in setting up a new business.

846.
"The Climber"
General Motors Corp., 6464 E. Twelve Mile Rd., Warren, MI 48090
16mm film, optical sound. 26 min. Color. 1975. LC Card No. 75-703592.
Outlines some of the problems of organizing and conducting a business operation by telling the story of Scott Stewart, who developed a successful ski clothing manufacturing business.

847.
"Credit Card Security: Merchant Training"
Summerhill Productions, Box 156, Stn. Q, Toronto, Ontario, Canada
16mm film, optical sound. 21 min. Color. 1977. Level C, A. LC Card No. 77-701146.
Presents a step-by-step analysis of a fraudulent credit card transaction.

848.
"Days of Reckoning"
Producer: Millbank Films
Distributor: International Film Bureau, 332 S. Michigan Ave., Chicago, IL 60604

16mm film, optical sound. 29 min. Color.
Dramatizes the problems of managing a small business by using the example of a small firm that is expanding.

849.
"Doing Business"
Document Associates, Inc., 1697 Broadway, Suite 802, New York, NY 10019
16mm film, optical sound. 15 min. Color. 1981. LC Card No. 82-700447.
Examines three small businesses in Atlanta: a workers' collective, a bakery, and a bean-sprout producer. Points out the problems and rewards of these and other small businesses.

850.
The Enterprise, a series
Producer: WGBH-TV, 125 Western Ave., Boston, MA 02134
Distributor: Learning Corporation of America, 1350 Ave. of the Americas, New York, NY 10019
16mm film, optical sound. 30 min. Color. 1981. Level C, A.
"Catfish Fever." LC Card No. 81-707543. Tells how, beset by the uncertainties of weather and the marketplace, cotton and soybean farmers in Mississippi are looking for a surer return on their labors, and that their latest hope is raising catfish. Points out that the demand is high now, but questions whether or not sales will continue to grow.
"Start-Up." LC Card No. 81-707547. Tells of the difficulties of starting a business as background to the story of John DeLorean, a former General Motors employee who started a company capable of competing with automobile industry giants.
"Wildcatter." LC Card No. 81-707537. Explains how small oil and gas prospectors are playing an increasingly vital role in America's search for energy. Tells the story of one such wildcatter, Bill Brodnax of Taurus Petroleum in Louisiana, as he drills a well in hopes of the big payoff.

851.

"Going Out of Business"

Christopher Gamboni, 29 Crystal Beach
   Blvd., Moriches, NY 11955

16mm film, optical sound. 15 min. Black/
   white. 1977. LC Card No. 79-700219.

Looks at the Griswold Machine Works,
Port Jefferson, New York, shortly before
the company went out of business.
Includes a history of the company, which
began as a small, general machine shop
in a vaudeville theater and eventually
turned to making motion-picture splicers
in response to the needs of an adjoining
movie theater.

852.

"Home and Property Protection"

Producer: Summerhill Productions, Box
   156, Stn. Q, Toronto, Ontario, Canada

Distributor: Aims Media, Inc., 626 Justin
   Ave., Glendale, CA 91201

16mm film, optical sound. 35 min. Color.
   1974. Level H–C, A. LC Card No. 75-
   700376.

Presents a criminologist, a security
expert, and an ex-burglar who discuss
crimes against homes, small business,
and property. Offers a number of pointers
to help owners protect their homes and
property against theft.

853.

"How to Lose Your Best Customer—Without
Really Trying"

Producer: Amer. Telephone and Tele-
   graph Co., Information Dept., 195
   Broadway, Room 07-1106, New York,
   NY 10007

Distributor: Wave, 826 N. Cole Ave.,
   Hollywood, CA 90038

16mm film, optical sound. 30 min. Color.
   1971. Level A. LC Card No. 75-713410.

Describes the problems of a small business whose employees have very bad
telephone habits. Presents and explains
proper telephone techniques.

854.

"The Huntsman"

National Film Board of Canada, 1251
   Ave. of the Americas, 16th floor, New
   York, NY 10020

16mm film, optical sound. 17 min. Color.
   1972. Level E–I. LC Card No. 72-
   702910.

When the difficulties of an unauthorized
enterprise outweigh its rewards, a young
entrepreneur abandons his project. Tells
the story of a ten-year-old boy who earns
money by collecting, cleaning, and
selling stray balls from a golf course, but
after learning that his occupation is
forbidden, the boy discards his collection
of balls and gives up the enterprise.

855.

"If the Fergi Fits, Wear It"

Producer: Dave Bell Assoc., 3211 Ca-
   huenga Blvd. West, Hollywood, CA
   90068

Distributor: Walt Disney Educational
   Media Co., 500 S. Buena Vista St.,
   Burbank, CA 91521

16mm film, optical sound. 23 min. Color.
   1975. Level I–H. LC Card No. 75-
   703571.

Presents the story of the first business
venture of a teenage brother and sister
who decide to sell silk-screen T-shirts.
Shows some of the responsibilities and
advantages of going into business.

856.

"International Operations"

National Film Board of Canada, 1251
   Ave. of the Americas, 16th floor, New
   York, NY 10020

16mm film, optical sound. 29 min. Color.
   1973. Level H–C, A.

Examines the arrival of a large supermarket on the outskirts of Paris, depicting the
impact it has on the shopping and eating
habits of the French and the problems of
adjustment by store employees, Paris
shoppers, and local merchants who see
their customers drifting away.

857.

"The Manager as Entrepreneur"

BNA Communications Inc., 9417 Decoverly Hall Rd., Rockville, MD 20850

16mm film, optical sound. 31 min. Color. 1971. LC Card No. 72-702879.

John Humble, noted for his management by objectives program, discusses with Peter Drucker the major tasks of the new manager.

858.

"Million Dollar Dreams"

Producer: Gannett Broadcast Group

Distributor: MTI Teleprograms, 3710 Commercial Ave., Northbrook, IL 60062

16mm film, optical sound. 30 min. Color. 1983. Level JC, A.

Looks at six Americans who started with nothing but an idea and a commitment to hard work. Shows how they became millionaires who make cookies, suntan lotion, computer programs, herbal tea, and cosmetics.

859.

"New Entrepreneur"

Producer: Paul Feyling Productions

Distributor: Aims Media, Inc., 626 Justin Ave., Glendale, CA 91201

16mm film, optical sound. 13 min. Color. 1974. Level I–C, A. LC Card No. 75-700379.

Examines the work of a young black woman in a small business that provides cars, drivers, and personalized service for travelers and business visitors. Shows the career possibilities in building and operating a small business.

860.

"Nine Dollars Plus One Dollar Equals Twenty Dollars—Shortchanged"

BNA Communications Inc., 9417 Decoverly Hall Rd., Rockville, MD 20850

16mm film, optical sound. 25 min. Color.

Features five actual situations showing unsuspecting cash-register operators being taken for $5 to $50 by professional count men. Reviews all five scenes, explains what is happening as it happens, and gives a tabletop demonstration of two of the examples emphasizing the trickery involved.

861.

"One Thing Leads to Another"

Producer: Educational Film Center, 5401 Port Royal Rd., N. Springfield, VA

Distributor: Agency for Instructional Television, Box A, Bloomington, IN 47401

16mm film, optical sound. 15 min. Color. 1980. Level I. LC Card No. 81-700138.

Describes the business problems faced by the Rocket Babysitting Service.

862.

"Organization"

Phillips Petroleum Co., Advertising Dept., 310 W. 5th St., Bartlesville, OK 74003

16mm film, optical sound. 29 min. Color. 1976. LC Card No. 76-702862.

Actor William Shatner portrays a dynamic entrepreneur discussing America's economic growth. Portrays organizational techniques such as mass production and mass marketing.

863.

"A Piece of the Pie"

Producer: EXXON Company, USA, Box 2180, Houston, TX 77001

Distributor: Modern Talking Picture Service, 500 Park St. N., St. Petersburg, FL 33709

16mm film, optical sound. 19 min. Color.

Tells the story of four minority group members who are in business for themselves. Provides insights into what the minority business owner must do to succeed in today's business world.

864.

"Planning and Goal Setting: Time-Waste or Management Tool"

BNA Communications Inc., 9417 Decoverly Hall Rd., Rockville, MD 20850
16mm film, optical sound. 22 min. Color.
Peter Drucker discusses the importance of planning and goal setting for small and large organizations.

865.
"The Right Location"
U.S. Small Business Administration, 1441 L St. NW, Washington, DC 20416
16mm film, optical sound. 16 min. Color. 1974. LC Card No. 74-702883.
Uses the experiences of a small businessman who tries to select a site for his first menswear store to dramatize the relationship of site selection to the success of a business and to identify some of the important factors in selecting a business site.

866.
"The Seventh Chair"
Producer: U.S. Small Business Administration, 1441 L St. NW, Washington, DC 20416
Distributor: U.S. National Audiovisual Center, General Services Administration, Washington, DC 20409
16mm film, optical sound. 13 min. Color. 1971. LC Card No. 74-705615.
Dramatizes the credit and collection problems of five small-business owners with a round-table discussion and flashbacks to their places of business.

867.
"Small Business Keeps America Working"
U.S. Chamber of Commerce, Audio Visual Dept., 1615 H St., NW, Washington, DC 20062
16mm film, optical sound. 28 min. Color. 1979. LC Card No. 79-701387.
Small-business owners discuss their experiences in business, their feelings about their work, and their problems and rewards. Features observations by an economic historian and the president of the U.S. Chamber of Commerce.

868.
"Westside Store"
Producer: Amitai Film, 117 E. Mt. Pleasant, Philadelphia, PA 19119
Distributor: Barr Films, 3490 E. Foothill Blvd., Pasadena, CA 91107
16mm film, optical sound. 23 min. Color. 1982. Level I, H. LC Card No. 82-700741.
Presents the economics of running a small business through a story about an ethnically mixed inner-city gang that turns from vandalism to operating its own legitimate business, a second-hand store.

869.
"What Is Business"
Producer: Sandler Institutional Films, Inc., 1250 Siskiyou Blvd., Ashland, OR 97520
Distributor: Barr Films, 3490 E. Foothill Blvd., Pasadena, CA 91107
16mm film, optical sound. 10 min. Color. 1973. Level H–C, A. LC Card No. 73-702609.
Acquaints the student with what a business is, how it operates, who operates it, and who is responsible for making short-term decisions and overall policy. Observes the operation of a one-man boutique leather shop in contrast with the operation of a large manufacturing company.

870.
"You're Gonna Have to Get Big to Be Heard"
National Federation of Independent Business, 150 W. 20th Ave., San Mateo, CA 94403
16mm film, optical sound. 16 min. Color. 1976. LC Card No. 76-703172.
Shows how the National Federation of Independent Business speaks for over 400,000 independent businesses around the United States and how the NFIB is lobbying in Washington to create legislation favorable to small businesses.

AUDIO TAPES

871.

"Authentic Selling: The Key to Sustained Sales Productivity"

American Society for Training and
    Development, 600 Maryland Ave. SW,
    Washington, DC 20024

Order number 5AST-M49.

State-of-the-art skills and ideas are offered to salespeople who want greater success and enjoyment in their work.

872.

"The Business Manager"

Center for Cassette Studies, Inc., 919
    Third St., New York, NY 10022

1⅞ ips cassette. 29 min. 1976. Level C, A.
Surveys the function of the business manager in joining resources, labor, and capital.

873.

"Competitive Marketing Strategy: Maintaining Your Edge in a Changing Economy"

American Society for Training and
    Development, 600 Maryland Ave. SW,
    Washington, DC 20024

Order number 5AST-TU24.

Maintain competitive edge through your company's strategic position with offered pragmatic methods and techniques.

874.

"Computer in Business—Its Advantages and Disadvantages"

Producer: Sound Seminars Division,
    Behavioral Science Assoc.

Distributor: McGraw-Hill, College Division, 1221 Ave. of the Americas,
    New York, NY 10020

3¾ ips tape.
Reviews the role of the computer in business management.

875.

"Conversational Selling: Sales Without Manipulation"

American Society for Training and
    Development, 600 Maryland Ave. SW,
    Washington, DC 20024

Order number 4AST-M1.

A useful, alternative method of selling for the sophisticated 1980s marketplace.

876.

"The Corporate Entrepreneur"

American Society for Training and
    Development, 600 Maryland Ave. SW,
    Washington, DC 20024

Order number 5AST-W50.

Shows how to measure entrepreneurial potential and how organizational development can encourage entrepreneurship in an organization.

877.

"Direct Response Marketing—A Practical Model for Training Telemarketing Professionals"

American Society for Training and
    Development, 600 Maryland Ave. SW,
    Washington, DC 20024

Order number 5AST-TU8.

Adapt existing skills to telemarketing and be the force in the achievement of your organization's marketing goals.

878.

"Fifty Ways to Make Money Without Leaving Home"

Communication Enterprises, 100 Hardy

Court Office, Suite 120, Gulfport, MS 39501
1⅞ ips cassette.
Presents case histories of 50 different home businesses.

879.
"How to Get Started Selling Your Arts and Crafts"
Communication Enterprises, 100 Hardy Court Office, Suite 120, Gulfport, MS 39501
1⅞ ips cassette.
Discusses how to make arts and crafts for profit as well as fun.

880.
"How to Open a Restaurant"
National Public Radio, 2025 M St., Washington, DC 20036
1⅞ ips cassette, 40 min.
Explains how to open a small restaurant, focusing on one couple's experience.

881.
"Managerial Data Processing"
Producer: Sound Seminars Division, Behavioral Science Assoc.
Distributor: McGraw-Hill, College Division, 1221 Ave. of the Americas, New York, NY 10020
3¾ ips tape.
Examines electronic data processing as the focal point of the management information system.

882.
"Professionalization of Selling"
American Society for Training and Development, 600 Maryland Ave. SW, Washington, DC 20024
Order number 5AST-M2.
In this world of sophisticated buyers, learn the professional way of approach.

883.
"Small Business/Big Business"
National Public Radio, 2025 M St., Washington, DC 20036

1⅞ ips cassette. 59 min.
Examines the impact of small business on the economy.

884.
"Small Businesses"
National Public Radio, 2025 M St., Washington, DC 20036
1⅞ ips cassette. 59 min. Level H–C, A.
Discusses the attempt to disband the Small Business Administration, looks at government regulations, and explores the special problems of blacks in small businesses.

885.
"Telemarketing Training Geared to the Marketplace of the '80s"
American Society for Training and Development, 600 Maryland Ave. SW, Washington, DC 20024
Order number 5AST-M80.
Examination of the telemarketer, marketing strategies, and the best training methods.

886.
"Winning the Marketing Challenge Through Strategic Planning"
American Society for Training and Development, 600 Maryland Ave. SW, Washington, DC 20024
Order number 5AST-TU45.
Through the use of a model involving a process, people, and information, learn about the sales/marketing competency of strategic planning.

887.
"Women in Today's Business World"
American Society for Training and Development, 600 Maryland Ave. SW, Washington, DC 20024
Order number 5AST-WO.
This is an examination of the socialization process that inhibits women from excelling in corporate positions; offers recommendations for change.

VIDEOTAPES

888.

"Another Bad Month at Grey's Grocery"
Coronet Instructional Films, 3710 Commercial Ave., Northbrook, IL 60062
¾- or ½-inch videocassette. 21 min. Color. 1977. Level H–C, A.
Gives insight into changing social values and increasing economic pressure that face small businesses by presenting interviews with store owners, customers, and a supermarket manager.

889.

"The Business Plan—for Small Businessmen"
Producer: U.S. Small Business Administration, 1441 L St. NW, Washington, DC 20416
Distributor: U.S. National Audiovisual Center, General Services Administration, Washington, DC 20409
Super 8mm cartridge, magnetic sound. 15 min. Color. 1972. LC Card No. 75-701696.
Uses a dialogue between two men engaged in a small business to dramatize the need for a management plan in achieving success. Cites the elements to be included in a plan for managing a small business.

890.

"Buying and Selling the Small Business with Professor John E. Moye"
National Practice Institute, 861 W. Butler Square, Minneapolis, MN 55403
¾- or ½-inch videocassette. 72 min.
Color. 1978. Level Prof. LC Card No. 80-706564.
Covers practical and legal considerations in evaluating, structuring, closing, and negotiating the sale of a small business.

891.

"A Case in Point"
Producer: U.S. Small Business Administration, 1441 L St. NW, Washington, DC 20416
Distributor: U.S. National Audiovisual Center, General Services Administration, Washington, DC 20409
Super 8mm cartridge, magnetic sound. 12 min. Color. 1969. LC Card No. 75-701700.
Tells of various services the Small Business Administration makes available to small-business owners.

892.

Case Studies in Small Business, a series
Producer: University of Mid-America, Box 82006, Lincoln, NE 68501
Distributor: Great Plains Instructional TV Library, University of Nebraska, Box 669, Lincoln, NE 68501
¾- or ½-inch videocassette. 30 min. Color. 1979. Level C, A.
Investigates the principles of small-business management by showing how real businesses successfully—or not so successfully—manage day-to-day operations. Titles in the series:

The Balancing Act
The Breaking Point
Dealing in Wheeling
The Downhill Slide
The Long Haul
Running the Show
Starting Up
Taking Off
Their Own Brand
The Venturer

893.
"Checking It Out"
Producer: Southwest Center for Educational Television, Austin, TX
Distributor: Great Plains Instructional TV Library, University of Nebraska, Box 669, Lincoln, NE 68501
¾- or ½-inch videocassette. 30 min. Color. 1983. Level I–H. LC Card No. 83-706605.
Profile of Juan Caballero, a 20-year-old entrepreneur who wants to be a millionaire at age 30. Presented in English and Spanish with English subtitles.

894.
"Chef's Special"
Producer: WGBH-TV, 125 Western Ave., Boston, MA 02134
Distributor: Learning Corporation of America, 1350 Ave. of the Americas, New York, NY 10019
¾- or ½-inch videocassette. 30 min. Color. 1983. Level C, A. LC Card No. 83-706276.
Establishment of a small restaurant shows what is involved in setting up a new business.

895.
"Days of Reckoning"
Producer: Millbank Films
Distributor: International Film Bureau, 332 S. Michigan Ave., Chicago, IL 60604
¾- or ½-inch videocassette. 29 min. Color.
Dramatizes the problems of managing a

small business by using the example of a small firm that is expanding.

896.
"Doing Business"
Document Assoc., Inc., 1697 Broadway, Suite 2, New York, NY 10019
¾- or ½-inch videocassette. 15 min. Color. LC Card No. 82-706540.
Offers a behind-the-scenes look at the pleasures and the difficulties of operating a small, self-managed business.

897.
"The Employer"
Producer: Coast Community College District, 1370 Adams Ave., Costa Mesa, CA
Distributor: Coast District Telecourses, 10231 Slater Ave., Fountain Valley, CA 92708
¾-inch videocassette. 29 min. Color. Level C, A.
Examines some of the difficulties in owning and operating a business. Uses a case study to explain some of the problems in obtaining licenses and permits. Covers legal and practical aspects of terminating a business.

898.
Enterprise, a series
Producer: WGBH-TV, 125 Western Ave., Boston, MA 02134
Distributor: Learning Corporation of America, 1350 Ave. of the Americas, New York, NY 10019.
¾- or ½-inch videocassette. 30 min. Color. 1981. Level C, A.
Discusses various aspects of business, finance, and banking using examples of actual companies. Titles in series:

Bankrupt
Boeing vs. the World
Catfish Fever
The Colonel Comes to Japan
Dogfight over New York

Fast Horse in a Bull Market
Gulliver's New Travels
The Kyocera Experiment
The Making of a Package Deal
Not by Jeans Alone
One Man's Multinational
Start-Up
Wildcatter

899.

Enterprise II, a series
Producer: WGBH-TV, 125 Western Ave.,
    Boston, MA 02134
Distributor: Learning Corporation of
    America, 1350 Ave. of the Americas,
    New York, NY 10019
¾- or ½-inch videocassette. Color. 1983.
    Level C, A.
Discusses various aspects of international
business, including the popularity of
video games, offshore oil leases, a company buyout by its employees, small
businesses, music promotion, and airline
bankruptcy. Titles in series:

All in the Game
Buck Stops in Brazil
Buy-Out
California Crude
Chef's Special
The Diamond Game
Fired
Hardball
Hong Kong Dresses Up
The New Space Race
The Selling of Terri Gibbs
Tailspin

900.

"Everyone's Business"
Producer: National Film Board of Canada,
    1251 Ave. of the Americas, 16th floor,
    New York, NY 10020
Distributor: Arthur Mokin Productions,
    2900 McBride Lane, Santa Rosa, CA
    95401
¾- or ½-inch videocassette. 21 min.
    Color. 1984. Level JC, A.

Features the Churchill Park Greenhouse,
where for eight years disabled or disadvantaged workers have produced vegeta-
bles for retail and wholesale markets.

901.

Export Development, a series
Producer: U.S. Industry and Trade
    Administration
Distributor: U.S. National Audiovisual
    Center, General Services Administra-
    tion, Washington, DC 20409
¾- or ½-inch videocassette. Color.
    "Doing Business in China." 45 min.
1979. LC Card No. 80-706633. Three
American businessmen who have been
doing business in China relate their
personal experiences.
    "E Is for Export." 16 min. 1978. LC
Card No. 80-706633. Uses the experiences
of a typical small company to show how
a small manufacturer can get into the
export market.
    "Export Opportunity." 16 min. 1978.
LC Card No. 80-706629. Explains how
three small manufacturers with market-
able products are successful in exporting
with the help of the Commerce Department trade specialists.
    "Information Please." 14 min. 1979.
LC Card No. 80-706632. Describes how to
develop export strategy by using the
marketing information on foreign markets
published by the Commerce Department.
    "Leiden Connection." 20 min. 1978.
LC Card No. 80-706631. Explains the
trade opportunity program administered
by the U.S. Industry and Trade Administration, which provides a computer
matching service bringing together U.S.
sellers with foreign buyers.

902.

"Family Business"
Producer: WQED, Metropolitan Pitts-
    burgh Educational TV, 42 Fifth Ave.,
    Pittsburgh, PA 15213
Distributor: Films Incorporated, 1213

Wilmette Ave., Wilmette, IL 60091
¾- or ½-inch videocassette. 90 min.
Color. 1982. Level JC, A.
Introduces Howie Snider who operates a
Shakey's Pizza franchise in Muncie,
Indiana, and works in the kitchen,
behind the counter, plays the banjo,
makes radio commercials, and tries to
arrange new financing for his economically shaky business. Questions what has
happened to the American dream of
owning a business with the additional
pressures of franchising and national
advertising.

903.
"Franchising/Smoke Detectors/Pensions"
Maryland Center for Public Broadcasting,
Owings Mill, MD 21117
¾- or ½-inch videocassette. Color.

904.
"Home and Property Protection"
Producer: Summerhill Productions, Box
156, Station Q, Toronto, Ontario,
Canada
Distributor: Aims Media, Inc., 6901
Woodley Ave., Van Nuys, CA 91406
¾- or ½-inch videocassette. 35 min.
Color. 1974. Level H–C, A.
Presents a criminologist, a security
expert, and an ex-burglar who discuss
crimes against homes, small business,
and property. Offers a number of pointers
to help owners protect their homes and
property against theft.

905.
"The Huntsman"
National Film Board of Canada, 1251
Ave. of the Americas, 16th floor, New
York, NY 10020
¾- or ½-inch videocassette. 17 min.
Color. 1972. Level E–I.
When the difficulties of an unauthorized
enterprise outweigh its rewards, a young
entrepreneur abandons his project. Tells
the story of a ten-year-old boy who earns

money by collecting, cleaning, and
selling stray balls from a golf course.
After learning that his occupation is
forbidden, the boy discards his collection
of balls and gives up the enterprise.

906.
"If the Fergi Fits, Wear It"
Producer: Dave Bell Assoc., 3211 Ca-
huenga Blvd., West, Hollywood, CA
90068
Distributor: Walt Disney Educational
Media Co., 500 S. Buena Vista St.,
Burbank, CA 91521
¾- or ½-inch videocassette. 23 min.
Color. 1975. Level I–H.
The story of the first business venture by
a teenage brother and sister who decide
to sell silk-screen T-shirts. Shows some
of the responsibilities and advantages of
going into business.

907.
"International Operations"
National Film Board of Canada, 1251
Ave. of the Americas, 16th floor, New
York, NY 10020
¾- or ½-inch videocassette. 29 min.
Color. 1973. Level H–C, A.
Examines the arrival of a large supermarket on the outskirts of Paris, depicting the
impact it has on the shopping and eating
habits of the French and the problems of
adjustment by store employees, Paris
shoppers, and local merchants who see
their customers drifting away.

908.
"It's Your Move"
Producer: U.S. Small Business Administration, 1441 L St. NW, Washington, DC
20416
Distributor: U.S. National Audiovisual
Center, General Services Administration, Washington, DC 20409
¾-inch videocassette. 13 min. Color.
1979. LC Card No. 79-707549.
Explains how small-business owners who

are faced with relocation problems can find help through the U.S. Small Business Administration and urban renewal offices.

909.
"Manager as Entrepreneur"
BNA Communications Inc., 9417 Decoverly Hall Rd., Rockville, MD 20850
Super 8mm cartridge, magnetic sound. 31 min. Color.
Defines the role of the entrepreneur in business and shows how managers can unleash the potential creativity and innovation in their organization.

910.
"Million Dollar Dreams"
Producer: Gannett Broadcast Group
Distributor: MTI Teleprograms, 3710 Commercial Ave., Northbrook, IL 60062
¾- or ½-inch videocassette. 30 min. Color. 1983. Level JC, A. LC Card No. 84-706143.
Looks at six Americans who started with nothing but an idea and a commitment to hard work. Shows how they became millionaires who make cookies, suntan lotion, computer programs, herbal tea, and cosmetics.

911.
"The Need to Achieve: Motivation and Personality"
Producer: National Educational TV, Inc., Indiana University, Bloomington, IN 47401
Distributor: Indiana University, Audio-Visual Center, Bloomington, IN 47405
¾- or ½-inch videocassette. 29 min. Black/white. 1963. Level H–C, A.
Dr. David McClelland of Harvard University explains his psychological theory—that the economic growth or decline of nations is dependent to a large extent upon the entrepreneurs of these nations. He seeks to substantiate his theory through motivational tests.

912.
"New Entrepreneur"
Producer: Paul Feyling Productions
Distributor: Aims Media, Inc., 6901 Woodley Ave., Van Nuys, CA 91406
¾- or ½-inch videocassette. 13 min. Color. 1974. Level I–C, A.
Examines the work of a young black woman in a small business that provides cars, drivers, and personalized services for travelers and business visitors. Shows the career possibilities in building and operating a small business.

913.
"On Key"
Producer: WGBH-TV, 125 Western Ave., Boston, MA 02134
Distributor: King Features Educational Division, 235 E. 45th St., New York, NY 10017
¾- or ½-inch videocassette. 30 min. Color. Level H–C, A.
Features the small business of Ned Steinberger, which has a single product: an innovative electric bass guitar. Tells how the business is perhaps too successful.

914.
"Planning and Goal Setting: Time-Waste or Management Tool"
BNA Communications Inc., 9417 Decoverly Hall Rd., Rockville, MD 20850
¾- or ½-inch videocassette. 22 min. Color.
Peter F. Drucker discusses the importance of planning and goal setting for small and large organizations.

915.
"A Portrait of a Small Hydro"
Producer: Neal Livingston, Mabou, Inverness County, Cape Breton Islands, Nova Scotia, Canada B0E-1XO
Distributor: Bullfrog Films, Inc., Oley, PA 19547

¾- or ½-inch videocassette. 28 min.
Color. 1984. Level JC, A.
Looks at the experiences of three hydro-
electric entrepreneurs who have bought
up old dam sites and are rebuilding them
for the production of power.

916.

Positive Shortage Prevention, a series
Anne Saum and Associates, 79 W. 12 St.,
New York, NY 10011
Super 8mm cartridge, magnetic sound. 16
min. Color. 1972. Level I.
"The Dollar Drain." LC Card No. 77-
702196. Overviews the inventory shortage problem and dramatizes the impact
of shortages on a store and its employees.
"First Line of Defense." LC Card No.
77-702197. Dramatizes the impact of a
store supervisor's behavior and practices
on those aspects of employee performance that contribute to inventory
shortage.
"The Losers." LC Card No. 77-
702199. Two case histories show how
store employees who steal merchandise
from their employer cause irreparable
damage to their own security, self-
respect, family, and future.
"Who, Me?" LC Card No. 77-702198.
Simulates situations in which store
employees' carelessness or failure to
follow established procedures causes loss
of merchandise or discrepancies in
records. Establishes the role of each
employee as an error controller and an
error detector.

917.

Running a Small Business, a series
Producer: MVM Enterprises
Distributor: Beacon Films, Box 575, 1250
Washington St., Norwood, MA 02062
¾- or ½-inch videocassette. Color. 1982.
Level H, C, A.
Shows basic principles of small-business
operations and basic skills and research
methods. Teaches principles of organi-

zing and sorting data relative to successful ventures. Titles in series:

> Basic Records for a Small Business
> Credit and Collections for a Small
> Business
> Evaluating a Small Business
> Financing a Small Business
> Insurance Needs for a Small Business
> Inventory Control for Manufacturers
> Merchandise Control for Retailers

918.

"Silicon Valley: The New Entrepreneurs"
Producer: WETA-TV, The Greater Washington Educational TV Association,
Inc., Box 2626, Washington, DC 20013
Distributor: Public Broadcasting Service,
475 L'Enfant Plaza SW, Washington,
DC 20024
¾- or ½-inch videocassette. 29 min.
Color.
Examines the electronics industry just
south of San Francisco and the American
entrepreneurs who created it. Emphasizes the beneficial side of industrial
development and technological advancement and raises questions about government regulation of the private economy.

919.

"Small Business"
Indiana University, Audio-Visual Center,
Bloomington, IN 47405
¾-inch videocassette. 21 min. Color.
1979. Level C, A. LC Card No. 80-
706235.
Stresses that the person considering
opening a small business should have
significant skills developed through work
experience and education. Presents a
bank loan officer commenting on financing a small business.

920.

The Small Business Administration, a series
Intercollegiate Video Clearing House,
Drawer 3300R, Miami, FL 33133
¾- or ½-inch videocassette.

"The Advertising Question." 15 min. Color. Designed to correct some of the misconceptions about the value of advertising.

"All or Nothing." 40 min. Black/white. A dramatization of a salesman faced with a problem of one dealer opening a branch in another's exclusive territory.

"Anything Is Possible with Training." 15 min. Color. Gives examples of successful training in a boatyard, a telephone answering service, a newspaper office, and a restaurant.

"Burglary Is Your Business." 15 min. Color. Depicts the investigation by police of a burglary at an appliance store. Points out security measures retailers should take.

"The Business Plan." 15 min. Color. Dramatizes the need for a business plan as a management tool for successful operation. Features a dialogue between a successful and an unsuccessful business owner.

"The Calendar Game." 15 min. Color. Illustrates advertising planning and budgeting by the owner of a dry cleaning shop to reach selected groups of people at specific times.

"The Follow-Up." 14 min. Color. Portrays partners in an appliance store discussing the follow-up on a radio commercial with store layout and point-of-purchase materials.

"The Heartbeat of Business." 15 min. Color. Shows two business owners discussing financial management. Uses flashbacks to illustrate good and bad practices.

"The Inside Story." 18 min. Color. Dramatizes steps to be taken to limit or prevent pilferage by plant employees. Shows how an old, trusted employee has been pilfering for years.

"It Can Happen to You." 18 min. Color. Shows a police lieutenant and a hardware store owner getting the facts about a pilfering problem and showing situations that encourage pilfering.

"The Language of Business." 15 min. Color. The owner of a radio and TV retail and service shop who wants to open a branch store asks his accountant to interpret his records to illustrate danger areas.

"Man or Woman for the Job." 15 min. Color. Dramatizes the importance of effective employee recruitment and selection procedures through the experiences of a small print shop owner.

"Man's Material Welfare." 30 min. Color. Features president of Amway Corporation addressing Dow Chemical executives on the fundamentals of the free-enterprise economic system as contrasted to socialistic systems.

"The Right Location." 14 min. Color. Designed to inform small-business owners faced with relocation problems, or new businesses, of the importance of site selection.

"The Seventh Chair." 14 min. Color. Discusses credit and collection problems of a large department store, a food caterer, a lumber dealer, a druggist, a haberdasher, and a florist.

"Step in the Right Direction." 15 min. Color. Discusses the importance of merchandise control procedures and techniques.

"They're Out to Get You." 14 min. Color. A jailed professional shoplifter makes plans to resume his trade when released. Points out preventive measures store owners should take.

"Three Times Three." 15 min. Color. Dramatizes nine keys to small-business success such as personal ability, use of assistance and information, insurance, regulation and taxes, business opportunity, sources of capital, records, financial factors, and organization and planning.

"Variations on a Theme." 15 min. Color. Dramatizes planning a sales event in a women's ready-to-wear shop. Shows the conflict of a cashier who is scornful of advertising and promotional themes.

"You and Your Customers." 15 min. Color. Dramatizes retailer's problem with customer relations.

921.

Starting a Business, a series
Producer: Soma Film Producers
Distributor: Beacon Films, Box 575, 1250
    Washington St., Norwood, MA 02062
¾- or ½-inch videocassette. Color. Level
    H–C, A.

"Are You an Entrepreneur?" 18 min. 1982. Explores three questions to arrive at successful entrepreneurship: What is an entrepreneur? What is an entrepreneur's role in starting a business? What are the personal qualities usually found in successful entrepreneurs? Presents costs and rewards of self-employment as career.

"How Can You Survive Business Crises?" 21 min. 1983. Explores why businesses fail, so strategies can be developed to avoid failure. Shows how entrepreneurs can deal with financial trouble and how to cope if failure does occur.

"How Do You Buy a Business?" 21 min. 1983. Advocates development of a strategic plan to buy an existing business. Identifies information sources, documents needed for analysis, ways to value a company, how to judge return on investment, and suitable approaches and strategies to acquisition.

"How Do You Buy a Franchise?" 21 min. 1983. Defines franchise business as a formalized legal marketing and distribution system. Shows how arrangement often results in entrepreneur's loss of freedom. Also interviews successful franchise owners.

"How Much Capital Will You Need?" 17 min. 1982. Explains how to determine what capital an entrepreneur needs to start, and clarifies basic financial tools

including pro forma cash flow, balance sheet, and profit and loss statement.

"How Will You Find Capital?" 21 min. 1983. Explores least understood of all elements in starting new business, stressing imperatives of entrepreneurs' knowing both the kinds of capital required and where to obtain it.

"How Will You Penetrate Your Market?" 16 min. 1982. Guides entrepreneur in developing marketing strategies. Covers six major areas of well-developed market plan, including specifics of product or service, sales and promotion methods, pricing, distribution, and location.

"What Will Your New Venture Demand?" 20 min. 1983. Challenges those planning careers to examine their strengths and interests and assess what role is best.

"What's the Best Business for You?" 16 min. 1982. Provides tools for the aspiring entrepreneur to assess a business idea, including personal considerations, possible growth, income, and market share.

"Who Will Help You Start Your Venture?" 20 min. 1983. Explores assistance needed by and available to starting business entrepreneurs. Lists sources of help and presents creative methods of getting information and evaluating assistance.

"Who Will Your Customers Be?" 18 min. 1982. Shows that market research clarifies the goals of a business, forming the basis for almost all other planning.

922.

"Success World"
Southerby Productions, 5000 E. Anaheim
    St., Long Beach, CA 90
¾- or ½-inch videocassette. 22 min.
    Color. Level I–A.
Art Linkletter comments on successful entrepreneurs.

923.

"Technical Venture Strategies"

Massachusetts Institute of Technology, 77 Massachusetts Ave., Cambridge, MA 02139

¾- or ½-inch videocassette. 49 min. Color.

Discusses entrepreneurial alternatives, investments in small companies, joint ventures and new-venture spin-offs, internal venture generation, and directions for enhancing new-venture results.

924.

"Teenage Entrepreneurs, Part I: Teenagers Learning About Entrepreneurship"

Social Issues Resources Series, Inc., P. O. Box 2507, Boca Raton, FL 33432

¾- or ½-inch videocassette. 25 min. Color. Level JC, A.

Focuses on teenage entrepreneurs who own their own business. Profiles four student businesses and discusses regulating competition on campus.

925.

"Teenage Entrepreneurs, Part II: Teenagers Design Programs for Home Computers"

Social Issues Resources Series, Inc., P.O. Box 2507, Boca Raton, FL 33432

¾- or ½-inch videocassette. 25 min. Color. Level JC, A.

Illustrates the increasing popularity among teenagers of designing computer programs and becoming involved in computer-related businesses.

926.

"Trader Vic's Used Cars"

Producer: Charles Braverman, P.O. Box 1048, Santa Monica, CA 90406

Distributor: Encyclopedia Britannica Educational Corp., 425 N. Michigan Ave., Chicago, IL 60611

¾- or ½-inch videocassette. 10 min. Color. 1976. Level JC.

Presents a film portrait of Victor Snyder, a Southern California used car dealer. Portrays Trader Vic, talks frankly about his business, and shares his secrets of success.

927.

"Westside Store"

Producer: Amitai Film, 117 E. Mt. Pleasant, Philadelphia, PA 19119

Distributor: Barr Films, 3490 E. Foothill Blvd., Pasadena, CA 91107

¾- or ½-inch videocassette. 23 min. Color. 1982. Level I–JC. LC Card No. 83-706626.

Presents the economics of running a small business through a story about an ethnically mixed inner-city gang that turns from vandalism to operating its own legitimate business, a second-hand store.

928.

"What Is Business"

Producer: Sandler Institutional Films, Inc., 1250 Siskiyou Blvd., Ashland, OR 97520

Distributor: Barr Films, 3490 E. Foothill Blvd., Pasadena, CA 91107

¾- or ½-inch videocassette. 10 min. Color. 1973. Level H–C, A.

Acquaints the student with what a business is, how it operates, who operates it, and who is responsible for making short-term decisions and overall policy. Observes the operation of a one-man boutique leather shop in contrast with the operation of a large manufacturing company.

929.

"Women Business Owners"

Martha Stuart, Anthony St., P.O. Box 127, Hillsdale, NY 12529

¾-inch videocassette. 28 min. Color. 1977. Level JC, A. LC Card No. 80-707156.

Features a group of women entrepreneurs talking about the rewards of a business career, as well as the motivations, doubts, guilts, and surprises they found along the way.

TEACHING MATERIALS

In this section are included 35mm filmstrips; prepared transparencies; and teaching kits consisting of slides or filmstrips with an audio cassette, record, or script. Many of the materials listed in Section 4 under Films, Audio Tapes, and Videotapes are also appropriate for instructional use.

930.

Business Organization, a series
Producer: Coronet Instructional Films
Distributor: Random House Inc., 400
    Hahn Rd., Westminster, MD 21157
Filmstrip. Color. 1972. Level H–C.
Titles in series:

> Accounting
> Management
> Marketing
> Production
> Services
> Types of Ownership

931.

Business Procedures: Service Area, a series
Producer: Hoffman Occupational Learn-
    ing Systems
Distributor: Prentice-Hall Media, 150
    White Plains Rd., Tarrytown, NY 10591
Filmstrip with cassette. Color.
Series titles: "Business Ethics and Com-
pany Policy," "Customer Relations."

932.

"Chance-Taking"
Guidance Association, Communications
    Park Box 3000, Mt. Kisco, NY 10549
Filmstrip with tape. 72 frames. Color.
    1974. Level H. LC Card No. 74-733691.

Discusses the issue of value judgments through the story of Tom, who's taking the risk of going into business for himself and cannot understand why his friend John won't join him.

933.

The Economics of Business, a series
Producer: Teaching Resources Films
Distributor: Random House, 400 Hahn
    Rd., Westminster, MD 21157
Filmstrip with record/cassette/script. 24
    frames. Color. Level H, C. LC Card No.
    73-733687.
The series examines business in America, ranging from the one-person operation to the giant conglomerate. Discusses product or service as related to profit and consumer goods, pricing, costs, plants, equipment, and raw materials. Describes the competitive marketplace. Titles in series: "Economics and Business Enterprise," "Business and the Public Interest."

934.

"Entrepreneur"
Guidance Association, Communications
    Park Box 3000, Mt. Kisco, NY 10549
Filmstrip with tape. 56 frames. Color.
    1974. Level JC. LC Card No. 74-735134.

935.

"Fergi Goes Inc.," Parts 1 and 2

Walt Disney Educational Media Co., 500
    S. Buena Vista St., Burbank, CA 91521
Filmstrip with record/cassette. 71 frames.
    Color. 1978. Level JC–H. LC Card No.
    78-730968.

Uses the story of a T-shirt business
started by a young man to explain the
differences between a partnership and a
corporation. Shows how Randy Ferguson's business incorporates and expands,
and deals with the business problems
created by expansion.

936.

"The Florist"

Society for Visual Education, Inc.,
    Division of the Singer Co., 1345 Diver-
    sey Parkway, Chicago, IL 60614
Filmstrip with record/script. 80 frames.
    Color. 1975. Level I–C. LC Card No. 76-
    730120.

Introduces many careers available in
floristry, featuring a flower shop manager
and describing his duties. Points out the
pressures involved in a successful operation, and the skills needed.

937.

"Franchising"

Lansford Publishing Co., P.O. Box 8711,
    1088 Lincoln Ave., San Jose, CA 95155
8 × 10 prepared transparencies. 13
    transparencies. Color.

Presents franchising as a system of
distribution enables the supplier to
arrange for a dealer to handle his or her
product or service under certain mutu-
ally agreed upon conditions. Shows that
phenomenal growth in the franchise
business has occurred since World War II.

938.

"How a Business Operates"

Society for Visual Education, Inc.,
    Division of the Singer Co., 1345 Diver-
    sey Parkway, Chicago, IL 60614

Filmstrip. Color. 1978. Level H, A. LC
    Card No. 79-730046.
Indicates the risks and amount of financing needed to start a business and shows
that the basic object of a business is to
make a profit.

939.

*Introduction to Business and Small Business
Management,* a series

Lansford Publishing Company, P.O. Box
    8711, 1088 Lincoln Ave., San Jose, CA
    95155
9 × 11 prepared transparencies. Color.
    1972.
Series titles: "Business Failure," "How to
Start Your Own Business and Succeed."

940.

"The Job Is Yours"

Walt Disney Educational Media Co., 500
    S. Buena Vista St., Burbank, CA 91521
Filmstrip with record/cassette. 53 frames.
    Color. 1977. Level E. LC Card No. 77-
    731103.

Describes how, when Gopher organizes a
work party to rebuild Kanga's living
room, the friends learn about the exchange of wages for labor services, the
advantages of specialized labor, the role
of the entrepreneur, and profits as payment for taking business risks.

941.

"Making It in Your Own Business," Parts 1
and 2

Current Affairs Films, Division of Key
    Productions, 346 Ethan Allen Hwy.,
    Ridgefield, CT 06877
Filmstrip with cassette. Color. Level J–A.
Gives examples of starting one's own
business and offers practical advice for
setting up moneymaking projects.

942.

"Music Retailing"

Producer: Activity Records, 1937 Grand
    Ave., Baldwin, NY 11510

Distributor: Educational Activities, Inc.,
P.O. Box 392, Freeport, NY 11520
Filmstrip with cassette/script. 67 frames.
Color. 1976. Level I–H. LC Card No. 77-
730224.

943.

**"Owning and Operating Your Own Business,"
Parts 1 and 2**
Pathescope Educational Films, Inc.,
Communications Park Box 6000, Mt.
Kisco, NY 10549
Filmstrip with cassette. 88 frames. Color.
1980. Level I–C, A. LC Card No. 80-
730250.
Part 1 includes interviews with people
who have opened their own businesses.
Part 2 introduces the concept of owning
and operating one's own business.

944.

"Productivity"
Society for Visual Education, Inc.,
Division of the Singer Co., 1345 Diver-
sey Parkway, Chicago, IL 60614
Filmstrip with cassette. 54 frames. Color.
1978. Level H, A. LC Card No. 79-
730046.

945.

"Sellers"
Producer: Columbia Broadcasting System,
51 W. 52nd St., New York, NY 10019
Distributor: Phoenix/BFA Films and
Video, Inc., 470 Park Ave. S., New York,
NY 10016
Filmstrip with record, cassette, script. 33
frames. Color. 1973. Level E–I. LC
Card No. 74-732720.
Tells a story about a man who decides to
form his own company to distribute jelly
beans in order to show the kinds of jobs
and duties that are performed by seller in
a company that makes and sells goods.

946.

"Small Business Owners"
Producer: Jam Handy School Service, Inc.

Distributor: Prentice-Hall Media, 150
White Plains Rd., Tarrytown, NY 10591
Filmstrip with record/cassette. 47 frames.
1974. Color. Level I–JC. LC Card No.
74-735003.

947.

"Sound Investment"
Encyclopedia Britannica Educational
Corporation, 425 N. Michigan Ave.,
Chicago, IL 60611
Filmstrip with cassette. 114 frames.
Color. Level H.
Presents the story of small-business
development. Shows three young people
who share a recording business and
discover that success encourages expansion. Looks at basic business concepts
such as working capital, productivity,
and public stock offerings.

948.

"Starting a New Business"
Producer: Hawkhill Associates, Inc.
Distributor: Random House, 400 Hahn
Rd., Westminster, MD 21157
Filmstrip with cassette. Color. Level H–C,
A.
Follows the initiation of a new business
venture. Discusses creation of a business
plan, financing a business, and the
legal, accounting, and insurance needs of
businesses.

949.

Store Organization, a series
Fairchild Visuals, 7 E. 12th St., New York,
NY 10003
Slides with cassette. Color. 1975. Level H,
C, A.
"Store Operations." 25 frames. LC
Card No. 80-72087. Focuses on the
various functions of a store's operations
team, including customer service, deliv-
ery traffic control, security, and mainte-
nance.
"Store Personnel." 24 frames. LC
Card No. 80-720825. Outlines the func-
tions of store personnel departments

from the initial interview to employee counseling services. Enumerates the responsibilities of the personnel manager and employment officers and discusses topics such as employment advertising, applicant testing, training programs, morale, and employee records.

950.
"Transparency Masters for *Business: Its Nature and Environment*"
South-Western Publishing Co., 5101 Madison Rd., Cincinnati, OH 45227
8 × 10 transparency master; 96 transparencies. Color. 1972. Level C. LC Card No. 72-733745.
Correlated with the textbook *Business: Its Nature and Environment—An Introduction*.

951.
"Types of Ownership"
Producer: Coronet Instructional Films

Distributor: Random House, 400 Hahn Rd., Westminster, MD 21157
Filmstrip with record or cassette. 50 frames. Color. 1972. Level H–C. LC Card No. 72-735079.
Explains four types of business ownership—sole proprietorship, partnership, cooperative, and corporation—and the advantages and disadvantages of each.

952.
"We Are the Economy"
Eye Gate Media, 3333 Elston Ave., Chicago, IL 60618
Filmstrip with tape. 49 frames. Color. 1973. Level I–H. LC Card No. 74-732569.
Shows how businesses are interconnected and how each action affects other businesses and the general public.

RECORDS FOR THE BLIND

953.
"The Garage Sale Manual—Alternate
Economics for the People"
Producer: American Printing House for
the Blind, P. O. Box 6085, Louisville,
KY 40206
Distributor: Library of Congress, Division
for Blind and Physically Handicapped,
1291 Taylor St. NW, Washington, DC
20542
8 rpm 10-inch record. 6 sides.
Examines the garage sale as a relatively
new and easy way of making extra cash.
Offers advice on starting such small
businesses as auctions, restaurants, and
real estate offices.

954.
"How to Start and Run a Successful Mail
Order Business"
Producer: American Foundation for the
Blind, 15 W. 16th St., New York, NY
10011
Distributor: Library of Congress, Division
for Blind and Physically Handicapped,
1291 Taylor St. NW, Washington, DC
20542
16⅔ rpm 10-inch record. 12 sides.
Explains the principles of successful
mail-order operations. Includes topics on
how to select, purchase, and price
suitable mail-order products, and how to
write and design effective advertise-
ments. Intended primarily for beginners.

955.
"The Worm Farm"
Library of Congress, Division for Blind
and Physically Handicapped, 1291
Taylor St. NW, Washington, DC 20542
1⅞ips cassette.
Tells how Charlie Morgan started and
built a family worm farm enterprise that
became a $20 million business. Gives
information on finances, selling and
buying, and supply and demand in the
worm business.

SECTION 5.

Computer Systems for Small Businesses

On-Line Information Sources   171
Software Packages   176

The computer age already has reshaped traditional methods of planning, analyzing, and managing business enterprises. Information, once painstakingly obtained, now explodes on CRTs or from printers in a multitude of facilitating formats shaped by software packages that can be tailored to the entrepreneur's personal specifications. Although nothing is more important than intelligent and experienced judgment, the ability to use computers wisely is an extremely valuable tool in almost every aspect of business management.

ALLAN A. KENNEDY
Author
Director, APM, Inc.
New York, New York

As society becomes more computer and telecommunications literate, the potential for innovation and improvement in our businesses will begin to explode. The smaller business will have virtually the same access to information and knowledge as the large firm. Everyone will learn of important developments, opportunities, and breakthroughs at the same time, opening the door for higher levels of innovation throughout the country. Becoming involved with electronic information sources is critical for all small-business operations.

Information is the energy that fuels entrepreneurship, and turning on that energy can help ensure the success of small businesses.

This section contains information about how entrepreneurs or small-business owner-managers can more effectively use their personal computer. Note that information on choosing and setting up a computer system for a small business appears in the chapter on Computers in Section 2. Ideas on moneymaking ventures using a computer you already own are found in Small-Business Opportunities in Section 1.

This section is subdivided into chapters describing on-line information sources and software packages particularly valuable to small businesses. On-line information sources allow the small-business owner to gain almost instant access to a variety of usable information, including credit ratings on suppliers and customers, general business news, business trends, and much more. The section on software applications provides a wide selection of packages, dealing with everything from accounting to inventory control to mailing lists and much more.

ON-LINE
INFORMATION SOURCES

Today, information can be obtained quickly and easily from a host of on-line data bases, all of which are accessible to anyone with a computer, a modem, and the appropriate password. Increasingly, it will be to this new source that entrepreneurs and small businesses will turn for insights, guidance, and practical information on their own operations and markets. In fact, the emergence of on-line data bases will bring new strength, vigor, and competitive energy to small businesses throughout the country.

What follows is a description of several specifically focused *business* data bases. While overwhelming in the amount of information available, this list only begins to scratch the surface. There are hundreds of other data bases—scientific, demographic, technical—available on-line. It is worth spending some time at your local library exploring the diversity of today's data bases. Most librarians can acquaint you with on-line information and help you get started. There are also several sourcebooks on on-line information; two that come highly recommended are:

Inc. Magazine's Databasics: Your Guide to Online Business Information, by Doran Howitt and Marvin I. Weinberger. New York: Garland Publishing, Inc., 1984. ISBN 0-8240-7290-1.

Directory of Online Databases, by Cuadra Associates, Inc., 2001 Wilshire Blvd., Suite 305, Santa Monica, CA 90403. ISSN 0193-6840.

It's important to understand that anyone can now obtain information that just a few years ago was available only to the wealthiest and largest organizations. Today, questions about a particular product or market, the latest technology, a specific company, advertising, or management techniques can all be answered using this new electronic library system. The real trick, of course, lies in asking the right questions and in securing the expertise needed to effectively search the data bases. It is possible, for example, to ask for the most recent sales figures and sales projections for your particular product or service. Or you can gather information on how others in your business are meeting new opportunities or problems. You can test an idea by searching to see if others have tried that particular idea or something similar. You may even be able to locate and actually purchase hard-to-find supplies through this versatile medium.

Much of the preliminary research for this handbook was accomplished through on-line searching by TRAC, Inc., of Alexandria, Virginia. For information on any of TRAC's electronic research services, write them at 300 N. Washington St., Suite 401, Alexandria, VA 22314.

Listings include the name of the data base; the type of information contained; the format type, whether reference (bibliographic) or full-text; the name of the producer and name of on-line service; and description of information, including frequency of updates.

956.
Bizdate
Business and industry; U.S. commodities; currency exchange rates; economic and finance news. Reference
Producer and On-Line Service: The Source
Contains nine files on U.S. financial, economic, and business news. In "The Board Room," groups such as the American Enterprise Institute, the Business Roundtable, the Media Institute, and private corporations offer information on subjects that affect business and business leaders. In "Business Horizons," current trends, research findings, economic conditions, and unusual business enterprises are reported upon. Other files include: Commodities Index; Currency Rates; Financial Headlines; Market Indicators; Stockcheck; U.S. News Washington Letter. Current information, updated throughout the day.

957.
Bliss
Administration and management. Reference
Producer: Gesellschaft fuer Betriebswirtschaftliche Information MbH
On-Line Service: FIZ Technik
Contains approximately 61,000 citations, with some abstracts, to German and international literature on business management. In German. Covers period from 1975 to date, updated with about 850 citations a month.

958.
Business
Business and industry; international trade. Reference

Producer: Online GmbH
Approximately 12,000 references, with summaries, to worldwide trade opportunities and business contacts. Covers a wide range of opportunities such as imports and exports, sales, services, research and development, technology, and cooperative ventures in manufacturing, marketing, and investment. In English, French, and German. Current information, updated throughout the day.

959.
Business and Law Review
Business and industry; law. Full text
Producer: Corporate Agents, Inc.
On-Line Service: CompuServe Executive Information Services
Full-text articles on a variety of U.S. business and legal topics. Current U.S. information, updated weekly.

960.
The Business Computer
Computers and computer industry. Full text
Producer: P/K Associates
On-Line Service: NewsNet, Inc.
Contains "The Business Computer," a syndicated column containing news, product reviews, forecasts of developments in the field of microcomputer hardware and software, and purchase recommendations. International data, from October 1983 to date, updated weekly. Monthly minimum of $15 to NewsNet.

961.
Business Credit Services
Finance commercial credit. Full text

TRW Information Services Division,
    Business Credit Services
Contains trade payment information on
over 8 million business locations representing all major industries in the United
States. Access restricted to companies
that have a legitimate business need for
the information. Updated continuously,
throughout the day; each company
provides data every 30 to 90 days.

962.

Business Information Wire
Business and industry news. Full text
Producer: The Canadian Press
On-Line Service: CompuServe Consumer
    Information Service; CompuServe
    Executive Information Service
International business news stories from
the Canadian Press wire service. Current
week's data, updated throughout the day.

963.

Business Periodicals Index
Business and industry. Reference
Producer: The H. W. Wilson Company
On-Line Service: Wilsonline
Contains 143,000 citations to articles and
book reviews in over 300 business
periodicals from Canada, Federal Repub-
lic of Germany, France, the Netherlands,
Switzerland, United Kingdom, and
United States. Covers June 1983 to date.
Updated twice a week; about 5,500
articles a month.

964.

Business/Professional Software Database
Computers and computer industry.
    Reference

965.

Business Review Weekly
Business and industry; economics and
    financial news. Reference
Producer: John Fairfax & Sons
On-Line Service: ACI Computer Services
Contains 4,000 citations, with abstracts,

to articles from the *Australian Business
Review Weekly*. Covers 1982 to date,
updated weekly. Monthly minimum of
$25 (Australian) to ACI for access to all
AUSINET data bases.

966.

The Business Wire
Computers and computer industry.
    Reference
Producer: Business Wire
On-Line Service: CompuServe Consumer
    Information Service; CompuServe
    Executive Information Service; Mead
    Data Central (as a NEXIS data base)
Provides full-text press releases from
publicly held U.S. companies traded on
major U.S. exchanges; emphasis on high-
tech companies. CompuServe provides
current information, updated continuously. Mead Data Central provides data
from September 1983 to date, and updates about 100 records a day.

967.

Canadian Business and Current Affairs
Business and industry; news. Reference
Producer: Micromedia Limited
On-Line Service: Dialog Information
    Services, Inc.
370,000 citations to articles in 175
English-language business periodicals
and 7 daily newspapers published in
Canada. Covers July 1980 to date; about
12,000 records a month updated.

968.

CBI (Canadian Business Index)
Administration and management; busi-
    ness and industry. Reference
Producer: Micromedia Limited
On-Line Service: QL Systems Limited
Over 170 citations in Canadian English-
language business and trade publications.
Subjects include business activities,
technical developments and new-product
announcements in all major manufacturing areas, corporate activities, finance,
computer science, industrial relations,

management, real estate, corporate taxation, service industries, and utilities. Covers July 1975 to July 1981; not updated.

969.
Corporate Acquisitions and Dispositions of Businesses
Corporations; taxes. Full text
Producer: Mark A. Stephens, Ltd.
On-Line Service: NewsNet, Inc.
Full text of *Tax Service for Corporate Acquisitions and Dispositions of Businesses*, a newsletter covering tax aspects of U.S. corporate reorganizations, incorporations, separations, liquidations, etc. Covers 1982 to date; updated monthly. Monthly minimum of $15 to NewsNet; differential charges for newsletter subscribers and nonsubscribers.

970.
Management and Marketing Abstracts
Administration and management; marketing. Reference
Producer: The Research Association for the Paper and Board, Printing and Packaging Industries
On-Line Service: Pergamon InfoLine Ltd.
Theoretical and practical areas of management and marketing, with abstracts. International citations from 1976 to date, with about 130 records updated every two weeks.

971.
Management Contents
Administration and management; business and industry. Reference
Producer: Management Contents
On-Line Service: BRS (Management Contents); BRS After Dark (Management Contents); Data-Star (Management Contents); Dialog Information Services, Inc. (Management Contents).
Citations with abstracts in business and management from over 725 journals, proceedings, books, courses, newsletters,

research reports, and tabloids. Wide range of topics, international scope. Covers September 1974 to date, with about 4,000 records a month updated.

972.
McGraw-Hill New Business Books/Software
Catalogs of books and periodicals. Reference
Producer: McGraw-Hill, Inc.
On-Line Service: NewsNet, Inc.
Lists software, books, films, and training materials available from McGraw-Hill Book Company. Users can place orders on-line at discounted prices. Covers July 1984 to date, updated every two weeks. Monthly minimum of $15 to NewsNet.

973.
Small Business Profit Digest (formerly Financial Management Advisor)
Administration and management. Full text
Producer: Newsletter Management Corporation
On-Line Service: NewsNet, Inc.
Full text of *Small Business Profit Digest*, a newsletter covering financial management of privately owned U.S. businesses. Covers June 1982 to date, updated monthly. Monthly minimum of $15 to NewsNet required; differential charges for newsletter subscribers and nonsubscribers.

974.
Small Business Reports
Small businesses and professional services. Full text
Producer: Stevens Features
On-Line Service: CompuServe Consumer Information Service; CompuServe Executive Information Service
Ideas and guidelines on how to operate a small business (up to $50 million in annual sales) or professional practice profitably. Practical ways to cut costs and increase profits are emphasized. Current information, updated weekly.

975.

Small Business Tax Review

Small businesses and professional
   services; taxes. Full text
Producer: Hooksett Publishing, Inc.
On-Line Service: NewsNet, Inc.
Provides full text of *The Small Business*
Tax Review, a newsletter that covers U.S.
tax news and developments affecting
small businesses. Covers October 1983 to
date, updated monthly. Monthly minimum of $15 to NewsNet; differential
charges for newsletter subscribers and
nonsubscribers.

SOFTWARE PACKAGES

Within a very short time the computer has changed the world. Every occupation, every organization, and every business has been affected in one way or another. From where we conduct our businesses and what we do there, to how and when we do it, the computer has revolutionized the very fabric of the business world. Quite literally, the ubiquitous computer is as necessary as yesterday's pencil, paper, and telephone. The computer, specifically the microcomputer, has become a business necessity. It can literally make the difference between failure and success.

Essentially nothing more than a box of plastic and steel, filled with circuit boards, microchips, and a spaghetti of rainbow-colored wires, the computer responds to our beck and call. Churning out financial reports and letters, it can manage accounts and keep track of everything from inventories and sales to personal appointment calendars. Across the board, the microcomputer allows us to manage information more effectively, whether that information is a financial report, a business letter, or an employee record. More important, the microcomputer can dramatically decrease response time in an environment where time is a critical factor.

Driving this great engine of change are hundreds of commercially available software programs—the set of commands and instructions that tell the computer how to operate. The last five years have witnessed an explosive growth in both the number and types of software programs. It would be impossible to list every software program that has a possible small-business application; that would be like presenting a list of all the types of paper and pens that have potential business applications. The software needs of a business depend on the nature of the business and the tasks that need to be done. However, software programs do differ radically in focus, application, system requirements, and price. Presented in this section is a selection of software packages that, according to their respective developers or marketers, are specifically oriented toward the small-business owner or manager.

The listings are organized by type of software (for example, all accounting packages are listed together). Each individual listing specifies the program's individual requirements such as type of computer, memory requirements, necessary hardware, language, and description, where available.

Accounting and Bookkeeping

976.
Account Keeper
Monument Computer Service, Village

Data Ctr., P.O. Box 603, Joshua Tree, CA 92252
Small-business accounting system that lets the user post to several accounts with one entry. Posting is done according to account, month, and summary of activity.

Also provides trial balance, complete check register, and monthly detailed report. Applesoft BASIC. Requires 48K. Runs on Apple II + , IIe.

977.
Account Pac II
Pacific Coast Software Corp., 3220 S. Brea Canyon Rd., Diamond Bab, CA 91765 (714) 594-8210
Checkbook manager for small business. Includes 100 user-defined accounts. For the Commodore 64.

978.
Accountant
Applied Scientific, 416 Arnold, Bozeman, MT 59715 (406) 586-1157
Software template for use with Apple-Works. Allows user to track personal cash, check, and credit card transactions. For the Apple IIc or IIe.

979.
Accounting for Micros—Small Business
James River Group, Inc., 125 N. First St., Minneapolis, MN 55401 (612) 339-2521
Set of interactive accounting programs designed for firms with under $2 million in sales per year. Includes general ledger, accounts receivable, accounts payable, inventory, payroll. Other modules include job costing and TMAN. Compiled BASIC. Requires 64K CP/M; 192K MS-DOS; or 256K Apricot and AT&T. Runs on Actrix; Apricot; Apple; AT&T; Columbia; Compaq; Corona; DEC Rainbow 100; Eagle; Epson QX-16, QX-10, Equity; Heath-Zenith Z-100, Z-150; HP 150 Touchscreen; IBM PC, PCjr, PC AT, PC XT; Kaypro 2, Kaypro 4, Kaypro 10, Kaypro 16; Morrow MD2, MD3, MD11; Osborne 1, Osborne Executive; Panasonic; Sanyo; Tava PC; TRS-80, Tandy; TeleVideo; Wang PC; Xerox 820.

980.
Accounting Partner Plus
Star Software Systems, 367 Van Ness Way, Torrance, CA 90501 (213) 533-1190
An accounting package designed to meet accounting and cost-control needs of the small-business owner. Modules include general ledger; accounts receivable, with invoicing; accounts payable, with purchasing; and payroll. Program also includes Calc Partner, a spreadsheet, and Popcorn Desktop, a resident calculator and calendar. Includes a utilities systems disk that lets users handle data errors without searching for programming solutions. Runs on IBM PC, PC XT, PC AT, and compatibles.

981.
Accounting System
Mark Data Products, 24001 Alicia Pkwy., Number 207, Mission Viejo, CA 92691 (714) 768-1551
Small-business accounting software for the TRS-80 Color Computer. Requires 32K, an 80-column printer, and one or more disk drives.

982.
Accounts Payable
Computerware, P.O. Box 668, Encinitas, CA 92024 (619) 436-3512
Helps users plan their business' growth by controlling expenditures and forecasting cash requirements. Assists a small business in managing and tracking its cash requirements liabilities by collecting vendor invoice information and reporting the business' cash commitments and payment history. Includes a check writer and payment forecast reports in addition to standard payables reports. Requires 64K. For the TRS-80 Color Computer with two disk drives.

983.
The Aviation Manager
Micro-Time Management System, Inc.,

17023 W. Ten Mile Rd., Southfield, MI
48075 (313) 557-6637

An integrated series of accounting software especially designed to serve the requirements of small business. Includes general ledger, accounts receivable with order entry, accounts payable with order entry, and mailing list processing. C-BASIC, CB-80. Requires 64K.

984.
Bank Account Manager

Innovative Educational Products, 10917 Sonja, Knoxville, TN 37922 (615) 483-4915

Checkbook accounting program can track two separate accounts for up to 25 separate expense categories. Allows for easy entry and for summary accounting information for each expense category for tax purposes. Will handle thousands of checks per year for a small business. Runs on Apple II, IIe, IIc.

985.
Basic Accounting System Accounts Payable

Hayden Software Co., 601 Kendall Square, Cambridge, MA 02139 (617) 494-1200

Allows a small business to manage its cash disbursements, keep on-hand cash to a minimum, and determine cash requirements. Compiled M-BASIC. Requires 46K. Runs on IBM PC, Apple III; requires two disk drives and printer.

986.
BK-2

Accountability, 1500 Adams, Suite 300, Costa Mesa, CA 92626 (714) 957-2976

Small-business bookkeeping software. Includes checkbook management and banking, loan calculations, loan payoff schedules, and display and print reports. For 64K MS-DOS 1.1 systems. Runs on IBM PC or compatible.

987.
Bookkeep

Dynacomp, Inc., 1064 Gravel Rd., Webster, NY 14580 (716) 442-8960

General ledger and financial statement preparation program designed for small business use. 5¼- and 8-inch disks available. Requires 56K. Runs on CP/M-based machines with C-BASIC.

988.
BPI Accounts Payable

Texas Instruments, Data Systems Group, P.O. Box 1444, Houston, TX 77251 (713) 895-4777

Enables small business to take advantage of computerized accounting techniques by providing cash-management tools like vendor control and check writing. M-BASIC. Requires 128K. Runs on TI Professional with Winchester second drive.

989.
Brantex Accounts Receivable

Brantex, Inc., Color Software Services Div., P.O. Box 1708, Greenville, TX 75401 (214) 454-3674

Designed to meet requirements of most small-business users. Functions as a stand-alone system or integrates with the Small Business Accounting package (see #1024). Requires 32K. Runs on TRS-80 Color Computer.

990.
Brantex Payroll

Brantex, Inc., Color Software Services Div., P.O. Box 1708, Greenville, TX 75401 (214) 454-3674

Designed for maintaining personnel and payroll data. Amounts can be transferred to Small Business Accounting package (see #1024) for financial reporting. System suited for all states except Oklahoma and Delaware. Requires 32K. Runs on TRS-80 Color Computer.

991.
Chequemate Plus
Masterworks Software, Inc., 2444 N. Palms, Long Beach, CA 90806 (213) 539-7486
Designed for small-business or home financial needs. Features include income statements, balance sheets, graphs, budgeting, accounts payable, automated teller transactions, cash control, and charge cards. Runs on IBM PC.

992.
Coco-Accountant
Federal Hill Software, 8134 Scotts Level Rd., Baltimore, MD 21208 (301) 521-4886
Lists and totals entries by month and by account, payee, or income source. Flags specified expenses and prints spread-sheets. Runs on TRS-80 Color Computer.

993.
Compact Basic Bookkeeping Course
ZYPCOM, P.O. Box 3421, Boise, ID 83703 (208) 345-2387
Thirty-lesson course covers all the basics of double-entry bookkeeping in a small-business environment. Self-testing questions and answers included. Re-quires 16K. Runs on Apple II, IIe with Applesoft; TRS-80 Model III, Model 4.

994.
Complete Personal Accountant
Futurehouse, Inc., 310 W. Franklin St., P.O. Box 3470, Chapel Hill, NC 27514
Five-program money management package for the home or small business. Runs on Atari 400, 800 (48K required); Commodore 64, VIC-20 (64K required); TRS-80 Color Computer (16K required for disk, 32K required for cassette).

995.
Compute!
Compute! Publications Inc., 825 Seventh Ave., New York, NY 10019 (212) 265-8360

Book of 13 programs for small-business accounting systems. For the Commodore 64.

996.
Continental Payroll
Software Guild, 2935 Whipple Rd., Union City, CA 94587 (415) 487-5900
Designed for small-business payroll needs, from printing payroll checks to employee lists. Runs on Apple II, II+; Franklin Ace 1000.

997.
Credit Card Tracking
Data Soft of New Hampshire, 22 Stevens Ave., Merrimack, NH 03054 (603) 424-5217
Small-business utility that allows user to enter card charges, payments, and fees or service charges for each credit card. Cassette. Requires 16K. For the TRS-80 Model I, Model III.

998.
Disk Double Entry
Custom Software Engineering Inc., 807 Minutemen Causeway (D-2), Cocoa Beach, FL 32931 (305) 783-1083
Accounting software for small-business use. Will handle up to 300 accounts. Produces reports and provides an average of 1,400 transactions per diskette. Re-quires 32K and Extended Color BASIC. Runs on IBM PC or compatible.

999.
Disk-O-Check
High Technology Software Products, Inc., 8200 N. Classen Blvd., Suite 104, P.O. Box 60406, Oklahoma City, OK 73146 (405) 848-0480
Personal accountant designed to handle small-business finances. User can record over 2,000 checks and deposits and access them at a later time. Program can handle multiple accounts. Categorizes checks by expense classifications. Pro-

vides user with a detailed report that summarizes the checks and the total amount spent for each category. User can search for a particular check number, amount, or check description. Applesoft BASIC. Requires 48K. Runs on Apple II+, IIe.

1000.
Dynamic Accountant
H & E Computronics, Inc., 50 N. Pascack Rd., Spring Valley, NY 10977 (914) 425-1535

Complete business accounting system specifically developed for small businesses with ten or fewer employees. Keeps track of all income and expenditures and prepares monthly, year-to-date, and annual summaries. Generates balance sheets, check register summaries, payroll register summaries, and profit and loss statements. Stores all information necessary for income tax forms and government-required payroll forms. Prints checks and automatically stores check information. BASIC. Requires 128K and two disk drives. Runs on AT&T; IBM PC and compatibles, PC XT, PCjr, PC AT.

1001.
Dynamic Check Register
H & E Computronics, Inc., 50 N. Pascack Rd., Spring Valley, NY 10977 (914) 425-1535

Stores every check detail necessary for small-business needs. Allows for automatic monthly payments, permits multiple account categories for each check, prints complete names and addresses of payees on checks, provides monthly and yearly totals of all tax-deductible and nondeductible transactions by category. BASIC. Requires 128K and two disk drives. Runs on AT&T; IBM PC and compatibles, PC XT, PCjr, PC AT.

1002.
Entrepreneur's Accountant III
Personal Software Co., 1580 E. Dawn Dr.,

Salt Lake City, UT 84121 (801) 943-6908

General ledger for the businessman or woman working at home or for any small, emerging company. Includes general journal, four special journals, ledgers, reports, graphs. Source code available. Compiled BASIC-A. Requires 128K. Runs on IBM PC, PC XT, PC AT.

1003.
EZ-Ledger
Highlands Computer Services, 14422 SE 132nd, Renton, WA 98056 (206) 235-1530

Recordkeeping system for running a small business. Requires 48K. Runs on Apple II.

1004.
Family Vehicle Expense
Atari Corp., 1196 Borregas Ave., Sunnyvale, CA 94088 (408) 745-2000

Information is stored on a monthly basis for a period of up to one year. The package allows up to 6 vehicles in 9 different expense categories. Will accommodate up to 10 credit cards and permits up to 12 fuel entries per vehicle per month. Requires 48K. For the Atari 800.

1005.
Financial Management System II
Roger Wagner Publishing, Inc., 10761 Woodside Ave., Suite E, P.O. Box 582, Santee, CA 92071 (619) 562-3670

For small-business accounting applications. Maintains multiple accounts, generates complete reports, and stores unlimited files. Global and specific search and automatic tax coding are featured. Requires 48K. For the Apple II.

1006.
Financial Management System II with CheckWriter
Computerized Management Systems, 1039 Cadiz Dr., Simi, CA 93065 (805) 526-0151

An accounting system designed for the small business. Account Auditor totals files by tax code for any one- to 12-month period with year-to-date totals. Account Manager is an error-avoiding entry system that includes edit, sort, reconcile, disk files, and balance. Budget Manager prints reports for any one- to 12-month period with summations. CheckWriter allows the user to enter checks from files. Search Records provides searches of all files; system utility designates up to 100 item and tax code macros. Requires 64K. For the IBM PC.

1007.

Financial Management System III
Computerized Management Systems, 1039 Cadiz Dr., Simi, CA 93065 (805) 526-0151
Maintains an unlimited number of checkbooks, savings accounts, petty cash, charge cards, and separate accounts. Through the use of file chaining, an unlimited number of records can be stored. All records can be edited for any previous month or year. Runs on IBM PC (requires 64K), Apple II + (48K).

1008.

Frontier Technologies Payroll
Frontier Technologies Corp., 3510 N. Oakland Ave., Milwaukee, WI 53211 (414) 964-8689
Calculates payroll checks and deductions and keeps track of year-to-date payroll figures for a small business of 100 or fewer employees. Requires 64K. Runs on IBM PC, PC XT.

1009.

Hardisk Accounting Series
Great Plains Software, 1701 SW 38th St., Fargo, ND 58103 (701) 281-0550
An accounting software program for small business. Includes general ledger with financial reporting and budgeting, accounts receivable, accounts payable, payroll, and inventory management with point-of-sale invoicing and job cost. UCSD Pascal. Requires 512K. Runs on Apple Macintosh.

1010.

The Home Accountant
Arrays, Inc., 6711 Valjean Ave., Van Nuys, CA 91406 (818) 994-1899
Small-business financial utility that keeps track of up to 200 budget categories. Five checkbooks, and all cash and credit card transactions. MS-BASIC, Z-BASIC. Runs on Apple II, II +, IIe, IIc, Macintosh (requires 48K); Atari 400, 800, 1200 with 850 interface card (40K); Compaq; Commodore 64; Epson QX-10 (64K); Executive (64K); Franklin Ace 1000; IBM PC, PC XT, PCjr (128K); Kaypro II, 4; Osborne (64K); TI Professional (128K); TRS-80 Model II, Model 4; Wang PC (128K); Zenith 110/120 (128K); requires two disk drives.

1011.

Home Accountant and Financial Planner
Arrays, Inc/Continental Software, 6711 Valjean Ave., Van Nuys, CA 91406 (818) 901-8828
Accounting and financial planning software for small-business use. For the Macintosh computer.

1012.

In-House Accountant
United Software Industries Inc., 8399 Topanga Canyon Blvd., Suite 200, Canoga Park, CA 91304
Accounting software for small-business and personal applications. For IBM PC, PC XT, and compatibles.

1013.

Micro Ledger
Data Consulting Group, 2311 W. 5700 S., Roy, UT 84067 (801) 773-8080
Assists in organizing the checking account of a small business. Helps plan and maintain budgets. Assists in balanc-

ing and reconciling checking accounts.
Searches and totals to any keyword.
Pascal. Requires 64K. Runs on Columbia,
Chameleon, IBM PC, PC XT and compatibles.

1014.
My Accountant
Ensign Software, 9522 Linstock, Boise, ID
83704 (208) 378-8086
A ledger program for small-business use,
which can handle up to 150 user-defined
accounts. Some features included are
macro codes, editing and updating
capabilities, as well as ability to print
flags for tax-deductible items, trend
charts, financial statements, and itemized
lists. A maximum of 16,384 entries can
be made. Data files are limited only by
disk drive size. Searches can be done by
date, item number, or amount. Compiled
BASIC. Requires 128K. Runs on IBM PC,
PC AT, PCjr.

1015.
PAM (Personal Accounts Manager)
S. E. Button, IBM PC Consultant, P.O. Box
837, Florissant, MO 63032 (314) 831-
8939
A financial accounting system specifically designed for small-business use.
Provides check writing and cash accounting. A sample of accounts for small
business is included in the documentation. Produces financial reports, audit
trails, master lists, maintenance lists, etc.
BASIC. Requires 64K. For the IBM PC.

1016.
Payroll Management
Timeworks Inc., 444 Lake Cook Rd.,
Deerfield, IL 60015 (312) 948-9200
Menu-driven accounting software for
payroll. Produces reports and can be
integrated with other Timeworks Man-
agement Information software. For the
Commodore 64.

1017.
Peachpak 4
Peachtree Software, Inc., 4355 International Blvd., Norcross, GA 30093 (404)
564-5700
Package of three interactive business
applications programs intended for small
business with limited microcomputer
capacity. Includes accounts receivable,
accounts payable, and general ledger
programs. M-BASIC, PC-BASIC. Runs on
Apple II, II+, IIe; IBM PC; requires
Language card, Z-80 softcard, 80- or 132-
column printer, and two disk drives.

1018.
Practical Accountant
Softlink, 3255-2 Scott Blvd., Santa Clara,
CA 95051 (800) 633-6300; (800) 222-
1244 in California
Single-entry, small-business accounting
software for Apple IIe, IBM PC, and
compatibles.

1019.
Property Management
HELU Software Corp., 627 Kaiemi St.,
Kailua, HI 96734
An accounting program for small business designed for rapid data manipulation and sorting. Complete tenant file
maintenance and preparation of aged ren-
tals-due summary and monthly statements are provided. Capable of updating
income and expense for each unit and
printing disbursement checks on pre-
printed forms. Custom modifications
available. Runs on IBM Displayer, IBM
PC, PC AT, PC XT, and NEC APC.

1020.
Sales Analysis Management
Timeworks Inc., 444 Lake Cook Rd.,
Deerfield, IL 60015 (312) 948-9200
Menu-driven accounting software for
sales analysis. Produces reports and can
be integrated with other Timeworks
Management Information software. For
the Commodore 64.

1021.

The Shoebox Accountant

CYMA–McGraw-Hill, 2160 E. Brown Rd.,
  Mesa, AZ 85203 (602) 835-8880
Offers small business a comprehensive,
fully integrated accounting system
including general ledger, accounts receiv-
able, accounts payable, and payroll.
CYMA C-OPT. Requires 128K. Runs on
Altos; Apple II, IIe, IIc; Cromemco; Data
General; DEC; Heath-Zenith; Hewlett
Packard; IBM PC, PC XT; NEC; North
Star; Osborne; TI Professional; TRS-80
Model I, Model II, Model III.

1022.

Sixty-Four Accounting

Software Design, Inc., 1945 Mitchell Ave.,
  Waterloo, IA 50702 (319) 235-1314
Provides essentials of effective money
management for small-business use, from
balancing checkbook to providing year-
end figures for taxes. Compiled BASIC.
Requires 180K and a printer. Runs on
Commodore 64.

1023.

Small Business Accountant

H & E Computronics, Inc., 50 N. Pascack
  Rd., Spring Valley, NY 10977 (914)
  425-1535
Small-business general ledger that will
track all income and expenditures and
prepare monthly summaries. Disk and
cassette available. BASIC. Requires 16K.
Runs on Apple II, III; Atari 800; Commodore; DEC; IBM PC; Kaypro; Osborne 1,
Executive; NEC; North Star; Sanyo;
SuperBrain; TeleVideo; TI; TRS-80 Model
I, Model II, Model III, Model 4, Model
12, Model 16; Xerox.

1024.

Small Business Accounting

Brantex, Inc., Color Software Services
  Div., P.O. Box 1708, Greenville, TX
  75401 (214) 454-3674
Sales-based package designed for the
nonaccounting-oriented businessperson.

Menu-driven format. Requires 32K. Runs
on TRS-80 Color Computer; TDP System
100.

1025.

Small Business Accounting

Howe Software, 14 Lexington Rd., New
  City, NY 10956 (914) 634-1824
Based on the Dome Bookkeeping Record
#612. Handles income, expenditures,
and payroll for a small business. Complete ledgers are maintained for income
and expenses on a monthly basis. Computes monthly, through-last-month, and
year-to-date summaries. Prints both
payroll and expense checks, and quarterly and year-to-date summaries. Can be
computed for all employees. BASIC.
Requires 48K TRS-80; 64K CP/M; 128K
MS-DOS. Runs on IBM PC, TRS-80,
Tandy.

1026.

Small Business Accounts Payable

Eastbench Software Products, 1290
  Cliffside Dr., Logan, UT 84321 (801)
  753-1084
Creates and maintains a list of paid bills
and open accounts payable. The list
contains: vendor number and name, un-
paid balance, date of last payment, etc.
Various reports can be generated from
this information. Cassette. Console
BASIC. Requires 16K. For the TI 99/4A.

1027.

Small Business Banking

The Professor, 4913 NW Second Terr.,
  Pompano Beach, FL 33064-2420 (305)
  427-5090
Keeps records of bank accounts and
provides analysis of receipts, payments,
and charges. Requires 48K. For the Apple
II, II +, IIe, IIc.

1028.

Small Business System

Dynacomp, Inc., 1064 Gravel Rd., Webster, NY 14580 (716) 442-8960

Handles accounting, examination, and scheduling in a professional practice. Requires 48K, two disk drives, and printer. Runs on Atari 400, 800.

Billing

Some all-purpose accounting software systems also include a billing (accounts receivable) function; see Accounting listings.

1029.
Computer Seen Accounts Receivable
The Computer Seen, Inc., 3272 E. Anaheim, Long Beach, CA 90804 (213) 494-4882
Designed to keep track of accounts receivable in a small business where there is limited accounting demand. With this package the user is able to age and generate bills on accounts electronically. With some user modification this package can be used to interface with other software to accomplish even more complex tasks. Requires 48K. Runs on Atari 800.

1030.
Instant Business
H & E Computronics, Inc., 50 N. Pascack Rd., Spring Valley, NY 10977 (914) 425-1535; (800) 431-2818 in New York
Time and billing software for accountants, doctors, consultants, and other professionals. Keeps track of billable and nonbillable time and supports up to 999 service codes. For IBM and compatibles.

1031.
The Invoicer-Plus II
Omni Software Systems, Inc., 146 N. Broad St., Griffith, IN 46319 (219) 924-3522
General billing system for accountants, lawyers, consultants, or any small business that sells a number of different

products. BASIC-A. Requires 128K. For the IBM PC.

1032.
Small Business Invoicing (Index Card)
H&E Computronics, Inc., 50 N. Pascack Rd., Spring Valley, NY 10977 (914) 425-1535
Identical to Small Business Invoicing (Rapidforms) (see next entry) except that receipts (invoices) are printed on 4 × 5 tractor-feed index cards. Prints any number of duplicate receipts or invoices. Additional receipts or invoice copies can be kept for business records. Disk or cassette available. BASIC. Requires 16K. Runs on Apple II, III; Atari 800; Commodore; DEC; IBM PC; Kaypro; Osborne 1, Executive; NEC; North Star; Sanyo; SuperBrain; TeleVideo; TI; TRS-80 Model I, Model II, Model III, Model 4, Model 12, Model 16; Xerox.

1033.
Small Business Invoicing (Rapidforms)
H&E Computronics, Inc., 50 N. Pascack Rd., Spring Valley, NY 10977 (914) 425-1535
Provides customers with invoices that are available through Rapidforms. Can be used in conjunction with small-business receivables. Disk and cassette available. BASIC. Requires 16K. Runs on Apple II, III; Atari 800; Commodore; DEC; IBM PC; Kaypro; Osborne 1, Executive; NEC; North Star; Sanyo; SuperBrain; TeleVideo; TI; TRS-80 Model I, Model II, Model III, Model 4, Model 12, Model 16; Xerox.

Financial Management

1034.
Budget Analysis Pac
H&E Computronics, Inc., 50 North Pascack Rd., Spring Valley, NY 10977

(914) 425-1535; (800) 431-2818 in New York

Software for financial statement preparation. Features balance sheet, comparative income statements, financial ratios, and cash-flow analysis. For use with Lotus 1-2-3 and Symphony software.

1035.
Dollars and Sense

Monogram, 8295 S. La Cienega Blvd., Inglewood, CA 90301 (213) 215-0529

Small-business financial planning software. Provides various reports and full-color graphs. Helps with tax preparation and loan applications. For IBM PC or compatible; Apple II, IIe.

1036.
Financial Calculator

Applied Scientific, 416 Arnold, Bozeman, MT 59715 (406) 586-1157

Software template for use with Apple-Works. Calculates simple and compound interest, present value, future value, and loan amortization. For the Apple IIe or IIc.

1037.
Financial Facts

Advanced Operating Systems, 4300 W. 62 St., P.O. Box 7092, Indianapolis, IN 46206 (317) 298-5566

Aids financial management in small-business accounting. Supports the calculation of manual, nominal, and effective interest rates; different amortization schedules such as straight-line, declining balance, and sum-of-years depreciation. Calculates required investment for future value, minimum investment for withdrawals, annuities. Apple-soft. Requires 48K. Runs on Apple II +, II, IIe.

1038.
Investment Portfolio

Applied Scientific, 416 Arnold, Bozeman, MT 59715 (406) 586-1157

Software template for use with Apple-Works. Summarizes stocks, mutual funds, bonds, and CDs. For the Apple IIe or IIc.

1039.
Job Cost System

Peachtree Software, Inc., 4355 International Blvd., Norcross, GA 30093 (404) 564-5700

Allows the small-business user to enter estimates and cost transactions, track costs and profitability on a job-by-job basis. Compiled M-BASIC. Requires 64K. Runs on AT&T PC 6300; Columbia MPC; Compaq Portable; Corona; Eagle PC, 1600; IBM PC, PC XT, PC AT; TI Professional; Zenith Z-100, Z-150.

1040.
Loan Application Pac

H&E Computronics, Inc., 50 North Pascack Rd., Spring Valley, NY 10977 (914) 425-1535; (800) 431-2818 in New York

Software computes interest, mortgage, and savings calculations. Includes loan amortization schedule, investment analysis, and cash-flow analysis. For use with Lotus 1-2-3 and Symphony software.

1041.
Real Estate Analysis

SimplexSoft Ltd., P.O. Box 445, Marion, IA 52302

Property investment analysis software for real estate and property investment agents. Available on disk for the Commodore 64.

1042.
SBA Loan Preparation/SBA Application Management System

SourceView Software International, 835 Castro St., Martinez, CA 94553 (415) 228-6228

Designed to develop and prepare Small Business Administration loan applications. For the IBM PC or compatibles.

1043.
Small Business Cash Flow Planner
The Professor, 4913 NW Second Terr.,
Pompano Beach, FL 33064-2420 (305)
427-5090
Monitors cash flow and projects future
available cash. Requires 48K. For the
Apple II, II+, IIe, IIc.

Inventory

1044.
IMP—Inventory Management Program
Dataconsulting, 2311 W. 5700 S., Roy, UT
84067 (801) 773-8080
Full-featured inventory program that
assists a small business in organizing and
tracking an inventory of commodities.
Handles organization from keeping track
of commodities to writing purchase
orders. Pascal. Requires 128K. Runs on
AT&T 6300; IBM PC or compatible.

1045.
Inventory Control
Timex Computer Corp., P.O. Box 2126,
Waterbury, CT 06720 (203) 573-5000
Allows a small business to track an
inventory of up to 150 items. Items are
identified by description and are associated with a supplier code, inventory
level, reorder level, and unit value. Tables
can be produced by supplier, by type, by
items under minimum stocking level, or
by complete inventory listing. Cassette.
BASIC. Requires 16K. For the Timex
Sinclair 6000 and 500 series.

1046.
Microinv
Compumax, Inc., P.O. Box 7239, Menlo
Park, CA 94026 (415) 854-6700
Series of programs that carry out the
inventory control functions of a small
business. Master file maintains information on inventory stock. Transaction file

monitors data on items received into
inventory or issued to jobs or locations.
Stock status report supplies status and
valuation of each item and cumulative
value for all items on hand; ABC analysis
categorizes inventory according to
frequency of usage; and job cost report/
materials shows total cost of materials
allocated to each job of issue. BASIC.
Requires two disk drives, 80-column
printer. Runs on Apple II+, IIe, III; IBM
PC XT.

1047.
Mini-Inventory
International Computer Products, 346 N.
Western Ave., Los Angeles, CA 90004
(213) 462-8381
Figures and prints inventory, sales, and
reorder data. A small-business user's
system, designed to update inventory
with the occurrence of each sale or item
restocked. 2,800 items listed by code,
name, purchase, and retail price. BASIC.
Requires 48K. For the TRS-80 Model III,
Model 4, Model 12.

1048.
PUFF: The Inventory Tracking System
Simply Systems, 1379 Lower Ferry Rd.,
Ewing Township, NJ 08618
Specially designed for cosmetic and drug
manufacturers to monitor raw materials
from the time they are received until they
are ready to ship as finished products.
Keeps track of raw materials by lot and
work in process. Helps fulfill FDA recordkeeping requirements. Informix-4GL.
Requires 1MB. Runs on IBM AT and
compatibles; Altos; most Unix/Xenix
computers.

1049.
Small Business Inventory
H & E Computronics, Inc., 50 N. Pascack
Rd., Spring Valley, NY 10977 (914)
425-1535
Allows user to access any inventory item.
Keeps track of reorder points and prints

out summaries of all items or individual items that need to be reordered. Disk or cassette. BASIC. Requires 16K. Runs on Apple II, III; Atari 800; Commodore; DEC; IBM PC; Kaypro; Osborne 1, Executive; NEC; North Star; Sanyo; SuperBrain; TeleVideo; TI; TRS-80 Model I, Model II, Model III, Model 4, Model 12, Model 16, Model 100; Xerox.

1050.

Small Business Inventory System

Mariah Computing, P.O. Box 513, Columbia, MO 65205 (314) 442-2500
Supplies ability to track retail inventory, print an inventory control sheet of all inventory data or price lists, and produce price labels. Inventory can be adjusted by receipt of stock or sale. Includes point-of-sale to supply sales slips to customers. Compiled BASIC-A. Requires 128K. For IBM PC with Colorgraphics.

1051.

Superinventory

Elcomp Publishing Inc., 53 Redrock Lane, Pomona, CA 91766 (714) 623-8314
Inventory software for small businesses; 1,000 items per disk. FORTH. For all Atari computers.

1052.

Your Home Inventory

Milo Software, P.O. Box 569, Boston, MA 02130 (617) 292-6465
Menu-driven program allows entry, editing, listing, finding, and printing of data. The user can enter name, location, serial number/miscellaneous, date of purchase, cost, and value. Designed for home or small-business use. For the Commodore 64.

List Management

Some all-purpose management software systems also include a mailing list function; see Management listings.

1053.

The Address Book

Omni Software Systems, Inc., 146 N. Broad St., Griffith, IN 46319 (219) 924-3522
Designed for use by a small business, a professional office, or any organization with several members that have a need to generate mailing lists and mailing labels. A group of programs and subroutines that store names, addresses, and telephone numbers on a disk. Prints mailing labels and various listings of the entire file. BASIC. Requires 128K and two disk drives. For the IBM PC and compatibles.

1054.

Datafile Manager

Jamestown Software, 2508 Valley Forge, Madison, WI 53719 (608) 271-5527
Data base management software for small business. Includes a build-file program for a 1,000-record mailing list, ZIP code label printing, and alphanumeric phone list printouts. For the Commodore 64 with one or two 1541 disk drives, monitor, and printer.

1055.

The Entrepreneur's Mailing List Workplate

Riverdale Systems Design, 3333 Henry Hudson Pkwy., Riverdale, NY 10463 (212) 549-1692
Automates the collection and maintenance of a corporate mailing list. Data entry, modification, sorting on any field, extraction of specific records, and printing tasks are all menu-driven. Users can choose from various label sizes or continuous-fed envelopes when printing the mailing list. Requires 256K. For IBM PC or compatible.

1056.

Mailpac II

H & E Computronics, Inc., 50 N. Pascack Rd., Spring Valley, NY 10977 (914) 425-1535; (800) 431-2818 in New York
Mailing list software capable of storing

up to 1 million names. Requires 48K and at least one disk drive. For TRS-80, Apple, IBM PC, NEC, DEC, or any CP/M computer.

Management

1057.
Busipack-1
Elcomp Publishing, Inc., 53 Redrock Lane, Pomona, CA 91766 (714) 623-8314
Small-business order entry, inventory, mailing, and invoicing package for use on Atari computers.

1058.
Computer Applications in Retail Management
Prentice-Hall, Inc., Rte. 9W, Englewood Cliffs, NJ 07632 (201) 592-2000. Orders to 200 Old Tappan Rd., Old Tappan, NJ 07675
Entrepreneurship for the IBM PC; entrepreneurship for the Apple II series.

1059.
The Entrepreneur's Assistant Workplate
Riverdale Systems Design, 3333 Henry Hudson Pkwy., Riverdale, NY 10463 (212) 549-1692
Personal almanac program provides templates that enable users to organize their phone books; keeps track of appointments for 12 months; lists their tasks-to-do file by priority, due date, or hours required; can write a memo and track the user's time and costs by client and project. Requires 256K. For the IBM PC and compatibles.

1060.
The Entrepreneur's Game
Avant-Garde Publishing Corp., 37B Commercial Blvd., Novato, CA 94947 (415) 883-8083

Teaches the rules, fundamentals, and tactics of entrepreneurial success and gives users an opportunity to test their skills in a simulated business environment. Runs on Apple II+, IIe, IIc (64K required); IBM PC (128K).

1061.
Essential Programs for Small Business
John Wiley & Sons, Inc., 605 Third Ave., New York, NY 10158 (212) 850-6418
Covers all aspects of markets, product and financial planning. For Apple II, IIc, IIe.

1062.
Memory Jogger
SourceView Software International, 835 Castro St., Martinez, CA 94553 (415) 228-6228
Data base management system for small-business use. For the TRS-80.

1063.
Milestone
Hewlett-Packard Co., 3410 Central Expwy., Santa Clara, CA 95051 (408) 865-6474
Project management and time-scheduling product using PERT/CPM techniques to increase productivity and management of small projects. Helps project leaders and small-business owners clarify the tasks at hand and communicate schedules and priorities. Stresses interactivity and comprehensive reporting. The list of associated activities provides a thread used to link all jobs together into an overall project schedule. Adding or changing activities is recomputed into the schedule and the results are immediately displayed on the screen. 3½- or 5¼-inch disk. For the HP 86/87 with CP/M system (HP 82900A).

1064.
Small Business Disk
The Computer Seen, Inc., 3272 E. Ana-

heim, Long Beach, CA 90804 (213) 494-4882

Designed as a productivity tool. Functions: mailing list generation, accounts receivable and payable, inventory data management, schedule/calendar coordination, and memo/letter writing. BASIC. Requires 48K. For the Atari 400, 800.

Marketing

1065.
The Entrepreneur's Marketing Workplate
Riverdale Systems Design, 3333 Henry Hudson Pkwy., Riverdale, NY 10463 (212) 549-1692

Set of ten templates designed to help the user answer questions concerning a product's market potential, performance, and optimal pricing strategies. The user can also track advertising dollars, gauge the effectiveness of ads, and create a message schedule. Requires 256K. For MS-DOS, PC-DOS systems.

1066.
The Entrepreneur's Sales Workplate
Riverdale Systems Design, 3333 Henry Hudson Pkwy., Riverdale, NY 10463 (212) 549-1692

Tool to help the user manage a sales effort. A sales order data base is created from which sales forecasts and performance analyses can be completed. Other functions include: a customer/prospect list, sales compensation analysis, sales plan/time allocation model, and staffing levels. Requires 256K. For IBM PC or compatible.

1067.
Mail Order Generator
Practical Programs, 1104 Aspen Dr., Toms River, NJ 08753 (201) 349-6070

Program designed to generate and modify orders for the small business or individ-

ual. Disk or cassette. BASIC. Requires 48K. For the TRS-80 Model I, Model III, Model 4, Model 4P.

Word Processing

1068.
Business Letter Library Series
Pacific Coast Software Corp., 3220 S. Brea Canyon Rd., Diamond Bar, CA 91765 (714) 594-8210

Library of 164 business letters on diskette. Compatible with many popular word processors. For the Commodore 64.

1069.
Mini Factory
Micro Lab, 2699 Skokie Valley Rd., Highland Park, IL 60035 (312) 433-7550

Includes many sort and search capabilities. Geared to small-business and home use. For the Apple II, IIe.

1070.
PIE Writer for the Apple
Hayden Software Co., 601 Kendall Square, Cambridge, MA 02139 (617) 494-1200

Features similar to Pie Writer for the IBM PC (see #1071). Requires 48K. Runs on Apple II, II +, IIc; Franklin Ace.

1071.
PIE Writer for the IBM PC
Hayden Software Co., 601 Kendall Square, Cambridge, MA 02139 (617) 494-1200

Includes standard merge and telecommunications features plus simultaneous split-screen editing of separate files in larger memory configuration. Permits file size exceeding 50K. Requires 64K (Hyperion), 128K (DOS 2.0). For IBM PC or compatible.

SECTION 6.

Organizations and Associations

The value of organizations and associations, especially as they relate to specific business ventures, cannot be overestimated. They provide invaluable statistics and other related general information to small-business owners, plus the opportunity to remain current on state-of-the-art developments within an industry through conferences, institutes, and annual trade shows. Entrepreneurs owe it to themselves to become associated with and gain the advantages available to them through the organizations and associations appropriate to their industry.

FRANK L. MORSANI
Former President U.S.
Chamber of Commerce
Washington, D.C.

This section includes many types of organizations: university, special interest for small business, organizations providing highly specific data bases, newsletters, and periodicals, and organizations that are proponents of the free-enterprise system. In some cases dues are necessary to participate in the organization; with many others, information is free for the asking.

The citations in this section include name of the organization, address and phone number (if available) to contact, date the organization was founded, number of members, number of staff, and an abstract describing the goals of the organization, including its publications.

1072.
The Advertising Council, Inc.
825 Third Ave., New York, NY 10022
Promotes voluntary citizens' action to solve national problems through multimedia advertising campaigns in the public interest.

1073.
Alpha Kappa Psi
3706 Washington Blvd., Indianapolis, IN 46205, (317) 925-1939
This professional fraternity in business administration and economics promotes the business concept in the college and university classroom and provides

speakers, tours, and on-the-job programs for members.

1074.
American Association of Black Women Entrepreneurs (formerly Task Force on Black Women Business Owners)
1326 Missouri Ave., Suite 4, Washington, DC 20011, (202) 231-3751
Founded 1982. Annual convention. 300 members.
Black women who own businesses in manufacturing, construction, service, finance, insurance, real estate, retail trade, wholesale trade, transportation, and public utilities. Objectives are to unite

black women entrepreneurs, encourage business ownership as a career option, serve as depository and distribution center for demographic and other data on black women business owners, promote business opportunities and businesses that are owned and controlled by black women and have predominately black staffs. Sponsors $10 Million Connection, Business Development Program; conducts Blueprint for Action, Training Institute for Business Strategy Planning.

Publications: *$10 Million Connection News*, monthly. *Legislative News*, quarterly. *Quarterly Business Tips*.

1075.

American Association of Community and Junior Colleges (formerly American Association of Junior Colleges)

National Center for Higher Education, One Dupont Circle, No. 410, Washington, DC 20036, (202) 293-7050

Founded 1920. Annual convention. 1,219 members.

Organization of community, technical, and junior colleges and individual and business associates interested in community college development. Business-related programs are Keeping America Working, Minority Business Enterprise, Small Business Training Network, and Veterans in Small Business.

1076.

American Association of MESBICs

915 15th St., NW,

Suite 700, Washington, DC 20005, (202) 347-8600

1077.

American Bankers Association

1120 Connecticut Ave., NW, Washington, DC 20036, (800) 424-2871; (202) 467-5288

To serve the needs and desires of the American public through enhancing the ability of banks and bankers.

Publications: *Construction Lending:*

Financing the Creation of Value and Entrepreneurship (1982). *Steps to Small Business Financing.*

1078.

American Entrepreneurs Association (formerly International Entrepreneurs Association)

2311 Pontius Ave., Los Angeles, CA 90064, (213) 478-0437

Founded 1973. 111,000 members, 55 staff.

People interested in business opportunities and in starting profitable businesses. Conducts in-depth research on new types of small businesses and disseminates information. Sponsors specialized education; maintains library.

Publications: *Entrepreneur Magazine*, monthly. Also publishes research reports.

1079.

American Entrepreneurs Association

2311 Pontius Ave., Los Angeles, CA 90064, (213) 478-0437

Goals are to help individuals discover the business that is right for them and to follow up with materials and counseling that will ensure success.

Publications: *Entrepreneur Magazine. Entrepreneurs Institute* (3 volumes). *Choices. The Most Profitable Businesses. 267 Ways to Start Your Own Business with Complete Step-by-Step Instructions.*

1080.

American Federation of Small Business

407 S. Dearborn St., Chicago, IL 60605, (312) 427-0207

Founded 1963. Annual convention, in January. 25,000 members, 12 staff.

Member firms include manufacturing, service, retail, construction, transportation, finance, and farming; individuals are professionals, property owners, resource developers, and self-employed. Opposes "big labor, big government and big business monopoly practices." Provides employer informational service on pending state and federal legislation; current events affecting small businesses; and radio and television appearances in support of small-business economic and nonpartisan views on current public affairs.

Publications: Bimonthly letters; also publishes statistical reports, significant reprints, and publications to help small business.

1081.

American Management Association
135 West 50th St., New York, NY 10020 (212) 586-8100
The AMA provides the training, research, publications, and information services required by managers to do a better job. It offers educational programs for managers through meetings, seminars, workshops, conferences, books, etc.

Publications: *CompFlash*, *Compensation and Benefits Review*, *Growth Strategies*, *Management Review*, *Management Solutions*, *Organizational Dynamics*, *Personnel*, *Supervisory Sense*, *Trainer's Workshop*.

1082.

American Woman's Economic Development Corporation
60 E. 42nd St., New York, NY 10165 (212) 692-9100
Founded 1976. 17 staff.
Nonmembership organization for women owning or planning to form small businesses. Sponsors 18-month training and technical assistance program. Provides management training, on-site analysis of businesses, volunteer advisers who work in specific problem areas, assistance in preparing a business plan, and continued support after the program is completed. National telephone counseling service for women not enrolled in the training program.

1083.

Asian Business League
760 Market St., Suite 914, San Francisco, CA 94102, (415) 788-4664
Founded 1980. Monthly meeting. 800 members.
Entrepreneurs, corporate professionals, small businesses, and large corporations. Goal is to promote local business and trade in the Pacific Basin. Acts as forum for networking, business development, acknowledgement of members' successes, and personnel placement.

Publications: *Asian Business*, monthly newsletter.

1084.

Association of Collegiate Entrepreneurs
Center for Entrepreneurship, Box 48, Wichita State University, Wichita, KS 67208, (316) 689-3000
Founded 1983. Annual convention, regional conferences.
A nonprofit corporation dedicated to bringing together the resources and information of the world's entrepreneurially minded young people. The organization is presently working with young people in all 50 states and 23 countries representing more than 300 universities. ACE is recognized as the trade association representing young entrepreneurs.

Publications: Monthly newsletter.

1085.

Association of Electronic Cottagers
677 Canyon Crest Dr., Sierra Madre, CA 91024, (818) 355-0800
Founded 1984.
Organization of salaried computer entrepreneurs and telecommuters working out of the home (electronic cottagers) and others interested in the field. Services include promotion and marketing support; business and consulting services such as editing services and hardware and software needs; expert assistance; updated information on issues affecting electronic cottagers and representation in

legislation; media exposure and assistance in starting a computer-based home business.

Publications: *MicroMoonlighter Newsletter,* monthly.

Computerized Services: CompuServe Information Service and on-line service providing expert consultation, an electronic bulletin board, data base, on-line membership directory.

1086.
Association of Private Enterprise Education
Box 709, Atlanta, GA 30301

1087.
Association of Venture Founders
521 Fifth Avenue, 15th Floor, New York, NY 10175, (212) 682-7373
Founded 1979. Quarterly conference. 150 members, 4 staff.
Successful entrepreneurs. Seeks to enhance the wealth, knowledge, and business success of members. Provides educational networking for the continuing education of members.

Publications: *Venture Magazine,* monthly; *Who's Who in AVF* (directory), annual.

1088.
Booker T. Washington Foundation
1010 Massachusetts Ave., NW, Suite 400, Washington, DC 20001, (202) 857-4800
Founded 1967. 100 staff.
Funded by federal agencies, foundations, and private corporations to provide policy research, technical assistance, and development and management expertise to minority entrepreneurs.

1089.
Bureau of Business Research
University of Texas at Austin, Box 7459, Austin, TX 78713, (512) 471-1616
Publications: 1986 *Directory of Texas Manufacturers. High-Technology Employment in Texas: A Labor Market Analysis.*

Metropolitan Profiles: Major Texas MSAs. The Impact of MCC: Economic, Population, and Land Use Trends.

1090.
Business Alliance on Government Competition
1615 H Street, NW, Washington, DC 20062, (202) 463-5500
Founded 1983. 44 members, 2 staff.
Trade associations, business federations, and organizations interested in promoting the "contracting out" of government work to business firms.

Publications: *Newsletter,* biweekly. *Legislative Status Sheet,* biweekly. *Alliance Update,* monthly.

1091.
Business and Professional Women's Foundation
2012 Massachusetts Avenue, NW, Washington, DC 20036, (202) 293-1200

1092.
The Business Council of New York
152 Washington Avenue, Albany, NY 12210

1093.
Business Education Alliance of S.E. Michigan
150 Michigan Avenue, Detroit, MI 48226, (313) 964-4000
Provides a structure through which business and education can work together to improve economic and career education in Detroit and southeastern Michigan.

1094.
Business Leader Group
c/o American Council for Coordinated Action, 1010 Vermont Avenue, NW, Suite 1010, Washington, DC 20005
Founded 1980. Quarterly meetings.
Coalition of business executives and entrepreneurs concerned about the future of the free-enterprise system, increasing government encroachment on individual

freedom, and "the liberal-left push for socialism." Sponsors Enterprise News Service, which disseminates articles on the need for private enterprise, tax reform, and reduced government spending to daily newspapers with a circulation of under 100,000.

1095.
The Business Roundtable
200 Park Avenue, New York, NY 10017, (212) 682-6370
Provides a forum in which the business leadership of the nation can exchange ideas and develops policy recommendations on major business, economic, and social issues. Fosters a higher public appreciation of the contributions by business to society and strengthens the voice of business on these problems.

1096.
Campus Studies Institute Division, World Research, Inc.
11722 Sorrento Valley Road, San Diego, CA 92121, (714) 755-9761

1097.
Carnegie-Mellon Innovation Center
5017 Forbes Avenue, Pittsburgh, PA 15213, (412) 578-2900

1098.
Center for Business Information, Inc.
90 Madison Street, Worcester, MA 01608, (617) 754-9425
Provides economic understanding courses and seminars for teachers, guidance counselors, and students; holds annual symposium for college students, faculty members, and business representatives.

1099.
Center for Entrepreneurial Management
83 Spring Street, New York, NY 10012, (212) 925-7304
Founded 1978. 2,500 members, 6 staff.

Serves as a management resource for entrepreneurial managers and their professional advisers. Selects and makes available published materials on developing business plans, organizing an entrepreneurial team, attracting venture capital, and obtaining patents, trademarks, and copyrights. Develops, collects, and disseminates current information on business trends, new laws and regulations, and tax guidance. Conducts intensive-study courses and seminars. Has identified stages of the entrepreneurial process and, through essays and audiocassettes, addresses problems pertinent to each stage. Maintains library of small-business and venture capital information.

Publications: *The Entrepreneurial Manager*, monthly newsletter.

1100.
Center for Entrepreneurs
Babson College, Babson, MA 02157, (617) 235-1200

1101.
Center for Family Business
Box 24268, Cleveland, OH 44124

1102.
Center for International Private Enterprise
1511 K Street, NW, Suite 334, Washington, DC 20005, (202) 463-5901
Founded 1983.
A division of the National Chamber Foundation, affiliated with the U.S. Chamber of Commerce. To encourage the growth of voluntary business organizations and private enterprise systems abroad, such as chambers of commerce, trade associations, employers' organizations, and business-oriented research groups, particularly in developing countries. Assists business communities abroad to strengthen their organizational capabilities; creates exchanges among business leaders and institutions to strengthen the international private enter-

prise system; encourages development of active business participation in the political process.

1103.
Center for Private Enterprise
820 N. Michigan Avenue, Chicago, IL 60611

1104.
Center for Private Enterprise Education
Box 922, Station A, 900 East Center Avenue, Searcy, AR 72143
The center engages in educational, developmental, and research activities pertaining to the private enterprise system, the process of entrepreneurship, and venture initiation.

1105.
Center for Venture Management
207 E. Buffalo Street, Suite 508, Milwaukee, WI 53202
A nonprofit organization devoted to serving small-business owners and managers with a number of publications.

1106.
Chamber of Commerce of the United States
1615 H Street, NW, Washington, DC 20062, (202) 659-6000
Founded 1912. Annual convention in Washington, DC. 1,400 staff.
National federation of business organizations and companies. Determines and makes known to the government the recommendations of the business community on national issues and problems affecting the economy and the future of the country. Works to advance human progress through an economic, political, and social system based on individual freedom and initiative. Informs, trains, equips, and encourages members to participate in policymaking at federal, state, and local levels and in legislative and political action at the national level.
Publications: *The Business Advocate,*

biweekly newspaper. *Business Action Network: Washington Watch,* monthly. *International Business Review,* monthly. *Nation's Business,* monthly magazine. *Analysis of Workers' Compensation Laws,* annual. *Employee Benefits,* annual. Also publishes special reports, studies, and research papers; distributes films and slide presentations.

1107.
Coalition of Women in National and International Business
Box 950, Boston, MA 02119, (617) 265-5268
Founded 1980. 1,700 members.
Full members are businesses at least 51 percent women-owned and -controlled; associate members are businesses less than 51 percent owned and controlled by women; affiliate members are women interested in owning their own businesses; and general members are men and women supporting the idea of women-owned and -controlled businesses. To encourage and develop women entrepreneurs and their associations; to expand the women's business network; to enhance communication among government, business, and women entrepreneurs. Keeps members informed on state and federal legislation affecting business. Maintains speakers bureau.
Publications: *Coalition Alert Newsletter,* for full members, monthly. *The Coalition* (for associate, affiliate, and general members), quarterly.

1108.
Commerce Clearing House, Inc.
4025 W. Peterson Avenue, Chicago, IL 60646
An organization devoted to compiling and publishing today's new tax and business law developments in periodic issues of current reports.
Publications: *Standard Federal Tax Reports. Payroll Management Guide. Employment Safety and Health Guide.*

Human Resources Management. Travel and Entertainment: Business or Pleasure?

1109.

Committee of 200

500 N. Michigan Avenue, Chicago, IL 60611, (312) 661-1700

Founded 1982. Annual convention. 250 members, 2 staff.

Women executives who are recognized as leaders in their industries. Encourages successful entrepreneurship by women and the active participation of women business owners and senior corporate executives in business, economic, social, political, and educational concerns.

1110.

The Conference Board, Inc.

845 Third Avenue, New York, NY 10022, (212) 759-0900

A business information service whose objective is to assist senior executives and other leaders in arriving at sound decisions. Many of the Board's associate members consist of labor unions, colleges and universities, government, agencies, libraries, and trade and professional associations.

    Publications: *Private Enterprise Looks at Its Image. Business and Education: A Fragile Partnership. Who Is Top Management?. Studying and Addressing Community Needs: A Corporate Case Book.*

1111.

Conference of American Small Business Organizations

407 S. Dearboarn Street, Chicago, IL 60605, (312) 427-3780

1112.

Control Data Business Information

2101 L Street, NW, Washington, DC 20036, (202) 789-6600

1113.

Corporation for Enterprise Development

1211 Connecticut Avenue, NW, Suite 710A, Washington, DC 20036, (202) 293-7963

Founded 1979. 10 staff.

To reduce unemployment by stimulating the development of business enterprises in poor communities and neglected markets. Devoted to the research, development, and dissemination of entrepreneurial policy initiatives at the local, state, and federal levels. Publishes and distributes resumes of MBAs seeking jobs in consumer advocacy, community development, economic analysis in natural resources, community organization, inner-city housing programs, international economic development, and in the administration of nonprofit organizations in the arts and education.

    Publications: *Entrepreneurial Economy,* monthly.

1114.

COSE (Council of Smaller Enterprises)

690 Huntington Building, Cleveland, OH 44115

1115.

Distributive Education Clubs of America

1908 Association Dr., Reston, VA 22091, (703) 860-5000

Purpose is to develop education in marketing and distribution and to promote understanding and appreciation for responsible citizenship in the competitive enterprise system. Distributive Education Clubs are school- and student-centered.

1116.

Economic Ecology Inc.

Holly Haven Farms, Houston, DE 19954, (302) 422-7724

1117.

Enterprise High

44001 Garfield Rd., Mt. Clemens, MI 48044, (313) 286-8800

A program for high school dropouts, Enterprise High operates on six campuses. Enterprise High lets students combine their academic learning with experience in running a small business of their own design.

1118.
Entrepreneurs Alliance
1333 Lawrence Expressway, Suite 150, Santa Clara, CA 95051

1119.
Entrepreneurs Club
University of Tennessee, Knoxville, TN 37916, (615) 974-0111

1120.
Entrepreneurs' Exchange Inc.
New York University, 100 Trinity Place, #706, New York, NY 10006, (212) 598-1212
Dedicated to the belief that entrepreneurship should be fostered within the public, private, and not-for-profit communities. The organization has actively assembled and used the resources of academic, business, and government communities to involve and expose students to the rigors of entrepreneurial ventures and to offer assistance and guidance to entrepreneurs.

1121.
The Entrepreneurship Institute
90 E. Wilson Bridge Road, Suite 247, Worthington, OH 43209, (614) 885-0585
An independent, nonprofit organization that assists and encourages entrepreneurial growth.
   Publications: *TEI's Business Planning Guide. Case Study Profile. Information Age Marketing Newsletter. Winning Images.*

1122.
The Foresight Institute
℅ The Naisbitt Group, 1101 30th Street, NW, Washington, DC 20007, (202) 333-3228
Conducts corporate programs on intracorporate entrepreneurship (intrapreneurship). Originally based in Sweden, the institute has recently begun to offer programs in the United States.

1123.
Future Business Leaders of America (Phi Beta Lambda)
1908 Association Dr., Reston, VA 22091, (703) 860-3334

1124.
Innovations Center
University of Utah, Salt Lake City, UT 84112, (801) 581-7200

1125.
Institute for Neighbor Reinvestment and Minority Business Research
800 18th Street, NW, Washington, DC 20005, (202) 347-7141

1126.
Institute for New Enterprise Development
Harvard Square, Box 360, Cambridge, MA 02238

1127.
Institute of American Enterprise
306 West Brooks, Norman, OK 73069, (405) 325-6333
Promotes economic literacy with varied activities including courses in regular curriculum and periodic seminars to target groups.

1128.
Institute of Certified Business Counselors
3301 Vincent Road, Pleasant Hill, CA 94523, (415) 945-8440
Annual convention. 250 members, 2 staff. Accountants, brokers, and attorneys involved in the buying and selling of business property. Offers training and advice on how to buy or sell a business

including information on what to look for in a prospective deal. Maintains speakers bureau.

Publications: *Certified Business Counselor*, bimonthly newsletter. *CBC Roster*, annual.

1129.
International Council for Small Business (formerly National Council for Small Business Management Development)
St. Louis University, 3642 Lindell Blvd., St. Louis, MO 63108, (314) 534-7232
Founded 1957. Annual conference in June. 1,500 members.
Management educators, researchers, government officials, and professionals. Holds annual conference to discuss problems, research, and the development of small-business management. Local members cosponsor small-business management seminars with universities and school systems throughout the world.

Publications: *Journal of Small Business Management*, quarterly. Quarterly newsletter. *Conference Proceedings*, annual. *List of Members*, annual. *Compendium*, biennial. *Small Business Research Topics*, biennial. Also publishes *Small Business Information Source*, bibliography.

1130.
International Franchise Association
1350 New York Avenue, NW, Washington, DC 20036, (202) 628-8000

1131.
Junior Achievement Inc.
550 Summer Street, Stanford, CT 06901, (203) 359-2970
Junior Achievement guides young people in practical business experiences, provides management skills, develops leadership, demonstrates sound economic and business principles, and helps evaluate careers.

1132.
Milwaukee Innovation Center
757 North Broadway, Milwaukee, WI 53202, (414) 277-5500

1133.
Mind Your Own Business at Home
2520 North Lincoln Avenue, #60, Chicago, IL 60614, (312) 472-8116
Information clearinghouse for home-based entrepreneurs. A newsletter provides information on financial, legal, managerial, marketing, and promotional aspects of running a business at home. Workshops are also offered.

1134.
Minority Business Enterprise Legal Defense and Education Fund
318 Massachusetts Avenue, NW, Washington, DC 20006, (202) 543-0040

1135.
Missouri Center for Free Enterprise
428 East Capitol Ave., Jefferson City, MO 65102, (314) 634-2414
The center is dedicated to preserving the freedom of the individual through a better understanding of the free-enterprise concept in our economic system.

1136.
National Alliance of Business
1015 15th Street, NW, Washington, DC, (202) 457-0040

1137.
National Alliance of Homebased Business Women
Box 95, Norwood, NJ 07648

1138.
National Association for the Cottage Industry
Box 14460, Chicago, IL 60614, (312) 472-9116
A trade association whose purpose is to encourage and emphasize professional

growth among home-based business-people; provide programs through conferences, seminars, and workshops; and share knowledge, experience, and insight on working from home. Offers a network that connects people running businesses or working for corporations out of their basements, kitchens, spare rooms, or garages, and informs others of the wide range of work that people do out of their homes. A directory of home-based businesses nationwide by region is available through a membership.

Publication: *Cottage Connection*, quarterly newsletter.

1139.
National Association for the Self-Employed
2121 Precinct Line Road, Hurst, TX 76054, (817) 656-6313
Founded 1981. 350,000 members, 10 staff.
Self-employed and small independent businesspersons. Objectives are to promote American small business in the free enterprise system for the self-employed, managers of small business, and owners of closely held corporations, and to protect and promote the economic and general welfare of American small business. Disseminates information to members; analyzes issues relating to the concerns and needs of the self-employed. Conducts tax and business seminars.

Publications: *Profitline*, monthly. Also publishes brochures and pamphlets.

1140.
National Association for Women in Commerce
Contemporary Management Consultants, 1333 Howe Avenue, Suite 100, Sacramento, CA 95825

1141.
National Association of Black Women Entrepreneurs
Box 1375, Detroit, MI 48231, (313) 963-8766

Founded 1979. Annual convention in October. 1,760 members, 3 staff.
Acts as a national support system for black businesswomen in the United States and focuses on the unique problems they face. Objective is to enhance business, professional, and technical development of both present and future black businesswomen.

Publications: *Making Success Happen*, bimonthly newsletter. Annual membership directory.

1142.
National Association of Development Companies
1511 K Street, NW, Suite 1100, Washington, DC 20005, (202) 737-4007
Founded 1981. Semiannual convention. 180 members, 1 staff.
Small Business Administration Section 503 certified development companies. Provides long-term financing to small and medium-size businesses. Represents membership in negotiations with the SBA, Congress, and congressional staff members. Provides technical assistance and information on special training programs, marketing techniques, audit checklists, and loan closing and processing procedures.

Publications: *News*, quarterly. Also publishes information packages.

1143.
National Association of Manufacturers
1776 F Street, NW, Washington, DC 20006, (202) 331-3700
NAM establishes official policy positions on national issues of importance to its members and communicates these positions to government agencies through a variety of programs.

1144.
National Association of Negro Business and Professional Women's Club
2861 Urban Avenue, Columbus, GA 31907

1145.

National Association of Small Business Investment Companies

1156 15th Street, NW, Suite 1101, Washington, DC 20005, (202) 833-8230

Founded 1958. Annual convention in October or November. 600 members, 6 staff.

Firms licensed as small-business investment companies (SBICs) under the Small Business Investment Act of 1958. Holds executive training seminars.

Publications: *NASBIC News*, semi-monthly. Annual membership directory.

1146.

National Association of Women Business Owners

645 N. Michigan Avenue, Chicago, IL 60611

An association of women business owners organized to assist in business startup and management situations. It is represented by 28 chapters throughout the United States.

1147.

National Association of Women Government Contractors

Box 5543, Washington, DC 20016, (202) 638-3336

Founded 1983. Annual convention. 84 members.

Women entrepreneurs seeking business growth and profitability through effective competition with other groups for government contracts. Compiles information on federal contract opportunities and awards and distributes such information to women entrepreneurs so that they may better compete in the federal and/or private sector markets for goods and/or services. Offers marketing assistance including identification of government and industry buyers and explanation of sales protection techniques. Sponsors seminars on the procurement process, bidding, and other topics; conducts panels and lectures.

Publications: Bimonthly newsletter. Annual directory.

1148.

National Business League

4324 Georgia Avenue, NW, Washington, DC 20011, (202) 829-5900

Maintains a file of minority vendors and a comprehensive list of corporate procurement and purchasing agents for constituents. Publishes a resource manual for use by corporate executives and minority entrepreneurs.

1149.

National Center for Neighborhood Enterprise

1367 Connecticut Avenue, NW, Washington, DC 20036, (202) 331-1103

Founded 1981. 10 staff.

Promotes community self-sufficiency through support of effective neighborhood mediating structures in low-income communities. Provides support and technical assistance to enable grass roots organizations to expand their role in the revitalization of urban communities. Objectives are to recognize, promote, and explain alternative approaches to community development; identify and analyze successful program principles, strategies, and techniques that may be transferable; identify needs for developing neighborhood groups and small-business leaders; simplify information technology and encourage grass roots organizations to make greater use of technological gains in solving problems; encourage financial support for programs; educate the public and private sectors; formulate policy recommendations to assist neighborhood revitalization.

Publications: *Policy Dispatch*, irregular.

1150.

National Council for Equal Business Opportunity

1221 Connecticut Avenue, NW, Suite 400, Washington, DC 20036, (202) 293-3960

Founded 1968. 7 staff.
Goal is to promote the ownership of competitive businesses by members of minority groups, including blacks, Puerto Ricans, and Mexican Americans. Helps to develop programs; bring together leaders from the minority and white business communities who have the necessary resources; obtain funds for the staff of the local organization and for seed money; develop criteria for employing staff and finding personnel; train the community organization's board members and staff; begin the local development company, small business investment company, and other institutions that will be needed, including furnishing both legal and financial advice.

1151.

National Development Council
1025 Connecticut Avenue, NW, Washington, DC 20036, (202) 466-3906
Founded 1972. 35 staff.
Brings innovative economic development financing programs to urban and rural communities interested in local business and industrial growth, commercial revitalization, and permanent job creation. Conducts intensive training program for economic development professionals with courses in business credit analysis, real estate financing, loan packaging, federal financing, and program management and implementation.
Publications: *Developments*, quarterly newsletter.

1152.

National Family Business Council
3916 Detroit Blvd., West Bloomfield, MI 48033, (313) 553-1000, Ext. 381
Publications: *Family Business Forum*.

1153.

National Federation of Independent Business
150 W. 20th Avenue, San Mateo, CA 94403, (415) 341-7441
Founded 1943. Quadrennial meetings.

560,000 members, 197 staff, 571 field staff.
Independent business and professional people. Presents opinions of small business to state and national legislative bodies. Members vote by ballot on issues; ballots are tabulated and results forwarded to Congress. Conducts surveys at the state level with area directors and government affairs representatives working with state legislatures. Maintains legislative, research, and public affairs office in Washington, DC.
Publications: *The Mandate*, 8 per year.

1154.

The National Management Association
2210 Arbor Blvd., Dayton, OH 45439, (513) 294-0421
Member programs include awards, career counseling, clinics, workshops, seminars, institutes, conferences, speakers service, film library, and community programs. NMA sponsors an aggressive American enterprise program through member chapters.

1155.

National Minority Supplier Development Council (formerly National Minority Purchasing Council)
1412 Broadway, 11th Floor, New York, NY 10018, (212) 944-2430
Founded 1972. Annual convention. 143 members, 11 staff.
Individuals, corporations, associations, foundations, and other organizations who are members of regional purchasing councils or who have agreed to participate in the program. Program provides, exclusively for educational purposes, consultative, advisory, and informational services and technical resources to minority businesses and to regional and local minority purchasing councils.
Publications: *Minority Supplier News*, 6/year. *Annual Report. Minority Vendor Directory* (published by regional

chapters), irregular. Also publishes *Public Law 95-507 Handbook*.

1156.
National Retail Merchants Association
100 West 31st Street, New York, NY
   10001, (212) 244-8780
   Publications: *Fair Credit Billing Act. Effective Stock Shortage Control. Retail Accounting* (revised). **Personnel Practices of the Retail Industry. Merchandise Control & Budgeting.**

1157.
National Science Foundation
Office of Small Business Research and
   Development, 1800 G Street, NW, Room
   1250, Washington, DC 20550, (202)
   357-9859

1158.
National Small Business Association (formerly National Small Business Men's Association)
1604 K Street, NW, Washington, DC
   20006, (202) 293-8830
Founded 1937. 50,000 members, 15 staff. Small businesses including manufacturing, wholesale, retail, service, and other firms representing more than 500 different kinds of business. Purposes are to promote a sound national economy and to foster the birth and vigorous development of independent small business.
   Publications: *Voice of Small Business*, monthly.

1159.
National Small Business Government Contractors Association
277 Fairfield Road, Suite 310, Fairfield, NJ
   07006, (201) 575-2533
Founded 1982. Annual convention. 50
   members, 1 staff.
Small businesses involved in federal government contracting; individuals with a professional interest in promoting the cause of small-business government contractors. Offers seminars on conducting business with the federal government.
   Publications: Monthly newsletter.

1160.
National Venture Capital Association
1655 N. Ft. Myer Drive, Arlington, VA
   22209, (703) 528-4370
The National Venture Capital Association was organized to foster a broader understanding of the importance of venture capital to the vitality of the U.S. economy. The Association is also interested in stimulating the free flow of capital to young companies. NVCA seeks to improve communications among venture capitalists throughout the country and to improve the general level of knowledge of the venturing process in government, in the universities, and in the business community. NVCA is open by invitation to all venture capital organizations, corporate financiers, and individual venture capitalists who are responsible for investing private capital in young companies on a professional basis.

1161.
North American Restaurant and Tavern Alliance
139 Day Street, Newington, CT 06111,
   (800) 243-8768
Founded 1979. 6,000 members, 5 staff. Independent restaurant and tavern owners. A trade alliance working to help businesses operate more profitably. Conducts research and seminars on topics concerning food service operations.
   Publications: *NARTA News Magazine*, bimonthly. *NARTA Newsletter*.

1162.
Pollock Divestitures
Box 19833, Oklahoma City, OK 73144

1163.
Potomac Institute
1501 18th Street, NW, Washington, DC
   20036, (202) 332-5566
Founded 1961. 3 staff.
Nonprofit, foundation-funded research

organization "concerned with developing human resources by expanding opportunities for racial and economically deprived minorities." Provides advisory and research services to government and private agencies involved in the development of programs to increase opportunities for minorities. Sponsors special-purpose conferences to explore problems affecting minority groups.

1164.

Professional Services Council
918 16th Street, NW, Washington, DC 20006, (202) 296-2030

1165.

Roundtable for Women in Foodservice
322 Eighth Avenue, Suite 1201, New York, NY 10001, (212) 206-7522
Founded 1983. Regional roundtables. 800 members, 3 staff.
Promotes advancement and success of women in the food industry. Acts as clearinghouse for food service, business, educational, and career information. Holds roundtable discussions to clarify issues and promote entrepreneurial opportunities; provides practical counseling service for members entering, reentering, or advancing in the industry.
Publications: Annual directory. Quarterly newsletter.

1166.

San Antonio Foundation for Free Enterprise
602 East Commerce, Box 1628, San Antonio, TX 78296, (512) 227-8181
Provides free-enterprise programs and materials for educators, students, employees, and the general public.

1167.

School for Intrapreneurs
c/o The Tarrytown Group, East Sunnyside Lane, Tarrytown, NY 10591, (914) 591-8200; (212) 933-1032

1168.

Service Corps of Retired Executives Association
1129 20th Street, NW, Suite 410, Washington, DC 20416, (202) 653-6279
Founded 1964. 12,000 members.
Volunteer program sponsored by U.S. Small Business Administration in which active and retired businessmen and businesswomen provide free management assistance to men and women who are considering starting a small business, encountering problems with their business, or expanding their business.

1169.

Small Business Assistance
7826 Eastern Avenue, NW, Washington, DC, (202) 829-0350

1170.

Small Business Association of Michigan
490 West South Street, Kalamazoo, MI 49005

1171.

Small Business Center
US Chamber of Commerce, 211 East 35th Street, New York, NY 10016

1172.

Small Business Foundation of America
20 Park Plaza, Boston, MA 02116, (617) 350-5096
Founded 1976. 30 staff.
Charitable organization that raises funds for education and research on small businesses. Conducts seminars; encourages youth economic education programs. Cosponsors conference on small-business research.
Publications: Exportise—A Handbook on Exporting.

1173.

Small Business High Technology Institute
1825 I Street, NW, Washington, DC 20006, (202) 293-8705

1174.

Small Business Legislative Council
1604 K Street, NW, Washington, DC
   20006, (202) 293-8830
Founded 1977. Annual convention in
   Washington, DC. 84 members, 3 staff.
Trade and professional associations
representing 4.5 million small businesses. Maximizes the influence of small
businesses; presents expert testimony
before Congress; works with executive
agencies on behalf of small-business
interests.
   Publications: Monthly newsletter.

1175.

Small Business Organizing and Financing
7826 Eastern Avenue, NW, Washington,
   DC, (202) 829-0350

1176.

Small Business Reporter
Bank of America, Department 3120, Box
   37000, San Francisco, CA 94137

1177.

Small Business Resources
Bentley College, Waltham, MA 02154,
   (617) 891-2000

1178.

Small Business United
1050 17th Street, NW, Washington, DC,
   (202) 775-0429
Founded 1981. Annual Washington
   presentation in January. 10 members.
Small-business associations whose
members represent the interests of small
firms in 35 states on national government
issues. Strives to shape government
policy and opinion to be supportive of
small business.

1179.

Smaller Business Association of New England
69 Hickory Drive, Waltham, MA 02154,
   (617) 890-9070
Founded 1938. Annual convention. 1,800
   members, 12 staff.
Organization of small to medium-size

businesses of all types in New England.
Represents members' interests in federal
and state legislation dealing with taxation, international trade, technological
innovation, employee benefits, hazardous
waste, government procurement, and
labor; assists management to become
more skilled; provides programs of
continuing education for executives in
small business.
   Publications: *Small Business News,*
monthly. *SBANE Enterprise,* 8 per
year. Annual membership directory. Also
publishes *Buyer's Guide.*

1180.

Society of Business Folk
c/o Dr. David Larson, 5600 W. Brown Deer
   Rd., Brown Deer, WI 53223, (414) 354-
   1290
Founded 1984. Semiannual convention.
Small-business proprietors. Purpose is to
represent the interests of small businesses (run by one or very few employees). Though currently active only in
Wisconsin, the group plans to expand
throughout the United States.
   Publications: Quarterly newsletter.

1181.

US Hispanic Chamber of Commerce
4900 Main, Kansas City, MO 64112, (816)
   531-6363
Founded 1979. Annual convention.
   40,000 members, 30 staff.
Hispanic and other business firms
interested in the development of Hispanic business and promotion of business leadership in the Hispanic community. Conducts business-related
workshops, conferences, and management training; compiles statistics.
   Publications: Monthly bulletin.
Bimonthly newsletter. *Who's Who in
Hispanic Business,* annual.

1182.

Volunteers in Technical Assistance (formerly
Volunteers for International Technical Assistance)

1815 N. Lynn Street, Suite 200, Arlington, VA 22209, (703) 276-1800
Founded 1960. 4,500 members, 35 staff. Private organization providing technical assistance to individuals and organizations in the United States and developing countries. Operates internationally with emphasis on helping local groups adapt, implement, and market technologies appropriate to given situations. Conducts one-day seminars in information resources, microcomputer applications, international development, and volunteerism.

Publications: *News*, quarterly magazine. *Annual Report*. Also publishes over 100 technical handbooks in different languages and a technical paper series.

1183.
Washington International Business Council
1625 I Street, NW, Washington, DC, (202) 872-8181

1184.
Women Entrepreneurs
2030 Union Street, Suite 310, San Francisco, CA 94123, (415) 929-0129
Founded 1974. 190 members.
Organization of women who actively own and operate a business (retail, service, manufacturing, consulting, publishing, or other) or who plan to start a business. Offers the woman business owner support, recognition, and access to vital information and resources. Conducts monthly programs featuring speakers and technical assistance educational seminars and workshops.

Publications: *Prospectus*, monthly newsletter. Annual membership roster.

1185.
Women's Equity Program
Nelson House, University of Massachusetts, Amherst, MA 01003, (413) 545-1558
Founded 1976. 6 staff.
Goals are to identify educational and economic equity issues of state, regional, and national importance and scope and to develop and disseminate model programs addressing those issues. Conducts research on women's centers, women's employment and small-business development, and teacher preparation. Conducts "Something Ventured, Something Gained," a training program in risk-taking for women business owners.

Publications: *Developing and Negotiating Budgets for Women's Programs*. *Developing Women's Programs*. *To Make a Difference: A Guide to Working with Feminist Organizations*. Also publishes reports, research summaries, and working papers on women and employment.

1186.
World Association of Women Business Owners
c/o Enterprising Women Magazine, 217 East 28th Street, New York, NY 10016
Although membership is limited to managing directors, or those assuming the day-to-day running and financial responsibility of businesses, the association provides several programs to aid women entrepreneurs.

SECTION 7.

Academic Programs

During the past decade, colleges and universities, as well as many private institutes and professional associations, have responded in growing numbers to the demand for formal academic programs and short-term learning experiences in entrepreneurship and small-business management. Opportunities tailored to the educational needs of any individual are available in almost every region of the United States, and institutions are eager to serve those needs. Aspiring entrepreneurs are but a telephone call or an inquiring letter away from making the initial contact with a school or program that can lead them to greater confidence in operating an enterprise.

DR. KARL VESPER
Professor and Chairman
Department of Management
and Organization
University of Washington

A surprising number of institutions of higher education now offer course work for academic credit that can be of significance to small businessmen and women. College and university programs are designed to prepare students for the small-business world through formal training in entrepreneurship, marketing, management, finance, and general accounting. A few offer undergraduate and graduate degree programs in entrepreneurship and small-business management. All institutions listed in this section provide some opportunities to those who wish to become involved in formal studies that combine theory with practice.

The scope of the listings that follow suggests that a program suitable to your needs is available within your immediate geographic area. Our thanks to Karl Vesper from the University of Washington; his book, *Entrepreneurship Education*, published in 1985 by the Center of Entrepreneurial Studies at Babson College, provided most of the information in this section. Listings include, as available, name of university, school that houses the program, mailing address and telephone number, and a description of program or courses taught.

The University of Alabama
Graduate School of Business
Box J
University, AL 34586
(205) 348-6517
Entrepreneurship: A course on new-venture initiation and the preparation of salable proposals. Covers the role of the entrepreneur in business society, characteristics of successful entrepreneurs, methods of identifying new opportunities for venture capital, market potential analysis for new products or services, acquiring seed capital, obtaining venture capital for growth or for purchase of an existing business, organization of the new

enterprise, and operation of the new business.

Arizona State University
College of Business Administration
Tempe, AZ 85281
(602) 965-3331
Entrepreneurship: Course focuses on the opportunities, risks, and problems associated with new-business development.

Auburn University
School of Business
Auburn, AL 36849
(205) 826-4000
Experiential Learning in Venture Creation.

Babson College
Management and Organizational
    Behavior
Babson Park, MA 02157
(617) 235-1200
Program in Entrepreneurship: Babson offers entrepreneurship courses at both undergraduate and master's levels; in the undergraduate program a major in Entrepreneurial Studies has been introduced. Its objectives are to teach students how to identify and evaluate the characteristics of prospective entrepreneurs and their environments in order to determine their chances of success, find potentially attractive new ventures, evaluate new ventures, and sell or merge a business interest.

Baylor University
Hankamer School of Business
Waco, TX 76798
(817) 855-3766
Hankamer offers two courses in the area of entrepreneurship, one undergraduate and the other graduate. *Venture Management* (undergraduate): Course includes an examination of the crucial factors involved in the conception, initiation, and development of new business ventures. An entrepreneurship concentration

within the BBA program also has been established. *Seminar in Entrepreneurship and Venture Initiation* (graduate). A course concentrating on entrepreneurship and enterprise development with particular attention to the formation and management of new business ventures. The Center for Private Enterprise and Entrepreneurship has research programs in the areas of government regulation of business, psychological characteristics of entrepreneurs, and women entrepreneurs. Research is currently pursuing two paths: comparative studies of psychological characteristics, and the prevalence of strategic planning in small business.

Boston College
School of Management
Chestnut Hill, MA 02167
(617) 552-3167
Graduate division has one course called *New Business Formation.* Other graduate and undergraduate courses include a field course on the SBA, a course in project management, and a course on management of new technologies.

Bradley University
College of Engineering and Technology
Peoria, IL 61625
(306) 676-7611
Engineering Administration Seminar (New Venture Plan): The capstone course in the Engineering Administration master's program. Objective is to develop new-venture plans for business areas selected by the class, working in small teams.

University of British Columbia
Faculty of Commerce and Business
    Administration
Vancouver, B.C., Canada
(604) 228-2191
Seminar in Small Business and New Venture Creation (MBA). Designed for people who wish to become involved in exploring the problem of developing their

own new business. Its main objectives are to (1) enable members to participate in the actual process of formulating, designing, and structuring a new venture, (2) assist course members to evaluate their own entrepreneurial potential and probable levels of commitment, (3) develop a set of feasible business plans, and (4) create some understanding of the character, problems, environment, and opportunities of the small-business sector in industrial countries.

University of California, Berkeley
School of Business Administration
Berkeley, CA 94720
(415) 642-1424
Business Development and Entrepreneurship.

University of California, Los Angeles
Graduate School of Management
Los Angeles, CA 90024
(213) 825-3045
Entrepreneurship and Venture Initiation: Presents various crucial aspects of exploring new-business opportunities and getting a business started. *Techniques for Establishing a New Enterprise:* Specifically for manufacturing and technically oriented service businesses.

University of California, Riverside
Graduate School of Administration
Riverside, CA 92521
(714) 787-5019
Entrepreneurial Management: A case-study course.

California State Polytechnic University, Pomona
School of Business Administration
Pomona, CA 91768
(714) 598-4211
Seminar in New Venture Creation: An interdisciplinary study and application of the general steps involved in preparing a preliminary venture feasibility analysis and initiating a small business.

Carnegie-Mellon University
School of Engineering and Public Policy
Pittsburgh, PA 15213
(412) 578-2672
Design and Entrepreneurship: Emphasis on the special problems of starting new service and manufacturing businesses. Topics include the nature of entrepreneurship, characteristics of new ventures, finding projects and services that can support new enterprises, raising capital, and preparing business proposals. *Design and Entrepreneurship (New Ventures):* Designed primarily for students who may wish to start their own business at some stage of their careers. Analyzes the role of the entrepreneur in our economy, and the risks and rewards of an entrepreneurial career. Several student group projects. The Enterprise Corporation of Pittsburgh, formed to encourage entrepreneurship in the Pittsburgh area, increases opportunities for students to interact with entrepreneurs and to serve as interns.

Case Western Reserve
The Weatherhead School of Management
Cleveland, OH 44106
(216) 368-2154 or 368-5004
New Enterprise Development; Innovations Research Issues; Innovations Management and Policy: The Entrepreneurial Assistance Group uses graduate MBA students to assist entrepreneurs and small businesses in making innovations become commercially viable.

Clarkson College of Technology
Potsdam, NY 13676
(315) 268-2204
Clarkson College Entrepreneurship Program: Directly involves students in the formation and operation of business and manufacturing. Teams of students work with Clarkson Small Business Institute as consultants to regional firms. The course has three component parts: (1) a strategic audit, (2) problem/opportunity definition, and (3) analysis and written reports.

University of Colorado
Graduate School of Business
  Administration
Boulder, CO 80309
(303) 492-5131
Small Business Strategy, Policy & Entrepreneurship: Emphasis is on planning, organizing, and operating small-business firms. Special attention is devoted to analysis of small business as a dynamic force in the American business system.

Colorado State University
Fort Collins, CO 80523
(303) 491-6471
Entrepreneurial Engineering: Students produce a business plan.

Columbia University
Graduate School of Business
New York, NY 10027
(212) 280-5553
Management of New Venture: A graduate-level course designed to offer students the opportunity to study the factors, variables, and conditions involved in the initiation and development of new ventures. Offers both classroom study and an intensive field research project centered on either entrepreneurial or business development activities.

University of Connecticut, Hartford
School of Business
Hartford, CT 06105
(203) 241-4742
Three courses in the Hartford MBA program: *Seminar in Entrepreneurial Planning; Corporate Venturing and Entrepreneurship; Starting New Ventures.*

Cornell University
Graduate School of Business and Public
  Administration
Ithaca, NY 14953
(607) 256-7248
The Entrepreneur and Small Business Enterprise: Deals with the formation of a new enterprise or the acquisition of

existing enterprises from the viewpoint of those who desire to become principal owners.

Cranfield School of Management
Cranfield, Bedford, England MK43 OAL
0234/751122

Dartmouth College
Thayer School of Engineering
Hanover, NH 03755
(603) 646-3318
Entrepreneurship: Deals with the formation of a new enterprise and certain special aspects of managing the small growing business. It considers the characteristics of the successful entrepreneur, methods of identifying new opportunity areas, creativity and invention, legal and tax aspects of starting a new enterprise, pros and cons of various forms of organization, acquiring seed capital, obtaining venture capital for growth or for purchase of an existing business, measuring market potentials for new products or services, and new-product development.

University of Delaware
Business Administration Department
Newark, DE 19716
(302) 451-2555
New Venture Planning: Groups identify a potential new-business opportunity, develop a complete business plan for the chosen venture, and present their plan to a panel of businesspeople.

DePaul University
Department of Management
25 East Jackson Blvd.
Chicago, IL 60604
(302) 321-8471
Entrepreneurship and New Venture Management: The focus is on new-venture initiation and the preparation of a business plan that can be used to generate financing and to begin operations.

Drexel University
College of Business Administration
8230 South Chestnut
Philadelphia, PA 19104
(215) 895-2354
New Product Development and Marketing: Covers all major facets of product development; students develop a product and a business they can launch if they choose. *Managing the Front End of Innovation:* An overview of the management functions in regard to innovation.

Duke University
Fuqua School of Business
Durham, NC 27706
(919) 684-4266
Center for Entrepreneurial Studies: Devoted to developing and studying entrepreneurs.

East Carolina University
School of Business
Greenville, NC 27834
(919) 757-6836
Entrepreneurship: Conception, initiation, and management of new enterprises and ventures. Consideration of the problems, risks, and opportunities associated with new enterprises and ventures.

Eastern Illinois University
School of Business
Charleston, IL 61920
(217) 581-2021
Enterprise Development: A practical exercise in the development, initiation, and management of an enterprise.

Ecole Polytechnique de Montreal
Department de Genie Industriel
Case Postale 6079, succursale "A"
Montreal, Quebec, Canada H3C-3A7
(514) 344-4868
Industrial Innovation: Part of the undergraduate Engineering program.

Emory University
Graduate School of Business
   Administration
Atlanta, GA 30322
(404) 329-6314
Entrepreneurship and New Venture Management: Studies the characteristics of effective entrepreneurs and the detailed actions necessary to start and manage a new venture; graduate and undergraduate courses.

Florida Atlantic University
College of Business and Public
   Administration
Boca Raton, FL 33431
(305) 393-3630
Introduction to Small Business: Fundamental principles involved in the management of a small business; emphasis on considerations involved in the initiation stage.

Fordham University
441 East Fordham Road
The Bronx, NY 10458
(212) 579-2000
The Entrepreneur and Small Business Management: Undergraduate course that focuses on starting a business from scratch. Working in teams, students develop new-business ideas.

George Washington University
School of Government and Business
   Administration
Washington, DC 20035
(202) 676-5818
Technical Enterprises: Essential features of technology-based companies from the entrepreneur's point of view. *Technological Entrepreneurship and Innovation:* Focus on new technology-based venture initiation. Special attention on technology-related topics such as R&D limited partnerships, patenting new technology, trade secrets, and managing technical people.

Georgetown University
School of Business Administration
Washington, DC 22057
(301) 942-7490

Entrepreneurship: Designed for students who desire to start their own business someday.

University of Georgia
College of Business Administration
Athens, GA 30602
(404) 542-2980
Entrepreneurship/New Venture Formation: The characteristics of the entrepreneur, a brief history of small business and its overall role in the economy, the factors operating in small-business success and failure, and the factors to be considered in starting up a new small business.

Georgia Institute of Technology
College of Engineering
Atlanta, GA 30332
(404) 894-3350
Analysis and Evaluation of Industrial Projects: Starting with the generation of ideas for new ventures, all steps involved in feasibility analysis are covered.

Georgia State University
School of Business Administration
University Plaza
Atlanta, GA 30303
(404) 658-3400
Entrepreneurship and Enterprise: Deals with the identification, development, and growth of the entrepreneur and his or her firm within the free-enterprise system. Selected business opportunities are appraised through identifying critical success factors in the design and implementation of a feasibility study.

University of Hartford
Barney School of Business & Public
  Administration
West Hartford, CT 06117
(203) 243-4241
Entrepreneurship: Designed to enable graduate students considering self-employment to examine realistically some of the characteristics, opportunities, risk taking, and decision making in new business, new enterprise, or self-employment ventures.

Harvard University
Graduate School of Business
Administration
Boston, MA 02163
(617) 495-6000
Entrepreneurial Management: Emphasis is on risk taking in new-business ventures, rather than on day-to-day management. Case studies. *Entrepreneurial Finance:* Focus is on the financial issues confronting managers in entrepreneurial settings.

University of Hawaii
College of Business Administration
2404 Maile Way
Honolulu, HI 96822
(808) 548-8377
Economics of Entrepreneurship: Critical appraisal of the role of entrepreneurship in process of industrialization. Examines major theories of entrepreneurial supply and determiners of entrepreneurial behavior.

University of Houston
College of Business Administration
Houston, TX 77004
(713) 749-3423 or 749-1126
Entrepreneurship: Overall goal is to move students closer to establishing their own businesses.

Humboldt State University
School of Business & Economics
Arcata, CA 95521
(707) 826-4203
Entrepreneurial Management Programs: Emphasis on integrating primary functional areas of business in a "managerial blueprint." Students develop a feasibility study and implementation plan for a new small business.

University of Illinois, Urbana and Champaign
Department of Business Administration
1206 South Sixth
Champaign, IL 61820
(217) 333-6129 or 333-4240
Entrepreneurship: Small Business Formation: For those with a serious interest in owning their own business within five years of graduation. Students prepare a comprehensive business plan for starting or acquiring such a business.

Indiana University
School of Business
Bloomington, IN 47405
(812) 335-3462
Small Business Entrepreneurship: Critical phases in the life of a small firm, planning a new business, the business plan, external sources of information, purchasing an existing business, choosing the legal structure, sources of funds for a new business, tax aspects of starting up, and franchising.

Insead
European Institute of Business Administration
77305 Fontainebleau
Cedex, France
6-422-4827
New Ventures: For MBA participants with a strong desire to run their own business. Case discussions, and a new-venture project requiring substantial field work.

University of Iowa
College of Business Administration
Iowa City, IA 52242
(319) 352-4960
Entrepreneurship and New Business Formation: Graduate students design a new business venture and present a proposal for financing it. Course emphasizes entrepreneurial history and the psychology of entrepreneurship, and the techniques of purchasing or selling a company.

Iowa State University
College of Engineering
Ames, IA 50011
(515) 294-5933
Entrepreneurship for Engineering: Furnishes an introduction and some practical guidelines for students interested in developing a private engineering enterprise.

Johns Hopkins University
Evening College and Summer Session
Baltimore, MD 21218
(301) 338-7192
Entrepreneurship and New Venture Management: Planning, organizing, and managing a new business venture. Particular emphasis on the concepts and actual practice of creating, financing, and marketing a new-business undertaking.

Keller Graduate School of Management
Center for Entrepreneurial Studies
Chicago, IL 60606
(312) 454-0880
Business Planning Seminar: Emphasis on preparation and presentation of new-business plans.

University of Kentucky
Department of Management
Lexington, KY 40506
(606) 257-7726 or 257-1185
Entrepreneurship and New Venture Creation: Intended for students who plan to pursue self-employment early in their careers.

Laurentian University
School of Commerce and Administration
Sudbury, Ontario, Canada P3E-2C6
(705) 675-1151
Entrepreneurship: Designed for students contemplating starting or purchasing a business at some time in their career.

Lehigh University
College of Business & Economics
Bethlehem, PA 18015
(215) 861-3434

Entrepreneurship and Business Policy:
Case study of the problem of creating
new ventures or managing family-owned
businesses.

Long Island University
School of Business
Greenvale, NY 11548
(516) 299-2361
The Venture Capital Game: One of the
capstone courses of the MBA program.
The game integrates the quantitative
approach with the behavioral sciences
and enables the students to consolidate
and bring together the tools and skills
acquired in the several disciplines within
the graduate program and apply them
directly to the problems of the raising of
venture capital. *Creating and Managing a
Small Business:* Designed to integrate the
functional areas of management, marketing, finance, and accounting within an
overall economic framework; business
students develop a comprehensive business plan.

Marquette University
Robert A. Johnson College of Business
    Administration
Milwaukee, WI 53233
(414) 272-5420
New Ventures and Entrepreneurship:
Students complete a sophisticated and
coherent business plan for a new busi-
ness, started and operated by them.

Massachusetts Institute of Technology
Innovation Center
Building W59-201
Cambridge, MA 02139
(617) 253-5180
MIT Innovation Center: A division of the
School of Engineering, the center offers a
variety of courses, four of which may be
considered standard: *Invention; Entrepre-
neurship; Development Laboratory;* and
*Internship in New Enterprise Develop-
ment.*

Miami (Ohio) University
School of Business Administration
Oxford, OH 45056
(513) 529-3631
Entrepreneurship: New Ventures: Designed to introduce students, through a
combination of complex cases, technical
notes, lectures, role playing, negotiations,
and guest speakers, to the problems and
opportunities involved in high-potential
business ventures.

University of Michigan
Graduate School of Business Administra-
    tion
Ann Arbor, MI 48109
(313) 764-2325
Seminar on Small Business Formation:
MBA students investigate the feasibility
of starting a small-business firm and
learn the problems of new-venture formation.

Milwaukee School of Engineering
College of Engineering, Management and
    Engineering Technology
P. O. Box 644
Milwaukee, WI 53201
(414) 277-7300
Technical Entrepreneurship: Designed to
develop a thorough understanding of
the requirements of successfully starting
and operating a manufacturing business.
Students choose a product and develop a
comprehensive business plan.

University of Minnesota
Department of Strategic Management and
    Organization
830 Management and Organization
    Building
Minneapolis, MN 55455
(612) 373-3846
Entrepreneurship and the Smaller Firm:
Assessment of opportunities and constraints in establishing and managing
one's own firm; topics include structuring a new venture, buying into an existing enterprise, owning an enterprise

versus becoming a principal employee in a new venture. Case method.

University of Missouri, Rolla
School of Engineering
Rolla, MO 65401
(314) 341-4568
Technical Entrepreneurship: Engineering student teams develop a complete business plan for a company to develop, manufacture, and distribute a real technical product or service.

University of Montana
Department of Management
Missoula, MT 59812
(406) 243-6644
Entrepreneurship: Studies methods of obtaining, investing, and managing personal wealth to achieve financial goals. *Management 690:* For students interested in starting a business or in learning about how new business ventures are started and developed.

University of Nebraska, Omaha
College of Business Administration
Omaha, NE 68182
(402) 554-2303
Entrepreneurship: Procedures and processes necessary to establish a new business. Stresses interrelationships among functional areas of business, assesses operating environments, and uses analytical management tools.

University of Nevada, Reno
Electrical Engineering Department
Reno, NV 89557
(702) 784-6927
Electrical Engineering Entrepreneurship: Primarily an engineering design project, but includes consideration of business aspects of the design as well. Business topics include marketing of new products, financial statements, venture capital, patents, obtaining assistance for small businesses, and insurance.

University of New Hampshire
Whittemore School of Business and Economics
Durham, NH 03824
(603) 862-2771
Exploration in Entrepreneurial Management: Focuses on the management of change and innovation, whether in new-venture formation or in new directions and methods for existing organizations.

University of New Mexico
Department of Mechanical Engineering
Albuquerque, NM 87131
(505) 277-2761
Entrepreneurial Engineering: Review of the necessary elements for successfully launching a technical business, with focus on technology, manufacturing, marketing, management, finance, and legal aspects.

New Mexico Highlands University
Division of Business and Economics
Las Vegas, NM 87701
(505) 425-7511 Ext. 344
Technological Entrepreneurship: Students prepare and present comprehensive business plans.

New Mexico Institute of Mining and Technology
Technological Innovation Program
Socorro, NM 87801
(505) 835-5953 or 835-5421
Technological Entrepreneurship.

University of New Orleans
College of Business Administration
New Orleans, LA 70148
(504) 286-6241
Marketing Management: Emphasis on preparing a thoroughly detailed plan for establishing a new business.

New York University
Center for Entrepreneurial Studies
100 Trinity Place
New York, NY 10006
(212) 285-6150

Entrepreneurship: Describes the entrepreneurial process, develops an analytic framework for analyzing new-venture situations, examines some of the typical problems encountered in new ventures, and prepares a business plan for a small business. *Corporate Entrepreneurship:* The unique problems and opportunities for entrepreneurs in corporations in the venturing process are examined with a view to reducing the cost of failure and increasing the chances of success.

University of North Carolina, Chapel Hill
School of Business Administration
Carroll Hall
Chapel Hill, NC 27599
(919) 962-2211
New Venture Management: Examines the entrepreneurial process of searching for new-venture opportunities, evaluating the potential of these opportunities, securing venture capital and permanent financing, managing the new enterprise, evaluating merger and acquisition opportunities, and going public.

North Carolina State University
Raleigh, NC 27695
(919) 737-2011
Starting Your Own Business: Designed for students interested in starting a business of their own or who are already operating a small business.

Northeastern University
College of Business Administration
Boston, MA 02115
(617) 437-4812
Entrepreneurship and New Venture Management.

University of Northern Iowa
School of Business
Cedar Falls, IA 50613
(319) 273-6304
Entrepreneurship and Small Business Management: An experience-based class including self-assessment, small-group

activities and discussions, interviews, research, and creative planning.

Northwestern Graduate School of Management
200001 Sheridan Road
Leverone Hall
Evanston, IL 60201
(312) 492-3300
Entrepreneurship and New Venture Formulation: Concentrates primarily on the initiation of new business ventures, although some attention is given to the problems of management and growth of the new venture after startup.

Nova University
School of Business & Economics
P.O. Box 170
Old Westbury, NY 11568
(516) 686-7580
Entrepreneurship and Venture Initiation: Offers the opportunity to study and research theories of business development and the multiplicity of factors peculiar to the launching of a new venture.

Ohio State University
College of Administrative Science
Columbus, OH 43210
(614) 486-6424
The Development of Entrepreneurs Through Vocational Education: Teacher Training Workshop: One of the first attempts to develop entrepreneurs through vocational-technical education.

The University of Oklahoma
College of Business Administration
Norman, OK 73019
(405) 321-7179
Venture Management: Skills needed to bring an idea for a product or service to the point of seeking financing for it.

Oklahoma State University
College of Business Administration
Stillwater, OK 74078
(405) 624-5200

Venture Management and Entrepreneurship: Graduate and undergraduate courses dealing with venture management and entrepreneurship.

Oral Roberts University
School of Business
Tulsa, OK 74171
(918) 495-7039
Special Problems in Entrepreneurship: A study of the art and science of entrepreneurship. Technical knowledge is developed through discussion of the tools needed to successfully start and operate a business. The primary emphasis, however, is on the more qualitative aspects of entrepreneurship.

University of Oregon
Graduate School of Management and
  Business
Eugene, OR 97403
(503) 686-3303
College of Business Administration operates an Innovation Center that includes the following courses: *Small Business Management; Venture Finance; Management of Creativity; Entrepreneurship; Technological Organizations.*

Oregon State University
School of Business
Corvallis, OR 97331
(503) 754-0123
Entrepreneurship: The search for, and the analysis of, new-venture possibilities, with emphasis on feasibility studies.

Pace University
Lubin Graduate School of Business
1 Pace Plaza
New York, NY 10038
(212) 488-1923 or 461-7515
Entrepreneurial Policy: Provides an understanding of entrepreneurship as applied to starting a new business or a new venture within an existing enterprise.

University of Pennsylvania
The Wharton School
Philadelphia, PA 19104
(215) 898-4856
Entrepreneurship and Venture Initiation: Self-chosen entrepreneurial activities are planned, presented, and executed to the extent feasible. A basic goal of the course is to develop and apply procedures and methods of corporate and strategic planning for the new and growing enterprise.

In addition, several courses are offered for the Entrepreneurship major in the Wharton Entrepreneurial Center, such as Entrepreneurial Decision Making; Mergers and Acquisitions; Consulting for Small Businesses; Economic Management of Small Business Systems; Technological Innovation and Entrepreneurship.

Portland State University
School of Business Administration
P.O. Box 751
Portland, OR 97207
(503) 292-8666
Venture Management for High-Technology Companies: Explores entrepreneurship and the entrance criteria and formation of new businesses.

Purdue University
Krannert Graduate School of
  Management
West Lafayette, IN 47907
(317) 494-9700
New Enterprises: Concerned with developing skills in starting and managing new enterprises.

Rensselaer Polytechnic Institute
School of Management
Troy, NY 12181
(518) 266-6834
Management of Technological Innovation: As part of the MBA concentration in the Management of Technology, course covers the process of technological innovation, from the initial idea to the suc-

cessful introduction into the market of a new product, process, or service.

University of Rhode Island
College of Business Administration
Kingston, RI 02881
(401) 792-4320
Entrepreneurship for Majors in Business.

Rice University
Jesse H. Jones School of Administration
P.O. Box 1892, Houston, TX 77251
(713) 827-8101
Entrepreneurship and the New Enterprise: For students who may wish to initiate their own businesses at some stage in their careers.

University of Rochester
Graduate School of Management
Rochester, NY 14627
(716) 442-0888
Entrepreneurship and New Venture Management: Personal qualities of successful entrepreneurs, suitable strategies for a new entrepreneurial business, and management problems unique to a new venture.

Rutgers University, the State University of New Jersey
Graduate School of Business
    Administration
Newark, NJ 07102
(201) 648-5287
Design of a Manufacturing Enterprise: The principles involved from conceptualization through establishment of a manufacturing enterprise.

St. John's University
College of Business Administration
Jamaica, NY 11439
(718) 990-6417
Administrative Planning: Student creates a business plan that includes an overall description of the new venture, a market survey, a time schedule, a manufacturing/service plan, a marketing plan, an organizational plan, and cash-flow earnings projections.

St. Louis University
School of Business Administration
St. Louis, MO 63108
(314) 658-3878
Entrepreneurship: Provides students with both the cognitive and effective components of the entrepreneur.

Saint Mary's University
Halifax, Nova Scotia, Canada
(902) 429-9780
Small Business Management: Students research their ideas for starting a small business, and prepare a comprehensive business plan to be used in gaining support (financial and otherwise) for the idea.

San Diego State University
College of Business Administration
San Diego, CA 92182
(619) 582-4436
Venture Management: The process of initiating, expanding, purchasing, and consolidating businesses. Investigates concepts, theories, and techniques of managerial innovation and implementation. Emphasizes unique managerial styles and strategies.

San Francisco State University
School of Business
1600 Holloway Ave.
San Francisco, CA 94132
(415) 469-1276
Entrepreneurial Management: Focus is on the risk/decision process of the innovative personality, developing an improved effectiveness.

San Jose State University
School of Business
San Jose, CA 95192
(408) 277-2305
Management of New Enterprises: For students who are considering investment

in a new business or who are interested in their own ventures.

University of Santa Clara
Graduate School of Business & Administration
Santa Clara, CA 96053
(408) 984-4580
Small Business Entrepreneurship: Seeks to examine the prerequisites for success as a small-business entrepreneur within a decision-making framework.

University of Saskatchewan
College of Commerce
Saskatoon, Saskatchewan, Canada S7N-0W0
(306) 343-3568
Entrepreneurship and Small Business Management: Examines the processes involved in and the skills required for the formation of new business ventures and the ongoing management of small businesses.

University of Sherbrooke
Department of Management
Sherbrooke, Quebec, Canada J1K-2R1
(819) 565-5970
Entrepreneurship and Venture Initiation: Emphasis is on evaluating the feasibility of a new business idea. Students conceptualize a profitable venture and prepare a detailed business plan outlining their level of commitment and specific competence toward the achievement of their goals.

Sonoma State University
Department of Management Studies
Rohnert Park, CA 94928
(707) 664-2377
Starting and Managing the Small Business: For prospective entrepreneurs wishing to start a new business or participate in the management of a small ongoing company during its early months.

University of South Carolina
Graduate School of Business
Columbia, SC 29208
(803) 777-5955
Initiation and Management of New Business Enterprise (undergraduate): Planning and establishing a business organization to exploit an opportunity; management of small business. *Small Business Management* (graduate): The problems involved in the organization and management of a small business, including legal forms, location, product market determination, production, and other operating conditions.

University of Southern California
School of Business Administration
Los Angeles, CA 90080
(818) 453-3307
Business Enterprise Development and Entrepreneurship Program: This graduate program helps develop the innovator who is skilled in the interrelated fields of (1) new-venture development and implementation and (2) small-business operation and development. Emphasizes the opportunity-creation aspects of business as well as problem solving; oriented toward the application of theory to practical situations.

Southern Illinois University, Carbondale
College of Business and Administration
Carbondale, IL 62901
(618) 453-3307
Entrepreneurship: Principles involved in locating market opportunities and developing growth plans for businesses requiring a relatively low initial capital investment. Taught from the point of view of the owner-manager, relying heavily upon case examples of successful entrepreneurship.

University of Southern Maine
Graduate School of Business Administration
96 Falmouth Street

Portland, ME 04103
(207) 780-4020
New Enterprise Institute.

Southern Methodist University
Edwin L. Cox School of Business
Dallas, TX 75275
(214) 692-3326
The SMU Entrepreneurial Experience:
Distinguished Entrepreneur Seminar;
Active Entrepreneur Seminar; Young
Entrepreneur Seminar.

Stanford University
Graduate School of Business
Stanford, CA 94305
(415) 497-2146
New Enterprise Management: Emphasis
is on the development and evaluation of
realistic, action-oriented business plans
to launch new enterprises.

Texas A. & M. University
College of Business Administration
College Station, TX 77843
(409) 845-1724
Entrepreneurship and New Ventures:
Includes *Small Business Formation;*
Special Studies in Entrepreneurship;
Internship in New Ventures; and *Entre-*
preneurship and New Ventures Society.

University of Tennessee, Knoxville
College of Business Administration
Knoxville, TN 37916
(615) 974-5061
Entrepreneurship: Managing the Small
Independent Enterprise: Introduction to
the elements in the process of initiating
and managing a new business enterprise.

University of Texas, Austin
Graduate School of Business
Austin, TX 78712
(512) 471-5921
Entrepreneurship: Focuses entirely on the
manifold aspects of beginning a new
business venture—from the genesis of an
idea for a potentially viable enterprise,

through a detailed feasibility analysis, to
the realities of implementing a rational
business plan.

Thiel College
Greensville, PA 16125
(412) 588-7700
The Entrepreneur, Small Business, and
Free Enterprise: Involves students in
starting and managing a small business,
and investigates the role of these enterprises in the community.

University of Toronto
Faculty of Applied Science and
    Engineering
Toronto, Ontario, Canada M4S-1A5
(416) 964-9515 or 978-2900
Innovation and Entrepreneurship: Emphasis is on identifying new-business
opportunities, and structuring and financing a new enterprise designed to
capitalize on one of the opportunities
selected.

Troy State University
School of Business
Troy, AL 36082
(205) 566-3000
Management Seminar.

Tulane University
Graduate School of Business
    Administration
New Orleans, LA 70118
(504) 865-5410
Entrepreneurship and the New Business
Enterprise: Includes an analysis of the
individual entrepreneur and the nature
and problems of establishing new enterprises.

University of Tulsa
College of Business Administration
Tulsa, OK 741
(918) 592-6000
New Ventures Management: The establishment, management, and operation of
a small business.

University of Utah
Graduate School of Business
College of Engineering
Salt Lake City, UT 84112
(801) 581-7785
Innovation and Entrepreneurship: Student teams develop a technical design for a new product.

University of Virginia
McIntire School of Commerce
Charlottesville, VA 22903
(804) 924-3214
Entrepreneurship: Deals with the formation of a new enterprise and certain special aspects of managing a small enterprise. Considers the characteristics of the successful entrepreneur, methods of identifying new opportunity areas, starting a new enterprise, tax and legal aspects of new business, and financing for initial capital.

University of Washington
School of Business Administration, DJ-10
Department of Management and Organization
Seattle, WA 98195
(206) 543-4367
Entrepreneurship: Focuses on entrepreneurship, both in the form of establishment of new independent businesses owned largely by those who manage them and initiation of new enterprises with exceptional autonomy within larger organizations that finance and own them. *Entrepreneurship II:* Focuses almost entirely on startup projects.

University of Waterloo
Faculty of Engineering
Waterloo, Ontario, Canada N2L-3G1
(519) 885-1211
The Engineer as an Entrepreneur: How an individual engineer may develop a new small business to supply goods or services to Canadian chemical industries; technical, economic, legal, and financial aspects.

The University of Western Ontario
London, Ontario, Canada N6A-3K7
(519) 679-3228
New Enterprise Management: Cases illustrate the opportunities, risks, and factors necessary for the success of the entrepreneur and the new enterprise.

Wichita State University
Center for Entrepreneurship
College of Business Administration
Wichita, KS 67208
(316) 689-3000
The center offers seven undergraduate courses (among them are *Small Business Management, Venture Creation,* and *Technical Entrepreneurship*) and several graduate-level courses, including *Small Business Practicum* and *New Venture Feasibility Seminar.* Special entrepreneurship seminars offered to local business owners and high school teachers.

Wilfrid Laurier University
School of Business and Economics
Waterloo, Ontario, Canada N2L-3C5
(519) 884-1970 Ext. 2532
New Venture Creation.

University of Wisconsin, Milwaukee
School of Business Administration
Milwaukee, WI 53201
(414) 963-4235
Venture Formation and Small Business Management.

Wright State University
College of Business and Administration
Dayton, OH 45435
(513) 873-3204
Entrepreneurship (graduate): Problems and perspectives in starting new ventures. Concepts and techniques of searching for market opportunities, screening and evaluating potentials, and financing.

Xavier University
Victory Parkway
Cincinnati, OH 45207
(513) 745-3491

Entrepreneurship: Emphasis is on problems, techniques, and methods relating to the search, screening, evaluating, negotiating, and financing needed to initiate or purchase a company. Other MBA-level courses in entrepreneurship which involve developing a new-venture concept, writing a business plan designed to aid in implementing the concept, and small-business consulting.

York University
Faculty of Administrative Studies
Toronto, Ontario, Canada
(416) 667-2532
New Small Business Ventures: Emphasis is on identifying personal goals and integrating them with a new venture plan, and ways to solve the problems of new-venture startups.

SECTION 8.

Government Information and Venture Capital Firms

The Small Business Administration   229
        National Association of Small Business
            Investment Companies   237
Private Venture Capital Companies   281

Entrepreneurs who feel the need of advice and assistance in the operation of their businesses can find help from a variety of sources. In addition to private sector accountants, attorneys, and other management consultants, both federal and state governments sponsor a wide variety of assistance. The Small Business Administration sponsors an effective network of public and semi-private assistance programs. Some of these are associated with selected colleges and universities, business associations, or state governments; others involve and utilize the expertise of both retired and active executives. The Internal Revenue Service periodically offers seminars on tax management and tax preparation. The wise entrepreneur knows his or her strengths and weaknesses and seeks help in filling any gaps.

JAMES ABDNOR
Administrator
U.S. Small Business Administration

THE SMALL BUSINESS ADMINISTRATION

For more than three decades, a network of public and private agencies has been developing programs that offer assistance to small businesses. This assistance comes in a variety of formats: publications, training programs, direct advising, and financial counseling and assistance. The cornerstone of this network is the Small Business Administration. It is supported by agencies such as colleges and universities, retired business executives, and private venture capitalists. Selecting the most appropriate medium through which to receive help often is a critical decision. The SBA maintains regional offices in most major cities, and SBA personnel are available to direct you to the best source available for a specific or general need.

Included in this section are a listing of all SBA offices by region, a compilation of SBA Business Development booklets and pamphlets, and a listing of the Association of Small Business Development Centers by state.

SBA Offices

National Office
Small Business Administration
1441 L St., NW, Room 317
Washington, DC 20416
(202) 653-6365

Region I
60 Batterymarch St., 10th floor
Boston, MA 02110
(617) 223-3204

Region II
26 Federal Plaza, Room 29-118
New York, NY 10278
(212) 264-7772

Region III
One Bala Cynwyd Plaza, West Lobby
Bala Cynwyd, PA 19004
(215) 596-5901

Region IV
1375 Peachtree St., NE
Atlanta, GA 30367
(404) 347-4999

Region V
230 S. Dearborn St.
Chicago, IL 60604
(312) 353-0359

Region VI
8625 King George Dr., Bldg. C
Dallas, TX 75235-3391
(214) 767-7643

Region VII
911 Walnut St., 13th floor
Kansas City, MO 64106
(816) 374-3163

Region IX
450 Golden Gate Ave.
Box 36044
San Francisco, CA 94102
(415) 556-7487

Region VIII
1405 Curtis St., 22nd floor
Denver, CO 80202
(303) 844-5441

Region X
2615 Fourth Ave., Room 440
Seattle, WA 98121
(206) 442-5676

SBA Business Development Publications

Booklets

Booklets in this series discuss specific management techniques or problems. The following list is reproduced from official SBA publications.

No.	Title	Stock No.	Price
	Small Business Management Series		
9.	Cost Accounting for Small Manufacturers	045-000-00162-8	$6.00
15.	Handbook of Small Business Finances	045-000-00208-0	4.50
20.	Ratio Analysis for Small Business	045-000-00150-4	4.50
25.	Guides for Profit Planning	045-000-00137-7	4.50
29.	Management Audit for Small Manufacturers	045-000-00151-2	4.25
30.	Insurance and Risk Management for Small Businesses	045-000-00209-8	5.00
31.	Management Audit for Small Retailers	045-000-00149-1	4.50
32.	Financial Recordkeeping for Small Stores	045-000-00142-3	5.50
33.	Small Store Planning for Growth	045-000-00152-1	5.50
35.	Franchise Index/Profile	045-000-00125-3	4.50
36.	Training Salesmen to Serve Industrial Markets	045-000-00133-4	2.50
37.	Financial Control by Time-Absorption Analysis	045-000-00134-2	5.50
38.	Management Audit for Small Service Firms	045-000-00203-9	4.50
39.	Decision Points in Developing New Products	045-000-00146-6	4.25
41.	Purchasing Management and Inventory Control for Small Business	045-000-00167-9	4.50
42.	Managing the Small Service Firm for Growth and Profit	045-000-00165-2	4.25
43.	Credit and Collections for Small Stores	045-000-00169-5	5.00
44.	Financial Management: How to Make a Go of Your Business	045-000-00233-1	2.50

Starting and Managing Series. This series is designed to help the small entrepreneur "look before leaping" into a business.

1.	Starting and Managing a Small Business of Your Own	045-000-00212-8	$4.75
101.	Starting and Managing a Small Service Business	045-000-00207-1	4.50
102.	Starting and Managing a Small Business from Your Home	045-000-00232-3	1.75
103.	Small Business Incubator Handbook: A Guide for Start-Up and Management	045-000-00237-3	8.50

Nonseries Publications

A Basic Guide to Exporting	003-009-00349-1	$4.50
U.S. Government Purchasing and Sales Directory	045-000-00226-8	5.50
Managing for Profits	045-000-00206-3	5.50
Buying and Selling a Small Business	045-000-00232-2	1.75
Women Business Owners: Selling to the Federal Government	045-000-00229-2	2.75

Business Basics. Each of the 23 self-study booklets in this series contains text, questions, and exercises that teach a specific aspect of small-business management.

1001.	The Profit Plan	045-000-00192-0	$4.50
1002.	Capital Planning	045-000-00193-8	4.50
1003.	Understanding Money Sources	045-000-00194-6	4.75
1004.	Evaluating Money Sources	045-000-00174-1	5.00
1005.	Asset Management	045-000-00175-0	2.57
1006.	Managing Fixed Assets	045-000-00176-8	4.75
1007.	Understanding Costs	045-000-00195-4	3.25
1008.	Cost Control	045-000-00187-3	4.75
1009.	Marketing Strategy	045-000-00188-1	4.75
1010.	Retail Buying Function	045-000-00177-6	4.50
1011.	Inventory Management—Wholesale/Retail	045-000-00190-3	4.75
1012.	Retail Merchandise Management	045-000-00178-4	4.50
1013.	Consumer Credit	045-000-00179-2	4.50
1014.	Credit Collections: Policy and Procedures	045-000-00180-6	4.75
1015.	Purchasing for Manufacturing Firms	045-000-00181-4	4.75
1016.	Inventory Management—Manufacturing/Service	045-000-00182-2	4.75
1017.	Inventory and Scheduling Techniques	045-000-00183-1	4.75
1018.	Risk Management and Insurance	045-000-00184-9	4.50
1019.	Managing Retail Salespeople	045-000-00189-0	4.75
1020.	Job Analysis, Job Specifications, Job Descriptions	045-000-00185-7	4.50
1021.	Recruiting and Selecting Employees	045-000-00186-5	4.50
1022.	Training and Developing Employees	045-000-00191-1	4.50
1023.	Employee Relations and Personnel Policies		4.50
		045-000-00196-2	

Pamphlets

The SBA publishes a growing list of pamphlets dealing with special topics and various aspects of starting and operating a small business; each is fifty cents per copy. The current list includes:

Financial Management and Analysis

MA 1.001   The ABC's of Borrowing
MA 1.004   Basic Budgets for Profit Planning
MA 1.009   A Venture Capital Primer for Small Business
MA 1.010   Accounting Services for Small Service Firms
MA 1.011   Analyze Your Records to Reduce Costs
MA 1.015   Budgeting in a Small Business Firm
MA 1.016   Sound Cash Management and Borrowing
MA 1.017   Keeping Records in Small Business
MA 1.018   Checklist for Profit Watching
MA 1.019   Simple Breakeven Analysis for Small Stores
MA 4.013   A Pricing Checklist for Small Retailers

General Management and Planning

MA 2.002   Locating or Relocating Your Business
MA 2.004   Problems in Managing a Family-Owned Business
MA 2.007   Business Plan for Small Manufacturers
MA 2.008   Business Plan for Small Construction Firms
MA 2.010   Planning and Goal Setting for Small Business
MA 2.014   Should You Lease or Buy Equipment?
MA 2.016   Checklist for Going into Business
MA 2.020   Business Plan for Retailers
MA 2.022   Business Plan for Small Service Firms
MA 2.025   Thinking About Going into Business
MA 2.026   Feasibility Checklist for Starting a Small Business of Your Own
MA 2.027   How to Get Started with a Small Business Computer
MA 2.028   The Business Plan for Homebased Business
MA 3.005   Stock Control for Small Stores
MA 3.010   Techniques for Problem Solving
MA 5.009   Techniques for Productivity Improvement
MA 6.004   Selecting the Legal Structure for Your Business
MA 7.007   Evaluating Franchise Opportunities

Crime Prevention

MA 3.006   Reducing Shoplifting
MA 5.005   Preventing Employee Pilferage

Marketing

MA 4.002   Creative Selling: The Competitive Edge
MA 4.005   Is the Independent Sales Agent for You?
MA 4.012   Marketing Checklist for Small Retailers
MA 4.015   Advertising Guidelines for Small Retail Firms
MA 4.018   Plan Your Advertising Budget
MA 4.019   Learning About Your Market
MA 4.023   Selling by Mail Order
MA 7.003   Market Overseas with U.S. Government Help

Personnel Management

MA 5.001   Checklist for Developing a Training Program
MA 5.007   Staffing Your Store
MA 5.008   Managing Employee Benefits

New Products/Ideas/Inventions

MA 2.013   Can You Make Money with Your Idea or Invention?
MA 6.005   Introduction to Patents
SBIR-T1   Proposal Preparation for Small Business Innovation Research

Miscellaneous

SBB 2   Home Businesses (includes text, but is mainly an in-depth bibliography on a
           wide range of books, newsletters, associations, etc.)

Association of Small Business Development Centers

The Small Business Development Center program provides a framework for combining resources of universities and colleges with those of government to strengthen the small-business community. The SBDC offers extensive assistance to entrepreneurs and the owner-managers of existing firms. It disseminates management information; performs services such as management audits, market studies, financial analyses, feasibility studies, and business planning; and provides business counseling and training with follow-on resources for the on-site implementation of recommendations.

Alabama
University of Alabama in Birmingham
School of Business
1717 - 11th Ave., South
Medical Towers Bldg., Suite 419
Birmingham, AL 35294
(205) 934-7260

Alaska
Small Business Development Center of Alaska
430 West 7th Ave.
Anchorage, AK 99501
(907) 274-7232

Arkansas
University of Arkansas at Little Rock
Small Business Development Center
Library, Room 512
33rd and University Ave.
Little Rock, AR 72204
(501) 371-5381

Connecticut
University of Connecticut
School of Business Administration
Box U-41D
Storrs, CT 06268
(203) 486-4135

Delaware
University of Delaware
Purnell Hall
Newark, DE 19711
(302) 451-2747

District of Columbia
Howard University
6th & Fairmount St., NW, Room 128
Washington, DC 20059
(202) 636-5150

Florida

Florida SBDC
University of West Florida
Bldg. 38
Pensacola, FL 32514-5752
(904) 474-3016

Georgia

University of Georgia
Small Business Development Center
Chicopee Complex
Athens, GA 30602
(404) 542-5760

Idaho

Boise State University
College of Business
1910 University Dr.
Boise, ID 83725
(208) 385-1640

Illinois

Small Business Development Center
Department of Commerce and Community
    Affairs
620 East Adams St., 5th floor
Springfield, IL 62701
(217) 785-6174

Indiana

Indiana Chamber of Commerce
One North Capitol, Suite 200
Indianapolis, IN 46204
(317) 634-6407

Iowa

Iowa SBDC
Chamberlynn Bldg.
Ames, IA 50010

Kansas

Wichita State University
Barton School of Business Administration
1845 Fairmount
Wichita, KS 67208
(316) 689-3193

Kentucky

University of Kentucky
18 Porter Bldg.
Lexington, KY 40506-0205
(606) 257-1751

Louisiana

Northeast Louisiana University
College of Business Administration
Administration Bldg. 2-99
Monroe, LA 71209
(318) 342-2464

Maine

University of Southern Maine
246 Deering Avenue
Portland, ME 04102
(207) 780-4420

Massachusetts

University of Massachusetts
School of Business Management
Room 203
Amherst, MA 01003
(413) 549-4930 ext. 303

Michigan

Wayne State University
2727 Second Ave., MCHT
Detroit, MI 48201
(313) 577-4848

Minnesota

Minnesota SBDC
1107 Hazeltine Blvd., Suite 451
Chaska, MN 55318
(612) 448-8810

Mississippi

Mississippi SBDC
3825 Ridgewood Rd.
Jackson, MS 39211
(601) 982-6760

Missouri
St. Louis University
3642 Lindell Blvd.
St. Louis, MO 63108
(314) 534-7204

Nebraska
Nebraska Business Development Center
University of Nebraska at Omaha
Omaha, NE 68182
(402) 554-3291

Nevada
Nevada SBDC
College of Business Administration
University of Nevada at Reno
Reno, NV 89557-0010
(702) 784-1717

New Hampshire
University of New Hampshire
110 McConnel Hall
Durham, NH 03824
(603) 862-3558

New Jersey
Rutgers University
Ackerson Hall, 3rd floor
180 University St.
Newark, NJ 07102
(201) 648-5950

New York
Research Foundation of the State of New
   York
SUNY Plaza
Albany, NY 12246
(518) 473-5398

North Carolina
Small Business and Technology Development
   Center
820 Clay St.
Raleigh, NC 27605
(919) 733-4643

North Dakota
North Dakota SBDC
Box 1576
Grand Forks, ND 58206
(701) 780-3403

Ohio
Ohio SBDC
P.O. Box 1001
Columbus, OH 43266-0101
(614) 466-5111

Oklahoma
Southeastern Oklahoma State University
517 West University
Durant, OK 74701
(405) 924-0121 ext. 427

Oregon
Lane Community College
Oregon SBDC Network
1059 Willamette St.
Eugene, OR 97401
(503) 726-2250

Pennsylvania
University of Pennsylvania
The Wharton School
3201 Steinberg Hall–Dietrich Hall 6374
Philadelphia, PA 19104
(215) 898-1219

Puerto Rico
University of Puerto Rico
P.O. Box 5253
College Station
Mayaguez, PR 00709
(809) 834-3590 or 834-3790

Rhode Island
Bryant College
Smithfield, RI 02917
(401) 232-6111

South Carolina
University of South Carolina
College of Business Administration
Columbia, SC 29208
(803) 777-4907

South Dakota
University of South Dakota
School of Business
414 East Clark St.
Vermillion, SD 57069
(605) 677-5272

Tennessee
Tennessee SBDC
Memphis State University
Memphis, TN 38152
(901) 454-2500

Texas
Gulf Coast SBDC
University of Houston
401 Louisiana, 8th floor
Houston, TX 77002
(713) 223-1141

Utah
University of Utah
Graduate School of Business
420 Chipeta Way, Suite 110
Salt Lake City, UT 84108
(801) 581-4869

Vermont
University of Vermont
Extension Service, Morrill Hall
Burlington, VT 05405
(802) 656-4479

Virgin Islands
College of the Virgin Islands
Grand Hotel Bldg., Annex B
P.O. Box 1087
St. Thomas, VI 00801
(809) 776-3206

Washington
Washington State University
College of Business and Economics
Pullman, WA 99164
(509) 335-1576

West Virginia
SBDC Division
GOCID, State Capitol Complex
Charleston, WV 25305
(800) 225-5982

Wisconsin
University of Wisconsin
602 State St., 2nd floor
Madison, WI 53703
(608) 263-7794

Wyoming
Wyoming SBDC
130 North Ash, Suite A
Casper, WY 82601
(307) 235-4825

NATIONAL ASSOCIATION OF SMALL BUSINESS INVESTMENT COMPANIES

Business organizations that are members of NASBIC include three main groups of firms:

1. Small-business investment companies (SBICs)
2. Minority enterprise small-business investment companies (MESBICs)
3. Associate Members and Sustaining Members; these are non-SBIC venture capitalists who also invest in small businesses or provide professional services to SBICs or MESBICs

SBICs and MESBICs are financial institutions created to make equity capital and long-term credit (with a maturity of at least five years) available to small businesses. SBICs are licensed by the SBA, but they are privately organized and privately managed firms that set their own policies and make their own investment decisions. In return for pledging to finance only small businesses, SBICs may qualify for long-term loans from SBA. Although all SBICs will consider applications for funds from socially and economically disadvantaged entrepreneurs, MESBIC companies normally make *all* their investments in this area. MESBIC companies are so identified at the end of each entry; others (unidentified) are SBICs.

In this section, SBICs and MESBICs are organized by state; Associate Members are listed alphabetically by company name. In using this directory, you should consider the following factors of each investment company: proximity, investment policy, industry preference, and size of financing. Contact any SBIC listed below for more information, or write the National Association of Small Business Investment Companies, 617 Washington Building, Washington, DC 20005.

Codes Used:

Preferred Limit of Loans or Investments

A Up to $100,000
B Up to $250,000
C Up to $500,000
D Up to $1 million
E Over $1 million

Investment policy

☐   Will consider either loans or investments
☐☐   Prefers to make long-term loans
☐☐☐   Prefers financings with right to acquire stock interest

Industry preferences

1   Communications and movies
2   Construction and development
3   Natural resources
4   Hotels, motels, and restaurants
5   Manufacturing and processing
6   Medical and other health services
7   Recreation and amusements
8   Research and technology
9   Retailing, wholesaling, and distribution
10   Service trades
11   Transportation
12   Diversified

NASBIC Members: SBIC and MESBIC Firms

Alabama

First SBIC of Alabama
David C. DeLaney, President
16 Midtown Park East
Mobile, AL 36606
(205) 276-0700
C ☐☐ 12

Hickory Venture Capital Corp.
J. Thomas Noojin, President and Chairman
699 Gallatin St., Suite A-2
Huntsville, AL 35801
(205) 539-1931
E ☐☐☐ 12

Remington Fund, Inc.
Lana Sellers, President
Box 10686
Birmingham, AL 35202
(205) 326-3509

Tuskegee Capital Corp.
A. G. Bartholomew, Vice-President and General Manager
4453 Richardson Rd.
Montgomery, AL 36108
(205) 281-8059
MESBIC   A ☐☐ 12

Alaska

Alaska Business Investment Corp.
James L. Cloud, Vice-President
Box 600
Anchorage, AK 99510
(907) 278-2071
B ☐ 12

Calista Business Investment Corp.
Nelson N. Angapak, President
516 Denali St.
Anchorage, AK 99501
(907) 277-0425
MESBIC   B ☐ 12

Arizona

FBS Venture Capital Co.
William McKee, President
6900 E. Camelback Rd., Suite 452
Scottsdale, AZ 85251
(602) 941-2160
C ☐ ☐ ☐ **1 5 6 8**

Norwest Growth Fund, Inc.
Robert F. Zicarelli, Chairman
8777 East Via de Ventura, Suite 335
Scottsdale, AZ 85258
(602) 483-8940
(main office in MN)
E ☐ ☐ ☐ **1 6 8 12**

Rocky Mountain Equity Corp.
Anthony J. Nicoli, President
4530 N. Central Ave., Suite 3
Phoenix, AZ 85012
(602) 274-7558
A ☐ ☐ **4 7 8 10**

Sun Belt Capital Corp.
Bruce Vinci, President
320 N. Central Ave., Suite 700
Phoenix, AZ 85004
(602) 253-7600
A ☐ ☐ ☐ **2 4 8**

VNB Capital Corp.
James G. Gardner, President
15 E. Monroe, Suite 1200
Phoenix, AZ 85004
(602) 261-1577
D ☐ ☐ ☐ **1 5 6 8 11 12**

Arkansas

Capital Management Services, Inc.
David L. Hale, President
1910 N. Grant, Suite 200
Little Rock, AR 72207
(501) 664-8613
MESBIC   A ☐ **12**

First SBIC of Arkansas, Inc.
Fred C. Burns, President
Worthen Bank Bldg.
200 W. Capitol Ave., Suite 700
Little Rock, AR 72201
(501) 378-1876
A ☐ ☐ ☐ **12**

Independence Financial Services, Inc.
John Freeman, President
Box 3878
Batesville, AR 72503
(501) 793-4533
B ☐ **6 9 12**

Kar-Mal Venture Capital, Inc.
Amelia S. Karam, President
2821 Kavanaugh Blvd.
Little Rock, AR 72205
(501) 661-0010
MESBIC   B ☐ ☐ ☐ **9**

Power Ventures, Inc.
Dorsey D. Glover, President
Hwy. 270 N., Box 518
Malvern, AR 72104
(501) 332-3695
MESBIC   A ☐ **12**

Loan limits: **A** $100,000   **B** $250,000   **C** $500,000   **D** $1 million   **E** Over $1 million

Policy: ☐ Loans or investments   ☐ ☐ Long-term loans   ☐ ☐ ☐ Financing with stock options

Industry: **1** Communications   **2** Construction and development   **3** Natural resources   **4** Hotels and restaurants   **5** Manufacturing and processing   **6** Health services   **7** Recreation   **8** Research and technology   **9** Retail, wholesale, distribution   **10** Service trades   **11** Transportation   **12** Diversified

Worthern Finance and Investment, Inc.
Ricor de Silveira, President
Box 1681
Little Rock, AR 72203
(501) 378-1082
MESBIC   C ☐☐ 4 5 6 9 10 11

California

Atlanta Investment Co., Inc.
Alan W. Livingston, President
141 El Camino Dr.
Los Angeles, CA 90212
(213) 273-1730
(main office in NY)
D ☐☐☐ 1 2 5 6 7 8

Bancorp Venture Capital, Inc.
Paul R. Blair, President
2082 Michelson Dr., Suite 302
Irvine, CA 92715
(714) 752-7220
E ☐☐☐ 12

BankAmerica Ventures, Inc.
Robert W. Gibson, President
555 California St., #3908, 42nd floor
San Francisco, CA 94104
(415) 622-2230
D ☐ 12

Bay Venture Group
William R. Chandler, General Partner
One Embarcadero Ctr., Suite 3303
San Francisco, CA 94111
(415) 989-7680
B ☐☐☐ 1 5 6 8

Brentwood Associates
Leslie R. Shaw, Vice-President of Finance
   and Administration
11661 San Vincente Blvd., Suite 707
Los Angeles, CA 90049
(213) 826-6581
E ☐☐☐ 1 12

Business Equity and Development Corp.
Ricardo J. Olivarez, President
1411 W. Olympic Blvd., Suite 200
Los Angeles, CA 90015
(213) 385-0351
MESBIC   B ☐ 1 5 12

California Capital Investors, Ltd.
Arthur Bernstein, General Partner
11812 San Vincente Blvd.
Los Angeles, CA 90049
(213) 820-7222
C ☐☐☐ 1 5 6 10 11 12

California Partners
Tim Draper, Vice-President and Chief
   Executive Officer
3000 Sand Hill Rd.
Bldg. 4, Suite 210
Menlo Park, CA 94025
(415) 854-7472
C ☐☐☐ 1 5 6 8

Camden Investments, Inc.
Edward G. Victor, President
9560 Wilshire Blvd., #310
Beverly Hills, CA 90212
(213) 859-9738
C ☐☐☐ 12

CFB Venture Capital Corp.
Richard J. Roncaglia, Vice-President
530 B St., 2nd floor
San Diego, CA 92101
(619) 230-3304
B ☐☐☐ 1 5 6 8

Charterway Investment Corp.
Harold Chuang, President
222 S. Hill St., Suite 800
Los Angeles, CA 90012
(213) 687-8534
MESBIC   B ☐☐☐ 2 4 5 7 9

CIN Investment Co.
Robert C. Weeks, President
444 Market St., 25th floor
San Francisco, CA 94111
(415) 398-7677
D ☐☐☐ 1 8

Citicorp Venture Capital, Ltd.
David A. Wegmann, Vice-President
2200 Geng Rd., Suite 203
Palo Alto, CA 94303
(415) 424-8000
(main office in NY, branch office in San
  Francisco)
E ☐☐☐ 1 5 6 8 11

Cogeneration Capital Fund
Howard Cann, Manager, General Partner
300 Tamal Plaza, Suite 190
Corte Madera, CA 94925
(415) 924-3525
D ☐ 8

Continental Investors, Inc.
Lac Thantrong, President
8781 Seaspray Dr.
Huntington Beach, CA 92646
(714) 964-5207
MESBIC   B ☐☐ 4 6 9 10 12

Crocker Ventures, Inc.
Ray McDonough
One Montgomery St.
San Francisco, CA 94104
(415) 983-3636
A ☐ 12

Crosspoint Investment Corp.
Max S. Simpson, President
1951 Landings Dr.
Mountain View, CA 94043
(415) 964-3545
B ☐☐☐ 1 5 8

Dime Investment Corp.
Chun Y. Lee, President
2772 W. 8th St.
Los Angeles, CA 90005
(213) 739-1847
MESBIC   A ☐ 5 8 9 12

Enterprise Venture Capital Corp.
Ernest de la Ossa, President
1922 The Alameda, Suite 306
San Jose, CA 95126
(408) 249-3507
B ☐ 1 5 8

First American Capital Funding Inc.
Luu Trankiem, President
9872 Chapman Ave., #216
Garden Grove, CA 92641
(714) 638-7171
MESBIC   B ☐ 12

First SBIC of California
Timothy Hay, President
650 Town Center Drive, 17th floor
Costa Mesa, CA 92626
(714) 556-1964
(branch offices in Pasadena and Palo Alto)
E ☐☐☐ 12

Loan limits: **A** $100,000   **B** $250,000   **C** $500,000   **D** $1 million   **E** Over $1 million

Policy: ☐ Loans or investments   ☐☐ Long-term loans   ☐☐☐ Financing with stock options

Industry: **1** Communications   **2** Construction and development   **3** Natural resources   **4** Hotels and restaurants   **5** Manufacturing and processing   **6** Health services   **7** Recreation   **8** Research and technology   **9** Retail, wholesale, distribution   **10** Service trades   **11** Transportation   **12** Diversified

Hamco Capital Corp.
William R. Hambrecht, President
One Post St., 4th floor
San Francisco, CA 94104
(415) 393-9813
C ☐ 1 5 6 8

Harvest Ventures, Inc.
(Bohlen Capital Corp.)
Harvey J. Wertheim, President
Bldg. SW3, 10080 N. Wolfe Rd., Suite 365
Cupertino, CA 95014
(main office in NY)
D ☐ 1 2 5 6 8

InterVen Partners
David B. Jones, President
445 S. Figueroa, Suite 2940
Los Angeles, CA 90071
(213) 622-1922
E ☐☐☐ 1 6 8 12

Ivanhoe Venture Capital, Ltd.
Alan Toffler, Managing General Partner
737 Pearl St., Suite 201
La Jolla, CA 92037
(619) 454-8882
B ☐☐☐ 1 5 6 12

JeanJoo Finance, Inc.
Frank R. Remski, General Manager
700 S. Flower St., Suite 3305
Los Angeles, CA 90017
(213) 627-6660
MESBIC   B ☐ 12

Lasung Investment and Finance Co.
Jung Su Lee, President
3600 Wilshire Blvd., Suite 1410
Los Angeles, CA 90010
(213) 384-7548
MESBIC   B ☐☐ 9 12

Latigo Capital Partners
Donald A. Peterson, General Partner
23410 Civic Center Way, Suite E2
Malibu, CA 90265
(213) 456-7024
C ☐ 1 4 5 6 7 8 9

Los Angeles Capital Corp.
Kuytae Hwang, President
606 N. Larchmont Blvd., Suite 309
Los Angeles, CA 90004
(213) 460-4646
MESBIC   B ☐ 2 4 5 12

MBW Management, Inc.
Doan Resources
James R. Weersing, Managing Director
350 Second St., Suite 7
Los Altos, CA 94022
(415) 941-2392
(main office in MI)
D ☐☐☐ 1 5 6 8

MCA New Venture, Inc.
W. Roderick Hamilton, President
100 University City Plaza
Universal City, CA 91608
(818) 777-2937
MESBIC   B ☐☐☐ 1 5 7

Merrill, Pickard, Anderson and Eyre
Steven L. Merrill, Managing Partner
Two Palo Alto Sq., Suite 425
Palo Alto, CA 94306
(415) 856-8880
E ☐☐☐ 1 6 8

Myriad Capital, Inc.
Chuang-I Lin, President
2225 W. Commonwealth Ave., #111
Alhambra, CA 91801
(818) 289-5689
MESBIC   B ☐ 1 2 5 8 9 10 11

Nelson Capital Corp.
Norman Tulchin, Chairman
10000 Santa Monica Blvd.
Los Angeles, CA 90067
(213) 556-1944
(main office in NY)
E ☐ 12

New Kukje Investment Co.
C. K. Noh, President
958 S. Vermont Ave., #C
Los Angeles, CA 90006
(213) 389-8679
MESBIC B ☐ 12

New West Ventures
Tim Haidinger, President
4350 Executive Dr., #206
San Diego, CA 92121
(619) 457-0722
(branch office in Newport Beach)
E ☐☐☐ 1 4 5 6 9 10 11

Opportunity Capital Corp.
J. Peter Thompson, President
50 California St., Suite 2505
San Francisco, CA 94111
(415) 421-5935
MESBIC B ☐☐☐ 1 5 11 12

Orange Nassau Capital Corp.
John W. Blackburn, Vice-President
Westerly Place
1500 Quail St., Suite 540
Newport Beach, CA 92660
(714) 752-7811
(main office in MA)
C ☐☐ 12

PBC Venture Capital, Inc.
Henry Wheeler, President and
  General Manager
Box 6008
Bakersfield, CA 93386
(805) 395-3206
A ☐☐☐ 2 5 6 8 9 12

PCF Venture Capital Corp.
Eduardo B. Cu-Unjieg, President
675 Mariner's Island Blvd., #103
San Mateo, CA 94404
(415) 574-4747
B ☐ 12

San Joaquin Capital Corp.
Chester W. Troudy, President
1675 Chester Ave., Suite 330
Box 2538
Bakersfield, CA 93303
(805) 323-7581
D ☐☐☐ 2 5 7 12

San Jose SBIC, Inc.
Robert T. Murphy, President
100 Park Ctr. Pl., Suite 427
San Jose, CA 95113
(408) 293-8052
C ☐ 1 6 12

Seaport Ventures, Inc.
Michael Stolper, President
525 B St., Suite 630
San Diego, CA 92101
(619) 232-4069
B ☐☐☐ 12

Loan limits: **A** $100,000 **B** $250,000 **C** $500,000 **D** $1 million **E** Over $1 million

Policy: ☐ Loans or investments ☐☐ Long-term loans ☐☐☐ Financing with stock options

Industry: **1** Communications **2** Construction and development **3** Natural resources **4** Hotels and restaurants **5** Manufacturing and processing **6** Health services **7** Recreation **8** Research and technology **9** Retail, wholesale, distribution **10** Service trades **11** Transportation **12** Diversified

Union Venture Corp.
Brent T. Rider, President
225 S. Lake Ave., #601
Pasadena, CA 91101
(818) 304-1989
(branch office in Irvine)
D ☐ ☐ ☐ **1 5 6 8**

Unity Capital Corp.
Frank W. Owen, President
4343 Morena Blvd., #3-A
San Diego, CA 92117
(619) 275-6030
MESBIC **A** ☐ ☐ **5 12**

VK Capital Co.
Franklin Van Kasper, General Partner
50 California St., #2350
San Francisco, CA 94111
(415) 391-5600
A ☐ **12**

Westamco Investment Co.
Leonard G. Muskin, President
8929 Wilshire Blvd., Suite 400
Beverly Hills, CA 90211
(213) 652-8288
C ☐ **12**

Wilshire Capital Inc.
Kyn Han Lee, President
3932 Wilshire Blvd., Suite 305
Los Angeles, CA 90010
(213) 388-1314
MESBIC **A** ☐ ☐ **12**

Wood River Capital Corp.
Peter C. Wendell, Vice-President
3000 Sand Hill Rd., Suite 280
Menlo Park, CA 94025
(415) 854-1000
(main office in NY)
D ☐ ☐ ☐ **1 5 6 10 12**

Worthen Finance & Investment Inc.
Ellis Chane, Manager
3660 Wilshire Blvd.
Los Angeles, CA 90010
(213) 480-1908
(main office in AR)
MESBIC **D** ☐ ☐ **12**

Yosemite Capital Investment
J. Horace Hampton, President
448 Fresno St.
Fresno, CA 93706
(209) 485-2431
MESBIC **A** ☐ ☐ ☐ **12**

Colorado

Colorado Growth Capital, Inc.
Nicholas Davis, Chairman and President
1600 Broadway, Suite 2125
Denver, CO 80202
(303) 831-0205
B ☐ **5 12**

Enterprise Financial Capital Development
    Corp.
Robert N. Hampton, President
Box 5840
Snowmass Village, CO 81615
(303) 923-4144
E ☐ **12**

FBS Venture Capital Company
Brian P. Johnson, Vice-President
3000 Pearl St., #206
Boulder, CO 80301
(303) 442-6885
(main office in AZ)
C ☐ ☐ ☐ **1 5 6 8**

InterMountain Ventures, Ltd.
Norman M. Dean, Vice-President
1100 10th St.
Box 1406
Greeley, CO 80632
(303) 356-3229
B ☐ ☐ ☐ **12**

Mile Hi SBIC
E. Preston Sumner, Investment Advisor
2505 W. 16th Ave.
Denver, CO 80204
(303) 629-5339
MESBIC A ☐ ☐ ☐ 1 5 6 8 12

UBD Capital Inc.
Richard B. Wigton, President
1700 Broadway
Denver, CO 80274
(303) 863-6329
B ☐ 12

Connecticut

Asset Capital and Management Corp.
Ralph Smith, President
608 Ferry Blvd.
Stratford, CT 06497
(203) 375-0299
A ☐ ☐ 2

Capital Impact
Kevin S. Tierney, President
961 Main St.
Bridgeport, CT 06601
(203) 384-5670
C ☐ 5 9 10 11 12

Capital Resource Co. of Connecticut
I. M. Fierberg, General Partner
Janice Romanowski, General Partner
699 Bloomfield Ave.
Bloomfield, CT 06002
(203) 243-1114
B ☐ ☐ 12

First Connecticut SBIC
David Engelson, President
177 State St.
Bridgeport, CT 06604
(203) 366-4726
D ☐ 12

Marcon Capital Corp.
Martin Cohen, Chairman
49 Riverside Ave.
Westport, CT 06880
(203) 226-6893
C ☐ ☐ ☐ 1 2 9 10 12

Northeastern Capital Corp.
Louis Mingione, President and Executive
    Director
61 High St.
East Haven, CT 06512
(203) 469-7901
A ☐ 12

Regional Financial Enterprises
Robert M. Williams, General Partner
George E. Thomassy III, General Partner
36 Grove St.
New Canaan, CT 06840
(203) 966-2800
E ☐ ☐ ☐ 1 5 6 8 9 12

SBIC of Connecticut
Kenneth F. Zarrilli, President
1115 Main St., #610
Bridgeport, CT 06604
(203) 367-3282
A ☐ 2 9 12

Loan limits: **A** $100,000   **B** $250,000   **C** $500,000   **D** $1 million   **E** Over $1 million

Policy: ☐ Loans or investments   ☐ ☐ Long-term loans   ☐ ☐ ☐ Financing with stock options

Industry: **1** Communications   **2** Construction and development   **3** Natural resources   **4** Hotels and restaurants   **5** Manufacturing and processing   **6** Health services   **7** Recreation   **8** Research and technology   **9** Retail, wholesale, distribution   **10** Service trades   **11** Transportation   **12** Diversified

District of Columbia

Allied Capital Corp.
George C. Williams, Chairman
1625 I St., NW, Suite 603
Washington, DC 20006
(202) 331-1112
E ☐☐☐ 1 5 6 9 10 12

American Security Capital Corp.
Brian K. Mercer, Vice-President
730 15th St., NW
Washington, DC 20013
(202) 624-4843
C ☐☐☐ 12

Broadcast Capital, Inc.
John Oxendine, President
1771 N St., NW, #404
Washington, DC 20036
(202) 429-5393
MESBIC A ☐☐☐ 1

Continental Investors, Inc.
Lac Thantrong, President
2020 K St., NW, Suite 350
Washington, DC 20006
(202) 466-3709
(main office in CA)
MESBIC B ☐ 4 6 9 10 12

D.C. Bancorp Venture Capital Co.
Allan A. Weissburg, President
1801 K St., NW
Washington, DC 20006
(202) 955-6970
C ☐☐☐ 5 6 9 10 12

Fulcrum Venture Capital Corp.
Divakar Kamath, President
2021 K St., NW, Suite 701
Washington, DC 20006
(202) 833-9590
MESBIC C ☐☐☐ 1 2 5 6 11 12

Syncom Capital Corp.
Herbert P. Wilkins, President
1030 15th St., NW, Suite 203
Washington, DC 20005
(202) 293-9428
MESBIC C ☐☐☐ 1

Washington Finance and Investment Corp.
Chang H. Lie, President
2600 Virginia Ave., NW, #515
Washington, DC 20037
(202) 338-2900
MESBIC A ☐☐☐ 2 4 10 12

Worthen Finance and Investment Inc.
Vernon Weaver, Manager
2121 K St., NW, Suite 830
Washington, DC 20037
(202) 659-9427
(main office in AR)
MESBIC C ☐☐ 4 5 6 9 10 11

Florida

Caribank Capital Corp.
Michael E. Chaney, President
255 E. Dania Beach Blvd.
Dania, FL 33004
(305) 925-2211
B ☐☐☐ 1 3 6 7 8 11

FAIC Capital Corp.
Joseph N. Hardin, Jr., President
2701 S. Bayshore Dr., Suite 402
Coconut Grove, FL 33133
(305) 854-6840
B ☐☐☐ 12

First Tampa Capital Corp.
Thomas L. du Pont, President
501 E. Kennedy Blvd., Suite 806
Tampa, FL 33602
(813) 221-2171
C ☐ 12

246

Ideal Financial Corp.
Ectore Reynaldo, General Manager
780 NW 42nd Ave., Suite 304
Miami, FL 33126
(305) 442-4653
MESBIC   A ☐ ☐ 12

J & D Capital Corp.
Jack Carmel, President
12747 Biscayne Blvd.
North Miami, FL 33160
(305) 893-0303
D ☐ 2 5 9 12

Market Capital Corp.
Ernest E. Eads, President
Box 22667
Tampa, FL 33630
(813) 247-1357
B ☐ ☐ 9

Small Business Assistance Corp.
Charles S. Smith, President
2612 W. 15th St.
Panama City, FL 32401
(904) 785-9577
B ☐ 4

Southeast Venture Capital Ltd. I
Clement L. Hofmann, President
One Southeast Financial Ctr.
Miami, FL 33131
(305) 375-6470
D ☐ ☐ ☐ 1 5 6 8 12

Universal Financial Services, Inc.
Norman Zipkin, President
3550 Biscayne Blvd., Suite 702
Miami, FL 33137
(305) 538-5464
MESBIC   B ☐ ☐ 12

Venture Opportunities Corp.
A. Fred March, President
444 Brickell Ave., Suite 650
Miami, FL 33131
(305) 358-0359
MESBIC   A ☐ ☐ ☐ 1 5 6 9 11 12

Verde Capital Corp.
Jose Dearing, President
255 Alhambra Circle, #720
Coral Gables, FL 33134
(305) 444-8938
MESBIC   B ☐ 12

Georgia

Mighty Capital Corp.
Gary E. Koryonski, Vice-President and
    General Manager
50 Technology Park, Suite 100
Norcross, GA 30092
(404) 448-2232
A ☐ 12

North Riverside Capital Corp.
Thomas R. Barry, President
5775-D Peachtree Dunwood Rd., Suite 650
Atlanta, GA 30342
(404) 252-1076
D ☐ ☐ ☐ 12

Hawaii

Bancorp Hawaii SBIC, Inc.
Thomas T. Triggs, Vice-President and
    General Manager
Box 2900
Honolulu, HI 96846
(808) 521-6411
A ☐ ☐ ☐ 12

Loan limits: **A** $100,000 **B** $250,000 **C** $500,000 **D** $1 million **E** Over $1 million

Policy: ☐ Loans or investments ☐ ☐ Long-term loans ☐ ☐ ☐ Financing with stock options

Industry: **1** Communications **2** Construction and development **3** Natural resources **4** Hotels and restaurants **5** Manufacturing and processing **6** Health services **7** Recreation **8** Research and technology **9** Retail, wholesale, distribution **10** Service trades **11** Transportation **12** Diversified

247

Pacific Venture Capital, Ltd.
Dexter J. Taniguchi, President
1405 N. King St., Suite 302
Honolulu, HI 96817
(808) 847-6502
MESBIC   A ☐ 12

Idaho

First Idaho Venture Capital
Ron J. Twilegar, President
Box 1739
Boise, ID 83701
(208) 345-3460
B ☐ ☐ ☐ 6 12

Illinois

Abbott Capital Corp.
Richard E. Lassar, President
9933 Lawler Ave., Suite 125
Skokie, IL 60077
(312) 982-0404
A ☐ ☐ ☐ 1 6 10

Alpha Capital Venture Partners
Andrew H. Kalnow, Managing Partner
3 First National Pl., Suite 1400
Chicago, IL 60602
(312) 372-1556
C ☐ 12

Amoco Venture Capital Co.
Gordon E. Stone, President
200 E. Randolph Dr.
Chicago, IL 60601
(312) 856-6523
MESBIC   C ☐ ☐ ☐ 3 8

Business Ventures, Inc.
Milton Lefton, President
20 N. Wacker Dr., Suite 550
Chicago, IL 60606
(312) 346-1580
B ☐ ☐ ☐ 12

Chicago Community Ventures Inc.
Phyllis E. George, President
104 S. Michigan, #215
Chicago, IL 60603
(312) 726-6084
MESBIC   B ☐ ☐ ☐ 4 5 12

Combined Fund, Inc.
E. Patric Jones, President
1525 E. 53rd St., #908
Chicago, IL 60615
(312) 363-0300
C ☐ 1 12

Continental Illinois Venture Corp.
John L. Hines, President
231 S. LaSalle St.
Chicago, IL 60697
(312) 828-8021
E ☐ ☐ ☐ 1 5 6 8 9 10

First Capital Corporation of Chicago
John A. Canning, Jr., President
Three First National Pl., Suite 1330
Chicago, IL 60670-0501
(312) 732-5400
E ☐ ☐ ☐ 1 5 6 9

Frontenac Capital Corp.
David A. R. Dullum, President
208 S. LaSalle St., #1900
Chicago, IL 60604
(312) 368-0044
E ☐ ☐ ☐ 12

Mesirow Venture Capital
James C. Tyree, Managing Director
350 N. Clark
Chicago, IL 60610
(312) 670-6000
E ☐ ☐ ☐ 1 2 3 4 5 6 7 8 9 10 11 12

Nelson Capital Corp.
Irwin B. Nelson, President
2340 Des Plaines Ave.
Des Plaines, IL 60018
(312) 296-2280
E ☐ 12

Northern Capital Corp.
Robert L. Underwood, President
50 S. LaSalle St.
Chicago, IL 60675
(312) 444-5399
D ☐☐☐ 12

Tower Ventures, Inc.
Robert T. Smith, President
Sears Tower, BSC 43-50
Chicago, IL 60684
(312) 875-0571
MESBIC B ☐☐☐ 12

Walnut Capital Corp.
Burton W. Kanter, Chairman
Three First National Plaza
Chicago, IL 60602
(312) 269-1732
C ☐ 1 5 6 8

Indiana

Circle Ventures, Inc.
Samuel Sutphin II, Vice-President
20 N. Meridian St., 3rd floor
Indianapolis, IN 46240
(317) 636-7242
A ☐☐☐ 12

Equity Resource Co., Inc.
Michael J. Hammes, Vice-President and
  Secretary
202 S. Michigan St.
South Bend, IN 46601
(219) 237-5255
B ☐☐☐ 5 12

1st Source Capital Corp.
Christopher Murphy III, President
100 N. Michigan
South Bend, IN 46601
(219) 236-2180
B ☐☐☐ 1 3 5 6 7 8 9 11

White River Capital Corp.
David J. Blair, President
500 Washington St., Box 929
Columbus, IN 47202
(812) 376-1759
B ☐☐☐ 1 5 9 10 12

Iowa

MorAmerica Capital Corp.
Donald E. Flynn, Executive Vice-President
300 American Bldg.
Cedar Rapids, IA 52401
(319) 363-8249
D ☐☐☐ 12

Kansas

Kansas Venture Capital, Inc.
Larry High, Vice-President
One Townsite Plaza
1030 First Nat'l Bank Towers
Topeka, KS 66603
(913) 233-1368
A ☐ 5

Loan limits: **A** $100,000   **B** $250,000   **C** $500,000   **D** $1 million   **E** Over $1 million

Policy: ☐ Loans or investments   ☐☐ Long-term loans   ☐☐☐ Financing with stock options

Industry: **1** Communications   **2** Construction and development   **3** Natural resources   **4** Hotels and restaurants   **5** Manufacturing and processing   **6** Health services   **7** Recreation   **8** Research and technology   **9** Retail, wholesale, distribution   **10** Service trades   **11** Transportation   **12** Diversified

Kentucky

Equal Opportunity Finance, Inc.
Frank Justice, President
420 Hursbourne Lane, Suite 201
Louisville, KY 40222
(502) 423-1943
MESBIC   B ☐ 12

Financial Opportunities, Inc.
Gary F. Duerr, General Manager
833 Starks Bldg.
Louisville, KY 40202
(502) 584-8259
A ☐ 9

Mountain Ventures, Inc.
L. Raymond Moncrief, President
911 N. Main St., Box 628
London, KY 40741
(606) 864-5175
C ☐ 1 5 6 10

Louisiana

Commercial Capital, Inc.
Milton Coxe, Acting President
Box 1776
Covington, LA 70434-1776
(504) 345-8820
A ☐ 12

Dixie Business Inv. Co., Inc.
L. Wayne Baker, President
Box 588
Lake Providence, LA 71254
(318) 559-1558
A ☐ ☐ 9 10 12

First Southern Capital Corp.
Charles Thibaut, Chairman and Chief
   Executive Officer
Box 14418
Baton Rouge, LA 70898
(504) 769-3004
D ☐ ☐ ☐ 12

Louisiana Equity Capital Corp.
Melvin L. Rambin, President
Louisiana Nat'l Bank
Box 1511
Baton Rouge, LA 70821
(504) 389-4421
C ☐ ☐ ☐ 1 5 6 12

Walnut Street Capital Co.
William D. Humphries, Managing General
   Partner
231 Carondelet St., #702
New Orleans, LA 70130
(504) 525-2112
B ☐ ☐ ☐ 12

Maine

Maine Capital Corp.
David M. Coit, President
70 Center St.
Portland, ME 04101
(207) 772-1001
A ☐ ☐ ☐ 12

Maryland

First Maryland Capital, Inc.
Joseph Kenary, President
107 W. Jefferson St.
Rockville, MD 20850
(301) 251-6630
A ☐ ☐ ☐ 12

Greater Washington Investors, Inc.
Don A. Christensen, President
5454 Wisconsin Ave., Suite 1315
Chevy Chase, MD 20815
(301) 656-0626
D ☐ ☐ ☐ 8 12

Suburban Capital Corp.
Henry P. Linsert, Jr., President
6610 Rockledge Dr.
Bethesda, MD 20817
(301) 493-7025
D ☐ ☐ ☐ 5 6 8 12

Massachusetts

Atlantic Energy Capital Corp.
Joost E. Tjaden, President
260 Franklin St., Suite 1501
Boston, MA 02110
(617) 451-6220
C ☐ 1 3 5 6 8 9 10 11 12

BancBoston Ventures, Inc.
Paul F. Hogan, President
100 Federal St.
Boston, MA 02110
(617) 434-5700
E ☐ 1 5 6 8

Boston Hambro Capital Co.
Robert Sherman, Vice-President
One Boston Pl., Suite 723
Boston, MA 02106
(617) 722-7055
(main office in NY)
C ☐☐☐ 1 5 6

Churchill International
Roy G. Helsing, Vice-President
9 Riverside Road
Weston, MA 02193
(617) 893-6555
(main office in CA)
D ☐☐☐ 1 8

First SBIC of California
Michael Cronin, Managing Partner
50 Milk St., 15th floor
Boston, MA 02109
(617) 542-7601
(main office in CA)
E ☐☐☐ 12

Fleet Venture Resources, Inc.
James A. Saalfield, Vice-President
60 State St.
Boston, MA 02100
(617) 367-6700
E ☐☐☐ 1 5 6 8 9 10 11 12

Narragansett Capital Corp.
265 Franklin St., 11th floor
Boston, MA 02110
(main office in RI)

New England Capital Corp.
Z. David Patterson, Executive Vice-President
One Washington Mall, 7th floor
Boston, MA 02108
(617) 722-6400
D ☐☐☐ 1 5 6 8 12

New England MESBIC, Inc.
Etang Chen, President
50 Kearney Rd., Suite 3
Needham, MA 02194
(617) 449-2066
MESBIC A ☐ 1 4 5 6 8 9 12

Orange Nassau Capital Corp.
Joost E. Tjaden, President
260 Franklin St., Suite 1501
Boston, MA 02110
(617) 451-6220
C ☐ 1 6 9 10 11 12

Loan limits: **A** $100,000   **B** $250,000   **C** $500,000   **D** $1 million   **E** Over $1 million

Policy: ☐ Loans or investments   ☐☐ Long-term loans   ☐☐☐ Financing with stock options

Industry: **1** Communications   **2** Construction and development   **3** Natural resources   **4** Hotels and restaurants   **5** Manufacturing and processing   **6** Health services   **7** Recreation   **8** Research and technology   **9** Retail, wholesale, distribution   **10** Service trades   **11** Transportation   **12** Diversified

TA Associates
(Advent Capital Co.)
(Chestnut Capital Corp.)
(Devonshire Capital Corp.)
David D. Croll, Managing Partner
45 Milk St.
Boston, MA 02109
(617) 338-0800
E ☐ ☐ ☐ 1

Transportation Capital Corp.
Jon Hirch, Assistant Vice-President
566 Commonwealth Ave., Suite 810
Boston, MA 02215
(617) 262-9701
(main office in NY)
B ☐ ☐ 11

UST Capital Corp.
Arthur F. F. Snyder, Chairman
30 Court St.
Boston, MA 02108
(617) 726-7138
B ☐ 1 5 6 8 9 12

Vadus Capital Corp.
Joost E. Tjaden, President
260 Franklin St., Suite 1501
Boston, MA 02110
(617) 451-6220
C ☐ 1 6 9 10 11 12

Worcester Capital Corp.
Kenneth Kidd, Vice-President and Manager
446 Main St.
Worcester, MA 01608
(617) 793-4508
A ☐ ☐ ☐ 1 6 8

Michigan

Comerica Capital Corp.
John D. Berkaw, President
30150 Telegraph Rd., Suite 245
Birmingham, MI 48010
(313) 258-5800
D ☐ 1 5 6 8 12

Doan Resources L.P.
Ian R. N. Bund, General Partner
2000 Hogback Road, Suite 2
Ann Arbor, MI 48105
(313) 971-3100
D ☐ ☐ ☐ 1 5 6 8

Metro-Detroit Investment Co.
William J. Fowler, President
30777 Northwestern Hwy., Suite 300
Farmington Hills, MI 48018
(313) 851-6300
MESBIC B ☐ 5 6 9

Michigan Capital and Service, Inc.
Mary L. Campbell, Vice-President
500 First Nat'l Bldg.
201 S. Main St.
Ann Arbor, MI 48104
(313) 663-0702
D ☐ ☐ ☐ 1 5 6 12

Michigan Tech Capital Corp.
Edward J. Koepel, President
Technology Park
17000 Duncan Ave., Box 529
Hubbell, MI 49934
(906) 487-2643
B ☐ ☐ ☐ 3 5 8

Motor Enterprises, Inc.
James Kobus, Manager
3044 W. Grand Blvd., #13-152
Detroit, MI 48202
(313) 556-4273
MESBIC A ☐ ☐ 5

Mutual Investment Co., Inc.
Timothy J. Taylor, Treasurer
21415 Civic Center Dr., Suite 217
Southfield, MI 48076
(313) 559-5210
MESBIC B ☐ ☐ 9

Regional Financial Enterprises
Barry P. Walsh, Senior Associate
315 E. Eisenhower Pkwy., Suite 300
Ann Arbor, MI 48104
(313) 769-0941
(main office in CT)
E ☐☐☐ 1 5 6 8 9 12

Minnesota

Control Data Capital Corp.
Doug C. Curtis, Jr., President
3601 W. 77th St.
Minneapolis, MN 55435
(612) 921-4118
D ☐ 1 5 6 8

Control Data Community Ventures Fund, Inc.
Thomas F. Hunt, Jr., President
3601 W. 77th St.
Minneapolis, MN 55435
(612) 921-4352
MESBIC   C ☐ 1 5 6 8 12

DGC Capital Co.
Jerry H. Udesen, Chairman
603 Alworth Bldg.
Duluth, MN 55802
(218) 722-0058
A ☐ 3 5 6 7 9 10

FBS Venture Capital Company
W. Ray Allen, Executive Vice-President
7515 Wayzata Blvd., Suite 110
Minneapolis, MN 55402
(612) 544-2754
(main office in AZ)
C ☐☐☐ 1 5 6 8

Northland Capital Corp.
George G. Barnum, Jr., President
Missabe Bldg. #613
227 W. 1st St.
Duluth, MN 55802
(218) 722-0545
B ☐☐☐ 12

North Star Ventures, Inc.
Terrence W. Glarner, President
100 S. Fifth St., #2200
Minneapolis, MN 55402
(612) 333-1133
D ☐☐☐ 1 5 6 8 12

North Star Ventures II
Terrence W. Glarner, President
100 S. Fifth St., #2200
Minneapolis, MN 55402
(612) 333-1133
D ☐☐☐ 1 5 6 8 12

Northwest Venture Partners
Robert F. Zicarelli, Chairman
222 S. Ninth St., #2800
Minneapolis, MN 55402
(612) 372-8770
E ☐☐☐ 12

Norwest Growth Fund, Inc.
Daniel J. Haggerty, President
222 S. Ninth St., #2800
Minneapolis, MN 55404
(612) 872-4929
A ☐☐ 4 9 11

Retailers Growth Fund, Inc.
Cornell L. Moore, President
2318 Park Ave.
Minneapolis, MN 55404
(612) 872-4929
A ☐☐ 4 9 11

Loan limits: **A** $100,000   **B** $250,000   **C** $500,000   **D** $1 million   **E** Over $1 million

Policy: ☐ Loans or investments   ☐☐ Long-term loans   ☐☐☐ Financing with stock options

Industry: **1** Communications   **2** Construction and development   **3** Natural resources   **4** Hotels and restaurants   **5** Manufacturing and processing   **6** Health services   **7** Recreation   **8** Research and technology   **9** Retail, wholesale, distribution   **10** Service trades   **11** Transportation   **12** Diversified

Shared Ventures, Inc.
Howard Weiner, President
6550 York Avenue, S, Suite 419
Minneapolis, MN 55435
(612) 925-3411
B ☐ ☐ ☐ 1 4 5 6 9 11

Threshold Ventures, Inc.
John L. Shannon, Vice-President
430 Oak Grove St., Suite 303
Minneapolis, MN 55403
(612) 874-7199
B ☐ ☐ ☐ 1 5 6 9 12

Mississippi

Columbia Ventures, Inc.
Maurice Reed, Chairman
Box 1066
Jackson, MS 39215

Invesat Capital Corp.
John Bise, President
Box 3288
Jackson, MS 39207
(601) 969-3242
D ☐ 12

Vicksburg SBIC
David L. May, President
Box 852
Vicksburg, MS 39180
(601) 636-4762
A ☐ 12

Missouri

Bankers Capital Corp.
Raymond E. Glasnapp, President
3100 Gillham Rd.
Kansas City, MO 64109
(816) 531-1600
A ☐ 12

Capital for Business, Inc.
James B. Hebenstreit, President
11 S. Meramec, #800
St. Louis, MO 63105
(314) 854-7427
(branch office in Kansas City)
C ☐ ☐ ☐ 1 5 6 8 9 10 12

Intercapco, Inc.
Thomas E. Phelps, President
7800 Bonhomme Ave.
Clayton, MO 63105
(314) 863-0600
C ☐ ☐ ☐ 12

MorAmerica Capital Corp.
Kevin F. Mullane, Vice-President
Commerce Tower Bldg., Suite 2724
911 Main St.
Kansas City, MO 64105
(816) 842-0114
(main office in Iowa)
D ☐ ☐ ☐ 12

United Missouri Capital Corp.
Joseph Kessinger, Executive Vice-President
    and Manager
928 Grand Ave., 1st floor
Kansas City, MO 64106
(816) 556-7115
B ☐ 5 6 8 10

New Hampshire

Granite State Capital, Inc.
Albert Hall III, Managing Director
10 Fort Eddy Rd.
Concord, NH 03301
(603) 228-9090
A ☐ 1 5 6 10 12

Lotus Capital Corp.
Richard J. Ash, President
875 Elm St.
Manchester, NH 03101
(603) 668-8617
B ☐ ☐ ☐ 1 6 8 12

New Jersey

Capital Circulation Corp.
Judy M. Kao, Director and Secretary
208 Main St.
Ft. Lee, NJ 07024
(201) 947-8637
MESBIC B ☐ 12

ESLO Capital Corp.
Leo Katz, President
2401 Morris Ave., Suite 220EW
Union, NJ 07083
(201) 687-4920
B ☐ 12

First Princeton Capital Corp.
S. Lawrence Goldstein, President
227 Hamburg Tpke.
Pompton Lakes, NJ 07442
(201) 831-0330
B ☐☐☐ 12

Monmouth Capital Corp.
Eugene W. Landy, President
Box 335—125 Wyckoff Rd.
Eatontown, NJ 07724
(201) 542-4927
C ☐ 4 5 7 12

New Management, Inc.
Doan Resources
Philip E. McCarthy, Managing Director
365 South St., 2nd floor
Morristown, NJ 07960
(201) 285-5533
(main office in MI)
D ☐☐☐ 1 5 6 8

Rutgers Minority Investment Co.
Oscar Figueroa, President
180 University Ave., 3rd floor
Newark, NJ 07102
(201) 648-5627
MESBIC B ☐☐☐ 12

Tappan Zee Capital Corp.
Jack Birnberg, Chairman
201 Lower Notch Rd.
Little Falls, NJ 07424
(201) 256-8280
D ☐ 12

Unicorn Ventures, Ltd.
Frank P. Diassi, General Partner
Arthur B. Baer, General Partner
6 Commerce Dr.
Cranford, NJ 07016
(201) 276-7880
D ☐☐☐ 12

New Mexico

Albuquerque SBIC
Albert T. Ussery, President
Box 487
Albuquerque, NM 87103
(505) 247-0145
A ☐☐☐ 12

Associated SW Investors, Inc.
John R. Rice, President
2400 Louisiana, NE, #4
Albuquerque, NM 87110
(505) 881-0066
MESBIC B ☐ 1 5 6 8

Loan limits: **A** $100,000 **B** $250,000 **C** $500,000 **D** $1 million **E** Over $1 million

Policy: ☐ Loans or investments ☐☐ Long-term loans ☐☐☐ Financing with stock options

Industry: **1** Communications **2** Construction and development **3** Natural resources **4** Hotels and restaurants **5** Manufacturing and processing **6** Health services **7** Recreation **8** Research and technology **9** Retail, wholesale, distribution **10** Service trades **11** Transportation **12** Diversified

Equity Capital Corp.
Jerry A. Henson, President
231 Washington Ave., Suite 2
Santa Fe, NM 87501
(505) 988-4273
B ☐ ☐ ☐ ☐ 5 9 12

Fluid Capital Corp.
George T. Slaughter, President
8421 B Montgomery Blvd., NE
Albuquerque, NM 87111
(505) 292-4747
C ☐ ☐ ☐ ☐ 1 2 4 5 6 12

Southwest Capital Inv. Inc.
Martin J. Roe, President
3500-E Commanche Rd., NE
Albuquerque, NM 87107
(505) 884-7161
C ☐ 12

New York

American Commercial Capital Corp.
Gerald J. Grossman, President
310 Madison Ave., Suite 1304
New York, NY 10048
(212) 775-9100
D ☐ ☐ ☐ ☐ 1 4 5 6 9 10 11 12

Atlanta Investment Co., Inc.
L. Mark Newman, Chairman
450 Park Ave., Suite 2102
New York, NY 10022
(212) 832-1104
D ☐ ☐ ☐ ☐ 1 2 5 6 7 8

Atlantic Capital Corp.
Herald Paumgarten, President
40 Wall St.
New York, NY 10005
(212) 612-0616
E ☐ ☐ ☐ ☐ 12

Boston Hambro Capital Co.
Edwin A. Goodman, President
17 E. 71st St.
New York, NY 10021
(212) 288-7778
C ☐ ☐ ☐ ☐ 1 5 6

BT Capital Corp.
James G. Hellmuth, Chairman
280 Park Ave.
New York, NY 10017
(212) 850-1916
E ☐ ☐ ☐ ☐ 5 10

The Central New York SBIC, Inc.
Albert Wertheimer, President
351 S. Warren St., Suite 600
Syracuse, NY 13202
(315) 478-5026
A ☐ ☐ ☐ ☐ 1 7

Chase Manhattan Capital Corp.
Gustav H. Koven, President
1 Chase Manhattan Plaza, 23rd floor
New York, NY 10081
(212) 552-6275
E ☐ ☐ ☐ ☐ 1 2 5 6 7 8 10 11 12

Chemical Venture Capital Corp.
Steven J. Gilbert, President and Chief
   Executive Officer
277 Park Ave., 10th floor
New York, NY 10172
(212) 310-4949
E ☐ ☐ ☐ ☐ 1 4 5 6 7 8 9 10 11 12

Citicorp Venture Capital Ltd.
Peter G. Gerry, President
153 East 53rd St., 28th floor
New York, NY 10043
(212) 559-1127
E ☐ ☐ ☐ ☐ 12

Clinton Capital Corp.
Mark Scharfman, President
419 Park Ave., S.
New York, NY 10016
(212) 696-4334
E ☐ ☐ 12

CMNY Capital Co., Inc.
Robert Davidoff, Vice-President
77 Water St.
New York, NY 10005
(212) 437-7078
C ☐ ☐ ☐ 1 5 9 10 12

College Venture Equity Corp.
Francis M. Williams, President
256 Third St., Box 135
Niagara Falls, NY 14303
(813) 248-3878
A ☐ ☐ 2 5 6 11 12

Croyden Capital Corp.
Victor L. Hecht, President
45 Rockefeller Pl., Suite 2165
New York, NY 10111
(212) 974-0184
B ☐ ☐ ☐ 12

Edwards Capital Co.
Edward Teitlebaum, Managing Partner
215 Lexington Ave., #805
New York, NY 10016
(212) 686-2568
A ☐ ☐ 11

Elk Associates Funding Corp.
Gary C. Granoff, President
600 Third Ave., #3810
New York, NY 10016
(212) 972-8550
MESBIC   B ☐ ☐ 11 12

Equico Capital Corp.
Duane E. Hill, President
1290 Avenue of the Americas, Suite 3400
New York, NY 10019
(212) 397-8660
MESBIC   C ☐ ☐ ☐ 12

Everlast Capital Corp.
Frank J. Segreto, Vice-President and Chief
    Executive Officer
350 Fifth Ave., Suite 2805
New York, NY 10118
(212) 695-3910
MESBIC   B ☐ 2 9 10

Fairfield Equity Corp.
Matthew A. Berdon, President
200 E. 42nd St.
New York, NY 10017-5893
(212) 867-0150
B ☐ 1 5 7 9

Ferranti High Technology, Inc.
Sanford R. Simon, President
515 Madison Ave., #1225
New York, NY 10022
(212) 688-9828
D ☐ 1 5 8 12

Fifth-Third Street Ventures
Patricia Cloherty, General Partner
Daniel Tessler, General Partner
420 Madison Ave., #1101
New York, NY 10017
(212) 752-8010
D ☐ ☐ ☐ 1 5 6 8

Loan limits: **A** $100,000   **B** $250,000   **C** $500,000   **D** $1 million   **E** Over $1 million

Policy: ☐ Loans or investments   ☐ ☐ Long-term loans   ☐ ☐ ☐ Financing with stock options

Industry: **1** Communications   **2** Construction and development   **3** Natural resources   **4** Hotels and restaurants   **5** Manufacturing and processing   **6** Health services   **7** Recreation   **8** Research and technology   **9** Retail, wholesale, distribution   **10** Service trades   **11** Transportation   **12** Diversified

J. H. Foster and Co., Ltd.
John H. Foster, Partner
437 Madison Ave.
New York, NY 10024
(212) 753-4810
E ☐ ☐ ☐ 6 10 11 12

Franklin Corp.
Allen Farkas, President
1185 Ave. of the Americas, 27th floor
New York, NY 10036
(212) 719-4844
E ☐ ☐ ☐ 5 6 8 9 11

Fundex Capital Corp.
Howard Sommer, President
525 Northern Blvd.
Great Neck, NY 11021
(516) 466-8550
D ☐ 12

GHW Capital Corp.
Jack Graff, President
489 Fifth Ave., 2nd floor
New York, NY 10017
(212) 687-1708
B ☐ 12

The Hanover Capital Corp.
John A. Selzer, Vice-President
Stephen E. Levenson, Vice-President
150 E. 58th St., Suite 2710
New York, NY 10155
(212) 980-9670
B ☐ 12

Harvest Ventures
Harvey Wertheim, General Partner
767 Third Ave.
New York, NY 10017
(212) 838-7776
D ☐ 1 3 5 6 8

Ibero-American Investors Corp.
Emilio L. Serrano, President and Chief
    Executive Officer
Chamber of Commerce Bldg.
55 St. Paul St.
Rochester, NY 14604
(716) 262-3440
MESBIC   B ☐ 5 9 12

Intergroup Venture Capital Corp.
Ben Hauben, President
230 Park Ave., Suite 206
New York, NY 10169
(212) 661-5428
A ☐ 12

Irving Capital Corp.
J. Andrew McWethy, Executive Vice-
    President
1290 Avenue of the Americas, 3rd floor
New York, NY 10104
(212) 408-4800
E ☐ ☐ ☐ 12

Key Venture Capital Corp.
John M. Lang, President
60 State St.
Albany, NY 12207
(518) 447-3227
B ☐ ☐ ☐ 12

Kwiat Capital Corp.
Sheldon Kwiat, President
576 Fifth Ave.
New York, NY 10036
(212) 391-2461
A ☐ ☐ 1 5 6 7 8 12

M and T Capital Corp.
Joseph V. Parlato, President
One M & T Pl., 5th floor
Buffalo, NY 14240
(716) 842-5881
D ☐ 1 5 6 8 9 11 12

Medallion Funding Corp.
Alvin Murstein, President
205 E. 42nd St., Suite 2020
New York, NY 10017
(212) 682-3300
MESBIC **B** ☐ ☐ **11**

Minority Equity Capital Co., Inc.
Donal Greene, President
275 Madison Ave., Suite 1901
New York, NY 10016
(212) 686-9710
MESBIC   **C** ☐ ☐ ☐ **1 5 6 9 11 12**

Multi-Purpose Capital Corp.
Eli B. Fine, President
31 S. Broadway
Yonkers, NY 10701
(914) 963-2733
A ☐ ☐ ☐ **12**

NatWest USA Capital Corp.
Orville G. Aarons, Senior Vice-President
175 Water St.
New York, NY 10038
(212) 602-1200
D ☐ **1 3 5 6 11**

Nelson Capital Corp.
Irwin B. Nelson, President
591 Stewart Ave.
Garden City, NY 11530
(516) 222-2555
E ☐ **12**

Norstar Bancorp
Raymond A. Lancaster, President
1450 Western Ave.
Albany, NY 12203
(518) 447-4492
D ☐ **12**

North American Funding Corp.
Franklin Wong, Vice-President and General
  Manager
177 Canal St.
New York, NY 10013
(212) 226-0080
MESBIC **B** ☐ **12**

North Street Capital Corp.
Ralph L. McNeal, Sr., President
White Plains, NY 10625
(914) 335-7901
MESBIC **B** ☐ ☐ ☐ **12**

NYBDC Capital Corp.
Marshall R. Lustig, President
41 State St.
Albany, NY 12207
(518) 463-2268
A ☐ **12**

Pan Pac Capital Corp.
Ing-Ping J. Lee, President
19 Rector St., 35th floor
New York, NY 10006
(212) 344-6680
MESBIC **A** ☐ ☐ **12**

Questech Capital Corp.
Earl W. Brian, Chairman
600 Madison Ave.
New York, NY 10022
(212) 758-8522
D ☐ **1 5 6 8**

R and R Financial Corp.
Martin Eisenstadt, Vice-President
1451 Broadway
New York, NY 10036
(212) 790-1400
A ☐ ☐ **12**

Loan limits: **A** $100,000 **B** $250,000 **C** $500,000 **D** $1 million **E** Over $1 million

Policy: ☐ Loans or investments   ☐ ☐ Long-term loans   ☐ ☐ ☐ Financing with stock options

Industry: **1** Communications   **2** Construction and development   **3** Natural resources   **4** Hotels and restaurants   **5** Manufacturing and processing   **6** Health services   **7** Recreation   **8** Research and technology   **9** Retail, wholesale, distribution   **10** Service trades   **11** Transportation   **12** Diversified

Rand SBIC, Inc.
Donald A. Ross, President
1300 Rand Bldg.
Buffalo, NY 14203
(716) 853-0802
C ☐ ☐ ☐ 1 5 6 7 8 9 10 12

Peter J. Schmitt Co., Inc.
Mark A. Flint, Manager
Box 2
Buffalo, NY 14240
(716) 821-1400
A ☐ ☐ ☐ 9

Small Business Electronics Investment Co.
Stanley Meisels, President
1220 Peninsula Blvd.
Hewlett, NY 11557
(516) 374-0743
A ☐ 12

Southern Tier Capital Corp.
Milton Brizel, President
55 S. Main St.
Liberty, NY 12754
(914) 292-3030
A ☐ 12

Tappan Zee Capital Corp.
120 N. Main Street
New City, NY 10956
(914) 634-8890
(main office in NJ)
D ☐ 12

TLC Funding Corp.
Philip G. Kass, President
141 S. Central Ave.
Hartsdale, NY 10530
(914) 683-1144
B ☐ ☐ 4 9 12

Transportation Capital Corp.
Melvin L. Hirsch, President
60 E. 42nd St., Suite 3126
New York, NY 10165
(212) 697-4885
MESBIC B ☐ ☐ 11

Transworld Ventures, Ltd.
Jack H. Berger, President
331 W. End Ave., Suite 1A
New York, NY 10023
(212) 496-1010
A ☐ ☐ ☐ 5 10 12

Triad Capital Corporation of New York
L. Jim Barrera, President
960 Southern Blvd.
Bronx, NY 10459
(212) 589-6541
MESBIC A ☐ 1 3 6 8 9 10

Vega Capital Corp.
Victor Harz, President
720 White Plains Rd.
Scarsdale, NY 10583
(914) 472-8550
D ☐ 12

Venture SBIC, Inc.
Arnold Feldman, President
249-12 Jericho Tpke.
Floral Park, NY 11001
(516) 352-0068
A ☐ ☐ 2 9 12

Walnut Capital Corp.
Julius Goldfinger, President
110 E. 59th St., 37th floor
New York, NY 10016
(212) 750-1000
(main office in IL)
C ☐ 1 5 6 8

Winfield Capital Corp.
Stanley Pechman, President
237 Mamaroneck Ave.
White Plains, NY 10605
(914) 949-2600
D ☐ 12

Wood River Capital Corp.
Elizabeth W. Smith, President
645 Madison Ave.
New York, NY 10022
(212) 750-9420
D ☐ ☐ ☐ 1 5 6 10 12

Worthen Finance and Investment, Inc.
Guy Meeker, Manager
535 Madison Ave., 17th floor
New York, NY 10022
(212) 750-9100
(main office in AR)
MESBIC   D ☐ ☐ 12

North Carolina

Carolina Venture Capital Corp.
Thomas H. Harvey III, President
Box 646
Chapel Hill, NC 27514
(main office in SC)
B ☐ ☐ ☐ 1 2 4 7 11 12

Delta Capital, Inc.
Alex B. Wilkins, Jr., President
227 N. Tryon St., Suite 201
Charlotte, NC 28202
(704) 372-1410
B ☐ 2 4 5 8 9 10

Falcon Capital Corp.
P. S. Prasad, President
400 W. Fifth St.
Greenville, NC 27834
(919) 752-5918
A ☐ ☐ ☐ 2 4 6 9 10

Heritage Capital Corp.
Herman B. McManaway, President
2290 First Union Plaza
Charlotte, NC 28282
(704) 334-2867
C ☐ ☐ ☐ 12

Kitty Hawk Capital, Ltd.
Walter H. Wilkinson, Jr., General Partner
One Tryon Ctr., Suite 2030
Charlotte, NC 28284
(704) 333-3777
C ☐ ☐ ☐ 1 5 6 8 12

NCNB SBIC Corp.
Troy McCrory, President
One NCNB Plaza, T05-2
Charlotte, NC 28255
(704) 374-5000
C ☐ 12

NCNB Venture Corp.
Mike Elliott, President
One NCNB Plaza, T39
Charlotte, NC 28255
(704) 374-0435
D ☐ ☐ ☐ 1 5 6 8 12

Ohio

A. T. Capital Corp.
Shailesh J. Mehta, President
900 Euclid Ave., T-18
Cleveland, OH 44101
(216) 687-4970
C ☐ 1 6 8

Capital Funds Corp.
Carl G. Nelson, Vice-President and Manager
127 Public Sq.
Cleveland, OH 44114
(216) 622-8628
C ☐ 1 5 6 9 12

Loan limits: **A** $100,000   **B** $250,000   **C** $500,000   **D** $1 million   **E** Over $1 million

Policy: ☐ Loans or investments   ☐ ☐ Long-term loans   ☐ ☐ ☐ Financing with stock options

Industry: **1** Communications   **2** Construction and development   **3** Natural resources   **4** Hotels and restaurants   **5** Manufacturing and processing   **6** Health services   **7** Recreation   **8** Research and technology   **9** Retail, wholesale, distribution   **10** Service trades   **11** Transportation   **12** Diversified

Clarion Capital Corp.
Morton Cohen, Chairman and President
3555 Curtis Blvd.
Eastlake, OH 44114
(216) 953-0555
C ☐ ☐ ☐ 1 3 5 6 8 10 12

First Ohio Capital Corp.
Michael J. Aust, Vice-President
606 Madison Ave.
Toledo, OH 43604
(419) 259-7146
B ☐ ☐ ☐ 12

Gries Investment Co.
Robert D. Gries, President
720 Statler Office Tower
Cleveland, OH 44115
(216) 861-1146
B ☐ ☐ ☐ 12

National City Capital Corp.
Michael Sherwin, President
623 Euclid Ave.
Cleveland, OH 44114
(216) 575-2491
C ☐ ☐ ☐ 12

River Capital Corp.
Peter D. Van Oosterhout, President
796 Huntington Bldg.
Cleveland, OH 44115
(216) 781-3655
(main office in RI)
D ☐ ☐ ☐ 12

SeaGate SBIC
Charles Brown, Vice-President
245 Summit St., #1403
Toledo, OH 43603
(419) 259-8397
A ☐ ☐ ☐ 5 6 12

Oklahoma

Alliance Business Investment Co.
Barry M. Davis, President
One Williams Ctr., Suite 2000
Tulsa, OK 74172
(918) 584-3581
C ☐ ☐ ☐ 1 3 5 6 7 9 11 12

First Oklahoma Investment Capital Corp.
David H. Pendley, President
120 N. Robinson, Suite 880C
Oklahoma City, OK 73102
(405) 272-4693
D ☐ ☐ ☐ 1 5 6 9 10 11 12

Southwest Venture Capital, Inc.
Donald J. Rubottom, President
2700 E. 51st St., Suite 340
Tulsa, OK 74105
(918) 742-3177
A ☐ ☐ ☐ 5 6 9 10

Western Venture Capital Corp.
William B. Baker, President and Chief
    Executive Officer
4900 S. Lewis
Tulsa, OK 74105
(918) 749-7981
D ☐ ☐ 12

Oregon

InterVen Partners
Wayne B. Kingsley, Chairman
227 SW Pine St., Suite 200
Portland, OR 97204
(503) 223-4334
(main office in CA)
E ☐ ☐ ☐ 1 6 8 12

Northern Pacific Capital Corp.
John J. Tennant, Jr., President
1201 SW 12th Ave.
Portland, OR 97205
(503) 241-1255
B ☐ ☐ ☐ 5 9 11

Norwest Growth Fund, Inc.
Anthony Miadich, Vice-President
1300 SW Fifth Ave., Suite 3018
Portland, OR 97201
(503) 223-6622
(main office in MN)
E □ □ □ 1 6 8 12

Trendwest Capital Corp.
Mark E. Nicol, President
Box 5106
Klamath Falls, OR 97601
(503) 882-8059
B □ □ □ 12

Pennsylvania

Alliance Enterprise Corp.
(The Sun Company)
Terrance Hicks, Vice-President
1801 Market St., 3rd floor
Philadelphia, PA 19103
(215) 977-3925
MESBIC   B □ 1 5

Enterprise Venture Capital Corp. of PA
Donald W. Cowie, Vice-President
227 Franklin St., #215
Johnstown, PA 15901
(814) 535-7597
A □ 12

First SBIC of California
Daniel A. Dye, Managing Partner
Box 512
Washington, PA 15301
(412) 223-0707
(main office in CA)
E □ □ □ 12

First Valley Capital Corp.
Matthew W. Thomas, President
One Center Sq., Suite 201
Allentown, PA 18101
(215) 776-6760
B □ 12

Greater Philadelphia Venture Capital Corp.,
   Inc.
Martin M. Newman, General Manager
225 S. 15th St., Suite 920
Philadelphia, PA 19102
(215) 732-1666
MESBIC   B □ □ □ 4 5 6

Meridian Capital Corp.
Knute C. Albrecht, President and Chief
   Executive Officer
Blue Bell West, Suite 122
Blue Bell, PA 19422
(215) 278-8907
B □ □ □ 12

PNC Capital Corp.
David M. Hillman, Executive Vice-President
5th Ave. & Wood St., 19th floor
Pittsburgh, PA 15222
(412) 355-2245
C □ □ □ 1 5 6 8 9 10

Puerto Rico

First Puerto Rico Capital, Inc.
Eliseo E. Font, President
Box 816
Mayaguez, PR 00709
(809) 832-9171
MESBIC   A □ 12

Loan limits: **A** $100,000   **B** $250,000   **C** $500,000   **D** $1 million   **E** Over $1 million

Policy: □ Loans or investments   □ □ Long-term loans   □ □ □ Financing with stock options

Industry: **1** Communications   **2** Construction and development   **3** Natural resources   **4** Hotels and
restaurants   **5** Manufacturing and processing   **6** Health services   **7** Recreation   **8** Research and
technology   **9** Retail, wholesale, distribution   **10** Service trades   **11** Transportation   **12** Diversified

North America Investment Corp.
S. Ruiz-Betancourt, President
Banco Popular Ctr., Suite 1710
Hato Rey, PR 00919
(809) 754-6177
MESBIC B ☐ ☐ 5 6 9 12

Rhode Island

Domestic Capital Corp.
Nathaniel B. Baker, President
815 Reservoir Ave.
Cranston, RI 02910
(401) 946-3310
B ☐ 4 5 11 12

Fleet Venture Resources, Inc.
Robert M. Van Degna, President
111 Westminster St.
Providence, RI 02920
(401) 278-6770
E ☐ ☐ ☐ 1 5 6 8 9 10 11 12

Narragansett Capital Corp.
Arthur D. Little, Chairman
40 Westminster St.
Providence, RI 02903
(401) 751-1000
E ☐ 1 5 7 8 9 12

Old Stone Capital Corp.
Arthur Barton, Vice-President
One Old Stone Sq., 11th floor
Providence, RI 02901
(401) 278-2559
D ☐ ☐ ☐ 1

River Capital Corp.
Peter D. Van Oosterhout, President
One Hospital Trust Plaza
Providence, RI 02903
(401) 278-8819
D ☐ ☐ ☐ 12

South Carolina

Carolina Venture Capital Corp.
Thomas H. Harvey III, President
14 Archer Rd.
Hilton Head Island, SC 29928
(803) 842-3101
B ☐ ☐ ☐ 1 2 4 7 11 12

Reedy River Ventures
John M. Sterling, General Partner
Tee C. Hooper, General Partner
Box 17526
Greenville, SC 29606
(803) 297-9198
B ☐ ☐ ☐ 1 5 9 12

Tennessee

Chickasaw Capital Corp.
Thomas L. Moore, President
Box 387
Memphis, TN 38147
(901) 523-6470
MESBIC D ☐ ☐ ☐ 2 5 6 9 10 12

Financial Resources, Inc.
Milton C. Picard, Chairman
2800 Sterick Bldg.
Memphis, TN 38103
(901) 527-9411
B ☐ ☐ ☐ 1 5 6 8 10 12

Leader Capital Corp.
Edward Pruitt, President
Box 708, 158 Madison Ave.
Memphis, TN 38101-0708
(901) 578-2405

Suwannee Capital Corp.
Peter R. Pettit, President
3030 Poplar Ave.
Memphis, TN 38111
(901) 345-4200
C ☐ ☐ ☐ 9

Tennessee Equity Capital Corp.
Walter S. Cohen, President and Chief
   Executive Officer
1102 Stonewall Jackson
Nashville, TN 37220
(615) 373-4502
MESBIC C ☐ ☐ ☐ 1 2 4 5 7 9 10 12

Valley Capital Corp.
Lamar J. Partridge, President
100 W. Martin L. King Blvd., #806
Chattanooga, TN 37402
(615) 265-1557
MESBIC B ☐ ☐ ☐ 1 5 6 9 11 12

West Tennessee Venture Capital Corp.
Osbie Howard, Vice-President
Box 300, 152 Beale St.
Memphis, TN 38101
(901) 527-6091
MESBIC B ☐ 1 5 6 7 10 11 12

Texas

Alliance Business Investment Co.
3990 One Shell Pl.
Houston, TX 77002
(713) 224-8224
(main office in OK)
C ☐ ☐ ☐ 1 3 5 6 8 11 12

Allied Bancshares Capital Corp.
Philip A. Tuttle, President
Box 3326
Houston, TX 77253
(713) 226-1625
D ☐ ☐ ☐ 1 6 8 9 11 12

Americap Corp.
James L. Hurn, President
7575 San Felipe, #160
Houston, TX 77063
(713) 780-8084
C ☐ ☐ ☐ 1 5 6 8 12

Brittany Capital Co.
Steven S. Peden, General Partner
2424 LTV Tower, 1525 Elm St.
Dallas, TX 75201
(214) 954-1515
B ☐ ☐ ☐ 12

Business Capital Corp. of Arlington
Keith Martin, President
1112 Copeland Rd., Suite 420
Arlington, TX 76011-4994
(817) 261-4936
A ☐ ☐ ☐ 12

Capital Marketing Corp.
John King Myrick, President
Box 1000
Keller, TX 76248
(817) 656-7380
E ☐ ☐ 2 9

Capital Southwest Venture Corp.
William R. Thomas, President
12900 Preston Rd., Suite 700
Dallas, TX 75230
(214) 233-8242
D ☐ ☐ ☐ 1 3 5 6 8 9 11 12

Central Texas SBIC
David G. Horner, President
514 Austin Ave., Box 2600
Waco, TX 76702-2600
(817) 753-6461
A ☐ ☐ 5 9 12

Loan limits: **A** $100,000 **B** $250,000 **C** $500,000 **D** $1 million **E** Over $1 million

Policy: ☐ Loans or investments   ☐ ☐ Long-term loans   ☐ ☐ ☐ Financing with stock options

Industry: **1** Communications **2** Construction and development **3** Natural resources **4** Hotels and restaurants **5** Manufacturing and processing **6** Health services **7** Recreation **8** Research and technology **9** Retail, wholesale, distribution **10** Service trades **11** Transportation **12** Diversified

Charter Venture Group, Inc.
Jerry Finger, President
2600 Citadel Plaza Dr., 6th floor
Houston, TX 77008
(713) 863-0704
B □ □ □ 12

Citicorp Venture Capital, Ltd.
Thomas F. McWilliams, Vice-President
Diamond Shamrock Tower, #2920-LB87
717 Harwood
Dallas, TX 75221
(214) 880-9670
(main office in NY)
E □ □ □ 12

Energy Capital Corp.
Herbert F. Poyner, Jr., President
953 Esperson Bldg.
Houston, TX 77002
(713) 236-0006
D □ □ □ 3

Enterprise Capital Corp.
Fred S. Zeidman, President
3501 Allen Pkwy.
Houston, TX 77019
(713) 521-4401
D □ □ □ 1 5 6 7 8 12

FCA Investment Co.
R. S. Baker, Jr., Chairman
3000 Post Oak Blvd., #1790
Houston, TX 77056
(713) 965-0077
D □ □ □ 5 6 8 9 12

The Grocers SBIC
Milton Levit, President
3131 E. Holcombe Blvd., #101
Houston, TX 77021
(713) 747-7913
B □ □ 9

Hickory Venture Capital Corp.
3811 Turtle Creek Blvd., #1000, LB33
Dallas, TX 75219
(214) 522-1892
(main office in AL)
E □ □ □ 12

InterFirst Venture Corp.
J. A. O'Donnell, President
901 Main St., 10th floor
Dallas, TX 75283
(214) 977-3164
E □ □ □ 12

Livingston Capital Ltd.
J. Livingston Kosberg, Partner
Box 2507
Houston, TX 77252
(713) 872-3213
B □ □ □ 12

Lone Star Capital, Ltd.
Stuart Schube, President
2401 Fountainview, Suite 950
Houston, TX 77057
(713) 266-6616
E □ 1 5 6 9 12

Mapleleaf Capital Corp.
Edward M. Fink, President
55 Waugh Dr., #710
Houston, TX 77007
(713) 880-4494
E □ □ □ 12

MESBIC Financial Corp. of Dallas
Thomas Gerron, Vice-President and
    Comptroller
12655 North Central Expwy., #814
Dallas, TX 75243
(214) 637-1597
MESBIC   C □ □ □ 12

MESBIC Financial Corp. of Houston
Richard Rothfeld, President
1801 Main St., Suite 320
Houston, TX 77002
(713) 228-8321
MESBIC   B ☐ 5 8 9 10 12

Mid-State Capital Corp.
Smith E. Thomasson, President
Box 7554
Waco, TX 76714
(817) 776-9500
B ☐ ☐ ☐ 12

MVenture Corp.
Joseph B. Longino, Jr., President
Box 662090
Dallas, TX 75266-2090
(214) 741-1469
D ☐ ☐ ☐ 1 5 6 10 11 12

Omega Capital Corp.
Ted E. Moor, Jr., President
755 S. 11th St., #250
Beaumont, TX 77701
(409) 832-0221
A ☐ ☐ ☐ 5 12

Orange Nassau Capital Corp.
Richard D. Tadler, Vice-President
One Galleria Tower
13355 Noel Rd., Suite 635
Dallas, TX 75240
(214) 385-9685
(main office in CA)
C ☐ ☐ 12

Red River Ventures, Inc.
D. W. Morton, President
777 E. 15th St.
Plano, TX 75074
(214) 422-4999
B ☐ 12

Republic Venture Group, Inc.
Robert H. Wellborn, President
Box 225961
Dallas, TX 75265
(214) 922-5078
D ☐ ☐ ☐ 1 3 5 6 12

Retzloff Capital Corp.
James K. Hines, President
Box 41250
Houston, TX 77240
(713) 466-4633
C ☐ ☐ ☐ 5 6 9 12

San Antonio Venture Group, Inc.
Tom Woodley, Investment Advisor
2300 W. Commerce
San Antonio, TX 78207
(512) 223-3633
B ☐ ☐ ☐ 4 5 6 9 10

SBI Capital Corp.
William E. Wright, President
Box 771668
Houston, TX 77215-1668
(713) 975-1188
C ☐ ☐ ☐ 1 5 6 8

Southern Orient Capital Corp.
Cheng Ming Lee, Chairman
2419 Fannin, Suite 200
Houston, TX 77002
(713) 225-3369
MESBIC   A ☐ 4 9 10 12

Loan limits: **A** $100,000   **B** $250,000   **C** $500,000   **D** $1 million   **E** Over $1 million

Policy: ☐ Loans or investments   ☐ ☐ Long-term loans   ☐ ☐ ☐ Financing with stock options

Industry: **1** Communications   **2** Construction and development   **3** Natural resources   **4** Hotels and restaurants   **5** Manufacturing and processing   **6** Health services   **7** Recreation   **8** Research and technology   **9** Retail, wholesale, distribution   **10** Service trades   **11** Transportation   **12** Diversified

Southwestern Venture Capital of Texas, Inc.
James A. Bettersworth, President
Box 1719
Seguin, TX 78155
(512) 379-0380
(branch office in San Antonio)
B ☐ 12

Sunwestern Capital Corp.
Thomas W. Wright, President
12221 Merit Dr., #1680
Dallas, TX 75251
(214) 239-5650
C ☐ ☐ ☐ ☐ 1 3 5 6 8 12

Texas Capital Corp.
David Franklin, Vice-President
1341 W. Mockingbird, #1250E
Dallas, TX 75247
(214) 638-0638
C ☐ ☐ ☐ 12

United Mercantile Capital Corp.
L. Joe Justice, Chairman
Box 66
El Paso, TX 79940
(915) 533-6375
A ☐ ☐ ☐ 5 11

United Oriental Capital Co.
Don J. Wang, President
908 Town & Country Blvd., #310
Houston, TX 77024
(713) 461-3909
MESBIC   B ☐ 12

Wesbanc Ventures, Ltd.
Stuart Schube, General Partner
2401 Fountainview, #950
Houston, TX 77057
(713) 977-7421
E ☐ 1 5 6 9 12

Virginia

East West United Investment Co.
Doug Bui, President
6723 Whittier Ave., Suite 206B
McLean, VA 22101
(703) 821-6616
MESBIC   A ☐ ☐ 4 9 12

Hillcrest Group
(James River Capital Associates)
(UV Capital Corp.)
A. Hugh Ewing III, General Partner
James B. Farinholt, Jr., General Partner
9 S. 12th St., Box 1776
Richmond, VA 23219
(804) 643-7358
C ☐ ☐ ☐ 12

Metropolitan Capital Corp.
S. W. Austin, Vice-President
2550 Huntington Ave.
Alexandria, VA 22303
(703) 960-4698
B ☐ ☐ ☐ 5 8

River Capital Corp.
1033 N. Fairfax St.
Alexandria, VA 22314
(703) 739-2100
(main office in RI)
D ☐ ☐ ☐ 12

Sovran Funding Corp.
David A. King, Jr., President
Sovran Ctr., 6th floor
One Commercial Pl.
Norfolk, VA 23510
(804) 441-4041
C ☐ ☐ ☐ 12

Washington

Peoples Capital Corp.
R. W. Maider, President
2411 Fourth Ave., Suite 400
Seattle, WA 98121
(206) 344-8105
B ☐ 1 6 9

Seafirst Capital Corp.
R. Bruce Harrod, President
Columbia Seafirst Center, 14th floor
Box C 34103
Seattle, WA 98124-1103
(206) 442-3501
C ☐ 2

Wisconsin

Bando-McGlocklin Inv. Co. Inc.
George Schonath, Chief Executive Officer
13555 Bishops Ct., Suite 205
Brookfield, WI 53005
(414) 784-9010
C ☐ ☐ 5 6 9 10 11

Capital Investments, Inc.
Robert L. Banner, Vice-President
744 N. 4th St.
Milwaukee, WI 53203
(414) 273-6560
C ☐ 1 5 9 12

M and I Ventures Corp.
Daniel P. Howell, Vice-President
770 N. Water St.
Milwaukee, WI 53202
(414) 765-7910
C ☐ ☐ ☐ 5 6 8 12

Madison Capital Corp.
Roger H. Ganser, President
102 State St.
Madison, WI 53703
(608) 256-8185
B ☐ 6 8 12

Marine Venture Capital, Inc.
H. Wayne Foreman, President
111 E. Wisconsin Ave.
Milwaukee, WI 53202
(414) 765-2274
C ☐ ☐ ☐ 12

MorAmerica Capital Corp.
Steven J. Massey, Vice-President
600 E. Mason St.
Milwaukee, WI 53202
(414) 276-3839
(main office in Iowa)
D ☐ ☐ ☐ 12

Super Market Investors, Inc.
John W. Andorfer, President
Box 473
Milwaukee, WI 53201
(414) 547-7999
A ☐ ☐ 9

Twin Ports Capital Co.
Paul Leonidas, President
1230 Poplar Ave., Box 849
Superior, WI 54880
(715) 392-5525
A ☐ 12

Loan limits: **A** $100,000 **B** $250,000 **C** $500,000 **D** $1 million **E** Over $1 million

Policy: ☐ Loans or investments ☐ ☐ Long-term loans ☐ ☐ ☐ Financing with stock options

Industry: **1** Communications **2** Construction and development **3** Natural resources **4** Hotels and restaurants **5** Manufacturing and processing **6** Health services **7** Recreation **8** Research and technology **9** Retail, wholesale, distribution **10** Service trades **11** Transportation **12** Diversified

Wisconsin Community Capital Inc.
Louis Fortis, President
14 W. Mifflin St., #314
Madison, WI 53703
(608) 256-3441
A ☐ 3 5 10

Wisconsin MESBIC, Inc.
Charles A. McKinney, Chairman
622 N. Water St., Suite 500
Milwaukee, WI 53202
(414) 278-0377
MESBIC   B ☐☐☐ 12

Wyoming

Capital Corporation of Wyoming, Inc.
Larry J. McDonald, President
Box 3599
Casper, WY 82602
(307) 234-5438
B ☐ 3 5 9 10 11 12

Non-SBIC Members

Robert B. Leisy, Consultant
14408 E. Whittier Blvd., #B-5
Box 4405
Whittier, CA 90605
(213) 698-4862

NASBIC Associate Members and Sustaining Members

Accel Partners
James R. Swartz, Managing Partner
Dixon R. Doll, Managing Partner
One Palmer Sq.
Princeton, NJ 08542
(609) 683-4500
E ☐ 1 5 6 8 9 10 12

Alimansky Venture Group, Inc.
Burt Alimansky, Managing Director
790 Madison Ave., Suite 705
New York, NY 10021
(212) 472-0502
E ☐☐☐ 1 3 5 6 7 8 9 10 11 12

R. W. Allsop & Associates
Robert W. Allsop, General Partner
Gregory B. Bultman, General Partner
2750 First Ave., NE, Suite 210
Cedar Rapids, IA 52402
(319) 363-8971
D ☐☐☐ 1 5 6 9 12

Allstate Insurance Co.
Leonard A. Batters, Senior Investment
   Manager
Allstate Plaza E-2
Northbrook, IL 60062
(312) 291-5681
E ☐☐☐ 1 4 5 6 8 10 11 12

Arthur Andersen & Co.
John Cherin, Managing Partner
8251 Greensboro Dr., #400
McLean, VA 22102
(703) 734-7300

Arthur Andersen & Co.
Brian P. Murphy, Partner
111 SW Columbia, #1400
Portland, OR 97201
(503) 220-6068

Arthur Andersen & Co.
Robert W. Philip, Partner
Box 650026
Dallas, TX 75265
(214) 741-8300

Arthur Andersen & Co.
Richard J. Strotman, Partner
33 W. Monroe St.
Chicago, IL 60603
(312) 580-0033

Arete Ventures, Inc.
Robert W. Shaw, Jr., President
990 Hammond Dr., Suite 620
Atlanta, GA 30328
(404) 396-2480

Atlantic Venture Partners
Robert H. Pratt, General Partner
Box 1493
Richmond, VA 23212
(804) 644-5496
D ☐ ☐ ☐ 12

The Babcock Group
Warner King Babcock, President
Box 1022
49 Locust Ave.
New Canaan, CT 06840
(203) 972-3579

Bain Capital
Geoffrey S. Rehnert, Senior Associate
Two Copley Pl.
Boston, MA 02116
(617) 572-3000
C ☐ ☐ ☐ 12

Baker & Kirk
Michael A. Baker, President
1020 Holcombe, Suite 1444
Houston, TX 77030
(713) 790-9316

Battery Ventures
Richard D. Frisbie, General Partner
60 Batterymarch St., #1400
Boston, MA 02110
(617) 542-0100
D ☐ ☐ ☐ 1

Beacon Partners
Leonard Vignola, Jr., Managing Partner
71 Strawberry Hill Ave., #614
Stamford, CT 06902
(203) 348-8858
D ☐ ☐ ☐ 1 4 5 6 7 9 11

Berry Cash Southwest Partnership
Harvey B. Cash, General Partner
Glenn A. Norem, General Partner
One Galleria Tower, Suite 1375
13355 Noel Rd.
Dallas, TX 75240
(213) 392-7279
D ☐ ☐ ☐ 1 8

William Blair Venture Partners
Samuel B. Guren, General Partner
135 S. LaSalle St., 29th floor
Chicago, IL 60603
(312) 236-1600
E ☐ ☐ ☐ 12

Brownstein, Zeidman and Schomer
Thomas C. Evans, Partner
1401 New York Ave., NW, #900
Washington, DC 20036
(202) 879-5760

Burton and Co., Inc.
Reginald C. Burton, President
Box 7319
Philadelphia, PA 19101-7319
(312) 263-6663

Camperdown Ventures
S. Cary Beckwith III, General Partner
115 E. Camperdown Way
Greenville, SC 29601
(803) 233-7770

Loan limits: **A** $100,000   **B** $250,000   **C** $500,000   **D** $1 million   **E** Over $1 million

Policy: ☐ Loans or investments   ☐ ☐ Long-term loans   ☐ ☐ ☐ Financing with stock options

Industry: **1** Communications   **2** Construction and development   **3** Natural resources   **4** Hotels and restaurants   **5** Manufacturing and processing   **6** Health services   **7** Recreation   **8** Research and technology   **9** Retail, wholesale, distribution   **10** Service trades   **11** Transportation   **12** Diversified

Capital Services and Resources, Inc.
Charles Y Bancroft, Treasurer
5159 Wheelis Dr., Suite 104
Memphis, TN 38117
(901) 761-2156
E ☐ 1 4 5 6 8 9

Cardinal Development Capital Fund I
Richard F. Bannon, Partner
155 E. Broad St.
Columbus, OH 43215
(614) 464-5550
E ☐ ☐ ☐ 1 5 6 8 9 10 11 12

Centennial Fund
G. Jackson Tankersley, General Partner
Steven C. Halstedt, General Partner
1999 Broadway, Suite 2100
Box 13977
Denver, CO 80202
(303) 298-9066
D ☐ ☐ ☐ 1 6 8

Cherry Tree Ventures
Gordon Stofer, General Partner
Tony Christianson, General Partner
640 Northland Executive Ctr.
3600 W. 80th St.
Minneapolis, MN 55431
(612) 893-9012
D ☐ ☐ ☐ 1 5 6 10

Colley Godward Castro Huddles and Tatum
James C. Gaither, General Partner
One Maritime Plaza, 20th floor
San Francisco, CA 94111
(415) 981-5252

Columbine Venture Management, Inc.
Mark Kimmel, President
5613 DTC Pkwy., #510
Englewood, CO 80111
(303) 694-3222

Coopers and Lybrand
Robert H. Stavers
One Almaden Blvd., #500
San Jose, CA 95113
(408) 295-1020
1 2 3 5 6 8 9

Corporation for Innovation Development
Marion C. Dietrich, President and Chief
   Officer
One N. Capitol Ave., Suite 520
Indianapolis, IN 46204
(317) 635-7325
C ☐ ☐ ☐ 1 5 6 8 9

Criterion Venture Partners
David Wicks, Jr., Senior Partner
333 Clay St., Suite 4300
Houston, TX 77002
(713) 751-2400
D ☐ ☐ ☐ 1 6 8 9 10 11 12

Dana Venture Capital Corp.
Gene C. Swartz, President
Box 1000
Toledo, OH 43697
(419) 535-4780
E ☐ 12

Deloitte Haskins and Sells
Sanford Antignas, Senior Consultant
1114 Ave. of the Americas
New York, NY 10036
(212) 790-0539

DeSoto Capital Corp.
William Rudner, Chairman
60 N. Third St.
Memphis, TN 38103
(901) 523-6894
A ☐ ☐ ☐ 5 12

Development Corp. of Montana
Richard L. Bourke, President
350 N. Last Chance Gulch, Box 916
Helena, MT 59624
(406) 442-3850
B ☐ ☐ ☐ 12

Development Finance Corp. of New Zealand
Chris C. Ellison, Manager
100 Spear St., Suite 1430
San Francisco, CA 94105
(415) 777-2847

DnC Capital Corp.
Jack A. Prizzi, Vice-President
600 Fifth Ave.
New York, NY 10020
(212) 765-4800
C ☐ ☐ ☐ 1 5 6 8 12

Early Stages Co.
Frank W. Kuehn, Partner
William Lanphear IV, Partner
244 California St., Suite 300
San Francisco, CA 94111
(415) 986-5700
C ☐ ☐ ☐ 6 7 9 10

El Dorado Ventures
Brent Rider, Partner
Gary Kalbach, Partner
2 N. Lake Ave., Suite 480
Pasadena, CA 91101
(818) 793-1936
D ☐ 12

Elf Technologies, Inc.
John H. Mahar, Executive Vice-President
High Ridge Park, Box 10037
Stamford, CT 06904
(203) 358-5120
E ☐ ☐ ☐ 3 5 8

Ernst and Whinney
Larry Gray, Partner
5941 Variel
Woodland Hills, CA 91367
(818) 888-0707

Fine and Ambrogne
Arnold M. Zaff, Partner
Exchange Place
Boston, MA 02109
(617) 367-0100

First Chicago Investment Advisors
Patrick A. McGivney, Vice-President
Three First National Plaza
Suite 1040, 9th floor
Chicago, IL 60670
(312) 732-4919
D ☐ ☐ ☐ 1 5 6 8 9

Fostin Capital Corp.
William E. Woods, President
Box 67
Pittsburgh, PA 15230
(412) 928-8900
C ☐ ☐ ☐ 1 6 8

Gatti Tomerlin and Martin Corp.
John Gatti, Chairman
405 N. St. Mary's, Suite 222
San Antonio, TX 78205
(512) 229-9028
E ☐ ☐ ☐ 1 3 5 6 9 10 12

General Electric Venture Capital Corp.
Harry T. Rein, President
3135 Easton Tpke.
Fairfield, CT 06431
(203) 373-3356
D ☐ ☐ ☐ 1 5 6 8 10 12

Loan limits: **A** $100,000 **B** $250,000 **C** $500,000 **D** $1 million **E** Over $1 million

Policy: ☐ Loans or investments ☐ ☐ Long-term loans ☐ ☐ ☐ Financing with stock options

Industry: **1** Communications **2** Construction and development **3** Natural resources **4** Hotels and restaurants **5** Manufacturing and processing **6** Health services **7** Recreation **8** Research and technology **9** Retail, wholesale, distribution **10** Service trades **11** Transportation **12** Diversified

Golder, Thoma and Cressey
Stanley C. Golder, General Partner
Carl D. Thoma, General Partner
Bryan C. Cressey, General Partner
120 S. LaSalle St., Suite 630
Chicago, IL 60603
(312) 853-3322
E ☐ ☐ ☐ 1 4 5 6 8 10 11

Grayrock Capital, Ltd.
W. J. Gluck, President
2 International Blvd.
Rexdale, Ontario M9W-1A2, Canada
(416) 675-4808
D ☐ ☐ ☐ 1 6 7 9 10

Great American Investment Corp.
James A. Arias, President
4209 San Mateo, NE
Albuquerque, NM 87110
(505) 883-6273
C ☐ ☐ ☐ 12

Heizer Corp.
E. F. Heizer, Jr., Chairman and President
261 S. Bluffs Edge Drive
Lake Forest, IL 60045
(312) 641-2200

Heller Financial Inc.
Robert Spitalnic, Senior Vice-President
101 Park Ave.
New York, NY 10178
(212) 880-7062
E ☐ ☐ ☐ 5 9 10 12

Helms, Mulliss and Johnston
B. Bernard Burns, Jr.
227 N. Tryon St., Box 31247
Charlotte, NC 28231
(704) 372-9510

HLPM Inc.
Robert W. Fletcher, President
545 S. Third St.
Louisville, KY 40202
(502) 588-8459

Houston Venture Partners
Howard Hill, Jr., General Partner
Thomas Fatjo, Jr., General Partner
401 S. Louisiana
Houston, TX 77002
(713) 222-8600
E ☐ 12

Hunton & Williams
C. Porter Vaughan III
Box 1535
Richmond, VA 23212
(804) 788-8200

Hutton Venture Investment Partners
James E. McGrath, President
1 Battery Park Plaza, #1801
New York, NY 10004
(212) 742-6486
D ☐ ☐ ☐ 1 5 6 8

IEG Venture Management, Inc.
Francis I. Blair, President
401 N. Michigan Ave., #2020
Chicago, IL 60611
(312) 644-0890
C ☐ ☐ ☐ 1 3 6 8

Indiana Capital Corp.
Samuel Rea, President
5612 Jefferson Blvd., W.
Ft. Wayne, IN 46804
(219) 432-8622

Institute of Private Enterprise
Rollie Tillman, Director
312 Carroll Hall, #012-A
Chapel Hill, NC 27514
(919) 962-8201

Interstate Capital Corp.
William C. McConnell, Jr., President
701 E. Camino Rea, #9A
Boca Raton, FL 33432
(305) 395-8466
B ☐ ☐ ☐ 3 5 6 8

Japan Associate Finance Co., Ltd.
Teiji Imahara, Chairman
Toshiba Bldg., 10th floor
1-1-1 Shibaura Minato-KU
Tokyo, Japan
(03) 456-5101
E ☐☐☐ 1 5 9 10

Jenkens, Huchison and Gilchrist
John R. Holzgraefe, Partner
Mark Wigder, Partner
1455 Ross Ave., 29th floor
Dallas, TX 75202
(214) 855-4500

Kirland and Ellis
Edward T. Swan
200 E. Randolph Dr.
Chicago, IL 60601
(312) 861-2465

Kleinwort, Benson (NA) Corp.
Alan L. J. Bowen, Sr., Vice-President
Christopher Wright, Vice-President
333 S. Grand, #2900
Los Angeles, CA 90071
(213) 680-2297
E ☐ 3 5 6 9 11 12

Knight and Irish Associates, Inc.
Joan S. Irish, President
420 Lexington Ave., Suite 2358
New York, NY 10170
(212) 490-0135

Lord, Bissell and Brook
John K. O'Connor, Partner
115 S. LaSalle St., #3500
Chicago, IL 60603
(312) 443-0615

Lubrizol Enterprises, Inc.
Donald L. Murfin, President
29400 Lakeland Blvd.
Wickliffe, OH 44092
(216) 943-4200
E ☐☐☐ 8

Madison Venture Capital Corp.
Norman C. Schultz, President
26515 Carmel Rancho Blvd., #201
Carmel, CA 93923
(408) 625-9650

Manufacturers Hanover Venture Capital
  Corp.
Thomas J. Sandleitner, President
140 E. 45th St., 30th floor
New York, NY 10017
(212) 350-6701
E ☐☐☐ 1 4 5 6 7 9 10 11 12

Mayer, Brown and Platt
Herbert B. Max
520 Madison Ave.
New York, NY 10022
(212) 437-7132

Med-Wick Associates, Inc.
A. A. T. Wickersham, Chairman and
  President
1902 Fleet National Bank Bldg.
Providence, RI 02903
(401) 751-5270

Menlo Ventures
Ken E. Joy, General Partner
3000 Sand Hill Rd.
Menlo Park, CA 94025
(415) 854-8540
E ☐☐☐ 12

Loan limits: **A** $100,000   **B** $250,000   **C** $500,000   **D** $1 million   **E** Over $1 million

Policy: ☐ Loans or investments   ☐☐ Long-term loans   ☐☐☐ Financing with stock options

Industry: **1** Communications   **2** Construction and development   **3** Natural resources   **4** Hotels and restaurants   **5** Manufacturing and processing   **6** Health services   **7** Recreation   **8** Research and technology   **9** Retail, wholesale, distribution   **10** Service trades   **11** Transportation   **12** Diversified

Michigan Investment Division, Treasury
   Department
Michael J. Finn, Administrator
Box 15128
Lansing, MI 48901
(517) 373-4330
D ☐ 12

Miller Venture Partners
William I. Miller, General Partner
Box 808
Columbus, IN 47202
(812) 376-3331
B ☐☐☐ 3 5 6 8 11

Moore Berson Lifflander, Mewhinney
Joel L. Berson
595 Madison Ave.
New York, NY 10022

Morgan Holland Ventures Corp.
James F. Morgan, Managing Partner
Daniel J. Holland, Managing Partner
1 Liberty Sq.
Boston, MA 02109
(617) 423-1765
E ☐☐☐ 1 5 6 8

Morgenthaler Ventures
David T. Morgenthaler, Managing Partner
700 National City Bank Bldg.
Cleveland, OH 44114
(216) 621-3070
E ☐☐☐ 1 5 6 8 10

Morrison and Forester
Tino Kamarck
Marco Adelfrio
2000 Pennsylvania Ave., NW
Washington, DC 20006
(202) 887-1500

MRI Ventures
Charles Moll, Vice-President
1650 University Blvd., NE, #500
Albuquerque, NM 87102
(505) 768-6200
D ☐☐☐ 1 5 6 8 12

NBM Participatie Beheer B. V.
Michiel A. de Haan, General Manager
Postbus 1800
1000 BV Amsterdam
The Netherlands, NL
020-543-3346
E ☐ 1 5 6 8 10 11

NEPA Venture Fund, L.P.
Frederick J. Beste III, President
Ben Franklin Advanced Technical Ctr.
Lehigh University
Bethlehem, PA 18015
(215) 865-6550
E ☐☐☐ 12

New Enterprise Associates
Charles Newhall III, General Partner
300 Cathedral St., Suite 110
Baltimore, MD 21201
(301) 244-0115
E ☐ 1 6

Nippon Investment and Finance Co. Ltd.
Yasutoshi Sasada, President
39 F, Nishi-Shinjuki 1-25-1
Shinjuku-ku
Tokyo 163 Japan
(03) 349-0961
E ☐☐☐ 12

Noro-Moseley Partners
Charles Moseley, General Partner
100 Galleria Pkwy., #1240
Atlanta, GA 30339
(404) 955-0020

North American Capital Corp.
Stanley P. Roth, Chairman
510 Broad Hollow Rd., #205
Melville, NY 11747
(516) 752-9696
E ☐ 12

North American Capital Group, Ltd.
Gregory I. Kravitt, President
7250 N. Cicero
Lincolnwood, IL 60646
(312) 982-1010
D ☐ ☐ ☐ 2 4 5 6 9 10

Olwine, Connelly, Chase
Roger Mulvihill
299 Park Ave.
New York, NY 10017
(212) 207-1831

Onondaga Venture Capital Fund, Inc.
Irving W. Schwartz, Executive Vice-President
327 State Tower Bldg.
Syracuse, NY 13202
(315) 478-0157
B ☐ ☐ ☐ 12

Oxford Partners
Kenneth Rind, General Partner
1266 Main St.
Stamford, CT 06902
(203) 964-0592
E ☐ ☐ ☐ 1 6 8

Ozanam Capital Co.
Janis L. Mullin, General Partner
Adam Robins, General Partner
4711 Golf Rd., #706
Skokie, IL 60076
(312) 674-2297
B ☐ ☐ ☐ 5 9

Pathfinder Venture Capital Fund
A. J. Greenshields, General Partner
7300 Metro Blvd., Suite 585
Minneapolis, MN 55435
(612) 835-1121
D ☐ ☐ ☐ 1 5 6 8

Peat, Marwick, Mitchell and Co.
Terrence D. Dibble, Partner
725 South Figueroa St.
Los Angeles, CA 90017
(213) 972-4000

Peat, Marwick, Mitchell and Co.
Ronald R. Booth, Partner
1700 IDS Center
Minneapolis, MN 55402
(612) 341-2222

Peat, Marwick, Mitchell and Co.
Michael E. Lavin, Partner
303 E. Wacker Dr.
Chicago, IL 60601
(312) 938-5043

Peat, Marwick, Mitchell and Co.
Edgar R. Wood, Jr., Partner
1800 First Union Pl.
Charlotte, NC 28282
(704) 335-5300

Pepper, Hamilton and Scheetz
Michael B. Staebler, Partner
100 Renaissance Ctr., Suite 3600
Detroit, MI 48243
(313) 259-7110

Peregrine Associates
Gene I. Miller, Partner
Frank LaHaye, Partner
606 Wilshire Blvd., Suite 602
Santa Monica, CA 90401
(213) 458-1441
E ☐ ☐ ☐ 1 5 6 8 9 10 12

Loan limits: **A** $100,000   **B** $250,000   **C** $500,000   **D** $1 million   **E** Over $1 million

Policy: ☐ Loans or investments   ☐ ☐ Long-term loans   ☐ ☐ ☐ Financing with stock options

Industry: **1** Communications   **2** Construction and development   **3** Natural resources   **4** Hotels and restaurants   **5** Manufacturing and processing   **6** Health services   **7** Recreation   **8** Research and technology   **9** Retail, wholesale, distribution   **10** Service trades   **11** Transportation   **12** Diversified

Pioneer Capital Corp.
Christopher W. Lynch, Partner
Frank M. Polestra, Partner
60 State St.
Boston, MA 02109
(617) 742-7825
D ☐ 12

Piper, Jaffray and Hopwood, Inc.
Frank Bennett
Piper Jaffray Tower
222 S. 9th St., Box 28
Minneapolis, MN 55402
(612) 342-6000
D ☐☐☐ 1 5 6 8 9 10

Piper, Jaffray and Hopwood
Gary L. Takacs, Vice-President
1600 IBM Building
Seattle, WA 98101
(main office in MN)
D ☐☐☐ 1 5 6 8 9 10

Primus Capital Fund
Loyal Wilson, Managing Partner
David A. DeVore, Partner
One Cleveland Ctr., #2140
Cleveland, OH 44114
(216) 621-2185
E ☐☐☐ 1 5 6 8 9 12

R and C Investments
Roger B. Collins
Box 52586
Tulsa, OK 74152
(918) 744-5604
B ☐ 1 3 4 5 9 10 11 12

RBK Management Co.
Robert B. Kaplan, President
140 S. Dearborn St., #420
Chicago, IL 60603
(312) 263-6058

Reprise Capital Corp.
Stanley Tulchin, Chairman
591 Stewart Ave.
Garden City, NY 11530
(516) 222-1028
E ☐☐☐ 12

Riordan & McKinzie
Michael P. Ridley
300 South Grand Ave., Suite 2900
Los Angeles, CA 90017
(213) 629-4824

Rothschild Ventures, Inc.
Jess L. Belser, President
One Rockefeller Pl.
New York, NY 10020
(212) 757-6000
E ☐☐☐ 1 5 6 8 12

Rust Capital Ltd.
Jeffery C. Garvey, President
114 W. 7th St., 1300 Norwood Tower
Austin, TX 78701
(512) 479-0055
D ☐☐☐ 1 4 5 6 12

Salomon Brothers, Inc.
Melvin W. Ellis, Vice-President
One New York Plaza
New York, NY 10004
(212) 747-6293
E ☐ 1 6 8

Santa Fe Private Equity Fund
A. David Silver, General Partner
524 Camino Del Monte Sol
Santa Fe, NM 87501
(505) 983-1769
D ☐☐☐ 6

SB Capital Corp., Ltd.
Mitch Kostuch, Executive Vice-President
85 Bloor St., E., #506
Toronto, Ontario M4W-1A9, Canada
(416) 967-5439
D ☐☐☐ 1 5 6 8 12

Scientific Advances, Inc.
Charles G. James, President
601 W. Fifth Ave.
Columbus, OH 43201
(614) 294-5541
D □ □ □

Security Pacific Business Credit, Inc.
Nicholas Battaglino, Vice-President
228 E. 45th St.
New York, NY 10017
(212) 309-9302
E □ □ 5 9 12

South Atlantic Venture Fund
Donald Burton, General Partner
Richard Brandewie, General Partner
220 East Madison, Suite 530
Tampa, FL 33602-4825
(813) 229-7400
D □ □ □ 1 5 6 8 10 12

Spensley, Horn, Jubas and Lubitz
Bruce W. McRoy, Partner
1880 Century Park, E., #500
Los Angeles, CA 90067
(213) 553-5050

Stephenson Merchant Banking
A. Emmet Stephenson, Jr., Senior Partner
100 Garfield St.
Denver, CO 80206
(303) 355-6000
E □ □ □ 1 5 6 9 10 11 12

S.W.S. Ltd.
Steven B. Schaffel, President
122 E. 42nd St.
New York, NY 10168
(212) 682-9550
E □ □ 4 11 12

Taylor and Turner
Marshall Turner, General Partner
William Taylor, General Partner
220 Montgomery St., Penthouse 10
San Francisco, CA 94104
(415) 398-6821
D □ 1 5 6 8

Taylor International
Don Snow
1801 Quincy St., NW
Washington, DC 20011
(202) 955-1330

Tektronix Development Co.
M. H. Chaffin, Jr., Vice-President and Manager
Box 4600, M/S 94-383
Beaverton, OR 97075
(503) 629-1121

Texas Infinity Corp.
C. Charles Bahr, Chief Executive Officer
Box 2678
Richardson, TX 75083
(214) 231-7070

3i Capital Corp.
David R. Shaw, President
99 High St., Suite 1530
Boston, MA 02110
(617) 542-8560

Tulsa Industrial Authority
Rick L. Weddle, General Manager
616 S. Boston
Tulsa, OK 74119
(918) 585-1201
D □ □ □ 1 5 6 8 11

Loan limits: **A** $100,000   **B** $250,000   **C** $500,000   **D** $1 million   **E** Over $1 million

Policy: □ Loans or investments   □ □ Long-term loans   □ □ □ Financing with stock options

Industry: **1** Communications   **2** Construction and development   **3** Natural resources   **4** Hotels and restaurants   **5** Manufacturing and processing   **6** Health services   **7** Recreation   **8** Research and technology   **9** Retail, wholesale, distribution   **10** Service trades   **11** Transportation   **12** Diversified

Venad Management Inc.
Joy London, Partner
375 Park Ave., #3303
New York, NY 10152
(212) 759-2800

Venco SBIC
Bill McAleir, Chairman
One Financial Sq.
Oxnard, CA 93030
(805) 656-4621
B ☐ 5 6 12

The Venture Capital Fund of New England
Richard Farrell, General Partner
100 Franklin St.
Boston, MA 02110
(617) 451-2575
C ☐☐☐ 1 5 8

Venture Economics, Inc.
Stanley Pratt, Chairman
16 Laurel Ave., Box 348
Wellesley Hills, MA 02181
(617) 431-8100

Venture Founders Corp.
Alexander Dingee, Jr., President
One Cranberry Hill
Lexington, MA 02173
(617) 863-0900
D ☐☐☐ 1 5 6 8

Whitehead Associates, Inc.
Joseph A. Orlando, President
15 Valley Dr.
Greenwich, CT 06830
(203) 629-4633
D ☐☐☐ 1 5 6 8 10 12

William Blair Venture Partners
Samuel B. Guren, General Partner
Scott F. Meadow, General Partner
135 S. LaSalle St., 29th Floor
Chicago, IL 60603
(312) 236-1600
E ☐☐☐ 12

Arthur Young and Co.
Robert J. Brennan, Director
1111 Summer St.
Stamford, CT 06905
(203) 356-1800

Arthur Young and Co.
John J. Huntz, Jr., Partner
235 Peachtree St., NE
2100 Gas Light Tower
Atlanta, GA 30343
(404) 581-1130

Arthur Young and Co.
Al Boos, Partner
6501 Americas Parkway, NE, Suite 400
Albuquerque, NM 87110
(505) 881-6363

Arthur Young and Co.
Dennis Serlen, General Partner
277 Park Ave.
New York, NY 10172
(212) 407-1611

Arthur Young and Co.
Paul E. Gricus
1100 Fleet Center
Providence, RI 02903
(401) 274-1800

Arthur Young and Co.
Edward B. Beanland, Partner
2121 San Jacinto, Suite 700
Dallas, TX 75201
(214) 969-8666

Arthur Young Entrepreneurial Services
Jerome S. Engel, Partner
Marc Berger, Partner
1 Sansome St., Suite 3300
San Francisco, CA 94104
(415) 393-2733

PRIVATE VENTURE CAPITAL COMPANIES

A business buildup requires great personal sacrifices by an entrepreneur who is willing to take risk in investment. And venture capitalists share that high risk in assisting entrepreneurs to meet adequate financing.

This listing includes the names of over 250 U.S. venture capital companies plus a few foreign venture capital companies at the end. They are private firms that are not members of NASBIC or affiliated with the Small Business Administration or other government agency. The listings, organized by state, include the name of the company, address, and telephone number, and are alphabetized by city within each state listing. Some listings may not be current, since venture capital companies appear and disappear with surprising frequency.

U.S. Venture Capital Companies

California

Security Pacific Capital Corporation
650 Town Center Dr., 17th floor
Costa Mesa, CA 92626
(714) 556-1964

Fairfield Venture Partners
650 Town Center Dr., Suite 810
Costa Mesa, CA 92626

Grace Ventures Corp.
20300 Stevens Creek Blvd., Suite 330
Cupertino, CA 95014
(408) 725-0774

Brentwood Associates
11661 San Vicente Blvd., Suite 707
Los Angeles, CA 90049
(213) 826-6581

Interscope Investments
10900 Wilshire Blvd., #1400
Los Angeles, CA 90024
(213) 208-8636

First Interstate Capital, Inc.
445 South Figueroa St., Suite 2940
Los Angeles, CA 90071
(213) 622-1922

City Ventures, Inc.
1880 Century Park East, Suite 413
Los Angeles, CA 90067
(213) 550-0416; (213) 858-5314

Union Venture Corporation
445 South Figueroa St.
Los Angeles, CA 90071
(213) 236-6292

SAS Associates
515 South Figueroa St., 6th floor
Los Angeles, CA 90071-3396
(213) 624-4232

Xerox Venture Capital
2029 Century Park East, Suite 740
Los Angeles, CA 90067
(213) 278-7940

U.S. Venture Partners
2180 Sand Hill Rd., Suite 300
Menlo Park, CA 94025
(415) 854-9080

Advanced Technology Ventures
1000 El Camino Real, Suite 210
Menlo Park, CA 94025-4327
(415) 321-8601

Technology Venture Investors
3000 Sand Hill Rd., Bldg. 4, #210
Menlo Park, CA 94025
(415) 854-7472

Churchill International
545 Middlefield Rd., Suite 160
Menlo Park, CA 94025

Bessemer Venture Partners
3000 Sand Hill Rd.
Menlo Park, CA 94025
(415) 854-2200

MenloVentures
3000 Sand Hill Rd.
Menlo Park, CA 94025
(415) 854-8540

Wood River Capital Corp.
3000 Sand Hill Rd.
Menlo Park, CA 94025
(415) 854-1005

Institutional Venture Partners
3000 Sand Hill Rd., Bldg. 2, Suite 290
Menlo Park, CA 94025
(415) 854-0132

Paragon Partners
3000 Sand Hill Rd., Bldg. 2, Suite 190
Menlo Park, CA 94025
(415) 854-8000

General Electric Venture Capital Corp.
3000 Sand Hill Rd., Bldg. 1, Suite 230
Menlo Park, CA 94025
(415) 854-8092

Mayfield Fund
2200 Sand Hill Rd., Suite 200
Menlo Park, CA 94025
(415) 854-5560

Sequoia Capital
3000 Sand Hill Rd., Bldg. 4
Menlo Park, CA 94025
(415) 854-3927

Bryan and Edwards
3000 Sand Hill Rd., Bldg. 2, Suite 215
Menlo Park, CA 94025
(415) 854-1555

Harvest Ventures, Inc.
3000 Sand Hill Rd., Bldg. 1, Suite 205
Menlo Park, CA 94025
(415) 854-8400

Hillman Ventures, Inc.
2200 Sand Hill Rd., Suite 240
Menlo Park, CA 94025

Continental Capital Ventures
3000 Sand Hill Rd., Bldg. 1, Suite 135
Menlo Park, CA 94025
(415) 854-6633

Glenwood Management
3000 Sand Hill Rd., Bldg. 3, Suite 250
Menlo Park, CA 94025
(415) 854-8070

Sierra Ventures Management Co.
3000 Sand Hill Rd., Bldg. 1, Suite 280
Menlo Park, CA 94025
(415) 854-1006

Dougery, Jones and Wilder
2105 Landings Dr.
Mountain View, CA 94043
(415) 968-4820

Bay Partners
1927 Landings Dr., Suite B
Mountain View, CA 94043
(415) 961-5800

Crosspoint Venture Partners
1951 Landings Dr.
Mountain View, CA 94043
(415) 964-3545

Hillman Ventures, Inc.
450 Newport Center Dr., Suite 304
Newport Beach, CA 92660

Investors in Industry
450 Newport Center Dr., Suite 250
Newport Beach, CA 92660
(714) 720-1421

Orange Nassau
1500 Quail St., Suite 540
Newport Beach, CA 92660
(714) 752-7811

Crosspoint Venture Partners
4600 Campus Dr., Suite 103
Newport Beach, CA 92660
(714) 852-1611

Vista Ventures
610 Newport Center Dr., Suite 400
Newport Beach, CA 92660

Schroder Venture Managers
755 Page Mill Rd., Bldg. A, Suite 280
Palo Alto, CA 94304
(415) 424-1144

Hewlett-Packard Co.
Box 10301
Palo Alto, CA 94303-0890
(415) 857-2314

Kleiner Perkins Caufield and Byers
2200 Geng Rd., Suite 205
Palo Alto, CA 94303
(415) 424-1660

TA Associates
435 Tasso St.
Palo Alto, CA 94301
(415) 328-1210

Asset Management Co.
1417 Edgewood Dr.
Palo Alto, CA 94301
(415) 321-3131

Arscott, Norton and Associates
375 Forest Ave.
Palo Alto, CA 94301
(415) 853-0766

Merrill, Pickard, Anderson and Eyre
Two Palo Alto Sq., Suite 425
Palo Alto, CA 94306
(415) 856-8880

Sutter Hill Ventures
Two Palo Alto Square, Suite 700
Palo Alto, CA 94306-0910
(415) 493-5600

Venrock Associates
Two Palo Alto Sq., Suite 520
Palo Alto, CA 94306
(415) 493-5577

Security Pacific Capital Corp.
155 North Lake Ave.
Pasadena, CA 91109

Continental Capital Ventures
555 California St., Suite 5070
San Francisco, CA 94104

Brentwood Associates
601 California St., Suite 450
San Francisco, CA 94108
(415) 788-2416

New Enterprise Associates, L.P.
235 Montgomery St., Suite 1025
San Francisco, CA 94104
(415) 956-1579

Burr, Egan, Deleage and Co., Inc.
Three Embarcadero Ctr., 25th floor
San Francisco, CA 94111
(415) 362-4022

Montgomery Medical Ventures Fund, L.P.
600 Montgomery St.
San Francisco, CA 94111
(415) 627-2000

BankAmerica Capital Corporation
555 California St.
San Francisco, CA 94104
(415) 622-2230

Kleiner Perkins Caufield & Byers
Four Embarcadero Ctr., Suite 3520
San Francisco, CA 94111
(415) 421-3110

Robertson, Colman and Stephens
One Embarcadero Ctr., Suite 3100
San Francisco, CA 94111
(415) 781-9700

Bryan & Edwards
600 Montgomery St., 35th floor
San Francisco, CA 94111
(415) 421-9990

Hambrecht and Quist Venture Partners
235 Montgomery St.
San Francisco, CA 94104
(415) 576-3333

Davis Skaggs Capital
160 Sansome St.
San Francisco, CA 94104
(415) 392-7700

Taylor and Turner
220 Montgomery St., Penthouse 10
San Francisco, CA 94104
(415) 398-6821

Weiss, Peck and Greer Venture Partners, L.P.
555 California St., Suite 4760
San Francisco, CA 94104
(415) 622-6864

Montgomery Securities
600 Montgomery St.
San Francisco, CA 94111
(415) 627-2000

Concord Partners
600 Montgomery St.
San Francisco, CA 94111
(415) 362-2400

Churchill International
444 Market St., 25th floor
San Francisco, CA 94111
(415) 398-7677

Accel Partners
One Embarcadero Ctr., Suite 2102
San Francisco, CA 94111
(415) 989-5656

Sprout Group
5300 Stevens Creek Blvd.
San Jose, CA 95129
(408) 554-1515

Matrix Partners, L.P.
224 West Brokaw Rd.
San Jose, CA 95110
(408) 298-0270

Oak Management Corp.
2055 Gateway Pl., Suite 550
San Jose, CA 95110
(408) 286-5233

InterWest Partners
2620 Augustine Dr., Suite 201
Santa Clara, CA 95054

Oxford Partners
233 Wilshire Blvd., Suite 730
Santa Monica, CA 90401

Adler & Company
1245 Oakmead Pkwy., Suite 130
Sunnyvale, CA 94086
(408) 720-8700

Alan Patricof Associates, Inc.
1245 Oakmead Pkwy., Suite 105
Sunnyvale, CA 94086-4041
(408) 737-8788

Colorado

Hill, Keeley and Kirby
885 Arapahoe Ave.
Boulder, CO 80302
(303) 442-5151

Stephenson Merchant Banking
899 Logan St.
Denver, CO 80203
(303) 837-1700

The Centennial Funds/Larimer and Co.
1999 Broadway, Suite 2100
Denver, CO 80202
(303) 298-9066

Columbine Venture Fund, Ltd.
5613 DTC Pkwy., Suite 510
Englewood, CO 80111
(303) 694-3222

Connecticut

General Electric Venture Capital Corp.
3135 Easton Tpke.
Fairfield, CT 06431
(203) 373-3333

MIP Equity Fund
47 Lafayette Place
Greenwich, CT 06830

Whitehead Associates
15 Valley Dr.
Greenwich, CT 06830
(203) 629-4633

Bridge Capital Advisors, Inc.
185 Asylum St., Cityplace
Hartford, CT 06103
(203) 275-6700

Grayrock Capital Inc.
36 Grove Street
New Canaan, CT 06840
(203) 966-8392

Anderson Investment Co.
39 Locust Ave., Box 426
New Canaan, CT 06840
(203) 966-5684

Regional Financial Enterprises
51 Pine St.
New Canaan, CT 06840
(203) 966-2800

Vista Ventures
36 Grove St.
New Canaan, CT 06840

DCS Growth Fund
Box 740
Old Greenwich, CT 06870
(203) 637-1704

Xerox Venture Capital
Box 1600
Stamford, CT 06904
(203) 329-8700

Saugatuck Capital Co.
999 Summer St.
Stamford, CT 06905
(203) 348-6669

Oxford Partners
1266 Main St.
Stamford, CT 06902
(203) 964-0592

Fairfield Venture Partners
1275 Summer St.
Stamford, CT 06905
(203) 358-0255

Prime Capital Management Co., Inc.
One Landmark Sq., Suite 800
Stamford, CT 06901
(203) 964-0642

Oak Management Corp.
257 Riverside Ave.
Westport, CT 06880
(203) 226-8346

General Electric Venture Capital Corp.
33 Riverside Ave.
Westport, CT 06880
(203) 373-3238

Florida

North American Company Ltd.
111 East Las Olas Blvd.
Fort Lauderdale, FL 33301
(305) 463-0681

North American Company Ltd.
Box 14758
Fort Lauderdale, FL 33302

Electro-Science Management Corp.
600 Courtland St., Suite 490
Orlando, FL 32804
(305) 645-1188

South Atlantic Capital Corp.
220 East Madison St., Suite 530
Tampa, FL 33602
(913) 229-7400

Iowa

R. W. Allsop and Associates
2750 First Ave., NE, Suite 210
Cedar Rapids, IA 52402
(319) 363-3719; (913) 451-3719 KS; (314)
434-1688 MO; (414) 271-6510 WI

Illinois

Prince Venture Partners
One First National Plaza, Suite 4950
Chicago, IL 60603
(312) 726-2232

Golder, Thoma and Cressey
120 South LaSalle St., Suite 630
Chicago, IL 60603
(312) 853-3322

Continental Illinois Venture Corporation
231 South LaSalle St.
Chicago, IL 60697
(312) 828-8021

First Chicago Investment Advisors
Three First National Plaza, Suite 0140
Chicago, IL 60670
(312) 732-4154

William Blair Venture Partners
135 South LaSalle St.
Chicago, IL 60603
(312) 853-8250

First Chicago Venture Capital
One First National Plaza, Suite 2628
Chicago, IL 60670
(312) 732-5400

Seidman Jackson Fisher & Co.
233 North Michigan Ave., Suite 1812
Chicago, IL 60601
(312) 856-1812

Ameritech Development Corporation
233 S. Wacker Dr., Suite 6960
Chicago, IL 60606
(312) 993-1900

Northern Capital Corporation
50 South LaSalle St.
Chicago, IL 60675
(312) 444-5399

Frontenac Venture Company
208 South LaSalle St., Suite 1900
Chicago, IL 60604
(312) 368-0044

Allstate Insurance Company
Allstate Plaza, Venture Capital E-2
Northbrook, IL 60062
(312) 291-5681

Vanguard Capital Corporation
5 Revere Dr., Suite 200
Northbrook, IL 60062
(312) 272-3636

Caterpillar Venture Capital, Inc.
100 NE Adams St.
Peoria, IL 61629-6170
(309) 675-5503

Maryland

T. Rowe Price Threshold Fund, L.P.
100 East Pratt St.
Baltimore, MD 21202
(301) 547-2179

ABS Ventures Limited Partnerships
135 E. Baltimore St.
Baltimore, MD 21202
(301) 727-1700; (301) 727-2154 (night line)

Broventure Capital Management
16 West Madison St.
Baltimore, MD 21201
(301) 727-4520

New Enterprise Associates, L.P.
1119 St. Paul St.
Baltimore, MD 21202
(301) 424-0115

Greater Washington Investors, Inc.
5454 Wisconsin Ave.
Chevy Chase, MD 20815
(301) 656-0626

Massachusetts

Elron Technologies, Inc.
12 Oak Park Dr.
Bedford, MA 01730
(617) 275-8990

VIMAC Corp.
12 Arlington St.
Boston, MA 02116
(617) 267-2785

Matrix Partners, L.P.
One Post Office Sq.
Boston, MA 02109
(617) 482-7735

Burr, Egan, Deleage & Co., Inc.
One Post Office Sq., Suite 3800
Boston, MA 02109
(617) 482-8020

General Electric Venture Capital Corp.
53 State St., Exchange Place
Boston, MA 02109
(617) 227-7922

Fleet Venture Partners
60 State St.
Boston, MA 02109
(617) 367-6700

Fidelity Venture Associates, Inc.
82 Devonshire St.
Boston, MA 02109
(617) 570-6450

Orange Nassau
One Post Office Sq., Suite 1760
Boston, MA 02109
(617) 451-6220

Commonwealth Partners
881 Commonwealth Ave., Suite 540
Boston, MA 02215
(617) 353-4550

New England Capital Corp.
One Washington Mall, 7th floor
Boston, MA 02108
(617) 772-6400

Morgan, Holland Ventures Corp.
One Liberty Sq.
Boston, MA 02109
(617) 423-1765

John Hancock Venture Capital
    Management, Inc.
John Hancock Pl., Box 111
Boston, MA 02117

Eastech Management Company, Inc.
One Liberty Sq., 9th floor
Boston, MA 02109
(617) 338-0200

Ampersand Management Co.
265 Franklin St., Suite 1501
Boston, MA 02110

TA Associates
45 Milk St.
Boston, MA 02109
(617) 338-0800

American Research and Development
45 Milk St.
Boston, MA 02109
(617) 423-7500

Venture Capital Fund of New England
100 Frank St.
Boston, MA 02110
(617) 451-2575

PaineWebber Venture Management Co.
265 Franklin St., Suite 1501
Boston, MA 02110
(617) 439-8300

Investors in Industry
99 High St.
Boston, MA 02110
(617) 542-8560

Faneuil Hall Associates
1 Boston Pl.
Boston, MA 02108
(617) 723-1955

The Charles River Partnerships
133 Federal St.
Boston, MA 02110
(617) 482-9370

Boston Capital Ventures
One Devonshire Pl., Suite 2913
Boston, MA 02109
(617) 227-6550

BancBoston Ventures
100 Federal St.
Boston, MA 02110
(617) 434-2442

Advanced Technology Ventures
Ten Post Office Square, Suite 1230
Boston, MA 02109
(617) 423-4050

Torchmark Venture Capital
Federal Reserve Plaza
Boston, MA 02210
(617) 722-6030

Greylock Management Corporation
One Federal St.
Boston, MA 02110
(617) 423-5525

Sprout Group
One Center Plaza
Boston, MA 02108
(617) 570-8720

John Hancock Venture Capital Management,
   Inc.
200 Clarendon St.
Boston, MA 02117
(617) 421-6231

First Chicago Venture Capital
133 Federal St., 6th floor
Boston, MA 02110
(617) 542-9185

Security Pacific Capital Corp.
50 Milk St., 15th floor
Boston, MA 02109
(617) 542-7601

Weiss, Peck and Greer Venture Partners
45 Milk St.
Boston, MA 02109
(617) 423-7500

Hambro International Venture Fund
Boston Place, Suite 923
Boston, MA 02108
(617) 722-7055

Memorial Drive Trust
20 Acorn Park
Cambridge, MA 02140
(617) 864-5770

Venture Founders Corporation
100 Fifth Ave.
Waltham, MA 02154
(617) 890-1000

Bessemer Venture Partners
83 Walnut St.
Wellesley Hills, MA 02181
(617) 237-6050

Churchill International
59 Riverside Rd.
Weston, MA 02193
(617) 893-6555

Palmer Organization
300 Unicorn Park Dr.
Woburn, MA 01801
(617) 933-5445

Michigan

Michigan Capital and Service, Inc.
500 First National Bldg., 201 S. Main
Ann Arbor, MI 48104
(313) 663-0702

Regional Financial Enterprises
315 East Eisenhower Pkwy., Suite 300
Ann Arbor, MI 48104
(313) 769-0941

Doan Associates
333 East Main St., Box 1431
Midland, MI 48640
(517) 631-2471

Minnesota

Cherry Tree Ventures
640 Northland Executive Center, 3600 W.
  80th St.
Minneapolis, MN 55431
(612) 893-9012

North Star Ventures, Inc.
100 South Fifth St., Suite 2200
Minneapolis, MN 55402
(612) 333-1133

Norwest Venture Capital Management
2800 Piper Jaffray Tower, 222 S. 9th St.
Minneapolis, MN 55402
(612) 372-8770

Piper Jaffray and Hopwood Incorporated
222 South Ninth St., Box 28
Minneapolis, MN 55440
(612) 342-6314

Pathfinder Venture Capital Funds
7300 Metro Blvd., Suite 585
Minneapolis, MN 55435
(612) 835-1121

Nevada

United Venture Capital, Inc.
Box 109, 2001 Foothill Rd.
Genoa, NV 89411
(702) 782-5114; (702) 883-6395

New Hampshire

Harvard Venture Capital
Box 746, 27 Loop Rd.
Merrimack, NH 03054
(603) 429-0858

New Jersey

DSV Partners
221 Nassau St.
Princeton, NJ 08542
(609) 924-6420

Johnston Associates, Inc.
179 Cherry Valley Rd.
Princeton, NJ 08540
(609) 924-3131

Accel Partners
One Palmer Square
Princeton, NJ 08542
(609) 683-4500

InnoVen Group
Park 80 Plaza West-One
Saddle Brook, NJ 07662
(201) 845-4900

New Mexico

MRI Ventures
1650 University Blvd., NE
Albuquerque, NM 87107
(505) 243-7600

Santa Fe Private Equity Fund
524 Camino Del Monte Sol
Santa Fe, NM 87501
(505) 983-1769

New York

Norstar Venture Capital Corp.
1450 Western Ave.
Albany, NY 12203
(518) 447-4050

Key Venture Capital Corp.
60 State St.
Albany, NY 12207
(518) 447-3181

AMEV Capital Corp.
One World Trade Center, 50th floor
New York, NY 10048-0024
(212) 775-9100

Welsh, Carson, Anderson and Stowe
45 Wall St.
New York, NY 10005
(212) 422-3232

Foster Management Co.
437 Madison Ave.
New York, NY 10022
(212) 753-4810

Warburg, Pincus Ventures, Inc.
466 Lexington Ave., 10th floor
New York, NY 10017
(212) 878-0600

Adler and Shaykin
375 Park Ave.
New York, NY 10152
(212) 319-2800

Elron Technologies, Inc.
1211 Avenue of the Americas
New York, NY 10036
(212) 819-1644

Drexel Burnham Lambert, Inc.
55 Broad St.
New York, NY 10004
(212) 480-6018

Sevin Rosen Management Co.
200 Park Ave.
New York, NY 10166
(212) 687-5115

J. H. Whitney and Co.
630 Fifth Ave., Room 3200
New York, NY 10111
(212) 757-0500

Sprout Group
140 Broadway
New York, NY 10005
(212) 504-3600

Euclid Partner Corp.
50 Rockefeller Plaza
New York, NY 10020
(212) 489-1770

Pioneer Ventures
113 E. 55th St.
New York, NY 10022
(212) 980-9090

Adler and Co.
375 Park Ave., Suite 3303
New York, NY 10152
(212) 759-2800

First Boston Corp.
12 East 49th St.
New York, NY 10017
(212) 909-4585

International Technology Ventures, Inc.
535 Madison Ave., 19th floor
New York, NY 10022
(212) 371-5895

Rothschild Venture Inc.
One Rockefeller Plaza
New York, NY 10020
(212) 757-6000

Sierra Ventures Management Co.
45 Madison Ave.
New York, NY 10022
(212) 758-8500

Bridge Capital Advisors, Inc.
50 Broadway
New York, NY 10004
(212) 514-6700

Northwood Ventures
420 Madison Ave.
New York, NY 10017
(212) 935-4679

Bessemer Venture Partners
630 Fifth Ave.
New York, NY 10111
(212) 708-9300

Instoria, Inc./Providentia, Ltd.
140 East 45th St., 34th floor
New York, NY 10017
(212) 687-7525

Hutton Venture Investment Partners, Inc.
1 Battery Park, Suite 1801
New York, NY 10004
(212) 742-6486

Venrock Associates
30 Rockefeller Plaza, Suite 5508
New York, NY 10112
(212) 247-3700

Prince Venture Partners
767 Third Ave.
New York, NY 10017
(212) 319-6620

Hambro International Venture Fund
17 East 71st St.
New York, NY 10021
(212) 288-7781

N.A.B. Nordic Investors, Ltd.
600 Fifth Ave.
New York, NY 10020
(212) 315-6532

Schroder Venture Managers
One State St.
New York, NY 10004
(212) 269-6500

ML Venture Partners, I
717 Fifth Ave.
New York, NY 10022
(212) 980-0410

Rain Hill Group, Inc.
90 Broad St.
New York, NY 10004
(212) 483-9162

Prudential Venture Capital Management, Inc.
717 Fifth Ave., Suite 1600
New York, NY 10022
(212) 753-0901

Quantum Venture Partners
650 Fifth Ave.
New York, NY 10017
(212) 975-1285

Harvest Ventures, Inc.
767 Third Ave.
New York, NY 10017
(212) 838-7776

Bernhard Associates/Hycliff Partners
1211 Avenue of the Americas
New York, NY 10036
(212) 921-7755

Chemical Venture Capital Corp.
277 Park Ave.
New York, NY 10172
(212) 310-4949

CW Group, Inc.
1041 Third Ave.
New York, NY 10021
(212) 308-5266

Alan Patricof Associates, Inc.
545 Madison Ave.
New York, NY 10022
(212) 753-6300

CM Capital Corporation
77 Water St.
New York, NY 10005
(212) 437-7080

Concord Partners
535 Madison Ave.
New York, NY 10022
(212) 906-7000

DeMuth, Folger and Terhune
One Exchange Plaza at 55 Broadway
New York, NY 10006
(212) 509-5580

Wood River Capital Corporation
645 Madison Ave., 11th floor
New York, NY 10022
(212) 750-9420

Horsley Keogh and Associates, Inc.
11 Tobey Office Park
Pittsford, NY 14534
(716) 385-9830

North Carolina

Venture First Associates
2422 Reynolda Rd.
Winston-Salem, NC 27106
(919) 722-9600

Ohio

Morgenthaler Ventures
700 National City Bank Building
Cleveland, OH 44114
(216) 621-3070

Primus Capital Fund
1375 East Ninth St., Suite 2140
Cleveland, OH 44114
(216) 621-2185

Scientific Advances, Inc.
601 West Fifth Ave.
Columbus, OH 43201-3195
(614) 294-5541

Cardinal Development Capital Fund I
40 South Third St., Suite 460
Columbus, OH 43215
(614) 464-5557

Lubrizol Enterprises, Inc.
29400 Lakeland Blvd.
Wickliffe, OH 44092
(216) 943-4200

Oregon

Cable, Howse, and Cozadd, Inc.
1800 One Main Pl., 101 SW Main
Portland, OR 97204

First Interstate Capital, Inc.
227 SW Pine St., Suite 200
Portland, OR 97204
(503) 223-4334

Norwest Venture Capital Management
1300 SW Fifth Ave., Suite 3018
Portland, OR 97201
(503) 223-6622

Pennsylvania

Butcher and Singer/Keystone Venture I
211 South Broad St.
Philadelphia, PA 19107
(215) 985-5519

Century IV Partners
1760 Market St.
Philadelphia, PA 19103
(215) 751-9444

Adler and Shaykin
1631 Locust St.
Philadelphia, PA 19103

Robinson Venture Partners
6507 Wilkins Ave.
Pittsburgh, PA 15217
(412) 661-1200

PNC Venture Corp.
Fifth Avenue & Wood St., 19th floor
Pittsburgh, PA 15222
(412) 355-2245

Taylor and Turner
% VenWest Inc., Gateway Center
Pittsburgh, PA 15222
(412) 642-5858

Fostin Capital Corp.
681 Andersen Dr.
Pittsburgh, PA 15220

Hillman Ventures, Inc.
2000 Grant Bldg.
Pittsburgh, PA 15219
(412) 281-2620

Fostin Capital Corp.
Box 67
Pittsburgh, PA 15230
(412) 928-8900

Security Pacific Capital Corp.
Box 512
Washington, PA 15301
(412) 223-0707

Rhode Island

Fleet Venture Partners
111 Westminster St.
Providence, RI 02903
(401) 278-6770

Narragansett Capital Corp.
40 Westminster St.
Providence, RI 02903
(401) 751-1000

Texas

New Business Resources II
4137 Billy Mitchell
Addison, TX 75001
(214) 233-6631; (512) 327-6095 (Austin)

Rust Ventures, L.P.
114 West 7th St.
Austin, TX 78701
(512) 479-0055

Lone Star Capital, Ltd.
3305 Graybuck Rd.
Austin, TX 78748
(512) 282-3882

Sunwestern Management, Inc.
6750 LBJ Freeway, One Oaks Plaza, Suite
    1160
Dallas, TX 75240
(214) 239-5650

InterWest Partners
13355 Noel Rd., Suite 1375/LB 65
Dallas, TX 75240
(214) 392-7279

Southwest Venture Partnerships
5080 Spectrum Dr., Suite 610 East
Dallas, TX 75248
(214) 960-0404

Capital Southwest Corp.
12900 Preston Rd., Suite 700
Dallas, TX 75230
(214) 233-8242

Citicorp Venture Capital, Ltd.
717 North Harwood, Suite 2920,
    Lock Box 87
Dallas, TX 75201
(214) 880-9670

Republic Venture Group, Inc.
Box 225961
Dallas, TX 75265
(214) 922-5078

MSI Capital Corp.
6510 Abrams Rd., Suite 650
Dallas, TX 75231
(214) 341-1553

Sevin Rosen Management Co.
5050 Quorum Dr., Suite 635
Dallas, TX 75240
(214) 960-1744

First Dallas Group, Ltd.
5950 Berkshire Lane, Suite 700
Dallas, TX 75225
(214) 891-3166

Dougery, Jones and Wilder
Two Lincoln Ctr., Suite 1100
Dallas, TX 75240
(214) 960-0077

Orange Nassau
3355 Noel Rd., Suite 635
Dallas, TX 75240
(214) 385-9685

Idanta Partners
201 Main St., Suite 3200
Fort Worth, TX 76102
(817) 496-9649

Tenneco Ventures Inc.
Box 2511, Suite T2919
Houston, TX 77001
(713) 757-8776

Criterion Venture Partners
333 Clay, Suite 4300
Houston, TX 77002
(713) 751-2400

Lone Star Capital, Ltd.
2401 Fountainview, Suite 950
Houston, TX 77057
(713) 977-7421

Curtin and Co., Inc.
2050 Houston Natural Gas Building
Houston, TX 77002
(713) 658-9806

The Sterling Group, Inc.
Eight Greenway Plaza, Suite 702
Houston, TX 77046
(713) 877-8257

Taylor and Turner
3800 Republic Bank Center
Houston, TX 77253
(713) 236-3180

Southwest Venture Partnerships
300 Convent Street, Suite 1400
San Antonio, TX 78205
(512) 227-1010

Virginia

Atlantic Venture Company, Inc.
801 North Fairfax Street
Alexandria, VA 22314
(703) 548-6026

Atlantic Venture Company, Inc.
815 Seventh and Franklin Bldg., Box 1493
Richmond, VA 23212
(804) 644-5496

Washington

Cable, Howse, and Cozadd, Inc.
999 Third Ave., Suite 4300
Seattle, WA 98104
(206) 583-2700

Piper Jaffray and Hopwood Incorporated
1700 IBM Tower
Seattle, WA 98101

Wisconsin

Lubar and Co. Incorporated
777 East Wisconsin Avenue
Milwaukee, WI 53202
(414) 291-9000

Foreign Venture Capital Companies

Belgium

BeneVenture Founders Management N.V.
Excelsiorlaan 21, Bus 4
1930 Saventem, Brussels
Belgium

Canada

Grayrock Capital Inc.
International Blvd.
Rexdale, Ontario M9W-1A2
Canada
(416) 675-4808

England

Venture Founders Ltd.
39 The Green, South Bar St.
Banbury, Oxon OX169AE
England
011-44-295-65881

Alan Patricof Associates, Ltd.
24 Upper Brook St.
London, WIY 1PD
England
493-3633

France

Alan Patricof Associes, S.A.R.L.
67 rue de Monceau
Paris 75008
France
563-3513

Scotland

Venture Founders Ltd.
Old Bank House, 42 Hardgate
Haddington, E. Loghian EH41 3JS
Scotland
011-44-62-082-4561

Netherlands

MIP Equity Fund
Bezuidenhoutseweg 27
P.O. Box 11592, 2502 An, The Hague
The Netherlands
70-814891

Indexes and List of Publishers

List of Publishers	301
Author Index	322
Title Index	329
Subject Index	339

LIST OF PUBLISHERS

ABA Professional Education Publishers
1155 East 60th St.
Chicago, IL 60637

Ablex Publishing Corporation
355 Chestnut St.
Norwood, NJ 07648
(201) 767-8450

Addison-Wesley Publishing Company
Jacob Way
Reading, MA 01867
(617) 944-3700

Allen & Unwin, Inc.
8 Winchester Place
Winchester, MA 01890

Allyn & Bacon, Inc.
7 Wells Ave.
Newton, MA 02159
(617) 964-5530

AMACOM
135 West 50th St.
New York, NY 10029

American Bankers Association
1120 Connecticut Ave., NW
Washington, DC 20036
(202) 467-4173

American Chemical Society
1155 16th St., NW
Washington, DC 20036
(202) 872-4600; (800) 424-6747

American Classical College Press
Box 4526
Albuquerque, NM 87106

American Enterprise Institute for Public Policy
Research
1150 17th St., NW
Washington, DC 20036
(202) 862-5800

American Entrepreneurs Association
Research Department
2311 Pontius Ave.
Los Angeles, CA 90064

American Institute of Certified Public
Accountants
1211 Avenue of the Americas
New York, NY 10046
(800) AICPANY; (212) 575-5696 in NY

American Management Association
135 West 50th St.
New York, NY 10020
(212) 586-8100

American Marketing Association
250 South Wacker Dr.
Chicago, IL 60606

American Philosophical Society
104 South Fifth St.
Philadelphia, PA 19106
(215) 627-0706

301

American Society for Training and
  Development
1630 Duke St., Box 1443
Alexandria, VA 22313
(703) 683-8107

Appleton-Century Crofts
1716 Locust
Des Moines, IA 50336

Arco Publishing Company, Inc.
219 Park Avenue South
New York, NY 10003
(212) 777-6300

Argus Communications
1 DLM Park
Allen, TX 75002

D. Armstrong Company, Inc.
2000-B Governor's Circle
Houston, TX 77092

Arno Press
3 Park Ave.
New York, NY 10016

Aronson, Charles N.
Rt. 1, 11520 Bixby Hill Rd.
Arcade, NY 14009
(716) 496-6002

Artech House, Inc.
685 Canton St.
Norwood, MA 02062
(800) 525-9977; (617) 326-8220 in MA

Ashish Publishing House
8/81 Punjabi Bagh
New Delhi 110026, India

Ashton Scholastic
PO Box 579, Gosford
NSW 2250, Australia

Ashton-Tate Books
10150 West Jefferson Blvd.
Culver City, CA 90230
(213) 204-5570

Atheneum
122 East 42nd St.
New York, NY 10017

Austin Press
Box 9774
Austin, TX 78766

Australiana Publishing
6511 Riviera Dr.
Coral Gables, FL 33146

Ballantine Books
400 Hahn Rd.
Westminster, MD 21157
(800) 638-6460

Ballinger Publishing Company
17 Dunster St., Harvard Square
Cambridge, MA 02138
(617) 492-0670

Bantam Books, Inc.
414 East Golf Rd.
Des Plaines, IL 60016

Barnes & Noble Books
10 East 53rd St.
New York, NY 10022
(212) 593-7141

Baron Publishing Co., Inc.
P.O. Box C-230
Scottsdale, AZ 85252

Basic Books Inc.
10 East 53rd St.
New York, NY 10022
(212) 207-7000

Beaufort Book Company
PO Box 1127
Beaufort, SC 29902

Beekman Publishers, Inc.
38 Hicks St.
Brooklyn Heights, NY 11201

Bell Springs Publishing Company
Box 640
Laytonville, CA 95454
(707) 984-6746

Matthew Bender
235 East 45th St.
New York, NY 10017
(212) 661-5050

Beresford Book Service
1525 East 53rd St., Suite 431
Chicago, IL 60615

Bermont Books
815-15th St., NW
Washington, DC 20005

Bihar Development Commissioner
Institute of Developing Economies
Small Scale Industries
Ministry of Development
India

Adams and Charles Black, Ltd.
35 Bedford Row
London WC1R 4JH, England

Blackwell Scientific Publishers Ltd.
Osney Mead
Oxford 0X2 0EL, England
52 Beacon St.
Boston, MA 02108
(617) 720-0761

Clark Boardman Company, Ltd.
435 Hudson St.
New York, NY 10014
(212) 929-7500

Bobbs-Merrill Company, Inc.
4300 West 62nd St.
PO Box 7083
Indianapolis, IN 46206
(317) 298-5400

Bolivar House
Stanford University
Stanford, CA 94305

Bookman House
Box 27108
Houston, TX 77277

Books in Focus
160 East 38th St.
New York, NY 10016

Boston Public Library
666 Boylston Street
Boston, MA 02117

Botany Books
1518 Hayward Ave.
Bremerton, WA 98310

Boyd & Fraser Publishing Co.
286 Congress St.
Boston, MA 02210

Brigham Young University Press
218 University Press Bldg.
Provo, UT 84602
(801) 374-1221

Brookings Institute
1775 Massachusetts Ave., NW
Washington, DC 20036
(202) 797-6254

Wm. C. Brown Company Publishers
2460 Kerper Blvd., Box 539
Dubuque, IA 52001
(319) 588-1451

L. Buchanan
2140 North Iris Lane
Escondido, CA 92026

Bureau of Business Research
University of Dacca
Bangladesh

Business Books Limited
2500 Hollywood Blvd., #302
Hollywood, FL 33020
(305) 925-5242

Business Publications Inc.
c/o Richard D. Irwin
1818 Ridge Rd.
Homewood, IL 60430

Business Research Services, Inc.
2 East 22nd St.
Suite 308
Lombard, IL 60148

Butterworth & Company
80 Montvale Ave.
Stoneham, MA 02180
(617) 438-8464

Calabasas Publishing Company
P.O. Box 9002
Calabasas, CA 91302-9002

Cambridge Corporation
Box K
Ipswich, MA 01938
(617) 356-0072

Cambridge University Press
32 East 57th St.
New York, NY 10022

Capital Publications
1300 North 17th St.
Arlington, VA 22209
(703) 528-1100

Capital Publishing Corp.
16 Laurel Ave.
Wellesley Hills, MA 02181

Carlton Press
11 West 32nd St.
New York, NY 10011
(212) 714-0300

Cassell, Ltd.
1 Vincent Square
London SW1P 2PN, England

CBI Publishing Company, Inc.
51 Sleeper St.
Boston, MA 02210
(617) 426-2224

CBS Educational and Professional Publishing
383 Madison Ave.
New York, NY 10017
(212) 750-1330

Center for Southeast Asian Studies
Kyoto University

Center for Entrepreneurial Management, Inc.
311 Main St.
Worcester, MA 01608
(617) 755-0770

Center for Venture Management
811 East Wisconsin Ave.
Milwaukee, WI 53202

Chandler & Sharp Publishers
11A Commercial Blvd.
Novato, CA 94947
(415) 883-2353

Cherokee Publishing Company
P.O. Box 1623
Marietta, GA 30061

Chicago Review Press
814 North Franklin
Chicago, IL 60610
(312) 337-0747

Chilton Book Company
201 King of Prussia Road
Radnor, PA 19089
(215) 964-4000

Phillip B. Chute Corp.
3585 Main St.
Riverside, CA 92501

Citizens Law Library, Inc.
Box 1745
7 South Wirt St.
Leesburg, VA 22075

Coalition of Northeastern Governors
400 North Capital Street, NW
Washington, DC 20001

Collier Macmillan, Ltd.
Stockley Close, Stockley Rd.
West Drayton, Middlesex UB7 9BE, England

Robert Collier Publishers, Inc.
P.O. Box 3684
Indialantic, FL 32903

Columbia Books, Inc.
1350 New York Avenue, NW
Suite 207
Washington, DC 20005
(202) 737-3777

Columbia University Press
562 West 113th St.
New York, NY 10025
(212) 516-7100

Commerce Clearing House, Inc.
4025 West Peterson Ave.
Chicago, IL 60646
(312) 583-8500

Comptere Group, Inc.
New York, NY

Computer BookBase
P.O. Box 1217
Cerritos, CA 90701

Concept Publishing
P.O. Box 500
New York, NY 14592

Concept Publishing Company
H-13 Bali Nagar
New Delhi 110015, India

Conference Board Inc.
845 Third Ave.
New York, NY 10022
(212) 759-0900

Consultant's Library
Box 309
Gunelg, MD 21737
(301) 531-3560

Consultants News
Templeton Rd.
Fitzwilliam, NH 03447

Contemporary Books, Inc.
180 North Michigan Ave.
Chicago, IL 60601
(312) 782-9181

Cordovan Press
5314 Bingle Rd.
Houston, TX 77092

Cornell University Press
124 Roberts Place
Ithaca, NY 14850
(607) 273-5155

Cornerstone Press
Box 28048
St. Louis, MO 63119
(314) 296-9662

Corporation for Enterprise Development
1725 K St., NW
Suite 1401
Washington, DC 20006
(202) 293-7963

Council of State Planning Agencies
400 North Capitol St.
Suite 291
Washington, DC 20001
(202) 624-5386

Council on East Asian Studies
Harvard University
Cambridge, MA 02138

Council on International and Public Affairs
60 East 42nd St.
New York, NY 10017

Crain Books
740 Rush St.
Chicago, IL 60611
(312) 649-5250

Creative Ventures, International
3341 Hidden Acres Dr.
Atlanta, GA 30340

Croom Helm Ltd.
Provident House, Burrell Row
Beckenham, Kent BR3 1AT, England

Thomas Y. Crowell Company
10 East 53rd St.
New York, NY 10022

Dataquest, Inc.
1290 Ridder Park Dr.
San Jose, CA 95131

Delmar Publishers Inc.
2 Computer Dr. West
Box 15015
Albany, NY 12212
(800) 833-3350; (800) 252-2550 in NY

Devin-Adair, Publishers/The Chatham Press
143 Sound Beach Ave.
Box A
Old Greenwich, CT 06870
(203) 637-4531

Direct Cinema Ltd.
Box 69589
Los Angeles, CA 90069
(213) 656-4700

Dodd, Mead & Company
79 Madison Ave.
New York, NY 10016
(212) 685-6464

Dolphin Books
501 Franklin Ave.
Garden City, NY 11530
(516) 873-4561

Adriaan Donker, Ltd.
Delta House, 111 Central St.
Houghton, Johannesburg, South Africa;

W. E. Donoghue & Company
Medway, MA

Doubleday & Company, Inc.
501 Franklin Ave.
Garden City, NY 11530
(516) 873-4561

Dow Jones—Irwin
1818 Ridge Rd.
Homewood, IL 60430
(312) 798-6000

Drake's Printing & Publishing
225 North Magnolia Ave.
Orlando, FL 32801

Duke University Press
6697 College Station
Durham, NC 27708
(919) 684-2173

E. P. Dutton & Co., Inc.
2 Park Avenue, 17th floor
New York, NY 10016
(212) 725-1818; (201) 387-0600

Eakin Publishing
P.O. Box 23066
Austin, TX 78735

Economic Institute
1030 13th St.
Boulder, CO 80302

Elcomp Publishing, Inc.
53 Redrock Lane
Pomona, CA 91766

Elsevere Science Publishing Company
52 Vanderbilt Ave.
New York, NY 10017
(212) 370-5520

EMC Corporation
180 East Sixth St.
St. Paul, MN 55101

Enterprise Publishing Company
725 Market St.
Wilmington, DE 19801
(302) 575-0440

Entrepreneur Press
1125 Missouri St.
Suite 109
Fairfield, CA 94533

Entrepreneurs' Library, Inc.
P.O. Box 8567
Newport Beach, CA 92658-8567
(714) 646-9400

Etc. Publications
700 East Vereda del Sur
Palm Springs, CA 92262
(619) 325-5352

Evans & Company, Inc.
216 East 49th St.
New York, NY 10017
(212) 688-2810

Exposition Press, Inc.
900 South Oyster Bay Rd.
Hicksville, NY 11801

Fairchild Books & Visuals
7 East 12th St.
New York, NY 10003
(212) 741-4280

Fairleigh Dickinson University Press
Box 421
Cranbury, NJ 08512

Farnsworth Publishing Company, Inc.
78 Randall Ave., Box 710
Rockville, NY 11570
(516) 536-8400

Federal Reserve Bank of Boston
Urban Finance Dept.
600 Atlantic Ave.
Boston, MA 02106

Frederick Fell, Inc.
386 Park Ave. South
New York, NY 10016

Folium Press, Ltd.
18 Regent Parade
Birmingham 1, England

Ford Foundation
320 East 43rd St.
New York, NY 10017
(212) 573-5000

Forecaster Publishing Company, Inc.
19623 Ventura Blvd.
Tarzana, CA 91356

Franchise Group Publishers
3644 East McDowell
Suite 214
Phoenix, AZ 85008
(602) 267-9409

Free Press
866 Third Ave.
New York, NY 10022

Gale Research Company
Book Tower
Detroit, MI 48226
(313) 961-2242

General Learning Press
250 James St.
Morristown, NJ 07960
(201) 285-7800

GHC Business Books
4214 North Post Rd.
Omaha, NE 68112

Gould Publications
199 State St.
Binghamton, NY 13901

Gower Publishing Company, Ltd.
Gower House, Croft Rd.
Aldershot
Hampshire GU11 3HR, England

Graphic Arts Center Publishing
2000 NW Wilson
Portland, OR 97209

Stephen Greene Press/Lewis Publishing
   Company
P.O. Box 1000, Fessenden Rd.
Brattleboro, VT 05301

Greenwillow Books
6 Henderson Dr.
West Caldwell, NJ 07006

Greenwood Press
88 Post Road West
Box 5007
Westport, CT 06881
(203) 226-3571

Grid Publishing, Inc.
4666 Indianola Ave.
Columbus, OH 43214

Grossett & Dunlap, Inc.
360 Park Avenue South
New York, NY 10010
(212) 481-5097

GTM Company
Box 776
Arnold, MD 21012

Guild of Tutors Press
1019 Gayley Ave.
Los Angeles, CA 90024

Guild Press
Box 22583
Robbinsdale, MN 55422

Gulf Publishing Company
Box 2608
Houston, TX 77001
(713) 529-4301

G. K. Hall & Company
70 Lincoln St.
Boston, MA 02111
(617) 423-3990

Harcourt Brace Jovanovich, Publishers
7555 Caldwell Avenue
Chicago, IL 60648
1250 Sixth Ave.
San Diego, CA 92101
(312) 647-8822; (800) 237-2665

Harper & Row Publishers, Inc.
10 East 53rd St.
New York, NY 10022
(212) 207-7000

Harrowood Books
3943 North Providence Rd.
Newtown Square, PA 19073
(215) 353-5585; (215) 649-7558

Harvard Common Press
The Common
Harvard, MA 01451
(617) 456-8615

Harvard University Press
79 Garden St.
Cambridge, MA 02138
(617) 495-2480

Haryana Development Commissioner
Institute of Developing Economies
Small Scale Industries
Ministry of Development
India

Hastings House Publishers, Inc.
260 Fifth Ave.
New York, NY 10001
(212) 889-9624

Hawthorn Books, Inc.
260 Madison Ave.
New York, NY 10016

Hayden Book Company
10 Mulholland Dr.
Hasbrouck Heights, NJ 07604
(800) 631-0856; (201) 393-6000 in NJ

D. C. Heath and Company
125 Spring St.
Lexington, MA 02173

Walter E. Heller Corp.
105 West Adams St.
Chicago, IL 60603

Herald Press
616 Walnut Ave.
Scottsdale, PA 15683
(412) 887-8500

Hofstra University
1000 Fulton Ave.
Hempstead, NY 11550

Holmes and Meier Publishers, Inc.
30 Irving Place
New York, NY 10003
(212) 254-4100

Holt, Rinehart & Winston, Inc.
383 Madison Ave.
New York, NY 10017
(212) 872-2000

Hoover Institution Press
Stanford University
Stanford, CA 94305
(415) 723-1754

Houghton Mifflin Company
2 Park St.
Boston, MA 02107

Howard University Press
2935 Upton Street, NW
Washington, DC 20008
(202) 686-6696

HP Books
Box 5367
Tucson, AZ 85703
(602) 888-2150

Indiana University
Bureau of Business Research
Bloomington, IN 47401
(812) 332-0211

Indiana University Press
Bloomington, Indiana 47401

Industrial Development Authority
Ireland

Industries and Commerce
Department of Andhra Pradesh
India

Info Press, Inc.
728 Center St.
Box 550
Lewiston, NY 14092
(716) 754-4669

Institute for Business Planning
IBP Plaza
Englewood Cliffs, NJ
(201) 592-2000

Institute of Developing Economies
Andhra Pradesh Development Commissioner
Small Scale Industries
Ministry of Development
India

Interbook, Inc.
131 Barick St.
New York, NY 10013
(212) 691-7248

Intermediate Tech Publishing
9 King St.
London WC 2E 8HN, England

International City Management Association
1120 G St., NW
Washington, DC 20006

International Council for Small Business
929 North Sixth Street
Milwaukee, WI 53203

International Labour Offices
Washington Branch
1750 New York Ave., NW
Suite 330
Washington, DC 20006

International Publications Service
114 East 32nd St.
New York, NY 10016
(212) 685-9351

Interstate Printers & Publishers, Inc.
19 N. Jackson Street
Danville, IL 61834-0050
(217) 446-0500

Richard D. Irwin, Inc.
1818 Ridge Rd.
Homewood, IL 60430
(312) 798-6000

Jai Press
P.O. Box 1678
Greenwich, CT 06836

Johns Hopkins Press
Johns Hopkins
Baltimore, MD 21218

Jossey-Bass Inc., Publishers
433 California St.
San Francisco, CA 94104

Augustus M. Kelley, Publisher
300 Fairfield Rd., Box 1308
Fairfield, NJ 07006
(212) 685-7202

Kent Publishing Company
20 Park Plaza
Boston, MA 02116
(800) 343-2204; (617) 542-1629 in MA

Kent State University Press
Kent, OH 44242
(216) 672-7913

Kentwood Publications
2515 Santa Clara Ave.
No. 103, P.O. Box 2787
Alameda, CA 94501

Key Books
147 McKinley Ave.
Bridgeport, CT 06606

Kluwer/Nijhoff NV
Somerssstraat 13-15,
B-2000 Antwerp, Belgium

Alfred A. Knopf, Inc.
201 East 50th St.
New York, NY 10022
(212) 751-2600

Robert E. Krieger Publishing Company, Inc.
P.O. Box 9542
Melbourne, FL 32901
(305) 724-9542

Lebhar-Friedman Books
425 Park Ave.
New York, NY 10022
(212) 371-9400

Lerner Publications Company
241 First Ave.
North Minneapolis, MN 55401
(612) 332-3345

Lewis Publishing Company, Inc.
15 Muzzey St.
Lexington, MA 02173
See also Stephen Greene Press

Lexington Books
125 Spring St.
Lexington, MA 02173
(617) 862-6650

Little, Brown and Company
34 Beacon St.
Boston, MA 02106
(800) 343-9204; (617) 890-0250

Livingston Publishing Company
18 Hampstead Circle
Wynnewood, PA 19096

Lomas Publishing Company
625 Ellis St.
Suite 301
Mountain View, CA 94043

Longman Financial Services Publishing, Inc.
78 Randall Ave.
Box 710
Rockville Center, NY 11570
(516) 536-8400
500 North Dearborn Street
Chicago, IL 60610-4975

Lorenz Press, Inc.
501 East Third St.
Dayton, OH 45401

MAC Publishing Inc.
P.O. Box 7037
Colorado Springs, CO 80933-7037

Macmillan Company of Canada, Ltd.
70 Bond St.
Toronto, Ontario, Canada

Macmillan Publishing Company
866 Third Ave.
New York, NY 10022

Madhya Pradesh Development Commissioner
Institute of Developing Economies
Small Scale Industries
Ministry of Development
India

Management Information Corp.
140 Barclay Center
Cherry Hill, NJ 08034

Manchester Press
P.O. Box 5368
Playa del Rey, CA 90296

Manchester University Press
Oxford Rd.
Manchester M13 9PL, England

Richard Marek Publ.
200 Madison Ave.
New York, NY 10016

Mason & Lipscomb
New York, NY

S. E. Mattox Corp.
Box 431
San Pedro, CA 90733

McGraw-Hill Book Company
1221 Avenue of the Americas
New York, NY 10020
(212) 997-1221

David McKay Company, Inc.
2 Park Ave.
New York, NY 10016

Meadow Press
Box 35
Port Jefferson, NY 11777

Memorial University of Newfoundland
Newfoundland, Canada

Merchants Publishing Company
20 Mills St.
Kalamazoo, MI 49001
(616) 385-1842

Merrill Publishing Co.
1300 Alum Creek Dr.
Columbus, OH 43216
(614) 258-8441

Methuen & Company, Ltd.
11 New Fetter Lane
London EC4P 4EE, England

Metro Publishing Co.
Box 270776
Houston, TX 77277

Michigan State University Press
1405 South Harrison Rd.
East Lansing, MI 48824
(517) 355-9543

Milady Publishing Company
3839 White Plains Rd.
Bronx, NY 10467

B. Minkow
7040 Darby Ave.
Reseda, CA 91335

Missouri Center for Free Enterprise
428 East Capitol Ave.
Jefferson City, MO 65101

MIT Press
28 Carleton St.
Cambridge, MA 02142

Monarch Press
1230 Avenue of the Americas
New York, NY 10013

Montgomery Ward & Company
Montgomery Ward Plaza
Chicago, IL 60671
(312) 467-2000

Morrison Publishing Co.
14 Brown St.
Warren, RI 02885

William Morrow & Company, Inc.
105 Madison Ave.
New York, NY 10016
(212) 889-3050

Mouton Publishers
200 Sawmill River Road
Hawthorne, NY 10532

John Murray Ltd.
50 Albemarle St.
London W1X 4BD, England

National Association of Accountants
10 Paragon Dr., Box 433
Montvale, NJ 07645-0433
(201) 573-6278

National Bureau of Economic Research
261 Madison Ave.
New York, NY 10016
(212) 682-3190

National Council for Small Business
Milwaukee, WI

National Financial Publications
Box 10344
Palo Alto, CA 94303
(415) 494-7448

National Industrial Conference Board
845 Third Ave.
New York, NY

National Retail Merchants Association
100 West 31st St.
New York, NY 10001
(212) 244-8780

Nelson Hall Publishers
35 West Jackson
Chicago, IL 60606

New American Library
1301 Avenue of the Americas
New York, NY 10019

New Guinea Research Unit
Australian National University
Australia

New York State School of Industrial and
    Labor Relations
Ithaca, NY

Newsweek Books
444 Madison Ave.
New York, NY 10022
(212) 350-2000

Nichols Publishing Company
155 West 72nd St.
New York, NY 10023
(212) 580-8079

Nolo Press
950 Parker St.
Berkeley, CA 94710

North-Holland Publishing Company
P.O. Box 1991
1000 BZ Amsterdam, Netherlands

W. W. Norton & Company, Inc.
500 Fifth Ave.
New York, NY 10036
(212) 354-5500

NTC Business Books
4255 West Touhy Ave.
Lincolnwood, IL 60646-1975
(312) 679-5500; (800) 323-4900

Oceana Publications
75 Main St.
Dobbs Ferry, NY 10522
(914) 693-1320

J. R. O'Dwyer Company, Inc.
271 Madison Ave.
New York, NY 10016
(212) 679-2471

OECD Publications Center
1750 Penn Avenue, NW, #1207
Washington, DC 20006
(202) 724-1857

Onaway Publishing
28 Lucky Dr.
San Rafael, CA 94904

OSHA
US Dept. of Labor
Third & Constitution Ave., Room N-3641
Washington, DC 20001

Ossin Publishing
Box 141
Fern Park, FL 32730
(305) 862-2392

Owner-Managed Business Center, Inc.
725 South Central Expressway, B-12
Richardson, TX 75080
(214) 669-1627

Oxford University Press
200 Madison Ave.
New York, NY 10016
(212) 679-7300

Parachuting Publications
Box 4232-R
Santa Barbara, CA 93103
(805) 968-7277

Parker Publishing Company
Englewood Cliffs, NJ 07632
(201) 592-2440

Peachtree Park Press
67 Peachtree Park Dr.
Atlanta, GA 30309

Penguin Books Ltd.
Bath Rd., Harmondsworth
Middlesex UB7 0DA, England

Penguin Viking
40 West 23rd St.
New York, NY 10010
(212) 807-7300

Pergamon-Maxwell
Fairview Park
Elmsford, NY 10523
(914) 592-7700

Pergamon Press
Headington Hill Hall
Oxford OX3 0BW, England

Phoenix Publishing
Canaan St.
Canaan, NH 03741

Phoenix Publishers
P.O. Box 210, Indooroopilly 4068,
Queensland, Australia

Pilot Books
347 Fifth Ave.
New York, NY 10016
(212) 685-0736

Frances Pinter, Ltd.
25 Floral St., Covent Garden
London WC2E 9DS, England

Pitman Publishing
1020 Plain St.
Marshfield, MA 02050
(617) 837-1331

Playboy Press
747 Third Ave.
New York, NY 10017
(212) 688-3030

Pocket Books
1230 Avenue of the Americas
New York, NY 10020

Bern Porter
22 Salmond Rd.
Belfast, ME 04915

Practicing Law Institute
810 Seventh Ave.
New York, NY 10019
(212) 765-5700

Praeger Publishing
383 Madison Ave.
New York, NY 10017
(212) 872-2000

Predicasts
11001 Cedar Ave.
Cleveland, OH 44106
(216) 795-3000

Prentice-Hall, Inc.
Route 9W
Englewood Cliffs, NJ 07632
(201) 592-2000

Presidents Publishing House
New York, NY

Princeton University Press
41 William St.
Princeton, NJ 08540
(609) 452-4900

Probus Publishing Company, Inc.
118 North Clinton
Chicago, IL 60606

Prudential Publishing Company
P.O. Box 10751
South Lake Tahoe, CA 95731

Public Affairs Press
419 New Jersey Ave., SE
Washington, DC 20003
(202) 544-3024

Publication Unit, Public Relations Dept.
Maharashtra Small Scale Industries
Ministry of Development
India

G. P. Putnam's Sons
200 Madison Ave.
New York, NY 10016
(212) 576-8811

Quadrangle
Key Stone Industrial Park
Scranton, PA 18512

Random House
201 East 50th St.
New York, NY 10022

Rawson Associates
115 Fifth Ave.
New York, NY 10003

A. H. & A. W. Reed, Books
Rutland, VT 05701

Reed Books
Morgan's Run
Danburg, NH 03230

Reed Publishers
4999 Kahala Avenue, Box 10667
Honolulu, HI 96816

H. Regnery Company
180 North Michigan Ave.
Chicago, IL 60601
(312) 782-9181

Reston Publishing Company, Inc.
c/o Prentice-Hall, Inc.
Route 9W
Englewood Cliffs, NJ 07632
(201) 592-2000

Rodale Press, Inc.
33 East Minor St.
Emmaus, PA 18049
(215) 967-5171

Ronald Press Co.
John Wiley & Sons, Inc.
605 Third Ave.
New York, NY 10158

Routledge & Kegan Paul
Victory House
14 Leicester Square
London WC2H 7PH, England

Rutgers University Press
New Brunswick, NJ 08903
(201) 932-1766

Sage Books
P.O. Box 205
Lenox Hill Station
New York, NY 10021

St. Martin's Press
175 Fifth Ave.
New York, NY 10010
(212) 674-5151

St. Martin's Gallery
New York, NY

St. Mary's University Press
Box 488, One Camino Santa Mar
San Antonio, TX 78284

Russell Sage Foundation
112 East 64th St.
New York, NY 10021
(212) 750-6000

Sage Publications, Inc.
275 South Beverly Dr.
Beverly Hills, CA 90212
(213) 274-8003

Howard W. Sams & Company
4300 West 62nd St.
Indianapolis, IN 46268
(317) 298-5564; (800) 428-3602

W. B. Saunders Company
210 West Washington Square
Philadelphia, PA 19105
(215) 574-4700

Scandinavian University Books
Bergen, Norway

Scarecrow Press, Inc.
52 Liberty Street, Box 4167
Metuchen, NJ 08840
(201) 548-8600

Schocken Books, Inc.
62 Cooper Square
New York, NY 10003
(212) 475-4900

Science Research Associates, Inc.
College & Vocational Studies Div.
115 North Wacker Dr.
P.O. Box 5380
Chicago, IL 60680-5380

Scope Publishing
P.O. Box 376
College Park, MD 20740

Charles Scribner's Sons
115 Fifth Ave.
New York, NY 10003
(212) 614-1300

Seybold Publications, Inc.
Box 644
Medea, PA 19063

Sherbourne Publishing
Box 12037
Nashville, TN 37212
(615) 254-5842

Simon & Schuster, Inc.
1230 Avenue of the Americas
New York, NY 10020
(212) 246-2471

R. D. Smith Associates
69 Gloucester St.
Toronto, Ontario M4Y-1L8, Canada

Soundview Executive Book Summaries
100 Heights Rd.
Darien, CT 06820
(203) 655-6795

South Asia Books
Box 502
Columbia, MO 65201
(314) 445-1493

South-Western Publishing Company
5101 Madison Rd.
Cincinnati, OH 45227
(513) 271-8811

Spectrum Books
see Prentice-Hall, Inc.

Springer Publishing Company
536 Broadway
New York, NY 10012
(212) 431-4370

Springer-Verlag Heidelberger
Platz 3, D-1000
Berlin 33, West Germany

Standard Oil Company (Indiana)
Box 5910-A
Chicago, IL 60680

State University of New York Press
University Plaza
Albany, NY 12246
(518) 473-1825

Sterling Publishing
2 Park Ave.
New York, NY 10016
(212) 532-7160

Storey Communications, Inc.
Schoolhouse Rd.
Pownal, VT 05261

TAB Books
P.O. Box 40
Blue Ridge Summit, PA 17214

Technology Management, Inc.
57 Kilvert Street
Warwick, RI 02886

Till Press
P.O. Box 27816
Los Angeles, CA 90027

Times Books
201 East 50th St.
New York, NY 10022
(212) 751-2600

Tinnon-Brown Publishing Company
1855 West Main St.
Alhambra, CA 91801

Traffic Service Corp.
1435 G Street, NW
Washington, DC 20005

Charles E. Tuttle Co.
Box 410
Rutland, VT 05701
(802) 773-8930

Umi Research Press
300 North Zeeb Rd.
Ann Arbor, MI 48106

Unipub
Box 1222
Ann Arbor, MI 48106
(800) 521-8110

University of California Press
2223 Fulton St.
Berkeley, CA 94720
(415) 642-4247

University of Cape Town
Graduate School of Business
Cape Town, South Africa

University of Chicago Press
5801 Ellis Ave.
Chicago, IL 60637
(312) 962-7722

University of Georgia Press
University of Georgia
Athens, GA 30602

University of Hull
Dept. of Economics and Commerce
Hull, Quebec, Canada

University of Illinois Press
54 East Gregory Dr.
Champaign, IL 61820
(217) 333-0950

University of Miami Press
Coral Gables, FL 33124
(305) 284-2211

University of Michigan
Center for Japanese Studies
Ann Arbor, MI 48109
(313) 764-1817

University of Michigan
Graduate School of Business Administration
Division of Research
438 Business Administration
Ann Arbor, MI 48104
(313) 764-1366

University of Michigan Press
438 Business Administration
Ann Arbor, MI 48104
(313) 764-1366

University of Minnesota Press
2037 University Ave., SE
Minneapolis, MN 55414

University of Missouri Press
Columbia, MO 65211
(314) 882-2121

University of Nebraska
Bureau of Business Research
200 CBA Bldg.
Lincoln, NE 68588

University of New Mexico Press
Albuquerque, NM 87131
(505) 277-0111

University of North Carolina Press
Box 2288
Chapel Hill, NC 27514
(919) 933-6481

University of Pennsylvania Press
Blockley Hall, 418 Service Dr.
Philadelphia, PA 19104
(215) 898-6261

University of Texas Press
Box 7819, University Station
Austin, TX 78713
(512) 471-7233

University of Utah Press
Bureau of Economics, Business and Research
Salt Lake City, UT 84112
(801) 581-6771

University of Washington Press
Seattle, WA 98105

University Press of Alabama
Box Ak
University, AL 35486
(205) 348-6191

University Press of Hawaii
2444 Dole St.
Honolulu, HI 96822
(808) 948-8111

University Press of New England
3 Lebanon St.
Hanover, NH 03755
(603) 646-3349

W. E. Upjohn Institute for Employment
  Research
300 South Westnedge Ave.
Kalamazoo, MI 49007
(616) 343-5541

US Department of Commerce
14th & E Sts., NW
Washington, DC 20230
(202) 377-4901

US Government Printing Office
North Capitol St. between
  G & H Sts., NW
Washington, DC 20402
(202) 783-3238

US News & World Report Books
2400 N St., NW
Washington, DC 20037
(202) 955-2000

US Small Business Administration
Financing Division
1441 L St., NW
Washington, DC
(202) 634-6083

Uttar Pradesh Development Commissioner
Small Scale Industries
Ministry of Development
India

Van Nostrand Reinhold Company
115 Fifth Avenue
New York, NY 10003
(212) 254-3232; (800) 543-2681

Vanderbilt University Press
2505 (Rear) West End Avenue
Nashville, TN 37203
(615) 322-3585

Vantage Press, Inc.
516 West 34th St.
New York, NY 10001

Venture Management Center
811 East Wisconsin Ave.
Milwaukee, WI 53202

Vikas Publishing House
5 Ansari Rd.
New Delhi 110 002, India

Wadsworth Publishing Company, Inc.
10 Davis Dr.
Belmont, CA 94002
(415) 595-2350

Warner Books
Division of Warner Communications
666 Fifth Ave.
New York, NY 10103

Warner Publishing Services
75 Rockefeller Plaza
New York, NY 10019

Watercress Press
111 Grotto
San Antonio, TX 78216

Watson-Guptill Publishers
1515 Broadway
New York, NY 10036
(212) 764-7300

Franklin Watts, Inc.
387 Park Ave. South
New York, NY 10016
(212) 686-7070

George Weidenfeld & Nicolson Ltd.
91 Clapham High St.
London SW4 7TA, England

West Press
P.O. Box 9917
San Diego, CA 92109

West Publishing Company
50 West Kellogg Blvd.
P.O. Box 3526
St. Paul, MN 55165
(800) 328-2209

Western Reserve Publishers
P.O. Box 675
Ashtabula, OH 44004

Wichita State University
Wichita, KS 67208
(316) 689-3456

John Wiley & Sons, Inc.
605 Third Ave.
New York, NY 10158

WPL Associates, Inc.
1105 Spring St., Suite G
Silver Spring, MD 20910
(301) 589-8588

Indexes

Author Index   322
Title Index   329
Subject Index   339

AUTHOR INDEX

[References are to entry numbers.]

Aaker, David A., 235
Adama, Paul, 593
Adler, Bill, 1
Albert, Kenneth J., 175
Alcorn, Pat, 306
Alexander, Don H., 487
Allen, Paul A., 594
Altman, Edward I., 488
Altschul, Selig, 526
Alves, Jeffrey R., 237
AMACOM, 403
American Institute of Certified Public Account-
    ants, 404, 405
American Management Associations, 308
Ames, Michael, 309
Anthony, Robert N., 406
Anthony, William P., 674
Archer, Maurice, 2, 310
Armstrong, Donald R., 311
Aronson, Charles N., 3
Aslund, Anders, 151
Avis, Warren E., 4

Bailey, Geoffrey, 5
Bailey, Ronald W., 135
Baker, Nancy C., 177
Balderston, Jack, 312
Ballas, George C., 6, 612
Barth, Frederick, 152
Bartlett, Roland W., 261
Bates, Timothy, 446
Batterson, Leonard A., 489
Baty, Gordon B., 7
Baumback, Clifford Mason, 8, 9
Baumer, William H., 709
Becker, Benjamin Max, 243
Behan, Raymond J., 407
Belew, Richard C., 490, 491
Bell, Chip R., 178
Bell, Robert W., 708
Bender, Marylin, 526
Bennett, Wilma E., 447
Bennis, Warren, 314
Benson, John, 262
Benton, F. Warren, 476
Berg, David N., 702
Bergash, Robert, 675
Berger, Peter L., 263

Berkery, Michael J., 448
Berman, Steve, 613
Bermont, Hubert, 179
Bernstein, Ilene Nagel, 264
Bhandari, Narendra C., 527
Bing, Gordon, 710
Birnbaum, Mark, 449
Blake, Gary, 614
Blake, Robert R., 315
Blanchard, Marjorie P., 180
Blue, Martha, 595
Blumenthal, Susan, 450
Bly, Robert W., 614
Boehm, Helen F., 121
Bolek, Raymond W., 448
Bonner, David M., 454
Bork, Robert, 693
Bos, Dieter, 10
Boseman, Glenn, 544
Boston Public Library, 572
Boswell, Jonathan, 694
Botkin, James, 573
Bracey, Hyler J., 316
Braden, Patricia L., 574
Bradley, Charles W., 451
Bradway, Bruce M., 615
Brandt, Steven C., 11, 317, 730
Brannen, William H., 616, 617, 618
Breen, George Edward, 619
Breen, James J., 181
Breuer, Miklos M., 528
Brodie, Earl D., 318
Brooks, Julie K., 12
Broom, H. N., 319
Brophy, David J., 265
Brown, Deaver, 13
Brownstone, David M., 182, 320, 620
Brunsson, Nils, 321
Bruch, John G., 15
Bunzel, John H., 14
Burrell, Berkeley G., 148
Burstiner, Irving, 16
Buskirk, Richard Hobart, 322
Butler, David H., 408

Caggiano, Michael N., 289
Cain, Louis P., 266
Calvin, Robert J., 621

Campbell, John Creighton, 153
Canape, Charlene, 184
Cancel, Adrian R., 279
Cantor, Mike, 185
Cantrell, J. A., 267
Carey, Omer L., 376, 409
Carlson, Linda C., 622
Carsberg, Bryan, 410
Carter, John Mack, 529
Carusone, Peter S., 378
Casey, William L., 268
Cassell, Dana K., 186, 623
Casson, Mark, 17
Cate, Joan M., 187
Cavanaugh, Gerald F., 147
Chamberlain, John, 18
Chamberlain, Neil W., 269
Champion, John M., 323
Channing, Peter C., 19
Chapin-Park, Sue, 377
Chappe, Eli, 624
Chase, Anthony G., 492
Childers, Peter, 188
Chipps, Genie, 126
Church, Nancy Sunway, 555
Church, Olive D., 254, 324, 530
Chute, Phillip B., 325
Clark, John J., 711
Clark, Leta, 189
Clark, Thomas D., 472
Clarke, Philip, 154
Clifton, David S., Jr., 20
Cohen, M. Bruce, 424
Cohen, William A., 326, 625, 626
Cohn, Theodore, 327, 651, 676, 677
Coleman, Bob, 328
Colman, Robert D., 717
Comiskey, James C., 21
Competere Group, 493, 494, 495
Conder, Joseph M., 329
Connor, Jr., Richard A., 627
Cook, James R., 23
Cook, Peter D., 23
Cooper, Arnold C., 531
Copeland, Lennie, 155
Copperman, Lois, 678
Copulsky, William, 731
Coutarelli, Spiro A., 156
Coxe, Weld, 628
Craig, Julia F., 129
Cramer, Clarence H., 270
Crawford, Nick, 582
Crego, Edwin T., 24
Crimmins, C. E., 25
Cross, Theodore L., 136
Cummings, Richard, 190
Curran, James, 330
Curry, Jess W., 454
Curtin, Richard T., 331

Dahl, Fred, 485
Dahlberg, Arthur, 271
Dailey, Charles A., 332
Danco, Leon A., 333, 334
Dataquest, 455
Davidson, Jeffrey P., 627
Davidson, Marion, 595
Davis, F. T., Jr., 712
Day, Theodore E., 411
Day, William, 335
Dayani, Elizabeth Crow, 130
Deal, Dr. Terrence E., 272
Deaton, Brian, 24
Deeks, John, 26
Deitzer, B. A., 391
Delaney, William A., 695
Diamond, Sidney A., 596
Dible, Donald M., 27, 336, 496
Dickey, Bill, 475
Dickinson, John R., 629
Dimancescu, Dan, 573
Doctors, Samuel I., 139
Dollar, William E., 337
Donoghue, William E., 412, 413
Dordick, Herbert S., 457
Dorff, Ralph L., 630
Dorland, Gilbert N., 28
Dougherty, James L., 679, 680
Doughtery, David E., 29
Drake Publishers, Inc., 30, 713
Dressler, Fritz R. S., 31
Droms, William G., 414
Drucker, Peter Ferdinand, 32, 575
Dunlop, W. J., 166
Dunnan, Nancy, 121
Durr, Frank L., 578
Dyer, Barbara, 299
Dyer, Mary L., 415
Dyer, William G., 681

Earl, Michael J., 338
Easton, Thomas A., 33
Eckert, Lee A., 339
Ellerbach, Richard J., 416
Ellman, Edgar S., 682
Elmore, Gregory Brooks, 636
Elster, Robert J., 270
Engel, Herbert M., 271
Enockson, Paul G., 456
Europa Publications Ltd., 157

Faber, Peter L., 597
Faivre, Milton I., 191
Falk, Howard, 457
Farrar, Lucien, 207
Faux, Marian, 192
Feeney, Joan, 529
Feinman, Jeffrey, 193
Feldstein, Stuart, 194

Fenno, Brooks, 632
Ferguson, James Milton, 273
Fierro, Robert Daniel, 35
Fiffer, Steve, 36
Figgie, Harry E., Jr., 417
Figueroa, Oscar, 279
Finn, Richard P., 556
Fisk, Raymond P., 631
Flamholtz, Eric, 342
Flexman, Nancy A., 37
Folsom, Burton W., Jr., 344
Fournies, Ferdinand F., 683
Fox, Jack, 190
Frank, A. L., 460
Frank, Susan, 647
Frantz, Forrest H., 196, 343
Fregly, Bert, 344
Freier, Jerold L., 714
Freiermuth, Edmond P., 345
Frenzel, Mary Anne, 615
Friday, William, 346
Friedberg, Ardy, 197
Friedman, Robert E., 275
Fritz, Roger, 38
Frost, Ted S., 696
Fucini, Joseph J., 39
Fucini, Suzy, 39
Fuld, Leonard M., 633

Gallup, Alec M., 40
Gallup, Jr., George, 40
Gardner, Ralph, 41
Gargan, John Joseph, 418
Gauld, Charles A., 158
Gautam, Vinayshil, 159
Gazvoda, Edward A., 198
Gearing, Phillip J., 199
Genfan, Herb and Taetzch, 200
Gerber, Michael E., 697
Geschka, H., 580
Gevirtz, Don, 276, 576
Gibb, Allan, 163, 701
Gibson, Glenn A., 458
Gibson, Mary L., 458
Gilder, George F., 347
Gill, Jr., Michael A., 590
Gill, M. D., Jr., 504
Ginalski, William, 559
Gitman, Lawrence J., 347
Gladstone, David John, 497
Goelz, Paul C., 278
Goffee, Robert, 122
Golden, Peggy A., 293
Goldman, Harold L., 384
Goldstein, Arnold S., 42, 201, 598, 698, 699
Goldstein, Jerome, 43, 44
Gough, J. W., 45
Gould Staff Editors, 577
Graham, John W., 634

Granick, David, 160
Gray, Bob, 46
Gray, Ernest A., 635
Green, Orville M., 578
Greene, Gardner G., 47
Greenfield, Sidney M., 48
Greisman, Bernard, 348
Grenier, Mildred, 202
Grieco, Victor A., 349
Griffin, Barbara C., 49
Griggs, Lewis, 155
Gross, Eugene L., 279
Gross, Harry, 557
Gross, Len, 203
Grousbeck, H. Irving, 103
Gruenwald, George, 579
Gumpert, David E., 204, 350
Gupta, Brijen, 137
Guthrie, Michael, 50

Haft, Robert J., 498
Hall, William E., 351
Haller, Leon, 419
Halliday, Thelma Y., 138
Hammer, Marian Behan, 51
Hammond, Alexander, 558
Hanan, Mack, 732
Hancock, William A., 579
Handy, Jim, 205
Hansen, John A., 685
Hanson, James M., 715
Harmon, Charlotte, 206
Harmon, Paul, 52
Harold, Victor, 716
Harper, Malcolm, 161, 162
Harrigan, Kathryn Rudie, 352, 353
Harris, Clifford C., 420
Harris, Herby, 207
Harvard Business Review Executive Books
    Series, 354, 355
Haskins, Gay, 163
Hayes, Rick Stephen, 499, 500, 636
Haynes, W. Warren, 637
Hazel, A. C., 356
Hebert, Robert F., 280
Hemphill, John Mearl, 68
Henderson, Carter F., 53
Henderson, James William, 501
Henke, Thomas R., 208
Hennessy, Elizabeth, 54
Henward, DeBanks M., III, 559
Hess, Robert P., 600
Heyel, Carl, 357
Hiatt, John, 235
Hicks, J. William, 601
Hilburn, R. E., 209
Hilton, Terri, 123
Hisrich, Robert D., 55, 124, 638
Hjelmfelt, David C., 560

Hockney, Donald, 459
Hodgson, Richard S., 639
Hogsett, Robert N., 421
Holbrook, Martin E., 597
Holland, Philip, 56
Hollas, David, 612
Holt, K., Geschka, H., 580
Holt, Robert Lawrence, 210
Holtz, Herman, 57, 211, 212, 502, 640, 641
Honkanen, Rober, 217
Hopkins, Gilbert N., 259
Horvitz, Paul M., 503
Hosmer, LaRue T., 57, 531
Hribar, Zvonimir, 422
Hubert, Tony, 163
Huff, Ann S., 139
Hughes, Jonathan R. T., 281
Hund, James M., 140

Ianni, Francis A. J., 288
Ichimura, Shin'ichi, 164
Imhoff, Eugene A., Jr., 642
Info Press, Inc., 561
Internal Revenue Service, 423
Isshiki, Koichiro R., 461

Jackson, Stanley G., 602
James, John H., 323
Japan Economic Journal, 165
Jessup, Claudia, 125, 126
Jewkes, John, 282
Johns, B. L., 166
Jones, Billy M., 532, 533, 534, 535
Jones, Leroy P., 167
Jones, Seymour, 354
Jones, Susan K., 564
Jones, Thomas B., 141
Jong, Steven F., 462

Kamoroff, Bernard, 425
Kao, Raymond W. Y., 359
Katchen, Carole, 213
Katz, Michael, 537
Kaufman, Bob, 426
Keast, Fred D., 678
Keim, Robert T., 463
Kelleher, Robert F., 643
Kelley, Robert E., 353
Kellogg, Marion S., 684
Kenney, David W., 440
Kent, Calvin A., 60
Keuls, Henry P. C., 536
Kiam, Victor, 62
Kirk, John, 603
Kirkpatrick, Frank, 214
Kirzner, Israel M., 63, 64, 284
Kishel, Gregory F., 65, 215, 360
Kishel, Patricia Gunter, 215

Klatt, Lawrence A., 361
Klein, Howard J., 216, 700
Kline, John B., 390
Kling, John R., 66
Kolve, Carolee Nance, 464
Konikow, Robert B., 644
Kozmetsky, G., 504
Kracke, Don, 217
Krause, William H., 218
Krauser, Peter M., 581
Kravitt, Gregory I., 705
Kreider, Carl Jonas, 67
Krentzman, Harvey C., 362
Kryszak, Wayne D., 219
Kuecken, John A., 220
Kuhn, Robert Lawrence, 363, 589
Kuriloff, Arthur H., 68, 91
Kurzweil, Edith, 168
Kuswa, Webster, 645

Lane, Byron, 69
Lane, Marc J., 427, 604, 605
Lane, Thorne, 221
Lasser, J., K., Tax Institute, 364
Lauenstein, Milton C., 365
Leavitt, Harold J., 70
Lee, Albert, 222
Lee, Donald D., 646
Lee, Roy F., 142
Lee, Steven J., 717
Leslie, Mary, 127
Lester, Mary, 128
Levering, Robert, 537
Levine, Mindy N., 647
Levinson, Jay Conrad, 71, 648
Levinson, Robert E., 366, 733
Levitan, Sar. A., 143
Lewis, H. Gordon, 649, 650
Lewis, John, 701
Lewis, Mack O., 562
Liebers, Arthur, 223
Light, Ivan H., 144
Liles, Patrick R., 538
Lindberg, Roy A., 327, 651, 676, 677
Linden, Eugene, 553
Lindsey, Jennifer, 506
Link, Albert N., 280
Linneman, Robert F., 367
Lipay, Raymond J., 428
Loffel, E. W., 507
Lopatin, Arthur D., 137
Lotus Development Corporation, 468, 469
Lowe, Julian, 582
Luisi, Billie, 224
Lulow, Kalia, 225
Lumley, James E., 652
Lund, Robert T., 685
Luther, William M., 653, 654
Lyons, Mary, 171

MacDonald, Stephen, 145
MacFarlane, William N., 368
Magaziner, Ira C., 285
Mahin, Philip William, 539
Makridakis, Spyros, 673
Mancuso, Joseph R., 9, 72, 73, 74, 75, 76, 508, 583
Mangold, M. A., 718
Mangum, Garth L., 142
Marthinsen, John E., 268
Martin, Michael J. C., 584
Masser, Barry Z., 226
McCaskey, Michael B., 299
McCready, Gerald B., 655
McDaniel, Carl, 347
McDavid, John E., 378
McGee, Robert W., 429
McGlynn, Daniel R., 465, 466
McGonagle, John J., 611
McKeever, Mike P., 509
McKenna, Regis, 656
McKiernan, John, 77
McLaughlin, Curtis P., 370
McLaughlin, Harold, 78
McNichols, Charles W., 467
McNitt, Jim, 468
McNulty, Herbert W., 731
McVicar, Marjorie, 129
Melo, Jose Luiz, 169
Mendelson, Martin, 563
Meredith, G. G., 79
Merrill, Ronald E., 371
Mermet, Jean P., 474
Metcalf, Wendell, 80
Meyers, Herbert S., 372
Meyers, M. Scott, 686
Midgley, David, 657
Miles, Raymond C., 720, 721
Miller, Harry M., 540
Miller, Murray, 297
Miller, William, 357
Mills, D. Quinn, 373
Minkow, Barry, 81
Mintzberg, Henry, 374
Mirvis, Philip H., 702
Molloy, James F., Jr., 475
Moore, Barbara H., 358
Moriarity, Shane, 541
Morris, Jane K., 512
Morrisey, George L., 375
Morrison, Robert H., 82
Morrison, Robert S., 83
Moscove, Stephen, 430
Moskowitz, Milton, 537
Moss, Laurence S., 268
Mouton, Jane S., 315
Mucciolo, Louis, 84, 85
Muffet, Deborah, 228
Murray, Jean Wilson, 229

Nadler, Leonard, 178, 687
Naisbitt, John, 734
Nanus, Burt, 314
National Association of Accountants Library, 431
Neels, Kevin, 289
Neely, Richard, 606
Nestlebaum, Karen, 542
Newcomb, Dwayne G., 230
Nicholas, Ted, 607
Norback, Craig T., 564
Norback, Peter G., 564
Northart, Leo J., 709
Novotny, Edward G., 516

O'Brien, Denis, 540
O'Brien, Richard E., 568
O'Connor, Joyce, 171
O'Flaherty, Joseph S., 510
O'Heffernan, Patrick, 697
Oakey, R. P., 170
Office of Minority Business Enterprise, 146
Olson, Dean Francis, 376
Osgood, William R., 86
Ossin, Archie and Myrna, 231
Ouchi, William, 290

Park, William R., 377
Peterlongo, G., 580
Peters, M. P., 638
Petrol, John V., 378
Pettit, R. Richardson, 503
Petty, J. William, II, 443
Piage, Richard E., 585
Pickle, Hal B., 379
Pilot Books, 511, 565, 566, 586
Pinchot, Gifford, 735
Platt, Harlan D., 703
Pollard, Robert, 299
Poppe, Fred C., 659
Porochnia, Leonard, 469
Porter, Michael, E., 172, 660
Poynter, Dan, 232, 470
Pratt, Shannon P., 722, 723
Pratt, Stanley E., 512
Predicasts, 471
Prentice-Hall, Inc., Information Services Division, 608
Price, Laurence W., 233
Pritchard, Robert E., 615
Proctor, William, 40
Proxmire, William, 380
Purcell, Theodore V., 147
Puth, Robert C., 291

Quince, Thelma, 671

Ragan, Robert C., 432, 433
Randall, Robert D., 472

Rausch, Edward N., 434, 435
Ray, Robert J., 339
Reagan, Alice E., 543
Reid, A. S., 356
Revel, Chase, 234, 235
Riccardi, Betty Rinehart, 130
Rice, Craig S., 688
Rice, Donald L., 236
Richard, Clement C., 237
Richards, Judith W., 513
Rivkin, Bernard, 587
Roberts, E. Wilson, 514
Roberts, Michael J., 103
Roman, Murray, 661
Ronen, Joshua, 87
Rosa, Nicholas, 473
Rosa, Sharon, 473
Rose, Tom, 381
Rosefsky, Robert S., 88
Rosenau, Milton D., Jr., 588
Rubel, Stanley M., 515, 516, 724
Ruhe-Schoen, Janet, 238
Ruland, William, 436

SaKong, Il, 167
Salm, Walter, 474
Sandberg, William R., 382
Sanderson, William D., 181
Scanlan, Thomas J., 37
Scarborogh, Norman M., 89
Scase, Richard, 90, 122
Schabacker, Joseph Charles, 239, 383
Schadewald, Robert J., 475
Schaller, Elmer O., 708
Scharf, Charles A., 725
Schellenberger, Robert E., 544
Schollhammer, Hans, 91
Scherer, Daniel J., 567
Scheuing, E. E., 662
Schiffrin, Peter D., 24
Schiliff, K. A., 391
Schmitz, Hubert, 545
Schoder, Judith, 241
Schweninger, Loren, 550
Seder, John W., 148, 437
Sedgwick, Henry D., 371
Seigel, David, 384
Seltz, David D., 127, 240, 568, 569
Serif, Med, 663
Sevareid, Eric, 292
Sexton, Donald L., 59, 92, 385
Shames, William H., 386, 517
Shebar, Sharon Sigmond, 241
Shenson, Howard L., 242, 243
Shilling, Dana, 10, 93
Shook, Robert L., 546
Sickman, John, 449
Siegel, G. M., 664

Siegel, William Lairy, 689
Silberstein, Judith A., 476
Silver, A. David, 94, 477, 518, 519, 620
Silver, Gerald A., 547
Simkin, Mark G., 430
Simon, Julian L., 244
Sipple, Charles J., 478
Siropolis, Nicholas C., 95
Slimmon, Robert F., 690
Small, Anne, 131
Small Business Computer News, 479
Small, Samuel, 96
Smilor, Raymond W., 504, 589, 590
Smith, Brian R., 387, 521, 666, 726
Smith, Cynthia S., 665
Smith, Dennis C., 245
Smith, Jerald R., 293
Smith, Randy Baca, 97
Smith, Richard D., 522
Smith, Roger F., 667
Smolin, C. Roger, 483
Sobel, Robert, 98
Soderberg, Norman R., 668
Sondeno, Stanley R., 388
Sonfield, Matthew C., 99
Speiro, Herbert T., 438
Stanford, Melvin J., 389
Stankiewicz, Rikard, 294
Stansfield, Richard H., 669
Stanworth, John, 260, 398, 571, 701
Starchild, Adam, 246, 439
Starling, Grover, 365, 366
Starr, Douglas P., 247
Stata, Ray, 573
Steckel, Robert C., 248
Stegall, Donald P., 390
Steiner, Barry R., 440
Steingold, Fred, 610
Steinhoff, Dan, 391, 392
Steinmetz, Lawrence L., 390
Sterling Publishing Co., Inc., 100, 570, 727
Stern, Alfred, 249
Stevens, Barry A., 12
Stevens, Lawrence, 320
Stevens, Mark, 101, 102, 704
Stevenson, Howard H., 103
Stewart, John, Jr., 705
Stickney, John, 104
Still, Jack W., 441
Stoll, Hans R., 411
Stone, Bob, 670
Storey, D. J., 105
Storey, David, 173
Strosberg, Linda, 485
Swann, Leonard Alexander, 549

Taetzsch, Lyn, 251
Taffi, Donald J., 106
Taggert, Robert, III, 143

Tansuhaj, Patriya S., 631
Tarrant, John J., 107
Tashakori, Maryam, 393
Tate, Curtis E., 108, 394
Taylor, Charlotte, 109
Taylor, Clarence R., 592
Taylor, Frederick John, 110
Taylor, John R., 395
Telchin, Charles S., 252
Temple, Mary, 253
Tepper, Ron, 254
Thomas, James P., 550
Thompson, Victoria, 86
Thomsett, Michael C., 255
Timmons, Jeffry A., 112, 204, 350
Tjosvold, Dean, 621
Tompkins, Bill G., 442
Torrence, Ronald W., 113
Townsend, Carl, 256
Traister, Robert J., 257

Uris, Auren, 692
U.S. Congress, House Committee on Banking, Finance, and Urban Affairs, 297
U.S. Congress, Joint Economic Committee, 298
U.S. Congress, Senate Committee on Small Business, 132
U.S. Government Printing Office, 396
U.S. Small Business Administration, 523
Uselding, Paul J., 266

Van Auken, Philip M., 385
Van Buren, Ernestine Orrick, 551
Van Der Wal, John, 28
Van Voorhis, Kenneth R., 114
Van Zandt, Joseph H., 260
Vatter, Harold G., 706
Vaughan, Roger J., 299, 444
Vaughn, Charles L., 571
Vaughn, Percy J., Jr., 252
Vella, Carolyn M., 611
Venable, Abraham S., 149
Vesper, Karl H., 59, 115, 300, 531

Wagener, Elaine Hoffman, 552
Walker, Ernest W., 397, 443
Walthall, Wylie A., 301
Wang, Dr. An, 553
Watkins, David, 330, 398, 671
Wayne, William, 707
Weaver, Peter, 116
Webb, Ian, 728
Webb, Terry, 302, 371
Webster, Bryce, 554
Wellsfry, Norval L., 309
Welsh, John A., 117, 399
West, C., 672
West, Thomas L., 726
Westrip, Ava, 398
Whaley, Robert E., 411
Wheelwright, Steven C., 673
White, Jerry F., 2, 117, 310, 399
White, Richard M., 118
Whitis, Rose Freeman, 258
Wiatrowski, Claude A., 486
Wichita State University, 150
Wik, Philip, 174
Wilbanks, Patricia M., 259
Wilken, Paul H., 119
Wilkens, Joanne, 133
Williams, Edward E., 120
Williams, W. P., 260
Wilson, Brian, 400
Wilton, John W., 524
Wingate, John W., 708
Winston, Sandra, 134
Woods, Gordon, 529, 729
Wortman, Leon A., 401

Young, Dennis R., 303
Young, Jerrald F., 402

Zabalaoui, Judith Cowan, 445
Zeigler, Harmon, 304
Zimmerer, Thomas W., 89
Zwick, Jack, 432

TITLE INDEX

[References are to entry numbers.]

Academic and Entrepreneurial Research, 264
Academic Entrepreneurs, 294
Accounting for Software Costs, 429
Accounting Information Systems, 430
Accounting Practice Management for Small Businesses, 422
Accounting Services for Your Small Business, 428
The Acquisition Decision, 729
Acquisition Search Programs, 714
Adjusting to an Older Work Force, 678
Administering the Closely-Held Company, 399
Advertising and Competition: Theory, Management, Fact, 273
Advertising and Sales Promotion, 616
The Advertising Manager's Handbook, 669
Advice, A High Profit Business, 211
AMA Management Handbook, 308
American Economic History, 291
American Enterprise—Free and Not So Free, 270
American Independent Business, 255
The American Small Businessman, 14
The Art and Science of Entrepreneurship, 92
The Art of Computer Management, 468
Audits of Small Business, 404

The Basic Book of Business, 65
Basic Business Appraisal, 720
Basic Management: An Experience-Based Approach, 361
Be Your Own Boss, 93, 228
Become a Top Consultant: How the Experts Do It, 254
Beginner's Guide to Small Business Computers, 474
Beyond Survival: A Business Owner's Guide for Success, 333
The Bibliography of Marketing Research Methods, 629
Big Decisions for Small Business, 485
Big Paybacks from Small Budget Advertising, 645
Big-Time Opportunities and Strategies That Turn Pennies into Millions, 196
Bill Adler's Chance of a Lifetime, 1
Black Business Enterprise, 135

Black Capitalism: Strategy for Business in the Ghetto, 136
Black Entrepreneurship, 140
Blacks in the Industrial World, 147
The Break-Even Handbook, 420
Breaking into Print, 199
Bringing High Tech Home, 476
Building Black Business, 149
Building Your Business Plan: A Step-by-Step Approach, 78
Business Acquisitions Deskbook with Checklists and Forms, 712
Business and Blacks, 145
Business Building Ideas for Franchising and Small Business, 663
Business Computers: Planning, Selecting and Implementing, 463
Business Enterprise and Economic Change, 266
The Business Idea—From Birth to Profitable Company, 28
Business Leaders in Brazil, 169
Business Loans: A Guide to Money Sources and How to Approach Them Successfully, 499
Business Merger and Acquisition Strategies, 711
Business Plan for America, 276
Business Planning for the Entrepreneur, 120
Business Resource Directory, 86
Business Start-Up Basics, 27
Business World, 277
Buy, Sell, Merge: How to Do It, 709
Buying Your Own Small Business, 726

Can Small Business Survive? 380
The Capitalist Revolution, 263
Cases from Management Accounting Practice, 541
Cases in Small Business Management, 527
Cash Management, 412
Cashing in on Cooking, 177
Cater from Your Kitchen: Income from Your Own Home Business, 180
The Chandlers of Kansas, a Banking Family, 532
The Changing Environment of Business, 295
Checklist/Guide to Selecting a Small Computer, 447

A Checklist Guide to Successful Acquisitions, 716

Choosing the Right Small Business Computer, 446

The Chosen Instrument, 526

The Christian Entrepreneur, 66

Clients and Consultants: Meeting and Exceeding Expectations, 178

Climate for Entrepreneurship and Innovation in the United States, 298

Clint, The Biography of Clinton Williams Murchison, 1895–1969, 551

Coaching for Improved Work Performance, 683

Compensating Key Executives in the Smaller Company, 676

Competition and Entrepreneur, 63

Competition in Global Industry, 172

Competitive Strategy, 660

Competitor Intelligence: How to Get It, How to Use It, 633

Complete Guide to Making Money with Your Ideas and Inventions, 585

The Complete Guide to Your Own Business, 108

Complete Handbook of Franchising, 568

The Complete Handbook of How to Start and Run a Money-Making Business in Your Home, 51

The Complete Legal Guide for Small Business, 593

The Computer Entrepreneurs, 537

The Computer Freelancer's Handbook, 197

Computer Power for the Small Business, 478

Computer Selection Guide, 470

Consultancy for Small Business, 161

Consultant's Edge: Using the Computer as a Marketing Tool, 640

Corporate Acquisitions, 710

Corporate Cultures: The Rites and Rituals of Corporate Life, 272

Corporate Human Resource Development, 687

Corporate Pathfinders, 70

The Cost Reduction and Profit Improvement Handbook, 417

Cost-Effective Telecommunications Management, 426

Creating the Successful Business Plan for New Ventures, 58

Credit and Collections, 437

Critical Incidents in Management: Decisions and Policy Issues, 323

Cutting Loose, 33

dBASE II Guide for Small Business, 475

The Decentralized Company: Making the Most of Entrepreneurial Management, 366

Decision Making for Small Business Management, 402

Deregulation and the New Airline Entrepreneurs, 286

Desk Book for Setting Up a Closely-Held Corporation, 600

Developing Business Strategies, 235

Diary of a Small Business, 548

Direct Mail and Mail Order Handbook, 639

Direct Response Marketing: An Entrepreneurial Approach, 625

Directory for State and Federal Funds for Business Development, 511

Directory of Franchising Organizations, 565

Directory of Operating Small Business Investment Companies, 523

Discovery and the Capitalist Process, 284

Do-It-Yourself Marketing Research, 619

Dollars on Your Doorstep: The Complete Guide to Homebased Businesses, 215

The Dow Jones–Irwin Guide to Franchises, 564

The Dynamic Small Firm: Selected Readings, 397

The E-myth: Why Most Businesses Don't Work and What to Do about It, 697

Earning Money Without a Job, 71

Economic Opportunity in the Ghetto: The Partnership of Government and Business, 143

An Economic Philosophy for a Free People, 278

Effective Purchasing and Inventory Control for Small Business, 337

Effective Small Business Management, 89

Electronic Mail: A Revolution in Business Communications, 453

The Emerging Business: Managing for Growth, 424

Encyclopedia of Entrepreneurship, 59

The Encyclopedia of Management, 357

The Encyclopedia of Small Business Resources, 204

Enterprise: The Making of Business in America, 292

Enterprise: A Simulation, 293

Enterprise and Society, 159

The Enterprising Americans: A Business History of the United States, 18

Entrechic: The Mega-Guide to Entrepreneurial Excellence, 25

The Entrepreneur: A Corporate Strategy for the '80s, 106

The Entrepreneur: An Economic Theory, 17

The Entrepreneur and Small Business Problem Solver, 326

The Entrepreneur in Local Government, 288

The Entrepreneur: Mainstream Views and Radical Critiques, 280

The Entrepreneurial Age: The Twenty-first Century Renaissance of the Individual, 31

The Entrepreneurial City: Innovations in Finance and Management for St. Paul, 289

The Entrepreneurial Function, 531

Entrepreneurial Health Care: How to Structure Successful New Ventures, 50

The Entrepreneurial Life: How to Go for It and Get It, 94

Entrepreneurial Management: Going All Out for Results, 332

Entrepreneurial Megabucks: 100 Greatest Entrepreneurs of the Last 25 Years, 547

The Entrepreneurial Middle Class, 90

Entrepreneurial Skills: Cases in Small Business Management, 539

Entrepreneurial Woman, 134

The Entrepreneurial Workbook, 109

Entrepreneuring, 11

Entrepreneuring in Established Companies: Managing Toward the Year 2000, 730

The Entrepreneur's Guide, 13, 56

The Entrepreneur's Guide to Capital, 506

The Entrepreneur's Guide to Restaurant Expansion, 240

The Enterpreneur's Manual, 118

Entrepreneur's Marketing Guide, 667

The Entrepreneur's Master Planning Guide, 117

Entrepreneurs in Cultural Context, 48

The Entrepreneurs, 54, 546

The Entrepreneurs: Explorations Within the American Business Tradition, 98

Entrepreneurship, 10, 15, 87

Entrepreneurship: A Comparative and Historical Study, 119

Entrepreneurship and the Corporation, 731

Entrepreneurship and National Policy, 300

Entrepreneurship and Small Business Management, 91, 114

Entrepreneurship and the New Firm, 105

Entrepreneurship and Venture Management, 19

Entrepreneurship for the Eighties, 7

The Entrepreneurship Handbook, 72

Entrepreneurship in a Mature Industry, 153

Entrepreneurship, Intrapreneurship, and Venture Capital, 55

Entrepreneurship, Productivity, and the Freedom of Information Act, 268

The Environment for Entrepreneurship, 60

Ethnic Enterprise in America, 144

The European Executive, 160

Everything You Need to Know about Raising Money for a New Business, 493

The Executive Challenge: Managing Change and Ambiguity, 299

The Executive Interviewer's Deskbook, 692

Expanding the Opportunity to Produce, 275

Experiences in Entrepreneurship and Small Business Management, 385

Failures in Organization Development and Change, 702

Family Business, Risky Business, 693

The Family-Owned Business, 313

Fast-Growth Management, 732

Finance and Accounting for Nonfinancial Managers, 414

Finance, Entrepreneurship, and Economic Development, 265

Finance for the Non-Financial Manager, 438

Financial Forecasting, 413

Financial Handbook, 488

Financial Keys to Small Business Profitability, 434

Financial Management for Small Business, 435

Financial Management of the Small Firm, 443

Financial Security and Independence Through a Small Business Franchise, 567

Financial Tools for Small Businesses, 409

Financing and Managing Fast-Growth Companies, 504

Financing Your Business, 507

Forecasting Methods for Management, 673

Franchise Annual, 1986, 561

Franchise Investigation and Contract Negotiation, 557

Franchise Opportunities: A Business of Your Own, 570

Franchisee Rights: A Self-Defense Manual, 558

Franchising, 571

A Franchising Guide for Blacks, 141

The Franchising Option: Expanding Your Business Through Franchising, 559

Free Enterprise, 3

Free Yourself in a Business of Your Own, 69

The Freelancer's Business Book, 225

From Technical Professional to Entrepreneur, 29

From Tennessee Slave to St. Louis Entrepreneur, 550

Fun and Guts, 73

Fundamentals of Development Finance: A Practitioner's Guide, 513

Fundamentals of Finance and Accounting for Nonfinancial Managers, 403

Fundamentals of Recordkeeping and Finance for Small Business, 432

Future Opportunities in Franchising, 555

George C. Vaughan, Early Entrepreneur, 552

Getting Free: How to Profit Most Out of Working for Yourself, 88

Getting into Business, 301

Getting It Together (Black Businessmen in America), 148

Getting Money: A Practical Guide to Financing Your Business, 522

Going for It! How to Succeed as an Entrepreneur, 62

Going International, 155

Going Public: The Entrepreneur's Guide, 510

The Gold Collar Worker, 283

Goldmine of Money-Making Ideas, 183

Government, Business, and Entrepreneurship in Economic Development, 167

The Great American Success Story, 40

Greedy Bastard's Business Manual, 82

Growing Concerns: Building and Managing the Smaller Business, 354

Guerrilla Marketing, 648

A Guide for Selecting Computers and Software for Small Businesses, 456

Guide to Buying, Selling and Starting a Travel Agency, 250

Guide to Buying or Selling a Business, 715

The Guide to Franchising, 563

A Guide to Managerial Accounting in Small Companies, 441

Guide to Selling a Business, 724

A Guide to Small Firms Assistance in Europe, 163

Guide to Venture Capital Sources, 515

Handbook for Manufacturing Entrepreneurs, 83

Handbook for Small Business, 396

Handbook of Computer Applications for the Small or Medium-Size Business, 457

Handbook of Mergers, Acquisitions and Buyouts, 717

The Harvard Entrepreneurs Society's Guide to Making Money, 198

Have You Got What It Takes?, 74

Helping Your Business Grow, 632

Her Own Business: Success Secrets of Entrepreneurial Woman, 133

High Technology Small Firms Regional Development in Britain and the United States, 170

High-Tech Start-Up Ventures in Japan, 165

House of Diamonds, 542

How Entrepreneurs Make Business Profits, 46

How Mail Order Fortunes Are Made, 249

How Small Businesses Use Computers, 479

How to Advertise and Promote Your Retail Store, 623

How to Advertise and Promote Your Small Business, 664

How to Be a Successful Inventor: Patenting, Protecting, Marketing, and Selling Your Invention, 592

How to Be Self-Employed: Introduction to Small Business Management, 344

How to Be Your Own Boss: A Complete Guide to Starting and Running Your Own Business, 110

How to Become a Successful Consultant in Your Own Field, 179

How to Borrow Money from a Bank, 487

How to Build a Small Advertising Agency and Run It at a Profit, 203

How to Buy a Small Business, 718, 719

How to Buy and Sell a Small Business, 713, 727

How to Buy (and Survive!) Your First Computer, 464

How to Buy the Right Small Business Computer System, 483

How to Capitalize on the Video Revolution, 184

How to Choose Your Small Business Computer, 449

How to Create and Market a Successful Seminar or Workshop, 242

How to Create Your Own Publicity and Get It Free, 613

How to Delegate—A Guide to Getting Things Done, 341

How to Develop, Install and Maintain Cost Reduction/Productivity Improvement Programs, 407

How to Do Business with the People's Republic of China, 174

How to Finance Your Small Business with Government Money: SBA and Other Loans, 500

How to Find and Buy Your Business in the Country, 214

How to Form Your Own Corporation Without a Lawyer for Under $50, 607

How to Franchise Your Business, 562

How to Get Big Results from a Small Advertising Budget, 665

How to Get Started as a Manufacturers' Representative, 218

How to Get Started in Your Own Franchise Business, 569

How to Handle Speechwriting Assignments, 247

How to Handle Your Own Public Relations, 649

How to Keep Your Company Out of Court, 594

How to Make Money at Home, 241

How to Make Money in Music: A Guidebook for Success in Today's Music Business, 207

How to Make Money with Your Home Computer, 237

How to Make Money Selling at Flea Markets and Antique Fairs, 206

How to Make Money with Your Microcomputer, 212, 256

How to Make the Transition from an Entrepreneurship to a Professionally Managed Firm, 342

How to Make Your Advertising Twice as Effective at Half the Cost, 650

How to Negotiate a Business Loan, 490

How to Open Your Own Shop or Gallery, 189

How to Organize and Operate a Small Business, 8

How to Own Your Own Newspaper, 221

How to Participate Profitably in Trade Shows, 644

How to Pick the Right Small Business Opportu-

nity: The Key to Success in Your Own
Business, 175
How to Plan and Finance a Growing Business,
496
How to Price a Business, 721
How to Proceed in Business—Legally: The
Entrepreneur's Preventive Law, 602
How to Profit from Your Arts and Crafts, 222
How to Prosper in Your Own Business, 387
How to Publish, Promote, and Sell Your Own
Book, 210
How to Publish Your Own Magazine, 236
How to Pyramid Small Business Ventures into a
Personal Fortune, 101
How to Raise and Invest Venture Capital, 516
How to Raise Capital: Preparing and Presenting
the Business Plan, 505
How to Raise Rabbits for Fun and Profit, 191
How to Run a Small Business, 348, 364
How to Run a Successful Specialty Foodstore,
182
How to Save Free Enterprise, 271
How to Save Your Business, 698
How to Sell to the Government: A Step-by-Step
Guide to Success, 626
How to Start a Family Business and Make it
Work, 43
How to Start a Profitable Retirement Business,
223
How to Start a Secretarial and Business
Service, 253
How to Start a Successful Restaurant: An
Entrepreneur's Guide, 181
How to Start a Typing Service in Your Own
Home, 259
How to Start and Manage Your Own Small
Business, 47
How to Start and Operate a Mail-Order Busi-
ness, 244
How to Start and Run a Profitable Craft Busi-
ness, 231
How to Start and Succeed in a Business of Your
Own, 395
How to Start, Expand and Sell a Business, 21
How to Start, Finance and Manage Your
Own Small Business, 75
How to Start, Run and Stay in Business, 64
How to Start Your Own Business . . . and
Succeed, 67
How to Start Your Own Craft Business, 200
How to Start Your Home Typing Business, 187
How to Start Your Own Horticulture Business,
233
How to Start Your Own Magazine, 260
How to Start Your Own Small Business, 100
How to Succeed in Business: A Resource Unit
on Understanding Business and Getting
Ahead in the Business World, 381

How to Succeed in Business When the Chips
Are Down, 707
How to Succeed in Your Own Business, 377
How to Test Your Million Dollar Idea, 216
How to Turn Your Idea into a Million Dollars,
217
How to Uncover Hidden Business Opportunities
That Make Money, 205
How to Use Your Business or Profession as a Tax
Shelter, 445
How to Win SBA Loans, 525
How to Win Profits and Influence Bankers: The
Art of Practical Projecting, 491
How to Win the Battle Against Inflation with a
Small Business, 227
How to Write a Business Plan, 24
How to Write a Marketing Plan, 653
How to Write a Successful Business Plan, 12
How, When and Where to Go Public with a
Small Company, 514

If Not for Profit, for What? 303
Impediments to the Use of Management
Information, 374
Improving Office Operations: A Primer for
Professionals, 312
In Business for Yourself, 44
In Print, 647
In the Owner's Chair, 113
An Income Tax Planning Model for Small
Businesses, 408
Incorporating: A Guide for Small-Business
Owners, 611
Incorporating Your Business, 603
Industrial Marketing and Sales Management in
the Computer Age, 643
Industrial Marketing Research: Technique and
Practices, 646
Industry Accounting Manuals, 431
Innovation and Entrepreneurship: Practice and
Principles, 575
Innovation and Entrepreneurship, 32
Innovation and New Product Marketing, 657
The Innovators: Rediscovering America's
Creative Energy, 573
Inside the Family Business, 334
Installing a Small Business Computer, 460
International Who's Who 1985–86, 157
Intrapreneuring, 735
Investment in People: A Small Business
Perspective, 675
The Irrational Organization, 251
Issues in Business and Society: Capitalism and
Public Purpose, 296
Italian Entrepreneurs: Rearguard of Progress,
168

James Nasmyth and the Bridgewater Foundry,
267

Japanese Entrepreneurship in the Early Stage of Economic Development, 164
John Roach, Maritime Entrepreneur, 549
Judicial Jeopardy: When Business Collides with the Courts, 606

Keeping America at Work: Strategies for Employing the New Technologies, 685
H. I. Kimball, Entrepreneur, 543
A Kiss for Your Computer, 486

The Last Titan: Percival Farquhar, American Entrepreneur in Latin America, 158
Leaders: The Strategies for Taking Charge, 314
Lectures for Inventors, 572
Legal Handbook for Small Business, 604
Legal Master Guide for Small Business, 610
Lessons: An Autobiography, 483
Limited Offering Exemptions: Regulation D, 1983, 601

Magic with Sand: AFG Industries, 534
Make Your Own Comics for Fun and Profit, 190
Making It Big on Your Own, 107
Making It in America, 81
Making It Legal: A Law Primer for the Craftmaker, 595
Making Money with Your Home Computer, 186
Making Money with your Microcomputer, 257
The Making of an Entrepreneur: Keys to Your Success, 6, 612
Making Sense of Accounting Information: A Practical Guide for Understanding Financial Reports and Their Use, 419
Making the Most of Entrepreneurial Management, 733
Management Buy-out: A Guide for the Prospective Entrepreneur, 728
Management by Objectives and Results for Business and Industry, 375
The Management of Nonprofit Organizations, 370
Management of Small Business: Text, Incidents and Cases, 352
Management Succession, 393
Manager's Guide to Productivity, Quality Circles and Industrial Robots, 436
Manager's Guide to Small Computers, 451
The Managerial Grid III, 315
Managing a Successful Business Turnaround, 705
Managing for Joint Venture Success, 352
Managing New Enterprises, 322
Managing Take-off in Fast Growth Companies, 589
Managing Technological Innovation and Entrepreneurship, 584
Managing Technology Products and Marketing Technology Products, 583

Managing the Small Business, 390
Managing the Survival of Smaller Companies, 286
Managing Today and Tomorrow with On-line Information, 392
Managing with Unions, 686
Managing Your Private Trucking Operation, 208
Manufacturing in the Backyard, 545
Marketing a New Product: Its Planning, Development and Control, 638
Marketing Architectural and Engineering Services, 628
The Marketing Book for Growing Companies That Want to Excel, 661
Marketing for the Small Manufacturer, 630
Marketing for Your Growing Business, 636
Marketing on a Small Budget, 672
The Marketing Plan: How to Prepare and Implement It, 654
Marketing Tactics Master Guide for Small Business, 655
Marketing Your Consulting and Professional Services, 627
Maverick, 5
Maximizing Small Business Profits with Precision Management, 265
Men in Business, 287
M-Form Society, The, 290
Microcomputer-Based Information and Decision Support Systems for Small Businesses, 467
Microcomputers in Small Business, 472
Milking Your Business for All It's Worth, 418
Milton Harris, Chemist, Innovator and Entrepreneur, 528
Minding America's Business, 285
Minding My Own Business, 129
Minding Your Own Business: A Contemporary Guide to Small Business Success, 372
The Minicomputer: To Buy or Not to Buy?, 469
Minorities in the Field of Business, 138
Minority Business Enterprise, A Bibliography, 146
Minority Enterprise and the President's Council, 139
My Story, 540

Need Assessment: A Key to User-Oriented Product Innovation, 580
The New American Entrepreneur, 35
The New Business Incubator, 590
New Business Ventures and the Entrepreneur, 103, 538
New Businesses Women Can Start and Successfully Operate, 127
The New Capitalism: How Cutting-Edge Companies Are Managing the Future, 279
The New Competitors, 373
New Enterprise Management, 389

The New Entrepreneurs: Innovation in American Business, 576
New Product Development: What Really Works, 579
New Product Management, 672
New Products and Diversification, 581
New Venture Creation: A Guide to Entrepreneurship, 112
The New Venture Handbook, 371
New Venture Performance: The Role of Strategy and Industry Structure, 382
New Venture Strategies, 115
The New Ventures: Inside the High-Stakes World of Venture Capital, 524
The Newest, Most Unique Ways People Are Making Money, 235
No One Gets Rich Working for Somebody Else, 38
The Nurse Entrepreneur, 130

Olive White Garvey: Uncommon Citizen, 535
The 100 Greatest Corporate and Industrial Ads, 659
100 Sure-Fire Businesses You Can Start with Little or No Investment, 193
168 More Businesses Anyone Can Start and Make a Lot of Money, 234
Open and Operate Your Own Small Store, 185
Opening Your Own Retail Store, 251
Opportunity Management: Strategic Planning for Smaller Businesses, 376
Organizing and Operating Profitable Workshop Classes, 238
Organizing Corporate and Other Business Enterprises, 609
Own Your Own: The No-Cash-Down Business Guide, 201

Participative Management, 674
Patenting and Marketing Your Invention, 587
Patents, 577
The Penny Capitalists, 262
People Management for Small Business, 689
Perception, Opportunity, and Profit, 64
Perfectly Legal: 450 Foolproof Methods for Paying Less Taxes, 440
Personal Computers for the Successful Small Business, 459
Personal Computing: Home, Professional and Small Business Applications, 465
Perspectives on a Decade of Small Business Research, 591
Perspectives on Management: A Multidisciplinary Analysis, 338
L. E. Phillips: Banker, Oil Man, Civic Leader, 533
Pilot's Question and Answer Guide to Successful Franchising, 566
The Place of Business in America's Future, 269

Planning and Budgeting for Higher Profits, 237
Planning and Financing Your New Business: A Guide to Venture Capital, 77
Planning Your Store for Maximum Sales and Profits, 252
Policy Formulation and Strategy Management: Text and Cases, 544
The Politics of Small Business, 304
Practical Bookkeeping for the Small Business, 415
A Practical Guide to Small-Scale Goatkeeping, 224
The Practical Inventor's Handbook, 578
Practical Marketing for Your Small Retail Business, 617
Practical Personnel Policies for Small Business, 677
The Practice of Entrepreneurship, 79
Pratt's Guide to Venture Capital Sources, 512
Preparing a Business Plan for Lenders or Investors, 494
Pricing Decisions in Small Business, 637
Principles of Small Business Management, 368
Principles of Venture Financing: Theory and Practice, 501
Private Enterprise in Eastern Europe, 151
Problems in Retail Merchandising, 708
Profit from Your Money-Making Ideas, 57
Profit Planning for Small Business, 421
Profitable Methods for Small Business Advertising, 635
Profitable Sales Management and Marketing for Growing Businesses, 621
Profitable Telephone Sales Operations, 248
Project Cost Control for Managers, 442
Project Feasibility Analysis (A Guide to Profitable New Ventures), 20
Promoting and Selling Your Art, 213
Protecting and Profiting from Your Business Ideas, 586
Public Relations for the Entrepreneur and the Growing Business, 668
The Publicity and Promotion Handbook, 622
Publicity: How to Get It, 658
Purchase and Sale of Small Businesses: Tax and Legal Aspects, 605
Put It in Writing, 682

The Quick and Easy Guide to Making Money at Home, 202

Raising Seed Money for Your Own Business, 521
Raising Venture Capital and the Entrepreneur, 489
A Reference Guide to Essentials of Accounting, 406
The Regis Touch: New Marketing Strategies for Uncertain Times, 656

Reinventing the Corporation, 734

Report of the Committee on Generally Accepted Accounting Principles for Smaller and/or Closely Held Businesses, 405

A Return to Free Market Economies?, 282

Revitalizing Your Business, 275

The Rise and Decline of Small Firms, 694

The Rise of the Entrepreneur, 45

The Role of the Entrepreneur in Social Change in Northern Norway, 152

Running Your Own Business, 37

Running Your Own Show: Mastering the Basics of Small Business, 261

S Corporation, 608

Sales Forecasting Systems, 642

The Secrets of Practical Marketing for Small Business, 641

Self-made: Braving an Independent Career in a Corporate Age, 104

The Self-Insurance Decision, 329

The Self-Publishing Manual—How to Write, Print and Sell Your Own Book, 232

Sell It by Mail: Making Your Product the One They Buy, 652

Selling by Mail, 634

Services Marketing: An Annotated Bibliography, 631

The Setting for Black Business Development, 142

Setting Up Shop, 97

Shirt-Sleeve Approach to Long-Range Planning for the Smaller, Growing Corporation, 367

Simplified Guide to Small Computers for Business, 466

A Small and Minority Business Management and Procurement Study for the Kansas Department of Economic Development, 150

Small Business: An Entrepreneur's Plan, 269

Small Business Computers, 461

Small Business Finance, 503

Small Business Financing: Federal Assistance and Contracts, 492

The Small Business Handbook, 16, 400

Small Business Ideas for Women and How to Get Started, 123

Small Business in the Third World: Guidelines for Practical Assistance, 162

Small Business in Australia: Problems and Prospects, 166

Small Business in the 1980s, 99

The Small Business Index, 219

Small Business Information Sources: An Annotated Bibliography, 239

The Small Business Legal Advisor, 599

The Small Business Legal Problem Solver, 598

Small Business: Look Before You Leap, 84

Small Business Management, 309, 319, 379, 392

Small Business Management: A Guide to Entrepreneurship, 95

Small Business Management: A Practical Approach, 52

Small Business Management: A Strategic Emphasis, 359

Small Business Management and Entrepreneurship, 324

Small Business Management: Concepts and Techniques for Improving Decisions, 308

Small Business Management: Essentials of Entrepreneurship, 361

Small Business Management Fundamentals, 392

Small Business Management Principles, 388

Small Business Marketing: A Selected and Annotated Bibliography, 618

The Small Business Owner's Practical Handbook, 320

Small Business Programs for the Commodore, 480

Small Business Programs for the IBM PC, 481

Small Business Research: The Development of Entrepreneurs, 671

Small Business Sourcebook, 340

The Small Business Survival Guide: A Handbook, 76, 328

Small Business Survival Guide: Source of Help for Entrepreneurs, 508

Small Business Systems for First-Time Users, 482

Small Business Systems Software, 471

Small Business Works! How to Compete and Win in the Free Enterprise System, 279

Small Businesses in Britain: How They Survive and Succeed, 154

Small Company Financial Reporting, 410

Small Computer Industry Service, 455

Small Computer Systems for Business, 477

Small Computers for the Small Businessman, 473

The Small Firm: An International Survey, 173

The Small Firm Owner-Manager: Entrepreneurial Behavior and Management Practice, 26

Small Time Operator: How to Start Your Own Small Business, Keep Your Books, Pay Your Taxes, and Stay Out of Trouble, 425

Some Aspects of the Problem of Small Enterprise As Seen in Four Selected Industries, 706

So You Think You Need Your Own Business Computer, 484

So You've Got a Great Idea, 36

Spare-Time Fortune Guide, 230

The Spirit of Enterprise, 277

Stanley Junction, 530

Start and Run Your Own Successful Business: An Entrepreneur's Guide, 23

Start Your Own Construction and Land Development Business, 246

The Start-up Entrepreneur: How You Can Succeed in Building Your Own Company into a Major Enterprise Starting from Scratch, 22

Start-up Manuals Series, 176

Start-Up Money, 439

Starting a Business After 50, 96

Starting and Building Your Own Accounting Business, 195

Starting and Managing the Small Business, 68

Starting and Managing a Small Business of Your Own, 80

Starting and Managing Your Own Engineering Practice, 220

Starting and Managing Your Own Small Business, 2, 310

Starting and Operating a Clipping Service, 245

Starting and Operating a Playgroup for Profit, 188

Starting and Operating a Vintage Clothing Shop, 258

Starting and Operating a Word Processing Service, 229

Starting and Succeeding in Small Business: A Guide for the Inner City Businessman, 137

Starting and Winning in Small Business, 85

Starting on a Shoestring: Building a Business Without a Bank Roll, 42

Starting Right in Your New Business, 111

State Tax Policy and the Development of Small and New Business, 444

Step-by-Step Bookkeeping, 433

Stimulating Small Firms, 398

Stop! You're Killing the Business, 700

Strategic Management, 355

Strategic Marketing, 615

Strategic Planning in Emerging Companies, 317

Strategies and Techniques for Saving the Financially-Distressed Small Business, 699

Strategies for Joint Ventures, 351

Strategies for Success in Small Business, 311

Strengthening Small Business Management, 383

Subchapter S Manual, 597

A Successful Business of Your Own and The Speculators Handbook, 49

Success and Failure in Small Business, 701

Success and Survival in the Family-Owned Business, 306

Success of Modern Private Enterprise, 261

The Successful Consultant's Guide to Fee Setting, 243

Successful Direct Marketing Methods, 670

Successful Electronics Servicing Business, 209

Successful Free-lancing, 192

Successful Management for One to Ten Employee Businesses, 346

Successful Marketing for Small Business, 666

Successful Pension Design for Small-to-Medium-sized Businesses, 690

Successful Selling Skills for Small Business, 620

Successful Small Business Management, 343, 394, 384, 401

Supergirls, 125

Survival and Growth: Management Strategies for Small Firms, 327

Survival of the Small Firm, 330

Take a Chance to Be First, 4

Talking to Lenders or Investors, 495

Talking with Employees: A Guide for Managers, 684

Tax Guide for Small Business, 423

Tax Havens for Corporations, 439

Tax Reduction Strategies for Small Business, 416

Taxation for Small Business, 427

Taxes, Financial Policy, and Small Business, 411

Team Building: Issues and Alternatives, 681

Technique and Strategies for Effective Business Management, 362

Technological Entrepreneurship, 574

Technology Licensing and the Small Firm, 582

Telephone Marketing: How to Build Your Business by Phone, 661

The Ten-Minute Entrepreneur, 102

Thirty-Six Small Business Mistakes and How to Avoid Them, 704

Thirty-Six Thousand Dollars a Year in Your Own Home Merchandising Business, 226

To Flourish Among Giants: Creative Management for Mid-Size Firms, 363

Touche Ross Guide to Selecting a Small Business Computer, 448

Trademark Problems and How to Avoid Them, 596

2001 Sources of Financing for Small Businesses, 502

Uncle Henry: The Autobiography of an Irrepressible Entrepreneur, 536

Understanding and Buying a Small Business Computer, 450

Understanding and Selecting Small Business Computers, 458

Understanding Franchise Contracts, 560

Union-Free Labor Relations: A Step-by-Step Guide to Staying Union Free, 679

Union-Free Supervisor, 680

Up and Running: The Small Business Computer Implementation Cookbook, 454

Up Front Financing: The Entrepreneur's Guide, 518

Up Your Own Organization!, 336
Urban Capitalists, 274

Valuing a Business: The Analysis and Appraisal of Closely-Held Companies, 722
Valuing Small Businesses and Professional Practices, 723
Venture Capital and Small Financings, 498
Venture Capital Handbook, 497
Venture Capital in Europe, 156
Venture Capital: The Complete Guide for Investors, 519
Venture Initiation in Irish Society, 171
Venture Management: The Business of the Inventor, Entrepreneur, Venture Capitalist and Established Company, 386, 517
The Vital Few: The Entrepreneur and American Economic Progress, 281

The Wealth of States: Policies for a Dynamic Economy, 299
What's Your Game Plan? Creating Business Strategies That Work, 365
When Your Name Is on the Door, 318
Where Have All the Wooly Mammoths Gone? A Small Business Survival Manual, 626

Who's Who in Venture Capital, 520
Why Companies Fail, 703
Why Small Businesses Fail—Don't Make the Same Mistake Once, 695
Winners, 53
Winner Take All, 554
Winning Government Contracts, 624
With a Little Luck—An American Odyssey, 121
The Woman Entrepreneur, 124
A Woman's Guide to Her Own Franchised Business, 131
A Woman's Guide to Starting a Small Business, 128
The Woman's Guide to Starting a Business, 126
Women Entrepreneurs, Their Success and Problems, 132
Women in Charge: The Experiences of Female Entrepreneurs, 122
Word Processing for Small Businesses, 462
Working Together to Get Things Done, 691

Young, Gifted, and Rich, 41
Your Business Is a Success, Now What?, 360
Your Fortune in Franchises, 556
Your Inc.: A Detailed Escape Route to Being Your Own Boss, 116

SUBJECT INDEX

[References are to entry numbers.]

accounting, 195, 255, 541

accounting for businesses. *See* Section 2 and Section 5, Accounting Software

acquisitions, 605, 890, 921, 1057

advertising, 203, 920, 1002, 1072

agriculture-related businesses, 191, 224, 233, 746

appraising a business. *See* valuations

arts and crafts, 189, 190, 200, 213, 222, 231, 525, 784, 785, 786, 787, 879

billing. *See* Section 5, Software Packages

biographies of entrepreneurs. *See* case histories

bookkeeping. *See* accounting

business plans, 12, 24, 28, 58, 78, 120, 494, 505, 843, 920, 889, 948. *See also* Section 1, The Entrepreneur

buying a business. *See* Section 2, Acquisitions

case histories, 3, 36, 38, 40, 41, 46, 89, 98, 125, 126, 129, 148, 158, 573, 579, 620, 700, 858, 892

computer-oriented businesses, 186, 197, 212, 237, 257, 755, 1085. *See also* typing and word processing businesses

computer use by small businesses, 429, 640, 685, 874, 881. *See also* Section 2

consulting, 161, 178, 179, 211, 243, 254, 255, 627, 640

cost control, 420, 442, 1039

credit management, 437

direct mail, 670

economic history and theory, 17, 18, 62, 63

exporting. *See* international sales

family businesses, 43, 306, 313, 334, 358, 693

farming, 850. *See also* agriculture-related businesses

financial management, 434, 435, 438, 443, 488, 703, 866, 920. *See also* Section 5, Financial software

financing, 20, 38, 55, 77, 792, 817, 828, 919, 921, 938, 948, 1076, 1077, 1141, 1144, 1159, 1194. *See also* Section 2

food-related businesses, 177, 180, 181, 182, 240, 840, 841, 845, 880, 894, 953, 1164

franchising, 96, 108, 131, 141, 663, 744, 755, 763, 814, 819, 902, 903, 921, 937, 1129. *See also* Section 2

high-technology businesses, 9, 31, 72, 220, 537, 804, 918, 925, 1174. *See also* computer-oriented businesses; Section 2, Innovation

home-based businesses. *See* Section 1, Small Business Opportunities

human resources, 920, 949

incorporating. *See* legal issues

incubators. *See* Section 2, Intrapreneurship

international sales, 901, 1083

intrapreneurs, 55, 874, 1121, 1166. *See also* Section 2

inventions. *See* Section 2, Innovation

inventory control. *See* Section 5, Inventory software

landscaping. *See* agriculture-related businesses

legal issues, 577, 587, 707, 806, 897, 948, 951, 1107. *See also* Section 2

loans. *See* financing

mailing lists, 1053, 1054, 1055, 1056

mail order, 244, 249, 625, 639, 652, 670, 775, 776, 954, 1067

management, general. *See* Section 1, The Entrepreneur, and Section 2

manufacturing businesses, 83, 846

marketing, 77, 579, 581, 587, 777, 812, 824, 873, 921, 1044. *See also* Section 2 and Section 5

mergers. *See* Section 2, Acquisitions

minority entrepreneurs, 742, 752, 765, 778, 779, 859, 863, 883, 893, 912, 1074, 1088, 1133, 1140, 1143, 1147, 1149, 1154, 1162, 1180

new-product development, 612, 657, 662. *See also* Section 2, Innovation and New-Product Development

patents. *See* inventions; legal issues

personnel. *See* human resources; Section 2, Human Resources Management

problems, 851, 854, 905, 921, 939

promotion. *See* publicity and public relations

public relations. *See* publicity and public relations

public stock offerings. *See* advertising; financing

publicity and public relations, 613, 614, 616, 622, 649, 658, 668, 783, 853. *See also* advertising

publishing, 210, 221, 232, 236, 260

research and development. *See* Section 2, Innovation and New-Product Development

restaurants. *See* food-related businesses

retailing, 184, 185, 251, 252, 258, 617, 623, 754, 757, 773, 789, 790, 831, 832, 833, 844, 847, 860, 865, 868, 869, 916, 920, 928, 942, 949, 1058, 1155

sales, 218, 244, 248, 871, 875, 877, 882, 885, 920, 1020. *See also* Section 2

secretarial services. *See* typing and word processing businesses

security concerns, 842, 852, 860, 904, 916, 920

selling a business. *See* Section 2, Acquisitions

small-business opportunities, 123, 127, 736, 747, 766, 816, 819, 878, 1073, 1080, 1132, 1137. *See also* Section 1

tax considerations, 408, 423, 425, 427, 436, 440, 444, 445, 605, 1107

trademarks. *See* inventions; legal issues

typing and word processing businesses, 187, 229, 253, 259, 1068, 1069, 1070, 1071

valuations, 720, 721, 722, 723

venture capital. *See* financing

women entrepreneurs, 750, 756, 815, 859, 887, 912, 929, 1174, 1175, 1091, 1106, 1108, 1139, 1140, 1143, 1145, 1146, 1164, 1183, 1184, 1185. *See also* Section 2

word processing. *See* Section 5, Word Processing Software

word processing service business. *See* typing and word processing businesses

writing, 199, 247